Tonic to the Nation

Long remembered chiefly for its modernist exhibitions on the South Bank in London, the 1951 Festival of Britain also showcased British artistic creativity in all its forms. In *Tonic to the Nation*, Nathaniel G. Lew tells the story of the English classical music and opera composed and revived for the Festival, and explores how these long-overlooked components of the Festival helped define English music in the postwar period. Drawing on a wealth of archival material, Lew looks closely at the work of the newly chartered Arts Council of Great Britain, for whom the Festival of Britain provided the first chance to assert its authority over British culture. The Arts Council devised many musical programs for the Festival, including commissions of new concert works, a vast London Season of almost 200 concerts highlighting seven centuries of English musical creativity, and several schemes to commission and perform new operas. These projects were not merely directed at bringing audiences to hear new and old national music, but share the broader goals of framing the national repertory, negotiating between the conflicting demands of conservative and progressive tastes, and using music to forge new national definitions in a changed postwar world.

Nathaniel G. Lew is Associate Professor of Music at Saint Michael's College in Colchester, Vermont, USA.

Tonic to the Nation
Making English Music in the Festival of Britain

Nathaniel G. Lew

LONDON AND NEW YORK

First published 2017
by Routledge
2 Park Square, Milton Park, Abingdon, Oxon OX14 4RN

and by Routledge
711 Third Avenue, New York, NY 10017

Routledge is an imprint of the Taylor & Francis Group, an informa business

© 2017 Nathaniel G. Lew

The right of the author to be identified as author of this work has been asserted by him in accordance with sections 77 and 78 of the Copyright, Designs and Patents Act 1988.

All rights reserved. No part of this book may be reprinted or reproduced or utilised in any form or by any electronic, mechanical, or other means, now known or hereafter invented, including photocopying and recording, or in any information storage or retrieval system, without permission in writing from the publishers.

Trademark notice: Product or corporate names may be trademarks or registered trademarks, and are used only for identification and explanation without intent to infringe.

British Library Cataloguing in Publication Data
A catalogue record for this book is available from the British Library

Library of Congress Cataloging in Publication Data
Names: Lew, Nathaniel Geoffrey, author.
Title: Tonic to the nation : making English music in the Festival of Britain / by Nathaniel G. Lew.
Description: Burlington, VT ; Farnham, Surrey, England : Ashgate, [2017] | Includes bibliographical references and index. | Description based on print version record and CIP data provided by publisher; resource not viewed.
Identifiers: LCCN 2015044326 (print) | LCCN 2015043212 (ebook) | ISBN 9781315550855 (ebook) | ISBN 9781317009870 (epub) | ISBN 9781472458230 (hardcover : alk. paper)
Subjects: LCSH: Music—Social aspects—Great Britain—History—20th century. | Music—Political aspects—Great Britain—History—20th century. | Concerts—Great Britain—History—20th century. | Nationalism in music. | Festival of Britain (1951 : Great Britain)
Classification: LCC ML3917.G7 (print) | LCC ML3917.G7 L49 2016 (ebook) | DDC 780.941/09045—dc23
LC record available at http://lccn.loc.gov/2015044326

ISBN: 978-1-472-45823-0 (hbk)
ISBN: 978-1-315-55085-5 (ebk)

Typeset in Times New Roman
by Florence Production Ltd, Stoodleigh, Devon, UK

In memory of

Wye Jamison Allanbrook

sine qua non

Contents

List of figures and tables ix
Acknowledgements xi

Introduction 1

1 Old music . . .: British repertory in London 23

2 . . . and new: Commissions and premieres 55

3 On stage . . .: Festival opera productions 75

4 . . . and off: The opera commissioning scheme 115

5 This is our moment: National elements in Festival operas 159

Afterword 177

Appendix 1: British music performed in the London Season of the Arts 181
Appendix 2: British works commissioned or premiered during the Festival of Britain 219
Appendix 3: Timeline of the open opera commissioning scheme 227
Bibliography 233
Index 239

Figures and tables

Figure

1.1 Works performed in the London Season of the Arts, arranged by birth decade of the composer 38

Tables

1.1 British composers with most works performed in the London Season of the Arts 41
5.1 New operas associated with the 1951 Festival of Britain 160

Acknowledgements

This book has been a long time in preparation, and a great many people have helped me along the way. I received essential grant and sabbatical funding from my home institution, Saint Michael's College, where, in addition, Susan Summerfield and Bill Ellis have been everything one could ever want in supportive colleagues. The staff of the Archive of the Arts Council of Great Britain and the BBC Written Archive Center offered invaluable research assistance, while Rachel O'Higgins actually made the Alan Bush archive available to me in her own dining room. John Pickard and the rest of the teaching and administrative staff of the Department of Music at the University of Bristol made me welcome as a Benjamin Meaker Fellow in 2012; thanks are also due to Susan Jim and the interns at the Meaker Fellowship Office. Pegram Harrison and Geoffrey Webber were my gracious hosts on other research trips too numerous to count, and Amy Werbel, in addition to her pep talks, offered one particular suggestion without which I probably would never have finished. I am very lucky to have found in the North American British Music Studies Association a group of colleagues who are also genuinely my friends; interacting with them regularly restored my motivation. Five extraordinary colleagues, friends, and family members read early versions of the manuscript and offered essential suggestions. These are Byron Adams, Stephen Banfield, Jenny Doctor, Danielle Fosler-Lussier, and Rivi Handler-Spitz. Byron and Stephen generously shared their boundless knowledge of British music with me in conversations and correspondence, and Stephen lent me his office in Bristol—blissfully free of wifi—where I wrote most of the first draft. For their part, Danielle and Rivi offered unwavering support and encouragement through hours of phone calling and reams of email. Finally, I am grateful without measure to my big man and my little man, Jason Paymar Lorber and Maxwell Elliott Lorber-Lew, who gave me time to work but also reminded me when it was time to come to dinner.

Introduction

On Thursday May 3, 1951, an orchestra assembled from members of five different London orchestras, along with the state trumpeters of the Royal Horse Guard and a chorus composed of members of ten London choirs, conducted in succession by Malcolm Sargent and Adrian Boult, opened the new Royal Festival Hall on the South Bank of the Thames. The program offered high points of English ceremonial music: George Frideric Handel's Coronation Anthem "Zadok the Priest", C. Hubert H. Parry's "Ode at a Solemn Music", Thomas Arne's "Rule Britannia" from *Alfred* (in the premiere of Sargent's now familiar arrangement), Ralph Vaughan Williams's "Serenade to Music", Edward Elgar's "Pomp and Circumstance" March no. 1 with chorus ("Land of Hope and Glory"), Henry Purcell's "Soul of the World" from *An Ode to Saint Cecilia*, and the choruses "Hallelujah" and "Amen" from Handel's *Messiah*.

This concert resembled many patriotic musical performances in England on ceremonial state occasions (and, more recently, at the Last Night of the Proms). The mostly familiar repertory served a function beyond baptizing a new concert hall and entertaining the invited audience: It created a portrait of musical Britain. The Coronation Anthem, Arne's chorus, and Elgar's march all express sovereignty and national identity, while the selections by Parry, Vaughan Williams, and Purcell take music itself as their subject, in the words of Milton, Shakespeare, and Nicholas Brady, respectively. All the music included the characteristic and nationally-marked practice of choral singing, and the concert closed with the most familiar selections from arguably the nation's most beloved work.

On the same evening, across the Thames at the Victoria and Albert Museum, the Jacques String Orchestra gave a concert including Vaughan Williams's already classic *Tallis Fantasia* and the London premiere of Peter Racine Fricker's violin concerto, which had just won a widely publicized competition for works by younger composers. Two days later, on May 5th, the Covent Garden Opera gave the third performance of Vaughan Williams's new opera, *The Pilgrim's Progress*, based on John Bunyan's 1678 allegory, whose premiere had occurred a week earlier on April 26th. The next afternoon at the Royal Albert Hall, the London Philharmonic Orchestra and the National Youth Orchestra together gave a concert consisting entirely of English music, including the premiere of George Dyson and Cecil Day Lewis's *Song for Festival*, a crib of Parry's famous setting of Blake's *Jerusalem* from the First World War.

2   *Introduction*

All these musical events, with their varied and rich associations, marked the opening of The Festival of Britain. For five months in the summer of 1951, the Government, in cooperation with towns and organizations across the country, mounted this celebration of British culture and its "contribution to civilisation," consisting of numerous performances and both fixed and traveling exhibitions. The immediate pretext for the Festival was the centennial of the 1851 Great Victorian Exhibition, which had been the occasion of the building of the Crystal Palace in Hyde Park. More proximately, the Festival offered a symbol of national recovery and renewal—moral, cultural, and material—from the destruction and privations of the Second World War.

"Conceived among the untidied ruins of war and fashioned through days of harsh economy" (Taylor 1951: 3), the Festival was designed to provide a large-scale optimistic public vision of Britain, a "great symbol of national regeneration" (Banks 1993: 2), particular useful to the government during the slow postwar period of reconstruction. In his comments at the Festival's opening ceremony at St. Paul's Cathedral, Geoffrey Fisher, the Archbishop of Canterbury, expressed this purpose in rolling phrases:

> The chief and governing purpose of the Festival is to declare our belief and trust in the British way of life, not with any boastful self-confidence nor with any aggressive self-advertisement, but with sober and humble trust that by holding fast to that which is good and rejecting from our midst that which is evil we may continue to be a nation at unity in itself and of service to the world. It is good at a time like the present so to strengthen, and in part to recover, our hold on the abiding principles of all that is best in our national life.
>
> (Taylor 1951: i)

The futuristic design of the main exhibitions on the South Bank of the Thames, the Festival's exclusive focus on the development and potential of one nation, and its underlying social idealism led the art historian Roy Strong to liken the Festival to French Revolutionary political festivals, which,

> with their apotheosis of the new ideals of society, of Liberty, Equality and Fraternity, attendants of the goddess Reason . . . are the most direct ancestors of 1951. They were truly secular state festivals in which governments set out to present to the masses the ideals and goals of a new society, framed within a view of history recast in the terms of romantic nationalism.
>
> (Banham and Hillier 1976: 6)

Similarly, Bevis Hillier compares the Festival to the Philadelphia Centennial Exposition of 1876, another anniversary celebration whose

> real motive was to boost morale after a chronically debilitating war . . . and to symbolize faith in the future, in the arrival of a new and happier era. Frank

Anderson Trapp ... has written of the 1876 exhibition that its organizers wished "to put the best possible face upon uncertain times and to call upon an idealistic vision of the past as the touchstone to the future". The description serves for the Festival of Britain.

(Banham and Hillier 1976: 13)

For Gerald Barry, the Festival's Director-General, the event clearly took on a deeper significance in difficult international circumstances. As the May 1951 opening of the Festival approached, the Cold War was at one of its hottest points; a return to full-scale war, this time with the Communist bloc, seemed a very real possibility. British casualties in Korea, the defection to the Soviet Union of the Cambridge spies Burgess and McLean one week after the opening of the Festival, and Iran's nationalization of the Anglo-Iranian Oil Company put psychological strain on the nation, occupying the public's attention and weakening the government. Where initially Barry had hoped to mount a celebration of peace and renewed prosperity, he now saw his work as a booster of national morale and a symbol of British freedom, reminiscent of the home front entertainments during the Second World War. He captured the uncertain nature of the entire affair when he seized on the description "a tonic to the nation"—the Festival as medicine for a recovering patient—a metaphor that Adrian Forty intensified in his critical account of the political background to the Festival when he wrote, "It might be more appropriate to describe the Festival as 'A Narcotic to the Nation'" (Banham and Hillier 1976: 26).

Whatever the nation's underlying weaknesses and concerns, the Festival was hugely successful with the public, breathing a mood of optimism and recovery into the air. Despite a cold and very rainy summer, eight and a half million people came to the South Bank before the exhibits closed in September, and the Festival Pleasure Gardens at Battersea Park also attracted eight million visitors. The total attendance at all official Festival locations was over 18 million, although, as Michael Frayn (1980: 324) points out, the Festival of Britain was not as successful as the 1851 Great Exhibition, which was seen, astonishingly, by one third of the English population of the time. Indeed, in the view of some, the Festival was the climax of the entire postwar period, "the single gigantic event which crystallizes the whole era" (Banham and Hillier 1976: 6).

Most people's mental image of the Festival was (and remains) the modernist pavilions of the world's-fair-like South Bank Exhibition in London, but of equal importance were the 22 official local festivals elsewhere throughout the United Kingdom, displaying all manner of artistic and cultural activities, two exhibitions traveling by ship and truck, and countless contributions and events in villages and towns throughout the realm. London and many other cities had been utterly devastated in the war, and in addition a large part of the Festival year's activity was a program of rebuilding and beautification.

The Festival of Britain has attracted intermittent academic attention over the years.[1] Scholars have analyzed the architecture and industrial design of the Festival and the social environment that it created, and have studied its planning and execution as representative of postwar Labourite British political culture. Assessments of the overall importance of the Festival of Britain to national culture vary: For some, the Festival was a watershed moment, for others, an irrelevant sideshow in postwar political and social developments. Most commentators note the significance of the South Bank Exhibition in design history. More recently, the contents and presentation of the Exhibition's didactic exhibits have come in for sophisticated analysis by Becky Conekin (2003).

From the Festival's beginnings, the fine arts were central to the goals of cultural celebration and reconstruction. However, the role of the fine arts in the Festival has attracted little attention in previous accounts. In an account of over 250 pages, for instance, Barry Turner (2011) scarcely mentions the fine arts at all. This neglect seems motivated by an assumption that the arts most notably on display shared neither the peculiar mix of forward and backward national definition that characterized the Festival exhibitions nor the ferment of invention and innovation that characterized the buildings and design. To critics focused on the most visible and documented contributions of the Festival to British culture, the fine arts merely continued existing pre-war forms of activity. For instance, Alan Sinfield and Andy Croft dismiss any consideration of the arts with the charge that the Festival of Britain was artistically reactionary, and that the elites who mounted it abandoned the "People's Culture" of the wartime years and effected a "drag back towards a traditional idea of culture" (Sinfield 1995: 189). Heather Wiebe (2012: 161), noting the preponderance of cultural heritage and religious drama in the arts festivals, more helpfully suggests that they performed "the major memory work of the Festival," in contrast to the emphasis on modernity and experimentation visible elsewhere. Clearly, the provision and meaning of high culture in the Festival deserve more methodical examination than has heretofore been attempted. Our understanding is incomplete without an appraisal of how the fine arts paralleled the drive to cultural redefinition evident elsewhere.

The United Kingdom underwent a political revolution in the years following the end of the Second World War and leading up to the Festival of Britain. The establishment of the Welfare State ushered in a new relationship between the government and the people. Along with comprehensive social welfare programs, this period also saw an unprecedented experiment in the involvement of the British government in the native production and performance of art. Indeed, this change was one of the most striking aspects of the postwar British scene, not an element of standard socialist dogma, although it grew out of the same ideals, as Alan Sinfield (1995: 183–184) describes:

> The underlying ideology that informed the postwar reforms was that the good things of life customarily enjoyed by the leisure classes were now to be available to everyone. All the people were to have a stake in society, an adequate share of its resources as of right—a job, a pension or social security, a roof over your head, healthcare, education. This, quite explicitly, was the pay-off for wartime suffering. And "good" culture, which hitherto had been the special prerogative of the leisure classes, was also to be available to

everyone. By the end of the war, state support for the arts was firmly on the agenda. . . . A key postwar assumption . . . was instituted at this point in the 1940s: that the condition of culture is in substantial part a responsibility of the State.

Just as the social welfare programs envisioned in the 1942 Beveridge Report served the goal of leveling class distinctions and drawing the populace up to a better lifestyle, the cultural programs used government intervention in a deliberate effort to edify the populace, to lead and extend popular taste. The agency authorized to implement arts policy and direct its public provision under the new dispensation was the newly chartered Arts Council of Great Britain. Thus when it came to the Festival of Britain, the government entrusted the planning and execution of the artistic programs to the Arts Council. The Council seized this opportunity to establish dominance in British culture, and generated an outpouring of all types of artistic creation, with special programs in painting, sculpture, poetry, and drama.

However, the extraordinary pains that the Arts Council took to extend and promote British achievement in classical music and opera surpassed those for all other genres and art forms in breadth and ambition. As a result, the Festival of Britain proved a defining moment in the history of English music, an unprecedented explosion of performances of native repertory and commissions that revived interest in older works and provided an incentive for a thorough evaluation of the canon of English music since the fourteenth century. The musical component of the Festival, unparalleled historically and unmatched in scope to this day, offered a bold repudiation, should any have been deemed necessary as late as 1951, of a lingering national insecurity. (As recently as 1914, the German author Oscar Schmitz had famously libeled England as "Das Land ohne Musik.")

Why did classical musical receive so much attention in the Festival in the first place? In part, as I discuss below, the enormous energy devoted to classical music derived simply from the social class and cultural expectations of the Festival's planners. It is characteristic of most people to believe in the value of their own culture, and to want to spread it. More significant, however, was the Festival's specific historical moment. While the Second World War disrupted all artistic endeavors, its impact on the performing arts was arguably greatest. (Even with paper shortages, authors could still write and publish, but orchestral concerts were largely out of the question during the Blitz.) When the end of the war brought a resumption of normal cultural life, thousands of professional musicians returned from military and home-front roles—including extraordinary wartime performance programs—to their performance careers, and the nation absorbed hundreds of émigré musical professionals as well. New performance ensembles, academies, and festivals proliferated.

Ironically, in Britain, as opposed to on the Continent, this normalized musical environment seemed novel. In the emerging music historiography of the time, the concert life of the thirties, however rich, had still been part of the English Musical Renaissance, which had seen the art sprout and bud anew from formerly barren soil starting in the late nineteenth century. The war, a tangible interruption of activities, marked the end of this phase. After 1945, English musical culture—its composers, performers, and institutions—could be declared mature and equal to any other country. In this environment, the Festival of Britain provided an opportunity and in fact an imperative to survey national achievement in music. A comparison with theater is illuminating in this regard. As with music, theatrical performance had suffered significant wartime disruption, but the English had long viewed drama as one of the jewels of their artistic genius. There was therefore no parallel need after the war to review their theatrical accomplishments, and the Arts Council mounted no projects in theater with the scope of their musical plans.

The present study recounts the story of classical music and opera in the Festival of Britain, in particular, the programs that created or presented English music. Although the repertory, scope, and outcomes vary, each project served a purpose similar to that of the opening concert at the Royal Festival Hall. Just as the Festival pavilions and exhibitions projected a vision of British culture combining machine-age modernism with an idealized past, the Festival concerts and operatic performances advanced an image of Britain as a truly musical nation, equal to any other, and also as a moderate nation: cultured and sophisticated but also inclusive and entertaining. Each chapter grapples with different accounts, problems, and critiques of postwar British music as the details of each project in turn raise questions about how music-making represented the nation at a time of transition and the forging of new identities. The Festival musical schemes intersected with a variety of postwar trends in British music, continuing certain prewar cultural values and essaying or instituting new ones. The works composed and performed fit in various ways into postwar musical life as it was imagined at the time.

But although national content and definition were present in the minds of the creators of the works examined here, this volume is not strictly a study of nationalism in music. My approach concentrates less on works and composers than on the roles of the institutions that placed commissions and organized performances. The narratives unfolded here rarely feature idiosyncratic composers and performers or the workings of popular taste, nor does my interest in musical texts lie in their intrinsic worth as exemplars of musical art.

Where the Festival of Britain had protagonists, they were cultural bureaucrats, highly musically educated although not always practicing musicians. While such figures necessarily made decisions, in the highly bureaucratized culture of mid-twentieth century Britain, authority for these decisions was functionally assigned to their committee or institution, which subsumed, obscured, protected, and often undermined the individuals' initiative. In a sense, then, the chief actors here are the bureaucracies and institutions themselves within which individual action functioned. Throughout history, and never more so than at events such as large state-sponsored festivals, such institutional actors are as significant as the composers and performers on whom musical history usually concentrates, and institutional norms and procedures are as significant as individual initiative in understanding the outcomes. Thus, a study of the Festival of Britain is necessarily also a study of British bureaucratic culture, with its ideology of anonymous civil service. In the largest sense, then, this volume is a case study of the state patronage of classical music in postwar Britain. I seek to uncover, compare, and evaluate the aims, policies, and mechanisms of government support for music, and how the imposition of such control affected the political and aesthetic environment in which actual works of art were produced and performed. To the extent, then, that the Festival of Britain provides examples of how government agencies do and do not stimulate the production of art, this is both a celebratory and cautionary tale.

My account focuses largely on the inner workings of the Arts Council of Great Britain as it prepared its Festival musical projects: its goals and decision-making processes where these are recoverable, the internal arguments used to frame and justify these goals, and the existing and new mechanisms used to achieve them. Although the context of the Festival bound the various proposals together, they reveal different purposes, institutional means, challenges, and levels of success. In each case, I investigate whether the particular institutional procedures impeded or advanced the goals of the project, and what effects—deliberate or unintended—they had on the role of concert music and opera, not merely in the Festival but in the broader culture of postwar Britain. The unfolding and outcome of each project expose institutional attitudes toward English (and British) music in this period, tying these questions back to the broader national issues at stake.

The people responsible for Festival music planning were for the most part established older cultural bureaucrats and composers who shared an upper-crust educational background and broadly condescending cultural outlook. These were representatives of the influential and well-meaning class whom Michael Frayn famously identifies having dominated postwar political and cultural developments:

> The radical middle-classes—the do-gooders; the readers of the News Chronicle, The Guardian, and the Observer, the signers of petitions; the backbone of the BBC In short the herbivores, or gentle ruminants, who look out from the lush pastures which are their natural station in life with eyes full of sorrow for less fortunate creatures, guiltily conscious of their advantages, though not usually ceasing to eat the grass.
>
> (1980: 307–308)

Their attitude toward both their qualification for and their work in the Festival was a classically "mandarin" one, to use a term introduced into English criticism in 1938 by Cyril Connolly (2008: 12) but developed by Robert Hewison (1988). In Hewison's analysis, the mandarin position was an aristocratic aesthetic that promoted "conservative, pastoral and genteel values": "[I]ts effect was to reassert the importance of hierarchy and tradition, and protect the influence of institutions that encouraged respect for such values" (64–65). Alan Sinfield (1989: 50–55), although he does not use the term "mandarin," marshals a sophisticated analysis of class markers and capitalist pressures to paint a similar portrait of a reactionary postwar cultural establishment.

But the term "mandarin" properly refers to the classical Chinese bureaucrats who were distinguished by their scholarly achievement, and in the context of the Festival of Britain, the mandarins' conservative cultural tastes are less important— and arguably less in evidence—than their paternalistic approach to the *provision* of culture. Never once did any figure in the narratives that follow question the guiding principle that a committee of worthies is the best agent to make artistic policy and guide the choice of both new and old repertory. Their planning of Festival music was emphatically "top-down," even to the level of individual concert programs.

Unquestionably, on a superficial level, some accusation of aristocratic values is warranted. In their funding decisions, the mandarins emphasized the high culture that they valued, and the development of public taste in this direction, as opposed to the commercial popular culture that was beginning to make headway at the same time. Classical music in the twentieth century was always an elite genre; any institution limiting its purview to concert music is already inherently reactionary in this sense. The Arts Council (and to an extent the BBC as well) set out to define and arrange a musical program which held little interest for a large portion of the British population, although the audience had broadened over the previous decades.

By contrast, popular musical styles of many kinds had a large and devoted audience in Britain, and had their own place in the Festival of Britain alongside the classical music under consideration here. Indeed, the role of popular music in the Festival of Britain deserves its own study: The BBC broadcast special popular-music programs throughout the Festival period, Noel Coward and others wrote satirical and celebratory songs about the Festival, and there was an extensive program of dance-band performances at the Battersea Pleasure Gardens (which were run by a private for-profit company).

We should not however ascribe the meager support that the Arts Council and the Festival as a whole offered such popular music solely to the prejudices of a few mandarins. Rather, an unquestioned distinction between art music and popular music was intrinsic to the culture of the period and built into the very institutions running the Festival. The Arts Council's royal charter limited its purview to the "fine arts exclusively," a term understood uncontroversially in the 40s to exclude jazz, dance hall, musical comedy, popular song, and the like. Furthermore, the charter permitted the Council to fund only organizations exempt from Entertainments Tax, as determined by H.M. Board of Custom and Excise, which reviewed entertainment organizations to determine whether they were "non-profit-distributing" and "partly educational". In practical terms, this qualification excluded most popular music, which was usually produced for profit and rarely for educational purposes.

There were occasional calls for the extension of official recognition to "low" genres—one example is the support that the composers Ralph Vaughan Williams and Thomas Wood gave to brass bands in the Festival commissioning scheme analyzed in Chapter 2—but it would be anachronistic to expect any more comprehensive crossing of cultural barriers at this time.

Rather than attempting to position Festival musical projects against a broad backdrop of British musical life generally, then, this study addresses the values that functioned within the sphere of concert music and opera, which still afford ample room for questions of style, breadth, progress, and reaction. Within such bounds, the mandarins, whose tastes outstripped those of the general populace and who disdained market-tested answers, could in fact be moderately progressive. Sinfield (1989: 41) refers to such figures as "middle-class dissidents." Contrary to the analysis of Hewison (1988: 65), for whom the postwar mandarins merely "hanker[ed] after an idealized earlier period, before modernism and before world wars, when cultural and social values seemed retrospectively more secure," the cultural bureaucrats who mounted the Festival of Britain worked open-mindedly and in good faith not only to encompass but also to advance Britain's musical culture. If they tempered their catholicity and enthusiasm for what one might term "respectable contemporaneity" with a care to avoid radicalism or anything truly avant-garde, the results were still impressively broad.

The Arts Council of Great Britain

The Arts Council of Great Britain received its royal charter in 1946 as the first permanent organ of state arts funding in British history. It grew out of the Council for the Encouragement of Music and the Arts (CEMA), which ran highly successful wartime programs for fostering culture—both on the small, local scale, and, increasingly as the conflict wore on, on a grander, metropolitan scale.[2] The Arts Council was not a government department, but rather a "quango" (quasi-autonomous non-governmental organization), granted money by the government but protected from government intervention, its decisions exempt from detailed questioning in Parliament, and in turn protecting the arts organizations it benefitted. This device of removing administrative control over the funds from the direct control of the government was known as the "arm's-length principle". Many analysts, however, most notably Raymond Williams (1989: 42–44) and Richard Witts (1998), have pointed out that the Arts Council was not truly an "intermediate body" as its advocates argued, and was never as independent of the government as it claimed.

In the period leading up to the Festival of Britain, the Arts Council consisted of the 16 members appointed by the Chancellor of the Exchequer, mostly prominent figures in the worlds of the arts, patronage, or the civil service, with few active politicians. The Council also maintained advisory panels in the chief art forms it subsidized: music, drama, visual art, and poetry. For a brief period in 1948, the Arts Council also convened an unsuccessful advisory panel on opera and ballet, which I discuss in Chapter 3. These advisory panels did in fact draw their members from among the most famous and accomplished artists in the country. For instance, in 1946, when the Arts Council came into official existence, the Music Panel included Benjamin Britten, Joan Cross, Myra Hess, Herbert Howells, Frank Howes (the music critic for the London *Times*), and Ninette de Valois; Michael Tippett had been invited to join. During the next five years, Lennox Berkeley, Edmund Rubbra, and Malcolm Sargent all served terms on the Music Panel.

As is often the case in such organizations, however, the real planning work of the Council was done by its professional staff, led by the Secretary-General and the Assistant Secretary, who supervised the work of directors in the areas covered by the panels, and by the regional directors, who convened local committees in various regions of the kingdom. These staff members and the chairs of the panels originated and crafted actual policies and decisions, and had much greater impact on the arts than the members of the Council itself. Mary C. Glasgow, the Arts Council's redoubtable first Secretary-General, who remained in that post until 1951, was thus a powerful figure in arts funding. Another of the pre-eminent figures developing ideas and driving decisions in the pages that follow was Eric Walter White, the Assistant Secretary of the Council from 1945 to 1971.

The duties of the Assistant Secretary in the Arts Council in this period were notably vague. In one sense White was simply an assistant to Mary Glasgow, but he was scarcely just an assistant or administrator. Born in 1905 and educated at Clifton College and Balliol, through a long career he issued a steady stream of works and lectures on music and poetry, including original compositions, poetry, and translations. He also had enormous enthusiasm for and significant expertise in the field of historical English opera; during his long tenure at the Arts Council, he published three carefully researched books on the subject. Furthermore, from his office, essentially independent of all of the Council's various panels and departments, he could advocate for the many opera projects reviewed here in Chapters 3 and 4. Indeed, because of his interest in early English music generally, he was also influential in transforming the London Season of the Arts into a historical panorama of English music, as reviewed in Chapter 1.

Although its original charter granted it purview over all the "fine arts", for many years the Arts Council limited its activities to the support of classical music, opera, ballet, drama, poetry, painting, graphic arts, and sculpture. This was in part a legacy of the highbrow tastes of the Council's founder, John Maynard Keynes. As Raymond Williams points out, this left out much of British art and culture:

> Socially, the original arts were the cultural interests of an older upper-middle and middle class: a limited governmental initiative ... would help to sustain them and to make them more widely accessible. But the cultural situation was rapidly changing. Radio was already the primary distributor of concert music and drama; television, if unevenly, was to become the major distributive channel of all arts, in terms of numbers.
>
> (1989: 47)

Furthermore, almost all of the Council's money went to *performers* and *exhibitors* of art in these fields, the means through which creative artists' work could reach the public, rather than to the creative artists themselves. Providers could commission or stimulate the creation of new works, and were sometimes encouraged to do so, but up until 1951 the Arts Council rarely viewed its role as a source of direct support to creative artists. As we will see, the Festival of Britain brought about a temporary but significant shift in this practice.

The work of the Arts Council fell for the most part into two categories. The smaller portion (less than 25 percent) of the Arts Council's money went to the direct organization, often undertaken by the regional offices, of artistic presentations such as concerts, play tours, and, especially, visual art exhibitions. This function was a continuation of the early practice of CEMA, but with the end of the war, as many performers returned from military service and professional companies started up again, the Arts Council found direct provision less necessary. Thus, for example, the number of directly provided concerts decreased steadily, from over 800 in 1945–1946 to a mere 138 in 1951–1952; instead, increased aid to symphony orchestras and chamber ensembles allowed such groups to tour more widely.

There was some concern at the announcement of the creation of the Arts Council that the agency might find itself in competition with other arts organizations. For this reason, the Arts Council explicitly announced in its first annual report (Arts Council Annual Report 1945–1946: 6) the policy of supporting independent producers rather than distributing arts directly through new state-run enterprises, and reiterated this policy frequently in subsequent annual reports:

> Except in the Art Department, "direct management" is a declining motive in the Council's work, the bulk of which will continue to be devoted to maintaining, guiding and encouraging the activities of existing bodies and thus acting as an independent instrument of State patronage of the Arts.
> (Arts Council Annual Report 1950–1951: 30)

The exception to this rule, as the quotation mentions, was in the visual arts, where the Arts Council continued to organize touring exhibitions throughout the country. The Arts Council even purchased and maintained its own collection of visual art for this purpose.

The larger portion of the Arts Council's money furnished grants, guarantees, and loans to associated professional non-profit artistic organizations exempt from Entertainments Tax, which in turn provided performances under their own management. (The requirement that performing institutions seeking Arts Council funding demonstrate that their work was "partly educational" could sometimes cause headaches.) Association with the Arts Council had to be renewed every year, and the associated organization had to accept the presence of a non-voting Arts Council assessor at its board meetings. Professional theater, opera, and ballet companies, museums, and orchestras all received grants, as did a number of festivals. Especially in its first years, the Arts Council played an active part in establishing professional repertory theater companies in provincial cities. It also helped to form the Orchestral Employers Association to enable the major orchestras to coordinate their programs and tours, and took over the management of the Wigmore Hall, the chief London venue for chamber music.

In the years leading up to the Festival of Britain, the financial clout of the Arts Council increased steadily. Over its first seven years, the Council's grant from the Treasury rose from an initial £235,000 in 1945–1946 to £675,000 in both 1950–1951 and 1951–1952 (approx. £9 million and £20 million respectively in 2013). The bulk of this grant went towards classical music concerts, art exhibitions, theater companies, opera, and ballet. Almost a quarter of this allocation went to support the opera and ballet companies at Covent Garden and Sadler's Wells.

Although both the literature on the Arts Council and that on the Festival of Britain report that the Festival was a major undertaking for the agency, the full scope of its Festival work has been neither recognized nor analyzed. In fact, the Festival was perhaps the most extensive coordinated undertaking in Arts Council's history, and arguably its defining moment. While the Arts Council always exerted some pressure on repertory indirectly by funding or not funding project proposals, and thus setting norms and expectations for future applications, for the Festival it staged an unprecedented intrusion into programming decisions of independent performers in order to achieve repertory goals conceived in-house.

The extensive literature critical of the Arts Council, most notably Richard Witts's irreverent "alternative history" (1998), repeatedly and effectively demonstrates the opportunistic and *ad hoc* nature of the Council's programs in the early years of its existence. According to these analyses, the Arts Council never succeeded in framing coherent policies and methods of evaluation to guide its funding decisions. Instead, it allowed a small set of seemingly permanent clients—chiefly the elite metropolitan performing organizations—to eat up the bulk of its grant without sufficient oversight, while at the same time taking up at the margins a shifting set of somewhat random new initiatives generated by the whims and enthusiasms of Council staff and members. The judgments passed by historians on the Council's functioning and results have been predictably severe.

Despite the sarcasm of commentators such as Witts about the integrity of almost everyone who ever worked at the Arts Council, the Council staff planning Festival music programs were conscientious in their attempts to program broadly and to avoid overt prejudice. The London Season of the Arts reviewed in Chapter 1 is representative of this balance; as a huge joint effort by many staff members and conductors and ensembles, it offered few opportunities for individual antipathies to unduly influence the outcome. This is not to say that the panels did not ever act unfairly. Chapter 2 recounts some missed chances in the commissioning scheme, and in the opera competition reviewed in Chapter 4 strong personal tastes and prejudices marred the work of the already problematic panel of judges. But a close analysis of the Arts Council's Festival projects offers a partial corrective to the almost universally negative appraisals of the agency in its early years. In the unique circumstances of the Festival of Britain, *ad hoc* decision-making—a charge fully borne out by the evidence I marshal here—could produce desirable results. Indeed, the Festival represents a rare triumph of the Arts Council's less-than-ideal methods. If, like the BBC, the Council in this period had maintained a set of clear objectives and working methods to guide it, it almost certainly would never have permitted itself to intrude so thoroughly into the work of so many of its clients and their performing plans. Ironically, then, the Festival of Britain provided the Arts Council, despite its overall early dysfunction, with the opportunity to do something right.

My attention here to the internal decision-making processes of the Arts Council is not meant to dismiss questions about the audience for all this music. Evidence of audience involvement, however, is notoriously hard to obtain. The Arts Council projects of this early period—and in subsequent periods as well—have attracted criticism for their scant consideration of or research into audience interest, and the Festival was no great departure from this norm. (The implied comparison is again with the BBC, which engaged in extensive audience research.)

The Arts Council's approach to art in the Festival was the classically mandarin position that dominated its thinking for many decades. The goal was to provide a broad survey of historical repertory and an impressive set of new works that Arts Council staff members themselves deemed necessary; there was little consideration of what audiences actually wanted to hear. Not surprisingly, the music that the Arts Council worked so hard to get performed in the Festival did not always draw large crowds eager to hear it; indeed, audiences were modest and often disappointing. But we should not judge the Arts Council too harshly for this outcome. Over the long term, mandarinism cut off from popular taste as a general policy is condemnable for an arts funding agency, as the Arts Council has discovered over its decades of controversy. But the very different task that the Arts Council conceived for itself in the special circumstances of the Festival was of considerable value: to celebrate native compositional achievement by presenting English music in its historical breadth and generating new repertory both in concert music and opera. That sort of project demands a top-down approach, because much of the music presented was necessarily unfamiliar to audiences.

Planning the Festival

Through its work on the Festival of Britain, the Arts Council of Great Britain truly came into its own as an agency promoting the arts and shaping their development in Britain. Although the organization of the Festival had to be carried out alongside the Council's regular programs in the years leading up to 1951, the Council staff threw themselves into the task of putting British visual art, music, and drama at the center of the Festival, adopting a combination of time-tested and novel methods and displaying both quick thinking and dogged perseverance.

The Arts Council became involved in the planning of the Festival very early both in the history of the Festival and in its own history. From the outset, it was clear that no one in Britain had ever attempted an arts festival on the proposed scale before. Therefore the government logically approached the fledgling Arts Council immediately as the most appropriate body to undertake it. According to the 1950–1951 Arts Council Annual Report (4), in 1947, only months after the Arts Council received its charter, the Chancellor of the Exchequer asked the Council for suggestions on commemorating the centennial of the Great Exhibition 1851, and specifically whether a national arts festival was feasible. As early as 1945, a Parliamentary Committee chaired by Lord Ramsden had looked into promoting exports through trade fairs and exhibitions, for which the centennial offered one opportunity. The first mention of the as-yet unnamed 1951 exhibition occurred at the Arts Council Executive Committee meeting on January 29, 1947. Mary Glasgow reported that the proposals of the Ramsden Committee were likely to be rejected, but that a cultural festival in London might take its place, with the Arts Council playing a central role. The minutes revealed an Arts Council eager to assume responsibility for the festival if invited to, so long as the resources provided for its other, ongoing work did not suffer, a sentiment reiterated on a number of later occasions.

14 *Introduction*

Even at this early date, the staff of the Arts Council could see that a national—or even just metropolitan—festival would boost their power and visibility. An internal Arts Council document, possibly drawn up by Steuart Wilson, then the Arts Council Director of Music, directly addressed the usefulness of the Festival to the Council, arguing that the Council:

> should seize the opportunity to establish themselves as organisers on a National Scale, with a view to increasing their prestige in the Country at large, and especially with the Government as their chosen instrument of carrying out Artistic Policy.
>
> (EL6/2, February 28, 1947)

Overstating the case slightly, the Arts Council Annual Reports later claimed that the agency had undertaken the entire Festival using their ordinary methods of operation, which were thereby shown to be equal to the largest cultural tasks.

So new was the Arts Council and so unprecedented the scale of the Festival, especially as it grew, that at times the Arts Council had to clarify the limits of its purview to the government. The initial 1947 plan for the Festival was tripartite: a trade exhibition, an arts festival, and a science exhibition. Since there was no existing agency to organize the science exhibition, this was at first offered to the Arts Council, which, however, refused to undertake it, as it was unrelated to its charter (EL6/1, n.d. [March 1947]). As a result, the government formed the Council of Science and Technology. Similarly, the British Film Institute took over responsibility for the film portion of the arts festival when the Arts Council made it clear that it had never considered film to be one of the "fine arts" under its jurisdiction.

Already by the Arts Council meeting of February 27, 1947, the basic outlines of the Council's role in the Festival were clear:

> The considered recommendation of the Council was that a Cultural Exhibition in London (and possibly other places) in 1951 was desirable, and that the Council would wish to be associated with it, if it were approved by the Government, on the following terms:
>
> a) That the occasion should take the form of a Festival of the Arts covering drama and music, including opera and ballet; the visual arts, including painting and sculpture, photography and films; books; and industrial design.
> b) That it should be centered, as far as possible, in existing buildings; but that -
> c) Everything possible should be done to improve these buildings by repairs and to press the completion of the new buildings already under consideration such as . . . one or more new Concert Halls in London.
> d) That the Arts Council should be provided with the necessary extra funds, extra accommodation and extra staff according to the need.

It was also the unanimous view of the Council that the events organised for the Festival should represent the British arts only.

(EL4/43, February 27, 1947)

The last point in this report strikes a new but important note in the Festival idea: Unlike previous festivals and world's fairs, the Festival of Britain (as yet unnamed), it was proposed, would be exclusively national. The report gave no reasoning behind this decision, but a later document refined the policy:

> The Festival should illustrate the arts of Great Britain only. This does not mean that only British plays and British music would be performed, or only British pictures and films shown, or even that only British artists would take part. It would mean that the resources of this country alone would be relied upon and no invitations issued to artists or organizations from abroad to take part.
>
> (Paper 86, EL4/66, n.d. [1948])

The consensus that the Festival, in whatever form it finally took, would focus exclusively on Britain, rested to an extent on fiscal constraints. At this early stage it was unclear what resources would be available to hire expensive foreign performers. A welfare-state mindset also underlies this policy: A seeming desire to restrict socialized benefits funded by tax-payers to British subjects arises in several instances where non-British musicians were considered for Festival honors. However, this nativist bias certainly also reflected the deliberate philosophical position of the planners: Britain, emerging from the War, could celebrate herself and show herself in her best colors without relying on foreigners. Of course, the same war had settled a large number of émigré creative artists and performers on British shores. The lack of clarity over the status of these immigrants in a purely national celebration inevitably generated problems.

As a whole, the Festival of Britain continued the tradition of exhibitions, world's fairs, and trade shows from earlier in the century. In its scope and ambition, the South Bank Exhibition in particular was the successor to the 1911 Festival of Empire at the Crystal Palace and the 1924–1925 British Empire Exhibition at Wembley, both of which featured a mix of novel architecture, cultural displays, and amusement similar to that of 1951. The 1924–1925 exhibition in particular, although mounted on a greater scale than the Festival of Britain, undoubtedly served as the main model for 1951 planners.

The musical program of the Festival of Britain owes a debt to the same precursors, but an impulse toward a higher class of performers, performance, and repertory tempered this influence. Jeffrey Richards (2001: 177–208) provides a thorough account of the musical events at the Empire exhibitions. Both, he writes, "made a specific attempt to promote British and Empire music as part of their propaganda offensive" (179). The opening concert in 1911 included works by Parry, Stanford, Elgar, Mackenzie, and Henry Wood. (A series of "Empire concerts" followed, with repertory representing in turn Canada, Australia, Scotland, South

Africa, Ireland, Wales, and New Zealand, although the national representation could be tenuous.) The 1924–1925 exhibition featured a similar pantheon of contemporary British composers in its concerts. Unquestionably, this trend of highlighting native music reached its pinnacle in the Festival of Britain. The events, however, differed in type: The concerts whose particular British content Richards describes continued the Victorian tradition of mass orchestra and choral performances or massed military bands, neither of which traditions dominated the Festival of Britain.

Furthermore, much of the new British music in the Empire exhibitions was not heard in concerts at all but accompanied the pageants that were the centerpieces of the program of performances. The Pageant of London (1911) and the Pageant of Empire (1924–1925), both produced by Frank Lascelles, the "Master of Pageants," were the largest, most famous, and most heavily attended pageants in a thirty-year period when pageants were very popular all across Britain. For both of these vast multi-day events, Lascelles and his team not only selected older British music but also commissioned new works and arrangements. Twenty composers, including many of the most prominent English composers of the day, contributed to the score of the Pageant of London; the Pageant of Empire was similar, and included a number of special commissions by Edward Elgar.

The musical selections in pageants were ordinarily subservient to the dramatic content of the scenes they underscored, and, at any rate, by 1951, the heyday of the pageant had passed. Even so, the music planners of the Festival of Britain undoubtedly relied on memories and records of the quantity and range of exhibition pageants for general inspiration. In particular, the Pageant of London, whose narrative spanned 2,000 years, included a sort of historical review of English music, albeit heavily filtered through the taste and understanding of the period and arranged for contemporary performing forces.

Another model for a program of coordinated but independent events could be found in the historical provincial music festivals: the Three Choirs Festival and the Norfolk and Norwich Festival, as well as the BBC's annual promenade concerts and more specialized festivals such as the annual series sponsored by the International Society for Contemporary Music. Indeed, although the Festival of Britain was conceived as a single massive event, the late forties saw a mania for founding new musical festivals in Britain. The Cheltenham Festival of Contemporary British Music began in 1945, followed by the Edinburgh International Festival—a sort of cosmopolitan antidote to the parochialism of the Three Choirs Festival—in 1947, and Benjamin Britten's Aldeburgh Festival and the Bath Festival in 1948. So the kind of programming that the Arts Council was undertaking was very timely.

In February 1948, Mary Glasgow appointed an Arts Council staffer, Duncan Guthrie, to be her assistant in Festival matters (EL4/95, February 4, 1948). In April, Guthrie prepared a ten-page memorandum entitled "Preliminary Suggestions for the Festival of the Arts" (Paper 247, EL4/48, April 16, 1948) This document differed from the earlier proposals for a "cultural exhibition in London" in that it now elaborated in detail the guiding principle of the Festival laid down by the Festival Council: decentralization. Guthrie's initial memorandum proved a remarkably precise blueprint for the form that the Arts Council's plans finally took. It envisioned a series of arts festivals dispersed throughout Britain, built around the existing annual festivals, but with the addition of other new festivals. Each festival would have a distinct character and focus, in accordance with local history and cultural traditions: for example, oratorios at the Three Choirs Festival in Worcester, Shakespeare at Stratford-upon-Avon, and religious drama at Canterbury. Furthermore, the component festivals would be spread out across the now-finalized May-to-September period so as to minimize overlapping; in theory, a traveler with sufficient time and funds should be able to visit all the official festivals. Beyond the official festivals, the Arts Council and the Festival Office would encourage other towns, societies, and associations to "indulge in the arts in one form or another," even in cases where the Arts Council could not directly support their events financially.

Guthrie stressed the need both to arrange spectacular offerings in London and also to make sure that the festivals in the provinces would not "be left with nothing more than the leavings of the London season". To this end, he recommended that the Council coordinate the touring schedules of the major performing groups. Similarly, he suggested that the Council lease the Royal Albert Hall for the entire summer and sublease it to individual performing organizations, thereby gaining the power to control the balance of performing groups and repertory. He also presciently pointed out that "the opportunity offered by 1951 for opening a new concert hall in London is of the first order. From a national point of view, the establishment of a new concert hall might well be the outstanding result of the Festival of Britain, 1951."

Guthrie further noted that the Festival afforded opportunities for the Arts Council to place commissions for the first time in its history: "Festivals have always been the occasion for commissioning. There has been a long tradition of works commissioned for Festivals and it would seem inappropriate to make any break with this tradition." He suggested some genres but advised against competitions, recommending instead placing commissions with composers chosen by the Arts Council in advance. Guthrie also proposed that in the case of musical commissions, guaranteed performances by reputable ensembles in different parts of the country could take the place of monetary payments to composers, but the Arts Council did not pursue this possibility.

In response to Guthrie's outline, Gerald Barry, the Director-General of the Festival, sent a series of 12 questions to the Arts Council in late April 1948, intended to stimulate their thinking (EL6/23, April 26, 1948). In addition to asking for a full list of component festivals with their themes and timing, Barry asked about the plans for London. He noted the proposal to commission music, and asked about similar plans for painting and sculpture. Finally, he asked, "In what other general ways does the Arts Council propose to make 1951 not merely a year of bigger and better festivals but one which will leave its own mark on history and if possible make some permanent contribution to the cause of the Arts in Britain?"

Meetings of the Arts Council panels refined Guthrie's draft in response to Barry's challenges. The next internal memorandum by Guthrie (Paper 84, EL4/66,

May 28, 1948) restated the "Purpose and Approach to Theme" that Barry had recently promulgated, and went on to give more detailed consideration of possible locations for the "decentralized Festivals", the list of which was still very much in flux. (For instance, the Aldeburgh Festival, which was brand new that year and whose continued existence could not be assumed, was added to the list only provisionally.) This second memorandum also incorporated recommendations for commissions and other programs generated by the specialist panels.

Guthrie's early memoranda served as the template for the much shorter official proposal forwarded by the Arts Council to the Festival of Britain Executive Committee (Paper 248, EL4/48, June 17, 1948). The basic outline of Arts Council activities was in place by this date. As initially envisioned, the existing festivals such as Edinburgh, Cheltenham, Three Choirs, and Aldeburgh fell within the Festival ambit, receiving extra money and help from the Arts Council to arrange special events. The Arts Council also encouraged the development of new local arts festivals. No initial proposal included the complete final tally of 22 regional festivals; the official list grew and changed almost up until the eve of the Festival, with Oxford and Cambridge included very late in the planning process. But, upon the approval of the official proposal, the Festival Office extended to every town on the list an invitation to hold a festival, or to associate its existing festival with the Festival of Britain, and Gerald Barry toured them all to encourage them to accept. The Arts Council regional directors and specialist art directors then began the complicated process of holding organizational meetings with the relevant local authorities to plan and coordinate events among the component festivals.

Eventually, as the body responsible for all the arts in all the local festivals around the nation in 1951, the Arts Council worked with the local committees planning the regional festivals to ensure a broad and varied program of artistic performances and exhibitions throughout the country. The individual festival committees proposed programming based on the local theme and the expertise of locally available performers. The Arts Council's chief duties were guidance, supervision, and encouragement in securing a good variety of works, with intervention only when plans seemed to take a wrong turn, as with Cambridge's operatic plans narrated in Chapter 3. Beyond this, the Arts Council coordinated the schedules of all the nation's main touring orchestras and theatrical ensembles, to ensure that they would be in the right towns at the right times and achieve a balance of repertory among these locales.

This coordination was a daunting task, but the largest part of the Arts Council's Festival work involved the offerings in London, curtailed from Guthrie's proposed three-month period of May through July to the eight weeks from May 3rd to June 30th, so as not to overlap excessively with the larger regional festivals later in the summer. There was no organizing committee through which to funnel funds, and participants included both commercial and non-profit promoters and both professional and amateur ensembles. To ensure a coherent festival in London, therefore, the Arts Council abandoned precedent and in effect became the London Festival Committee, with full responsibility for coordinating all the offerings. The

London Season of the Arts, as the period came to be called, was both more extensive and more diffuse than the regional festivals, encompassing exhibits of paintings, drawing, and sculpture, and drama, music, and dance performances by major and minor troupes and ensembles, mainly British but also from abroad.

The present study focuses chiefly on the work of the Arts Council in London precisely because it was so extensive and so direct, but does not neglect performance elsewhere, particularly when the repertory was subject to close supervision by the Council. The first two chapters explore the ways that the Arts Council, and to a lesser extent, the BBC and performing ensembles, formulated an appropriate repertory of national music for Festival concerts, largely in London. Chapter 1 examines the broad historical repertory of English music in the London Season of the Arts. This was the largest festival of English music in history, showcasing an unprecedented variety: approximately 200 performances containing over 800 works by over 160 composers from 1350 to 1950, all crammed into eight weeks. I analyze the planning and repertory of English music in both the London Season of the Arts and the BBC's Promenade Concerts that followed, with consideration of the tensions between traditional and more innovative programming, and the canon of English music as it stood in 1951. Chapter 2 addresses the imperative to have new national music in the Festival, and what the Festival's designers believed that new music should be. I investigate the chief commissioning and competition schemes for concert works and interpret the resulting works in the light of their expressly national, public, and celebratory purpose.

The latter three chapters turn their attention to the operas produced around the nation in the Festival year. Opera had played a somewhat peripheral role in British culture for centuries, and the Festival appeared to offer an opportunity to rehabilitate the genre. The Arts Council and performing organizations around the nation gave particular attention and resources to operatic projects for the Festival of Britain, with the result that 1951 saw a record number of English opera revivals, premieres, and commissions. Chapter 3 details the commissioning and preparation of the new operas premiered during the Festival. The Covent Garden Opera Company mounted premieres of large-scale works by the nation's two foremost composers, while Sadler's Wells Opera and smaller companies staged premieres and significant revivals of English operas in London and the provinces. Chapter 4 turns to the highly publicized competition conducted by the Arts Council to further stimulate opera production. This commissioning scheme, the most ambitious plan concocted by the Arts Council for the Festival, was plagued by delays and eventually devolved into a near-fiasco: Not only was the Arts Council unable to arrange performance of the winning works, but the revelation of the winners' names raised questions of nationality and suitability for native audiences, in both theme and musical style. Finally, Chapter 5 turns from analysis of bureaucratic methods and results to an analysis of the operas composed for and presented at the Festival. Bound together by temporal proximity and given prominence by their Festival context, these works form a repertory striking in its projection of elements of national identity, both positive and negative, as well as the ever-present legacy of the Second World War.

20 *Introduction*

Terms and Citations

In a work of this kind, some difficulty arises with the use of national terms. Both the public and private documentation of the Festival of Britain unwaveringly stressed its British qualities. Becky Conekin (2003: 30–33) has sensitively and thoroughly analyzed the ways in which the Festival represented a British nationality that encompassed and obscured ethnic differences within the United Kingdom. However, such an idealistic—and ideological—approach to nationality did not really function in the realm of art music, where the historical and contemporary supremacy of the English was both assumed and explicitly represented.

Musical nationalism of the nineteenth century variety in Britain focused on ethnic identities—English, Scottish, Welsh, Irish and, in certain cases, Cornish—rather than on British identity. However, the English not only dominated the kingdom politically but had the largest population, the greatest educational resources, the most prestigious performing institutions, and the most significant metropolis. Thus, the term "English" could have a more restrictively ethnic connotation, but it was usually an unmarked general term. In this usage, "English" applied to works and composers with national reputations or positions in the central institutions of British musical life, even when they were assimilated into that identity through education and station (Charles Villiers Stanford) or sought to escape it (Arnold Bax).

By contrast, ethnic terms such as "Scottish" and "Welsh" drew attention to a composer's or a work's difference or position outside the "English" mainstream. Often, the peripheral musical traditions were assumed to be largely folkloric or working-class ones, outside the "fine arts" purview of the Arts Council. Welsh music, for instance, though respected as a highly developed art, entered the Festival of Britain solely through church singing and the eisteddfodau (performance festivals) until the Welsh committee specifically requested a commissioning scheme for its local classical composers, and from the evidence of the Festival documents one would conclude that Scottish art music did not exist at all. This erasure of ethnic identity was possible because most of the composers with national reputations could be classed as "English" in the broader sense. As necessary, this category included not merely Welsh and Scottish composers with positions in London or the universities, but figures such as the Russian-born cosmopolitan Albert Coates, the London-educated Australian Arthur Benjamin, and the Cornwall-born Welsh-American George Lloyd.

Because of this general meaning of the term "English," historical documents are notably unsystematic, using the terms "English" and "British" somewhat interchangeably in discussions of national music. More legalistic guidelines speak of the "British nationality" of eligible composers, while most other documents refer to the classical art tradition in question simply as "English music" and its practitioners as "English composers." The term "British music" usually has a political cast aligned with the Festival of Britain's erasure of ethnic difference, while "British composer" occurs most often in discussions of institutional challenges. However, the status of immigrants rendered even the term "British" problematic at this period. The Second World War brought to Britain a number of prominent middle- and eastern-European composers whose national status remained unclear.

With regard to opera, the use of national terms is equally vexing. In the decade following the Second World War, prominent British musical figures expressed a strong desire to establish "English opera" on a newly firm foundation. But depending on the individual using the term, it encompassed not merely repertory, but performance and training institutions, performance traditions, and the performers themselves. Even setting aside institutional definitions (companies, schools, and theaters), the term "English opera" has a wide range of meanings with regard to repertory, as Steven Martin (2010: 12–14) points out. These include (1) works by composers of any nationality sung in English translation, (2) works by born or naturalized Britons usually (but not exclusively) sung in English, (3) works in English based on English subjects or sources, and (4) works with specifically English (as opposed to Scottish, Welsh, or Irish) characteristics. The phrase "British opera" raises similar problems.

Thus, the question of what "English" and "British" mean for different individuals and constituencies at different times in the process of preparing the music of the Festival of Britain forms one of the secondary themes of this study. For my part, I have tried to be as systematic as possible with these terms while avoiding monotony.

Finally, for ease of reading, I have abbreviated the citations in this study by leaving out the archive names. All shelf-marks beginning with "EL" or "ACGB" are internal documents of the Arts Council of Great Britain housed in the Archive of Art and Design, a division of the Victoria and Albert Museum; those beginning with "WORK" are Festival Office documents housed in the National Archive in Kew; and those beginning with "R" are BBC documents from the Written Archive Centre in Caversham. "AROHCG" is the Archive of the Royal Opera House, Covent Garden, "BPF" is th Britten-Pears Foundation, and "CUL" is the Cambridge University Library. Published sources are listed in the bibliography.

Notes

1 The foundational texts for all studies of the Festival of Britain are Michael Frayn's essay "Festival" (Frayn 1980) and the materials collected by Mary Banham and Bevis Hillier in *A Tonic to the Nation* (1976) to accompany the 25th anniversary exhibit of Festival design at the Victoria and Albert Museum. Another important contribution is Alan Sinfield's 1995 essay "The Government, the People and the Festival". More recent years have seen the publication of Becky Conekin's *The Autobiography of a Nation* (2003), the only sustained academic study of the Festival, and Barry Turner's *Beacon for Change* (2011), the first thorough journalistic account. The literature on the Festival's cultural output is more limited. The most significant contributions are Elain Harwood and Alan Powers's 2001 volume, which provides a thorough history, review, and critique of the Festival's architecture, Sarah Street's 2012 essay analyzing Festival films, and Graham Saunders 2012 essay on the playwriting competition.
2 The history of CEMA and the early years of the Arts Council is a contentious topic, largely because of a significant shift in focus from community-based art around the

nation towards support for the elite institutions, mostly in London. Because the Arts Council (in various guises) has remained a powerful and controversial force in British culture, the extensive literature on it almost universally expresses partisan opinion based on the events of the time that the author in question is writing. Nevertheless, this literature reveals much about the strange origins and procedures of the Council. For the period leading up to the Festival, Eric Walter White's 1975 history of the Arts Council provides good a summary of its structure and functioning of the Council. Lindsay 1945 and Ifor Evans and Glasgow 1949, along with the Arts Council's own annual reports, also provide early pictures of the agency. Minihan 1977, Hutchison 1982, Raymond Williams 1989, Leventhal 1990, Croft 1995, Sinclair 1995, Sinfield 1995, and Witts 1998 all analyze and critique the Arts Council from various points of view. See also Wiebe 2012: 24–30. The best source on the career of Mary Glasgow, the Council's powerful Secretary General, is David Sheridan's 2007 Ph.D. dissertation.

1 Old music...
British repertory in London

William Weber (1999: 336–341) has made a useful distinction between *performance canons* in music, driven by the taste of patrons and audiences, and *scholarly canons*, driven by instructors and scholars. In its attempt in the London Season of the Arts to mount a comprehensive display of English musical creativity covering seven centuries, the Arts Council of Great Britain deliberately and with great specificity proposed a canon of national music. Indeed, as a rare attempt both to define *and perform* an entire canon, or as much of it as practical considerations would allow, the London Season of the Arts falls between Weber's two types. The contributors to the planning process were musical professionals, musically educated civil servants, and academics, with none of these categories strongly outweighing any other. These different constituencies used every mechanism at their disposal, and developed new means when necessary, to direct repertory selection and balance. The concert promoters and ensembles proposed works that particularly interested them or that would be popular with audiences; the musicologists advocated little-heard works of scholarly interest; the bureaucrats individually and in committees balanced these suggestions and further supplemented them with their own lists of unjustly neglected works that audiences may had heard of, but which were neither studied or performed on a regular basis. The result was the largest festival of English music in history, encompassing hundreds of works.

Like all canons, the repertory of the London Season of the Arts had its ideological boundaries. This chapter investigates those boundaries and the aesthetic commitments of the institutions and individuals who policed them. A comparison of the London Season of the Arts with the BBC's smaller but still impressive series of Promenade Concerts (Proms) at the Royal Albert Hall later in the official Festival period illuminates the two institutions' differing approaches to choosing native repertory, stemming in part from their contrasting goals and management styles.

Careful analysis of this extensive concert repertory reveals tensions between traditional and progressive musical values, and between impulses toward exclusivity and inclusivity, both at mid-century and in later historiography. In an era more cynical or politicized about the concept of national music, an institution with the cultural authority of the Arts Council might have established far more rigid aesthetic boundaries. In fact, with some exceptions, the ideologies at work in the London Season of the Arts were internalized and unconsidered; genuine good will and at least an effort at broad-mindedness motivated the chief planners of the London Season, moderated more often by a sense of prudence than by overt disapproval. The process of selection offered countless opportunities to rehabilitate unfamiliar or neglected composers and works, and to limit the excessive exposure of others. Still, in retrospect, and even to an extent at the time, the results reinscribed or only modestly expanded the existing canon of British music, rather than forging a challenging counter-narrative. This tendency raises questions about whether such omissions, deliberate or not, resulted from bureaucratic processes, individual narrow-mindedness, or other causes, and how they represent broader cultural and musical trends of the time.

British music in the Twentieth Century

To the extent that the recent and newly prominent music performed in the London Season of the Arts appears stylistically unadventurous, with few incursions from composers identified with alternate high-modern or culturally marginal traditions, the culture of committees and planning reports that generated the Festival must bear some responsibility. Even admitting the broadness of their goals and the influence of enthusiastic individuals in institutions such as the Arts Council and the BBC, British bureaucratic culture took a cautious approach to aesthetic risk-taking. Indeed, although the conservatism of the Festival's contemporary music seems to contrast with the progressive tendencies of its architecture, most of the forms of Festival design, while novel in the blitzed environment of 1951 Britain, were in fact based on established pre-war Scandinavian models (see Banham and Hillier 1976; Harwood and Powers 2001).

But bureaucratic restraint alone is not sufficient explanation for the staid profile of the Festival musical repertory. Any analysis of the Festival repertory must first contend with the undue emphasis on atonality in the historiography of twentieth century music, and the question of how modernism functions as a useful category in discussions of English music. In the period leading up to the Festival of Britain, the avant-garde exerted increasing authority in Western Europe, where the end of the Second World War led in many spheres to calls for a fresh start: In music, this rebirth was marked by a rejection of the legacy of tonal harmony and classical genres, and was promoted at contemporaneous European festivals. But one can easily exaggerate the importance of avant-garde repertory to the general classical music audience. Works in tonal styles exhibiting forms and gestures derived from common-practice and early modern composers still dominated mainstream concert music on both sides of the English Channel.

Even if we correct for the overemphasis on avant-garde music, British music of the period still may appear stylistically conservative. European modernist trends—whether Viennese, Stravinskian, or other—were received and disseminated warily in Britain.[1] In 1951, most British composers had an ambivalent relationship with continental varieties of stylistic modernism in this period, and were characterized, in Arnold Whittall's terms (1995: 17), by "the suspicion of the extravagant, the expressionistic, the experimental" The historiography of British music has amply demonstrated that when we judge British composers' output by outmoded standards of progressive style, the entire nation unfairly appears to come up short.

There are several reasons why adherents of the musical avant-garde in Britain were relatively few and obscure compared to their continental brethren at this time. One reason was the curriculum of British conservatories in the late 19th and early 20th centuries, which hewed to traditional lines in technique, style, and genre (this state of affairs created an environment which inspired hopes in some young British composers of crossing the Channel to broaden their horizons). The historiography of music in Britain supplies another source for postwar aesthetic caution. Unlike continental countries with centuries of musical history both to celebrate and then to reject during postwar reconstruction, Britain in 1951 had very recently forged its narrative of national musical history. The history of British music current after the Second World War saw the period starting around 1880 as an English Musical Renaissance, when the art of composition in England, languishing in the depths of foreign domination and amateurism since the death of Henry Purcell in 1695, sprang to new life. England's return to the musical stage was thus far too recent to warrant wholesale rejection by impresarios or composers; her romantic art-music tradition represented twentieth century strength, not nineteenth century decadence.

Furthermore, as Matthew Riley (2010: 6–9) points out, quoting Stefan Collini, the British experience of the transition to the twentieth century differed from that of continental countries in other ways. Britain escaped most of the social and cultural shock that rocked Europe in the nineteenth century: Britain suffered no military invasion; political reform kept up with social change, dampening revolutionary political movements; and more advanced industrialization held off economic upheaval. As a result, there was less fodder for the development of a violently oppositional avant-garde. The transition to modernist ideas and styles proceeded more as a continuity than as a rupture with the past. Riley (2010: 28–30) also credits the survival of nineteenth century liberal British critical attitudes, including a longstanding mistrust of professionalism in music, with the muted approach to modernism in the first half of the twentieth century.

The ideology of Musical Renaissance was not merely a mode of music-historical awareness; it also affected the reception of musical style. Although the maturation of teaching and performing institutions, rather than specific stylistic developments, arguably generated the "English Musical Renaissance," a loose set of nationally marked stylistic and compositional categories did coalesce between the wars into what seemed to many an English national or pastoral school. The stylistic elements that characterized this repertory were neither uniform nor ubiquitous, and no composer exemplifies all of them throughout his or her works, but among them were harmonic and melodic markers based on the revivals of folksong and Tudor polyphony before the First World War and programmatic focus on symbols central to British national identity, such as the sea and the rural countryside.[2] Ralph Vaughan Williams was most closely identified with this trend, along with composers such as Gerald Finzi and Herbert Howells. This pastoral trend, such as it was, had its heyday in the twenties and thirties. In Arnold Whittall's analysis (1995: 13–14), the proponents of the trend defended it as an alternative, British form of modernism based on cultural rather than structural principles; no doubt, the "sane and socially responsible" values Whittall identifies with the modernism of Vaughan Williams would have surprised many artists on the Continent who valued rupture and individualism.

Audiences take longer to adapt to change than do composers. Even after the Second World War, audiences and critics both in Britain and abroad continued to recognize the stylistic characteristics of the pastoral repertory as historically, even essentially English. To their minds, for music to claim status as national, it had to sound English, which meant to refer to this style. The historical understanding and stylistic prejudices of English-Musical-Renaissance thinking inform the institutional decision-making of the Festival, as well as the journalistic responses to the performances.

There were also dissenting voices between the wars, of which the dominant group drew on Stravinsky, Jazz, and French music, rather than the more extreme innovations coming from German-speaking lands. These include the early William Walton as well as composers associated with the ballet: Arthur Bliss, Lord Berners, and Constant Lambert. By 1951, however, the mainstream had integrated their music, and Walton's style had lost some of its acerbic wit. Alan Bush was unusual among Englishmen for having received German training, and he experimented between the wars with a severe contrapuntal style unlike most of his compatriots, but, by the forties he too had mellowed into a far more nationally-marked style. In her magisterial study *Romantic Moderns*, Alexandra Harris (2010: 10–11) descries a "turn towards home" among English literary and visual artists at mid-century, just when cultural trends in Western Europe were heading ever farther afield. It is scarcely surprising to find a parallel impulse among composers.

To be sure, by the time of the Festival of Britain, a new and more diverse and cosmopolitan generation of British composers was making inroads into the repertory, but in the assessment of Peter Evans (1995: 207) the composers who dominated the landscape remained a restrained, competent crew uninterested in radical change:

> In Britain, insulation from the European radicals, the celebrated "time lag", allowed the 1900s generation some sense of creative adventure, but in essence they were as cautious as their colleagues abroad; there was no explorer among them to match Holst, and until Tippett's full maturity, no visionary prepared, like Vaughan Williams, to risk charges of monumental bungling rather than lower his aim. A respectable level of technical skill was common, though its source might be diverse; the standard orchestra served their needs well, symphony and concerto being preferred to the freer, programmatic forms. . . . Several of them showed a capacity for self-renewal which prevented their merely pandering to the expectations of the growing, but essentially wary, audience for orchestral concerts in Britain.

Stephen Banfield (private communication) has similarly argued that after the war the tonal composers who remained successful with audiences were precisely those such as Gordon Jacob and Malcolm Arnold who continued to reference a recognizably stylistic Englishness. Others, such as George Lloyd (discussed in Chapters 3 and 5), whose tonal styles, while conservative, were more individualistic or derived from Continental models, and who eschewed the markers of musical Englishness such as folksong and modalism, generated neither the frisson of the new nor the comfort of nostalgia, and fell into obscurity in the postwar period.

A final factor guiding the profile of contemporary music in the Festival that is quite separate from questions of style was the relative cultural authority of the composers. The recognition that the Arts Council granted individual composers sometimes depended more on their educational background, their association with central cultural institutions, and even the details of their wartime service, than on the kind of music they wrote. Not surprisingly, the closer a composer was—professionally, socially, and geographically—to the institutions of power such as the Arts Council, the BBC, or one of the prestigious universities or London conservatories, the better he or she was represented in 1951. As we shall see in Chapter 2, the Arts Council placed all its Festival commissions with composers well known to its own staff and easily approached by them; some were actually serving on the Music Panel. The modest Festival roles afforded certain modernists, such as Elisabeth Lutyens, Humphrey Searle, and Peter Racine Fricker, are scarcely surprising, as all three of these composers maintained ties with London teaching and performing institutions. Benjamin Britten's prominent position in Festival programs—despite a musical style that, while not high modernist, sometimes exceeded the expectations and appreciation of mainstream audiences—stems in part from his mastery of self-promotion, which included his own opera company and music festival and unwavering support from his powerful London publisher, Boosey and Hawkes (Kildea 2002).

Concert planning for the London Season of the Arts

The London Season of the Arts encompassed all the fine arts under the purview of the Arts Council. London museums and galleries, including the South Bank Exhibition, mounted 30 special exhibits of paintings, drawings, and sculpture (Hewison 1988: 51–54). Book exhibits and lecture series represented literature. There were screenings of classic and newly commissioned films, while commercial and non-profit theater companies staged both classic works by Shakespeare and Shaw and new plays. All the major metropolitan and touring opera and ballet companies performed. In addition to performances and exhibitions, the University of London offered a summer school on "Literature, the Visual Arts, and Music in Britain To-Day". This summer school included a series of nine public lectures in June and July on "British Artists, Composers, and Writers", although it is unclear how broad the coverage of music was in this series: The only composers mentioned in the publicity flier are Vaughan Williams and Britten (EL6/166).

Among all these cultural riches, the musical component was the London Season's extraordinary feature. Provision was made for broad tastes; in addition to classical music, the London Season guide included announcements of musical comedy, music hall, brass bands, revue, dance bands, and even fireworks, not to mention the comprehensive season by the D'Oyly Carte Company, even though these were neither planned nor financially supported by the Arts Council (in 1949, the Arts Council had even ruled against funding light music in the Festival). Becky Conekin (2003: 119–120) argues that the Arts Council strove to make the London Season of the Arts accessible to people of all incomes and classes, and a retrospective publication entitled *The Story of the Festival of Britain* (Festival Council 1952: 19) reported: "The musical programmes were planned to give a comprehensive survey of all important types of music-making in Britain." This is an overstatement; many forms of British music were unrepresented, but nonetheless the offerings were certainly wide-ranging.

The Arts Council published schedules and lists of all these performances, but the effort of collecting this information paled beside the preparation of the art-music concert schedule, given the great expense of musical performance and the logistical difficulty of coordinating so many separate organizations and venues. Naturally, much of the music performed at festival concerts was not by British composers, but, given the extent to which the Festival celebrated all things British, and especially British creativity, the Arts Council strove to represent British music not just richly, but comprehensively. In the words of *The Official Book of the Festival of Britain* (Taylor 1951: 16), "In its work in connection with the London Season the Arts Council has set out to arrange a full representation of the history and practice of British music, the work of orchestras, singers, players and musical societies from every part of the kingdom and the variety of the nation's musical life, professional and amateur." The Council staff used both encouragement and coercion to achieve this breadth, exercising unprecedented authority over concert programs. They urged performers to investigate unfamiliar repertory, approached musical scholars for suggestions, and made their own lists of native works, old and new, familiar and obscure, by major and minor British composers.

The musicological activity sponsored by the Arts Council bore fruit not only in performance activities, but also in a related Festival publishing project. An early Arts Council memorandum had pointed out that the Festival "could provide an ideal opportunity for the commissioning of research or 'realisation' work on some old masterpiece" (EL6/45, n.d. [1948]). The project became *Musica Britannica*, whose first volumes, announced for the Festival, were the Mulliner Book of Tudor keyboard music, Matthew Locke and Christopher Gibbons's music for *Cupid and Death*, and Thomas Arne's music for John Milton's *Comus*.

The task of piecing together the concert program of the London Season began in earnest in early 1949, when the Council called two meetings, one on April 4th with the professional London ensembles, concert organizers, and promoters, and the other on April 7th with amateur musical organizations.[3] At these meetings, John Denison, the Arts Council's Music Director, explained the structure of the upcoming Festival—the regional festivals and the London season—and invited the organizations to consider what part they could play in both areas. Recognizing that many ensembles would wish to tour the provinces during the Festival year, Denison presented the Arts Council's plans to coordinate the content of the regional festivals. He outlined the state of London's concert halls (discussed below), and laid out preliminary financial plans and the publicity campaign for the Festival as a whole (EL6/80).

Denison also made a pitch for programming British music, mentioning the Arts Council's plans to commission new works and stressing the Council's desire to have these works performed throughout the nation during the Festival. To encourage the performance of rarely heard British music, he explained, the Arts Council would make available special guarantees for concerts including such repertory, but emphasized that the Council would not provide 100 percent guarantees, since promoters had to take some risk. He asked the organizations to submit proposals specifying the type of program, the hall wanted, the date, and financial estimates to the Arts Council by June 1949, so that the Council could organize them into a coherent program and ensure sufficient breadth of repertory.

In August, the Arts Council called another meeting with the major metropolitan and provincial orchestras to initiate coordination of London performances, touring schedules, and repertory. By October, a subcommittee of the Arts Council's Music Panel had received eighty concert proposals and began piecing together the Festival and the London Season, planning the concerts, in the words of the Council's 1950–51 Annual Report (5), "in such a way as to ensure that our own composers and our own musical habits and traditions [are] all substantially represented."

Ensembles and promoters entered willingly into the spirit of the Festival, and probably in some cases surpassed the Council's expectations for creative and broad exploration of the national repertory; several announced plans to commission new works for the Festival.[4] But even so, the Arts Council's commitment to diversity and innovation in programming required arrogating to the Arts Council some of the performers' autonomy. Where the Council identified over-exposure of popular works, or neglect of necessary ones, they demanded changes to the programs as a condition of a subsidy for the concert. In Paul Kildea's words (2002: 121), the Arts Council, "demand[ed] innovative programming—rescinding guarantees if this innovation was not forthcoming." For instance, Ernest Pooley, the Chairman of the Arts Council, wrote to the English Opera Group offering a larger Festival grant if they agreed to perform Brian Easdale's new opera, *The Sleeping Children*, during the Festival (Kildea 2002: 104).

One obstacle facing this early Festival concert planning in the capital was the absence of a proper concert hall. London's main concert hall, the Queen's Hall, had been destroyed during the Blitz, leaving the city with only the vast Royal Albert Hall, famous for its pronounced echo, for orchestral performances. In 1948, as the Arts Council's plans began to materialize, the need for a new concert hall became urgent. Although in June 1948 opinion within the Arts Council leaned toward the rebuilding of the Queen's Hall (EL4/48), the London County Council announced its intention to build a concert hall on the South Bank to be ready by

1951. As the Festival developed, the location of the new concert hall within the precincts of the Festival Exhibition became a great point in the hall's favor.

While it appeared for a time that the Queen's Hall would be rebuilt as well, by late 1949, as the first detailed plans for the London Season emerged, it was clear that the Festival Hall (the new South Bank concert hall, not yet so named), and not a rebuilt Queen's Hall, would be the only new venue for orchestral music. Therefore, in an enterprising move adapting Duncan Guthrie's suggestion in his original planning memorandum, the Arts Council paid almost £14,000 to secure the lease on the new hall for the full eight weeks of the London Season. Although it was not possible to secure a parallel long-term lease of the Albert Hall, the management of the Albert Hall was "well-disposed" to the Arts Council's plans and negotiated a similar arrangement for the same period, effectively giving the Council authority over bookings there. (Arts Council 1950–1951 Annual Report, 5; ACGB 50/28) In this way, since the Council already managed the Wigmore Hall, London's premiere chamber-music venue, it alone could choose which groups would sublet each hall each night, commanding not only the balance of ensembles but also their repertory, and guaranteeing that the offerings were representative and varied. For the duration of the London Season, all of the capital's major concert venues, including its only proper concert hall, were protected from the vagaries of the marketplace.

Such control inevitably pitted ensembles against one another. For instance, almost all the major London choral societies lobbied the Arts Council to be chosen to perform Handel's *Messiah*. The Arts Council bestowed this honor upon the London Choral Society, which together with the Council sponsored an exhibition at the British Museum of Handel's autograph score and the copies used at early performances (EL6/144). Similarly, the London *Times* music critic Frank Howes (1951: 2) reported, somewhat in jest, that almost all the national choral societies included Edward Elgar's *Dream of Gerontius* in the proposals they submitted to the Arts Council (both Southwark Cathedral and the Royal Choral Society gave performances of this work in the London Season).

With the music programs of London churches, where the Arts Council staff could not influence repertory directly, they resorted to advocacy and persuasion, calling for a comprehensive review of English choral tradition over the course of the summer. Then, as if cajoling conductors, ensembles, and church musicians were not enough, in January 1950, to further expand the repertory offered at the London Season concerts beyond what the independent concert-promoting bodies proposed, the Arts Council decided to mount three special concert series of their own. The first series of eight concerts offered music in all genres by Henry Purcell, the second devoted eight concerts to English music from 1300 to 1750, and the third, arranged jointly with the BBC and broadcast live, displayed English art song since the Renaissance over six concerts.

By May 1950, the Arts Council had scheduled so many special and notable performances and exhibitions in London that they could not be left to attract audiences merely as an intensification of the city's ordinary summer concert life. Some additional publicity was necessary to attract the larger audiences of both locals and domestic and international tourists necessary to fill seats. Therefore, the Council recommended that the Festival Office package and publicize them as a London Festival, even though the program of events was broader and looser than the other official exhibitions and regional festivals, and not organized around any particular theme (Papers 122 and 127, EL4/100). After some consideration of other names, the Festival Office chose the designation "London Season of the Arts," and issued a special program book like those for the exhibitions with a listing of every event offered by organizations sponsored by the Arts Council flanked by essays on the various arts by prominent figures such as Ralph Vaughan Williams, T. S. Eliot, and Thomas Beecham. The Arts Council even suggested extending the program guide's coverage beyond sponsored events to include contributions by profit-making and independent professional organizations, but the Festival Office did not take this step. (The Arts Council on its own released lists of such non-sponsored events.)

In March 1950, the composer Herbert Murrill assumed full responsibility for the musical content of the London Season. Murrill was a good choice for the job. Although not an Arts Council staff member, he was a member of the Arts Council's Music Panel. More importantly, he had worked at the BBC since 1936 and was therefore far better acquainted with large-scale seasonal programming than the regular Arts Council staff, to whom direct provision of professional musical performances and balance of repertory on such a scale was a novel undertaking. Indeed, the concerts of the London Season resemble an overgrown BBC quarterly music programming plan, and, in fact, while working on the London Season, Murrill was promoted to BBC Head of Music. (The resulting workload may have been too much for him; he died in 1952.)

By June 1950 Murrill's plans called for celebrity afternoon recitals at the Festival Hall, 25 major choral concerts, 45 orchestral concerts, between 20 and 30 string orchestra concerts, the three special series, competitive festivals, band concerts, music in parks, chamber music, and church music: over 200 performances in 56 days. In Murrill's understated assessment, "The music programme, as a whole, should provide a fair representation of British musical practice and achievement" (WORKS 25/2/A1/A2/13, report 17).

For the eight weeks of London Season of the Arts, the Arts Council transformed London concert life. From its usual haphazard mix of audience-driven programs with occasional noble efforts at reviving old works and presenting new ones, the entire London musical scene became an organized, planned presentation of British music history. The London Season of the Arts, in other words, had become the musical analogue of the South Bank Exhibition, with a share of that exhibition's didacticism and pretension to narrative coherence. This is scarcely surprising. The Arts Council drew its staff from the same Oxbridge-educated cultural elite as the Exhibition planners, and they shared the postwar Labourite commitment to educating the masses in the greatness of high culture. They were inspired by the narrative approach that Gerald Barry declared for the Festival. Adopting the matronly tone common in Festival documents, the notes for the London Season's publicity plan charged, "It is necessary for the public to be brought to realize that, in much the same as the scientific and architectural contributions are to be represented in the ... exhibitions, so the artistic life and contribution of the nation will be represented in the London Festival of the Arts" (WORKS 25/2/A1/A2/13, report 15).

In June 1950, the final piece of the Arts Council's influence over programming fell into place. The government granted the Council the extraordinary right to provide guarantees against loss (although not grants or loans) to commercial for-profit ensembles for the Festival period (EL6/78). This license exceeded the Council's established role and almost certainly violated the terms of its charter. Although the Arts Council did not in the end make much use of this new and short-lived power, and never again distributed money to commercial performing groups, in several cases such guarantees may have eased commercial companies' worries about ticket sales and allowed them too to take risks on unfamiliar repertory. By September, to toast the planning already accomplished and to disseminate information about the final stages of arrangements, the Arts Council gave a reception at the Royal Opera House for representatives of all the London theater companies, concert promoters, and art galleries.

Plans for the London Season of the Arts were largely complete by Christmas 1950 when the last months before the Festival's opening brought an unexpected public controversy over the Royal Festival Hall that played right into the Arts Council's hands. According to the original timetable, the London County Council would hold the Hall's gala opening on Monday April 30th followed by a week of special concerts, during which, on Thursday May 3rd, the South Bank Exhibition was slated to open next door, and the nationwide Festival and the London Season would both begin. After this first week of county-sponsored concerts the Arts Council's tenancy of the hall would commence.

Two problems intervened. On August 1, 1950, the Festival Subcommittee of the Arts Council's Music Panel had met and expressed the opinion that the Royal Festival Hall opening should "be entrusted to a large composite choir and orchestra selected from the London musical organisations, and Sir Thomas Beecham, Sir Adrian Boult, and Sir Malcolm Sargent should be invited to take part" (Paper 145, EL4/101). Such a concert, with its emphasis on native performers, would constitute a suitable opening of the London Season of the Arts.

Instead of accepting such a proposal, however, the London County Council—which in the run-up to the Festival seemed to delight in thwarting the Arts Council whenever possible—proposed to engage Arturo Toscanini to conduct the BBC Symphony in a concert of standard European repertory works. Announcement of this proposal early in 1951 sparked an outcry among those who felt that a new concert hall in London, for the use of British orchestras, inaugurated just before a British festival, should be opened by a British conductor. A letter of protest "on behalf of Thomas Beecham" appeared in the *Daily Telegraph* in mid-February, and Beecham himself wrote a typically intemperate letter a few days later, in which he specifically complained about the opening concert. In a public reply, Isaac J. Hayward of the London County Council tried to justify the Council's decision, explaining that they had invited the various British conductors to submit concert proposals for later in the opening week. The controversy attracted attention, with some newspaper readers expressing concerns that there was insufficient British music in the opening week of concerts, and others continuing to complain that the invitation to Toscanini was an insult to British conductors (EL6/66–67).

The London County Council was still trying to justify its decision when the second problem arose: George VI made it clear that he would not attend a concert hall opening on the South Bank before the day that the Festival of Britain itself opened there, which was May 3rd. There was no arguing with the monarch, and the London County Council had to move back the opening of the hall to that date. The Festival officially opened in the morning with a ceremony of thanksgiving at St. Paul's Cathedral attended by the royal family. After this service, the royal party traveled to the South Bank site to officially open the exhibitions, and then attended the gala concert in the evening. The enforced coincidence of the opening of the Royal Festival Hall and the South Bank Exhibition brought the opening concert within the official period of the London Season of the Arts, and offered the Arts Council an opportunity to re-impose its vision. Fortuitously, Toscanini dropped out due to his own illness and that of his wife Carla (Dyment 2012: 202–208), and the London County Council invited Sargent, Boult, and Beecham to conduct. True to form, Beecham, despite his earlier caviling, declined to share the podium. The Arts Council assembled the special combined orchestra and chorus and helped devise the program of British ceremonial music discussed in the Introduction, although the London County Council vetoed the inclusion of Edmund Rubbra's *Festival Te Deum*, which the Arts Council had commissioned for the Festival.

The week of county-sponsored performances in the hall was moved back as well, so that the Arts Council's tenancy began on May 10th. In the ensuing eight weeks, there were almost 300 musical performances in the Capital, including operas, ballets, and around 200 orchestral, choral, and chamber music concerts. For comparison, a modern-day series of Proms includes around 90 concert events over nine weeks; the London Season was approximately four times as dense with performances. Both the Royal Festival Hall and the Royal Albert Hall offered concerts almost every night. The five London orchestras all appeared, as did six provincial British orchestras, 20 choral societies (most from London), and dozens of other ensembles. There were daily recitals in the Wigmore Hall, concerts of sacred music in churches, and numerous music events of all kinds at other venues. The performances included the finals of the National Competitive Music Festival and the Schools Music Association gala concert. The National Brass Band Club and the British Federation of Music Festivals participated as well. In the words of Desmond Shawe-Taylor (1951: 617), "Das Land ohne Musik has become das Land mit almost too much Musik."

This was an expensive undertaking. For the fiscal year containing the Festival, the Treasury increased the Arts Council's funding by more than half, from £675,000 to £1,075,000, or around £32 million in 2013 currency. In 1949, Mary Glasgow, the Secretary General of the Arts Council, had estimated expenses of £40,000 for the London Season. In the final accounting, they had in fact disbursed over £35,000, over £1 million at current values. Of this, £1,090 was rent for the Festival Hall, another £8,000 spent on the special concert series, and an astonishing £26,518 in guarantees against loss for concerts. The Royal Philharmonic and London Philharmonic Orchestras received £2,000 each (EL6/167). The Council also provided an additional £36,000 in special Festival guarantees and grants—above the regular annual maintenance grants—to opera companies located in or performing in London, although some of the supported performances fell outside the London Season proper.

The London Season of the Arts gave a tremendous boost to the performance of national music. It did not, however, draw the audiences that its planners had hoped for. Not surprisingly, the zeal of performers and organizers outstripped the interest of the public. Already in October 1950, concert and performance planning had progressed so far that Arts Council staff raised concerns that too much was being arranged, and that there would not be sufficient audience to attend all the events (EL4/95). Similarly, a Festival Executive Committee memorandum from March 1949 expressed the concern that there would be too many exhibitions in 1951 for either the exhibition industry to construct or public interest to support (EL6/23).

The concerns about concerts turned out to be at least partially justified. The 1950–51 Arts Council Annual Report (5–6) crowed that "the concert season as a whole was successful beyond expectation," citing attendance at concerts at the Festival Hall during the Arts Council's tenure that averaged 85 percent capacity. (Concert attendance was doubtless encouraged by the fact that, since the Festival Hall was on the exhibition grounds, ticket-holders got into the Festival Exhibition as well.) But financial reports on the grants and guarantees show that most of the other concerts—especially those by smaller organizations—were undersold, sometimes to an extreme extent, and lost money; in some cases, but not all, the performers had naively estimated expenses using sellout figures. For example, the special concert of British music at Central Hall in Westminster, at which the London Choral Society and the Tobin Chamber Orchestra performed Arthur Bliss's *Pastorale: Lie Strewn the White Flocks*, the *Magnificat* of Ralph Vaughan Williams, Handel's *Ode for St Cecilia's Day*, and the premiere of *Twelfth Night: An Entertainment* by Geoffrey Bush attracted only a tiny audience (EL6/145).

Simply put, there were too many concerts in London in the summer of 1951 for even the most eager audiences. The Festival of Britain Office, with the assistance of the British Council, engaged in as much overseas publicity as possible given its meager budget, but despite their best efforts, poor weather and a lack of adequate tourism infrastructure limited international tourism. The South Bank Exhibition attracted tourists, but these were mostly Britons rather than foreigners, and in the evening they were more likely to return home or spend the evening at the Battersea Pleasure Gardens than take in a classical concert. And without a large increase in the concert-going public, music-loving Londoners would have had to greatly increase their concert attendance to fill the halls. But there is also some evidence that, contrary to the Arts Council's hopes that the Festival context of celebrating all things British would bring out the public, the unusually broad concert repertory actually deterred audiences. At the BBC, Julian Herbage, in his annual report on the 1951 Proms, expressed both the ambition and the challenge of the London Season concerts: "[T]he Festival itself has been something of a gamble, or should we say a brave gesture? Taking music alone, the plans for the Festival have been on an almost crazily inflated scale. Where were the audiences to come from? How would they cope, in particular, with this surfeit of British art when the surest way of emptying a concert hall is to play one (or even worse, two) major British works? And then the competition between two concert halls, the Festival Hall offering not only the advantage of novelty, but also the bonus of a free view of the Exhibition?" (R79/115/40).

British repertory in the London Season of the Arts

So, what was this "surfeit of British art" of which Herbage spoke? The opening concert only hinted at the breadth of British music to come. The London Season of the Arts program book and the National Archives together contain hundreds of concert programs from the London Season of the Arts.[5] Naturally, much of the repertory consisted of established continental fare. But due to the Arts Council's successful advocacy and arm-twisting, the enthusiasm of performers and promoters, and the three special concert series, in the eight weeks of the London Season of the Arts, audiences heard over 750 individual works, familiar and obscure, by almost 170 British composers, major and minor, spanning 700 years (the earliest piece was "Sumer is icumen in," followed by works of Roy Henry, Dunstable, Fayrfax, and Davy).

Appendix 1 collects information from these concert programs and announcements on individual works performed during the London Season. Although the impressive week-long festival of English sacred music mounted by the Choir of Westminster Abbey in the first week of July came after the official end of the London Season of the Arts on June 30th, in the spirit of ecumenism I have included it in the data to balance the similar exercise conducted by the Choir of Westminster Cathedral in June. English church music was also heard in daily services at the Festival Church, St. John's Waterloo, in two evening concert series there, one on Thursday evenings devoted to English sacred music and the other on Saturdays tracing the development of English hymnody, but the programs for these series are available neither in the Arts Council archive nor in the National Archive.

In reviewing this vast repertory, it makes sense to start with the three special series produced by the Arts Council, which were all exclusively British. The eight concerts in the Purcell series included 69 separate works, covering almost every genre essayed by the composer. These included, in addition to more familiar choral and vocal works, quite a number of fantasias, in nomines, keyboard suites, and trio sonatas. The origins of this series remain obscure, but the 250th anniversary of the composer's death had prompted a thorough re-evaluation of his oeuvre in 1945, giving his music a boost in popularity and familiarity. However, the instrumentation of most of Purcell's music matched neither the large orchestras and choral societies nor the established chamber-music ensembles, so the planning committee likely found Purcell's contribution underrepresented in the early concert proposals it received. It is characteristic of the Arts Council's Festival methods that they leapt so enthusiastically at the chance to fill this void.

The second series traced English music from 1300 to 1750 over eight concerts, encompassing an impressive selection of genres and composers. The early-music scholar and Third Programme producer Basil Lam drew up the detailed plans for these performances. The series concentrated on the Tudor "Golden Age," with both the first and last concerts focused on the period 1550–1650. This was wise; the Tudor period was widely held to be one of the few historical periods when English style and technique matched those on the continent. This concert series thus represents a culmination of the early twentieth century revival of interest in Tudor music that had been so important in the nascent musical nationalism of composers such as Holst and Vaughan Williams. The promoters could expect some interest in and appreciation of Byrd, Weelkes, Morley, and Gibbons, but the same could not be said of Dunstable and Davy, not to mention the host of little-known works by Renaissance and Baroque composers on other evenings: a pavyon by Master Newman, virginals works by Benjamin Cosyns and Martin Peerson, and violin sonatas by Andrew Parcham and Joseph Gibbs. The press release announcing this series unintentionally emphasized the obscurity of the material by reassuring readers, with somewhat forced jollity, that "this series of concerts of English music, some of which will be performed after centuries of neglect, is no dull academic jamboree for the pundits and musical snobs, but will be a rich and exciting experience—a festive occasion for the music-lover during the Festival of Britain" (EL6/136, March 1951). In fact, the series amounted to overt advocacy, a reclaiming of a substantial portion of the nation's musical patrimony for the benefit (or edification) of average concert-goers. Although the BBC considered broadcasting the concerts, in the end they rejected the idea because the concerts duplicated existing series on the Third Programme such as the on-going "History of European Music and Sound" and the special series of "English Music of the Fifteenth Century" mounted for the Festival, and because of disagreement with Lam's chronological approach to the material (R27/11/5).

The third series offered six concerts of English art songs from the Renaissance through the twentieth century. Cosponsored and broadcast by the BBC, these concerts featured some of the foremost British singers of the day. Balancing the repertory of orchestral and choral works in regular concerts, and selecting from Purcell's catalogue had proven relatively straightforward, if time-consuming, and for the early music series, the Arts Council had relied on Basil Lam, an outside programmer. The performers in the other two series had been glad for the patronage and a national stage, and readily accepted proposed repertory. But in crafting a program of over 100 English art songs, the Arts Council found itself out of its depth, so the staff consulted with the performers. Perhaps unsurprisingly, accommodating the performers' interests proved problematic and contentious. In particular, Benjamin Britten and Peter Pears, who agreed to give the first two recitals, saw themselves as assisting the Arts Council and BBC, rather than the other way around, and were not easily influenced.

The draft programs that the Arts Council forwarded to the BBC do not survive, but a lengthy memorandum from December 1950 written by Leonard Isaacs of the BBC Third Programme in response to these proposals demonstrates both the BBC staff's greater experience in assembling such programs and their greater knowledge of the repertory (R27/500/5). Isaacs's memo identifies serious shortcomings, given the London Season's overall pretensions to comprehensiveness. He starts by noting the surprising omission of songs by Ernest J. Moeran, Frederick Delius, Arthur Somervell, Granville Bantock, Roger Quilter, and Cecil Armstrong Gibbs, while most of the rest of his critique stems from the excessive influence that Benjamin Britten and Peter Pears had exercised over the selection of works. Although supportive of including the composer's *Michelangelo Sonnets*, Isaacs objects to Britten's disproportionate presence as performer, composer, and arranger. He argues against the inclusion of Britten's folk-song settings on the grounds that they are neither art songs nor balanced by arrangements by other composers such as Cecil Sharp and John Fuller Maitland. Isaacs also objected to the composer's quirky realizations of songs by Henry Purcell. The emphasis on Britten, Isaacs felt, devalued Ralph Vaughan Williams, whose *On Wenlock Edge* was absent from the program. In a later, February 1951 memorandum, Isaacs recognized that the folk-song settings might be unavoidable and asked if any other singer could be found to tackle a few of the *Michelangelo Sonnets*, since Britten and Pears were unwilling to include them (R27/500/6).

In revising the plans, the Arts Council accepted most of Isaacs' suggestions: *On Wenlock Edge* was heard at the fourth concert, and songs by all the neglected composers except Bantock included. But Britten and Pears could only be bidden so far. They performed a set of eight Purcell realizations and nine folksong settings, but only two of the composer's original works, the W. H. Auden setting "Fish in the Unruffled Lakes" and the Canticle "My Beloved is Mine." Despite Isaacs' urging, neither they nor any performer performed even one of the *Michelangelo Sonnets*. They did however give the premiere of Tippett's new cycle "The Heart's Assurance," composed for them.

In spite of these difficulties, the English Song series was admirably broad, presenting more than 130 songs stretching from Morley and Dowland to works by Geoffrey Bush and Antony Hopkins, both in their early thirties. Kathleen Ferrier was to have premiered Arthur Bliss's scena "The Enchantress" on June 11th, but in the event she was too ill to perform. (She sang the premiere in 1952.) Positive response to the concerts led Leonard Isaacs to propose a similar series of concerts of English chamber music for the autumn of 1951. The proposal shows a continuation of the Festival ethos in the BBC, but initial response within the BBC hierarchy was unfavorable, and although the Third Programme developed the idea, they did not broadcast a strictly British series.

A global consideration of the repertory of the London Season of the Arts paints a vivid picture of the canon of British music in 1951. Numerical analysis of concert programs is a rough tool, but does reveal some broad trends. Figure 1.1 arranges 784 performances of works by British composers given during the London Season of the Arts and the Westminster Abbey concert series according to the decade of

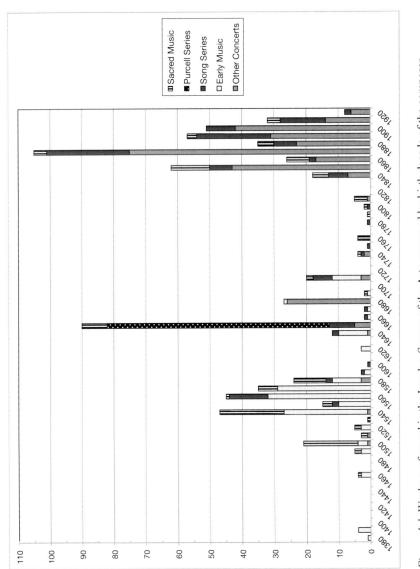

Figure 1.1 Works performed in the London Season of the Arts, arranged by birth decade of the composer

the composer's birth. The data excludes anonymous works, operas, operettas, and other theatrical works with music that received multiple performances.[6]

The figure shows that the admirable catholicity of Murrill and the Arts Council staff had its limits, and not just ones based on practical considerations. Conventional mid-century historiography dominates the results. Despite the early music series, and allowing for the nine anonymous works from early centuries excluded from the table, medieval English music largely awaits rediscovery. The works on offer cluster readily into a Tudor Golden Age with birth years from the 1540s through the 1580s (preceded by Tallis in 1505), a spike of Purcellian glory in 1659, a Handelian interlude in 1685, and the so-called English Musical Renaissance rising from composers born in the 1840s into the contemporary period. The only modest surprises on the chart are the spikes for John Blow in 1649 and Thomas Arne and William Boyce in the 1710s, all three of whom were featured in the early music series. The underrepresentation, indeed almost total lack, of Georgian and Victorian music is not surprising for 1951, as it parallels the contemporaneous denigration of Victorian architecture and décor at this time. For instance, the series of English song since the Renaissance, despite its claims of breadth, included just five works between Thomas Arne and Hubert Parry: one song each by William Boyce, James Hook, Thomas Linley Jr., Henry Bishop, and John Hatton. It is hard to determine whether this tiny sample represents knowledge of and interest in nineteenth century music that had been preserved or where it was beginning to take root.

Reckonings of sacred music are incomplete since the archives record only works performed in concerts and official church services (the latter not included here), not the anthems and service music chosen by the many London church choirs or even the special series at the Festival Church. If church music lists were available—even just the music lists from the Festival church—sacred composers from the Tudor period and the "English Musical Renaissance" would of course rank even higher. The numbers for the nineteenth century would also rise, since the Church preserved a certain amount of Victorian repertory (by, for example, the Wesleys). Even in the absence of such records, however, compositions from before 1650 comprise over a quarter of all the works performed. Although most of these works are short, that is still an enormous share for a festival in the early 1950s, and testifies both to a growing awareness and acceptance of early music, willingness to recover music from "lost" periods in English music history, and the missionary zeal of Basil Lam and the Arts Council in organizing the early music series.

Except in the case of Purcell and arguably, Byrd (given the coverage he received in the Early Music series), the Arts Council's broadening of the national repertory consisted mostly of the rehabilitation of unperformed composers, not works. Frank Howes, the music critic for the London *Times*, indirectly registered his support for this approach when, in an assessment of the coverage of British music, he regretted not the absence of specific pieces, but inadequately representation of Granville Bantock (Howes 1951: 62, 236). As a result of this policy, the Festival repertory consists almost entirely of the better-known works by as many composers as possible, rather than neglected works of acknowledged masters. We find multiple performances of the symphonic works and late oratorios of Elgar, but his piano quintet was the only chamber work performed, and *Sea Pictures* the only earlier vocal-orchestral work. Older and more established living composers were represented by their most familiar works (for example, Vaughan Williams's symphonies, Ireland's piano concerto and cantata *These Things Shall Be*), and contemporary figures who wrote works specifically for the Festival were often represented by those works alone. The same principle applied to the song series, in which, although there were novelties, composers tended to be represented by their best-known works.

Because of the entire series devoted to him, more of Henry Purcell's oeuvre—at least 86 separate works—received performance than that of any other composer. Table 1.1 lists the other composers with the largest number of works performed in (a) ordinary concerts, (b) the early music series, (c) the song series, and (d) the series of sacred music given by Westminster Cathedral, Westminster Abbey, the St. Bartholomew Choir, the St. Michael's Singers, and the Renaissance Singers taken together as a single category. After Purcell, the most performed composers are Byrd, Vaughan Williams, and Elgar. Dividing the lists into Ancients and Moderns, Stanford, Charles Wood, and C. H. H. Parry are unsurprisingly the only Moderns in the cathedral series, while Purcell is the only Ancient near the top of the song series. Perhaps unexpectedly in 1951, Thomas Arne, with five songs, did slightly better in the that series than Thomas Campion or John Dowland, each of whom had only four songs.

Of the top-ranking Moderns in the concert-music table, half were still alive during the Festival of Britain, and indeed about a quarter of all the works performed in the London Season were by living composers, an impressive showing. Of these, John Ireland stands out since his stature has fallen below that of the other top Moderns since 1950. Stanford's place in the concert table is misleading, as it is based mostly on short choral works; *Songs of the Fleet* and *Songs of the Sea* were his only major concert works performed. Not surprisingly, the list contains only 18 works by ten separate women composers. About half of these are songs, but Rebecca Clarke, Elisabeth Lutyens, Elizabeth Maconchy, Ivy Priaulx Rainier, and Ethel Smyth were all represented by larger-scale works.

Handel's third-place position is similarly boosted by shorter works or works performed only in part. *Messiah* and *Solomon* were the only oratorios presented in full, although with two complete performances and excerpts on two other concerts, *Messiah* was one of the pieces most often heard. It is not clear whether Murrill's committee discouraged performances of other Handel oratorios, or if choral societies didn't even propose them. Of course, in both of these tables, one must take into account the varying length of a work for different composers. All 19 of Dowland's works heard on the Early Music series would take up less time than a single Handel oratorio. For total performance time Handel or Elgar may in fact have placed first.[7]

Even so, the numbers show the decline of the historical Handel cult and perhaps even some squeamishness on the part of postwar Britons about claiming him as

Table 1.1 British composers with most works performed in the London Season of the Arts (each individual work counted only once)

A.	Concerts not in special series (living composers in italics)
Vaughan Williams, Ralph	29 (+6 repeat performances)
Elgar, Edward	24 (+10 repeat performances)
Handel, George Frideric	18 including excerpts (+7 repeat performances)
Holst, Gustav	9 (+3 repeat performances)
Britten, Benjamin	9
Walton, William	8 (+4 repeat performances)
Delius, Frederick	8
Stanford, Charles Villiers	8
Ireland, John	7 (+4 repeat performances)
Armstrong Gibbs, Cecil	7
Bax, Arnold	7
Moeran, Ernest John	7 (Moeran died 1 December 1950.)

B.	Early Music series
Byrd, William	26
Dowland, John	19
Morley, Thomas	9 (+1 repeat performances)
Weelkes, Thomas	9 (+1 repeat performances)
Blow, John	7
Farnaby, Giles	6
Gibbons, Orlando	6
Arne, Thomas	5
Bull, John	5
Wilbye, John	5

C.	Song series ("Ancients" in italics)
Warlock, Peter	13 (mostly arrangements)
Britten, Benjamin	11 (2 are original, 9 are arrangements)
Moeran, Ernest John	10 (7 are "Seven Poems of James Joyce")
Vaughan Williams, Ralph	10 (6 are "On Wenlock Edge")
Purcell, Henry	8
Ireland, John	7
Parry, C. H. Hubert	6
Stanford, Charles Villiers	5 (+1 repeat performances)
Arne, Thomas	5

D.	Combined sacred music series ("Ancients" in italics)
Byrd, William	17 (+3 repeat performances)
Tallis, Thomas	10 or more
Gibbons, Orlando	10
Stanford, Charles Villiers	9 (+1 repeat performances)
Purcell, Henry	7 (+1 repeat performances)
Wood, Charles	5 (+1 repeat performances)
Parry, C. H. Hubert	5
Tye, Christopher	5

British. The vigorous promotion of Purcell in his own series—the only composer so honored—suggests that by midcentury, the strategy of replacing Handel with Purcell as The Representative English Baroque Master was well established. Indeed, at the 1951 Three Choirs Festival in Worcester, Handel and Mendelssohn were largely laid aside (all but *Messiah*), and every concert included a work by a British composer; the large repertory of English choral works included both Elgar's *Kingdom* and *The Dream of Gerontius*, Ralph Vaughan Williams's *Sancta Civitas*, Gustav Holst's *Hymn of Jesus*, Gerald Finzi's *Intimations of Immortality*, and Herbert Howells's *Hymnus Paradisi.*

Most works other than operas and ballets were heard only once. Several works did receive multiple performances, but none of them are surprises. Aside from *Messiah,* Festival commissions such as William Alwyn's *Festival March* and George Dyson's *Song for a Festival*, and several perennially popular anthems, the most-performed concert works were by Elgar. *The Enigma Variations* and *Cockaigne* received four performances, the Introduction and Allegro three, as did Vaughan Wiliams's *Benedicite* and *Tallis Fantasia*, Walton's *Scapino*, Ireland's *London Overture* and Holst's ballet music from *The Perfect Fool*. All of these are popular orchestral showpieces except for *Benedicite*, a moderate-length work less challenging than a full-scale oratorio and thus well suited to second-tier choruses.

The BBC

Of secondary importance in an analysis of London concerts in 1951 are the activities of the BBC, especially the Promenade concerts, which dominated London concert life after the London Season of the Arts had ended. The Arts Council made up its rules as it went along, and expanded its reach and function through its Festival initiatives. The British Broadcasting Corporation, by contrast, had originally been organized on quasi-military lines (Doctor 1999: 22–25). It had a clear operations and management hierarchy for making decisions and well regulated mechanisms for vetting proposals for broadcasts, balancing content, and reviewing past broadcasts. Reporting procedures tracked audiences for broadcasts, and the staff used predictions of audience interest based on this data to plan future broadcasts. At the same time, the staff also believed in their mandate to educate the public beyond its current tastes, and the tension between these two goals on the broadest level is one of the central themes of the entire history of the Corporation. The BBC managed its Festival of Britain content by means of these ordinary procedures, and eschewed the large-scale improvisations that characterized the Arts Council's approach.

Founded in 1922, the BBC broadened its reach and services after the end of the Second World War, most notably introducing in 1946 the Third Programme, devoted to classical music, radio drama, and highbrow talks on art, culture, and politics. By 1951 the BBC was the most pervasive and widespread provider of culture and information to the nation. Its division into three programs was well established, and reflected the class system and the hierarchy of taste within British society. The Light Service, with its emphasis on entertainment, catered to the least educated strata of society, while the BBC expected the usual audience for the Home

Service to be drawn from the large more educated middle sector of the population. The Third Programme was designed to appeal to the most discriminating listeners, who, although described by the BBC as the "intelligent receptive people in all classes", naturally tended to be drawn from the grammar-school-, public-school-, and university-educated elites. The Third Programme rejected the ideas of "adult education" and "crutches" for listeners, and sought to encompass both a larger, European or Continental culture than was available elsewhere on British radio and also a deeper exploration of British culture. For instance, while listener numbers had weight on the Home and Light Services, planners for the Third Programme concerned themselves little with such considerations. The cultural aspirations of the BBC Third Programme were comparable to those of the Arts Council, its close contemporary; in fact, in an effort to attract writers, composers, and critics to participate in broadcasts, Third Programme producers cultivated ties with the Arts Council, which promised to be a meeting-place for eminent figures of high culture.

The BBC involved itself in the Festival of Britain on every level, but its focus was chiefly on reportage, local color, and information. Particularly for Britons unable to visit the metropolis or one of the Festival centers, the BBC was a dominant force in shaping conceptions of the Festival. It did this through a series of broadcasts from Festival locations and events throughout the summer. The BBC 1951 annual report and accounts for the year (5–6) claim that "in aiming to play its full part in this event, the BBC was engaged in a bigger protracted effort than it had previously devoted to a single enterprise. Apart from news coverage, it reflected the Festival in a total of some 2,700 programmes. . . . [T]he BBC tried to ensure that, during the period of the Festival, broadcasting in its whole range should provide the best that Britain could offer. Certainly nothing that the BBC had done in any previous summer could compare in quality of output with its programmes in the summer of 1951." Internal reports compiled at the end of the season by the different divisions list hundreds of Festival events from around the United Kingdom that the BBC had broadcast live.

Among these events, naturally, was a staggering amount of classical music. But even in ordinary times, the BBC always engaged in musical broadcasting. It is impossible to tabulate all the music broadcast during the Festival period or to answer the question "What was the BBC's contribution to the Festival of Britain in the area of classical music?" The BBC broadcast too much music over that five-month period, spread out over the three main frequencies, not to mention the regional services, to collect and analyze. Furthermore, unlike the Arts Council, the BBC did not approach the Festival as an opportunity to conduct a systematic review of national music or make significant additions to the repertory. (The BBC did mount just such a systematic review in the 1995 Fairest Isle Festival, celebrating the 300th anniversary of the death of Henry Purcell.)

Rather, considering the abundance of new music commissioned by other institutions available for broadcast, the BBC took a cautious approach to placing its own Festival commissions. An April 1949 suggestion to commission a series of works from major world composers for the 1951 Proms, mentioned in early documents (R30/2657/1; R30/880/1) went nowhere. The only prominent new music the BBC paid for during the Festival was a set of eight fanfares by Frederick Curzon and recorded by the Royal Artillery Band for announcing various Festival broadcasts (R44/148). Furthermore, the BBC's Festival planning documents are largely procedural in tone, with little articulation of guiding visions or values. Although one would expect the BBC to have "sold" its Festival programming through its widely circulated print journals, the year's run of the *Radio Times* and the *Listener* never draws attention to particular music broadcasts as expressing the theme of the Festival.

Instead, without significantly altering its existing procedures for classical music programming, the BBC brought much of the existing Festival music within the bounds of its ordinary operations. From its beginnings, the BBC's efforts in the cause of high culture had been most clearly directed in the realm of music, toward which it felt a special duty, recognizing the role that it could play in the dissemination of musical knowledge. From the moment of its founding the BBC was the foremost provider of classical music to the British public. By the late forties, with over 500 musicians on its payroll, and with a number of different orchestras of different sizes and styles (including regional orchestras), the BBC was the largest employer of musicians in Britain. The BBC also maintained and expanded its ties with external classical musical organizations. It sponsored and broadcast the Promenade Concerts every summer, and broadcast performances from concert halls throughout the nation, the Glyndebourne opera festival, Covent Garden, Sadler's Wells, and the International Society for Contemporary Music, among many others.

The Music Division engaged in unceasing programming activity, as the planning for all broadcasts, including music, ran on a quarterly schedule, with the coming quarter under development as the current quarter took its course. The music staff of the BBC developed their broadcasts in a number of ways. One important category of music broadcast consisted of frequent live relays of concerts presented and promoted by other bodies from venues outside the BBC studios. Staff in London and the regions kept track of the concert life of the entire nation, and sent up proposals for Outside Broadcasts ("OBs" in Corporation jargon) when a concert of interest was announced. During the Festival of Britain, the Arts Council's industry supplied the BBC with a groaning board of options for Outside Broadcast: the hundreds of concerts in the London Season of the Arts and the regional festivals. The staff of the Music Department had to make difficult decisions about which of these concerts to broadcast, considering the balance of performers and repertory on offer, as well as their sense of what audiences of the various services would want and be willing to hear. During the Festival summer, in addition to the six concerts their own orchestras gave, the BBC broadcast the opening ceremony at the Festival Hall, three of the opening week concerts there, and 11 of the London Season concerts, including the massed brass band concert and the children's concert (on the Light Service). Among the professional concerts, the Music Department preferred those with participation of a superstar soloist or conductors performing standard repertory (Victoria de los Angeles, Yehudi Menuhin, Witold Maluczynski, Rafael Kubelik, Victor de Sabata) to those with conspicuously British repertory.

In a process analogous to OB proposals, members of the musical staff would identify gaps in the repertory or opportunities and would propose studio broadcast projects, either single concerts or series with a thematic connection, performed by one of the Corporation's several orchestras and choirs, or by invited prominent performers or ensembles in the studio. Managers considered the balance of repertory and performers in the proposed OBs against one another and also against proposed studio performances. In comparison with the vast opportunities for OBs, and perhaps because of them, the BBC offered relatively few special studio broadcasts of classical music during the Festival. A series of eight concerts of English Cathedral Music throughout the summer featured major cathedral and college choirs performing mainstream sacred repertory. The Third Programme broadcast motets by Renaissance Scottish composers Robert Carver and Robert Johnson from Dunkeld Cathedral and a rather daring series of English motets, mass movements, and paraliturgical compositions from the fifteenth century, while the Light Service offered programs such as "Song of Britain: A Festival of Choirs from all parts of Britain" (R27/11/5–6; WORKS 25/233/EL1/C2/1).

1851 Week

The chief contribution that the Third Programme made to the Festival of Britain came during the week before its official opening.[8] In characteristically highbrow fashion, the Third Programme designated the week of April 23–29 as "1851 Week", and broadcast only things that could have been heard in 1851. This included news reports that, over the course of the week, covered the highlights of that year's events, talks by eminent mid-Victorian politicians and scholars read by actors, and adaptations of contemporary dramas.

The 1851 Week presented the music programmers with a challenge, but also stimulated their adventurous and scholarly approach to repertory. Continental repertory dominated the English concert scene in 1851, as always, but it would have been awkward for the BBC to have completely neglected native repertory, especially with the Festival of Britain about to commence. Still, few musicians in 1951 had any expertise in Victorian musical practices, nor could the BBC count on much audience enthusiasm for neglected English music of the period. An article in the *Radio Times* for the week unintentionally demonstrated the prevailing ignorance. The piece, titled "Britain's Music in 1851" and written specially for the issue by Robert Sterndale Bennett, scarcely mentions native composers or works at all, even those by the author's own grandfather, the composer William Sterndale Bennett. Instead, it offers a brief overview of music-making, teaching, organists, and repertory from abroad.

But broadcasters needed to find real music, and the performances that they put together paint a better picture of the music of the period than Sterndale Bennett's article did. The orchestral and chamber concerts were conventional, dominated by Bach, Mozart, Beethoven, Rossini, Spohr, and Meyereer. Although they include no works by British composers, Mendelssohn, favorite composer of the period in Britain and a personal friend of Queen Victoria and Prince Albert, surpasses all other composers in the number of works performed. Mendelssohn was represented by a dozen works: the fourth symphony, the cello sonata, three part-songs, six songs without words, and, most unusually, excerpts from the opera *Son and Stranger* (*Die Heimkehr aus der Fremde*). *Israel in Egypt*, by Handel, Mendelssohn's predecessor in the hearts of the British public, also received a complete performance.

For representative English music, the programmers concentrated on the lighter genres widespread in the mid-nineteenth century for two special broadcasts, each one repeated. The first, a reproduction of the 110th anniversary concert given by the Madrigal Society on January 10, 1851, featured "ancient" repertory, mostly Tudor, while the other consisted of "contemporary music" in the form of drawing-room songs and ballads. The madrigal concert—a program devised not by the BBC but replicated from 1851—offered the more familiar fare: works of John Bennet, William Byrd, Thomas Ford, Orlando Gibbons, Christopher Tye, Thomas Weelkes, and John Wilbye, as well as one work by Alessandro Striggio in an English-language version. Slightly out of place with these madrigalists, the program closed with a sole representative of the late seventeenth century, Henry Purcell's ever popular chorus "In these delightful pleasant groves" from *The Libertine*.

The popular-song program included songs both sentimental and humorous by John Beuler, Jonathan Blewitt, Michael Bruce, Henry Farmer, Stephen Glover, Wellington Guernsey, John Hatton, and Joseph Robinson, plus one song by Alexander Varlamov arranged by Henry Bishop. On a separate "vocal and instrumental concert"—a miscellany in the nineteenth-century manner where all the instrumental selections were continental—this English repertory was expanded with four songs in a more serious register: John Braham's "The Death of Nelson", William Shield's "The Wolf", Michael Balfe's "I'm a Merry Zingara", and Henry Bishop's Shakespeare setting "Lo! Here the Gentle Lark."

Unfortunately, records do not show who assembled these impressive programs, or how they made their selection, but the BBC staff involved clearly researched this repertory carefully. It is unlikely that even assiduous audiences heard any other music by most of these composers in the Festival year, or indeed any other year. While a few much later Victorian parlor songs, such as Sullivan's "Lost Chord," remained sentimental favorites after the Second World War, having been popularized within the memories of the older generation, the earlier repertory heard during 1851 Week was almost entirely in eclipse.

The true rarity of the 1851 Week, however, was not any of the forgotten parlor songs but rather came during the re-creation of a concert given on May 13, 1851 at Buckingham Palace. This program was a typical melange of arias and songs by Beethoven, Hérold, Mozart, Stradella, Meyerbeer, and Rossini. But it closed with the ten-minute-long cantata *Invocation to Harmony* by Prince Albert, orchestrated for its BBC incarnation by Philip Sainton. The work was probably receiving its first radio broadcast and would have been unknown to practically all the listeners.

The Proms

The most important Festival performances planned in-house at the BBC were not studio broadcasts but the series of Promenade concerts at the Royal Albert Hall. Although structurally similar to Outside Broadcast, the Proms were planned in every detail by the BBC, a task similar to that of the Arts Council in the London Season of the Arts. Despite its attention to British music-making, the Festival season did not simply buoy the Proms; indeed, as a number of observers within the BBC pointed out, in 1951 the Proms competed with the Festival concerts. The documents surrounding the planning and assessment of the 1951 Proms reveal an awareness of both congruence and conflict with the Festival of Britain. Unlike performances arranged chiefly for broadcast, promenade concerts were commercial events in a huge venue where ticket receipts mattered. The planners of the Proms worried whether there would be any audience interest in another series of 49 orchestral concerts coming so soon after the extravaganza of orchestral concerts in the London Season of the Arts. Two other serious concerns were that evening festivities at the South Bank Exhibition and the Battersea Pleasure Gardens would draw away the casual summertime audience that typically attended promenade concerts, and that, with the return of a second concert hall, there would be competing concerts for the first time in years.

The planning and execution of the Proms always formed one of the largest undertakings for the Music Department of the BBC, and the concerts were a showcase for British music. The Festival context placed extra emphasis on the national element of the 1951 season: In comparison with the relatively modest plans for broadcast music earlier in the summer, the BBC made a particular effort to increase the quantity and seriousness of British repertory in Festival Proms. Although initially inspired to consider a broad exploration of the national repertory on the model of the London Season, the BBC staff eventually opted instead for only a modest increase in this content. The BBC's greater experience with programming, highly bureaucratic decision-making, and, crucially, its habit of keeping statistical records of every aspect of its operations, all contributed to this more cautious approach.

The musicologist Julian Herbage, a member of the BBC music staff from 1927 to 1946, helped organize the Proms up until 1961, and each year he prepared an evaluative report after the season was over. Herbage's 1951 report describes the BBC's approach to British repertory in the Festival Proms:

> The programmes were, let it at once be admitted, a gamble, but a gamble based on a system. It was essential for the 1951 Proms to reflect the Festival year, and they have certainly done so. Over 25% in time of the music played (30 minutes a night) has been British. British contemporary composers have been more fully represented (and with their most important symphonic works) than in any previous Promenade season. The accent has also been laid on significant works first produced at the Proms, and so this season's programmes have achieved a historic aspect. And they have achieved it as comparatively

little cost to the box-office, when all other Festival factors are taken into consideration.

(R79/115/40)

The path to the modestly successful outcome that Herbage described was circuitous. At an early stage in the planning process for 1951, members of the Music staff drew up lists of British orchestral works for consideration. One of these documents lists 48 pieces by 32 composers, the other lists an extraordinary 84 pieces by 50 composers (R79/115). The focus is on the "modern school", or the "English Musical Renaissance": Almost all the composers are mainstream, none earlier than Arthur Sullivan, and with certain exceptions such as Eric Coates and Edward German, most are "serious", although the works listed include many overtures, suites, and other "lighter" genres.

These lists were useful as an exercise in brainstorming, but they obviously had to be pared down to a more manageable scale. The programs as finally designed included 64 works (not including arrangements) by 30 British composers. The average of 30 minutes a night mentioned by Herbage (for a total of almost 25 hours) represents an increase from the previous year, but the extraordinary breadth of coverage envisioned in the early lists had been almost entirely abandoned. Cooler heads had prevailed, and instead formulated a solid, mainstream season. Although the Proms did include three composers *not* on the original lists—William Alwyn, Maurice Johnstone, and Daniel Jones—they completely eliminated 24 of the composers on the initial lists.[9] Furthermore, fully half the British repertory performed was composed by just five proven composers: Delius, Elgar, Ireland, Vaughan Williams, and Walton, all of whom had five or more pieces. There were also six works by Handel. As Herbage's report confirms—and echoing the Arts Council's practice in the London Season of the Arts—even within the oeuvres of these composers, the BBC avoided lesser-known works, emphasizing the core repertory of British symphonies. The programs included both of Elgar's essays in the genre, all of Vaughan Williams's except the *Pastoral*, Walton's first (his only symphony in 1951), and Bax's seventh (his most recent), as well as the premiere of Peter Racine Fricker's first.

Of the 11 "novelties"—works receiving their world or regional premiere in the Proms—in the 1951 season, seven were by British composers, in keeping with the past two seasons, although representing a drop from the first years after the War:

1. Alan Bush, Symphonic suite, *Piers Plowman's Day*
2. Peter Racine Fricker, Symphony
3. Gordon Jacob, *Galop joyeux*
4. Maurice Jacobson, Symphonic suite for strings
5. Maurice Johnstone, Cumbrian rhapsody, *Tarn Hows*
6. Daniel Jones, Five pieces for orchestra
7. Philip Sainton, *Serenade fantastique* for oboe and strings

Of these, only the Sainton and Jones works were true first performances; the rest had received performances already abroad or in regional festivals. The BBC tracked the average length of the novelties. This was a measure of how substantial the works were, since a season packed with new fanfares and short concert overtures would draw this number down sharply At a respectable 18 minutes, the 1951 average was in line with previous seasons. Even so, a post-mortem memorandum from W. W. Thompson, the BBC Concert Manager, to Herbert Murrill on October 10, 1951 (R79/115/40) expresses dissatisfaction with the selection of premieres and even suggests that composers were avoiding the Proms:

> Regarding the inclusion of new works I do not consider we are making the best of the Prom 'shop window'. An earlier start [to the selection process] would undoubtedly help as for one thing composers might be persuaded to offer first performances to the Proms rather than elsewhere. And first performances are of infinitely more value than first London or first Concert performances. Further I would suggest that a special Jury should be brought into being for the express purpose of selecting works for Proms only.
> (R79/115/40)

Economics provide some explanation for the drastic simplification of the British offerings in the 1951 Proms. After all, excessively adventurous repertory would jeopardize ticket sales. The BBC carefully analyzed the financial results of repertory choice. The same memorandum groups the concerts into four categories: "Popular Saturdays", "Beethoven programmes", "Composer programmes (whole or part)", and "Miscellaneous programmes". The miscellaneous programs were the home of most British music other than lighter Saturday fare. With their interesting and unfamiliar repertory, these concerts were most popular with critics, but considerably less so with paying audiences. To increase the quantity of British music for the Festival, the BBC increased the number of miscellaneous programs from ten in 1950 to 16 in 1951. A table of receipts shows that on average the miscellaneous concerts took in only £411 each compared with £738 for all other concerts. Despite Herbage's sanguine report and Herbert Murrill's assertion after the season was over that the influence of the London Season of the Arts earlier in the summer and the ongoing South Bank exhibition had made little difference in Proms audiences (R79/115/40), total receipts for the 1951 series were down significantly (16.4 per cent) from the previous year, and this drop was concentrated in these "miscellaneous" concerts. "Here," wrote Thompson, "is proof positive I think that if the Festival of Britain affected the Proms it was only on the nights when the programmes were slightly above the heads of the general public so to speak" (R79/115/40).

In a similar vein, Herbage gives an example of a program that performed dismally at the box office:

> Wagner, Overture to *The Flying Dutchman*
> Moeran, Violin Concerto

Dvorak, Symphony no. 2 (No. 7 in D Minor)
Ireland, *The Forgotten Rite*
Tchaikovsky, *Francesca da Rimini*

About this program, Herbage commented: "The Moeran concerto is hardly helped out by the Forgotten Rite, and Dvorak no. 2 only draws an audience when there is a full house already. Obviously the Moeran concerto was the primary cause of the bad house, yet the Moeran concerto was an essential ingredient of the 1951 series" (R79/115/40). Sadly, of course, it was precisely nights like this when the Proms were most *British*, but the Arts Council had faced a similar problem in the London Season of the Arts. (As mentioned earlier, Herbage himself fully appreciated this quandary.)

Consideration of the Proms as national broadcasts rather than public concerts in London reveals the BBC's commitment to British music in the Proms to be even more modest than presented above. With the resumption of Proms after the Second World War, the BBC ordinarily broadcast only the first halves of the concerts and then returned to non-musical studio programming, in part to avoid preempting the nine o'clock news broadcast. This practice was controversial, and would eventually be abolished, but as we have seen, the special Festival circumstances of 1951 did not justify alterations to standard Corporation practices. As a result of this truncation, unfamiliar and native repertory after the intermission was denied a broadcast audience. As a result, only 34 of the 64 British works were actually broadcast, including only one of the seven British premieres (Gordon Jacob's *Galop joyeux*). The Light Service made an exception to this rule, relaying the Saturday "popular concerts" in their entirely (including The Last Night of the Proms). As a result, Light Service listeners could have actually heard 18 British works, including the Jacob score, more than what the listeners of the other two services combined could have heard.

Herbage, in his post-mortem report, decried the policy of post-intermission truncation –in particular its effect on broadcasting of British music—in comments worth quoting at length:

> In the good old days when the BBC stepped in and took over the Proms as a national cultural duty, every note, I believe was broadcast, despite the fact that the BBC did not then have the luxury of Home, Light and Third Programme. The sacrosanct nine o'clock news was altered to 9.40 to accommodate the traditional eight o'clock start. Broadcasting, in those days, both did the Proms proud and also took full program value from them. This situation, as far as I remember, existed up to the beginning of World War II. Since then, the whole attitude to the broadcasting of the Promenade Concerts seems to have changed. Instead of its being realised that here is a mine of musical material that can be exploited with the least possible cost to broadcasting, the general attitude is that the Proms merely have program nuisance value. Far better musical entertainment must be available from Salzburg, Edinburgh, Bayreuth, the Three Choirs Festival—anywhere except the Proms. Is this really so, and are the Proms so devoid of suitable broadcasting material? Let us take a look at some

of the musical works that the Proms offered the three Services but which none of them cared to broadcast. Walton's "Sinfonia Concertante", Delius' "Idyll", Elgar's "Music Makers", Tippett's Concerto for Double String Orchestra, Rawsthorne's Piano Concerto, Bax's 7th Symphony, Rawsthorne's Violin Concerto, Delius's "Sea Drift" and "Paris", Bartok's Violin Concerto, Walton's "Belshazzar's Feast", Racine Fricker's Symphony, Bliss's "Music for Strings". Was better musical material—and better performed—really available from other sources? I doubt it. And this list does not include the main classical works, such as Schubert's C major Symphony, Beethoven's Pastoral Symphony, and Tchaikovsky's 5th Symphony, none of which, also, were broadcast. Does any Festival, given anywhere else in the world, offer such attractive musical materials as these, the scattered and unbroadcast crumbs of the Promenade Season? This wastage is so colossal that it surely demands an immediate reorientation of policy. After all, the BBC sponsors and pays for the Proms, and yet makes the minimum use of the available broadcast material.

(R79/115/40)

In summary, the Proms organizers abandoned their more wide-reaching repertory proposals in favor of tried and true composers. They brought a decent collection of British music into the series, including a number of solid new pieces, but failed to ensure that these works would be heard by the radio audience. In this mixed outcome we see the moderating influence of elaborate planning procedures as well as a certain timidity that characterized the Corporation at this time. Arguably, these characteristics hemmed in the BBC and rendered the British content of the Proms less impressive than one would have expected for the Festival year. Certainly, and despite Herbage's attempt in his report to put the best face on the results, in this respect the Proms pale in comparison with the London Season of the Arts.

At the end the summer of 1951, the *Radio Times* ran a preview of the upcoming quarter's broadcasts. Although the concerts under review fell outside the Festival of Britain entirely, the comments of Herbert Murrill suggest that the BBC had a relatively complacent attitude towards the programming of both contemporary and British music that may explain the failings of the 1951 Proms:

I have not attempted to draw attention to modern music as such or to British music as such. It is sufficiently gratifying that, in 1951, these categories tend less and less to be artificially segregated. The names of British composers, old and new, naturally take their place alongside the great internationals, without special pleading. When a composer, today, launches a new opera, concerto, symphony, he sends it out to take its chance and to win its place alongside the great and accepted masterpieces of this and previous ages.

(Murrill 1951: 6)

It is odd to find such an optimistic picture of the British composer's prospects in the words of Murrill, who led the planning of the London Season of the Arts. As I demonstrate later in this study, the contention in the final sentence is not truly warranted in the case of opera, and arguable for the other genres. Perhaps Murrill should have known better, but he was writing in the afterglow of the London Season, when British music seemed to be everywhere.

Assessment

If we take the 1951 publicity at its word, and accept that the Arts Council aimed at a "full representation of the history and practice of British music," we must consider the extent to which they succeeded and failed, and why. What image of musical Britain did this extraordinary program of concert music present? What did it reveal and obscure? To begin with, the low turnout at many concerts indicates a discrepancy between the zeal of the organizers and the interest of the potential audience. The problem was not so much that the Arts Council staff and their associates were wholly out of touch with what the audience wanted. Rather, the evidence suggests that the process developed its own momentum, and in the excitement of planning lost touch with reality. The mandarinate putting the London Season together extrapolated their own enthusiasm for British classical music to a much larger potential public than could reasonably be expected, even in a Festival season. With the exception of school, massed band, and competitive concerts, the target (and real) audience for concerts was limited to the educated middle- and upper classes, a fact which the Arts Council treated as either obvious or irrelevant. The archives contain no proposals for audience development schemes such as providing inexpensive tickets or bringing in groups from schools and working-class neighborhoods and organizations. Wishful thinking and the putative inherent appeal of innovative programming—an "If you build it, they will come" mentality—ruled, and audiences were small as a result.

In the realm of programming, the Festival concert season had conflicting aims: A desire to educate the public in the full historical repertory of British music coexisted with an unwillingness to perform truly obscure works, although in some cases, it is difficult to distinguish genuine unwillingness from ignorance of the repertory or lack of availability of scores. The concerts were not organized purely as a "museum of the best" divorced from audience interest. Of course, if the Arts Council had permitted the performers to set their own programs based on what would bring in audiences, the results would have been even more conventional than what emerged, but while they did encourage and even demand innovative programming, they still had to plan to sell tickets. Market realities required a balance between the familiar and the unfamiliar. There would have been little virtue in concerts so abstruse or bizarre—whether historical or contemporary—that they attracted little audience and drove away those who did attend. As Julian Herbage pointed out, the BBC faced these realities of the marketplace even more strongly in the Proms, and its programming was consequently even less inventive than that of the Arts Council.

Thus, bureaucratic caution countervailed mandarin enthusiasm. For instance, despite all their research and organizing, the Festival planners showed little interest in rehabilitating marginalized composers such as John Foulds, Rutland Boughton, or Havergal Brian, or in inviting "dissenting and experimental composers" (Witts 1998: 162) into the fold. No one, for instance, thought to make overtures to Kaikhosru Sorabji (who had by 1951 banned performance of his works). The inability of the programmers to see past the fairly close circle of professional acquaintance and interaction that characterized British music at this time is one of the whole endeavor's most serious flaws. If ever there was a time to rehabilitate a work by Boughton, or rediscover Foulds or Brian, the Festival of Britain was surely that time, yet despite all the work put into researching and expanding the repertory, no such attempt was made.

Along with such avant-garde and marginal figures, the concerts also excluded most British music composed between 1640 and 1880. The almost total absence of Victorian secular music in the Festival (outside the BBC's 1851 Week), if regrettable, is really not surprising: The dominant narrative of English Musical Renaissance branded such repertory derivative and irrelevant. But a few works were performed, and these show where knowledge and interest was beginning to take root. That is, as Figure 1.1 shows in graphic form, the London Season of the Arts, with its pretensions to historical breadth, provides an uncommonly detailed picture of the mid-twentieth century educated conception of the British repertory.

In other words, conceding that such gaps are deficiencies when viewed from a contemporary perspective, we can interpret them historically as evidence not of injustice or institutional failure but of canonicity. The Festival presented the Arts Council the opportunity to become not only the "chosen instrument of carrying out Artistic Policy" (EL6/2, February 28, 1947), but also the Framer and Policer of Canons. The London Season was a curatorial exercise. The mandarin worthies who made up the panels and committees, headed eventually by Herbert Murrill, undertook to acknowledge, define, and broaden the mainstream of British concert repertory by wielding their institutional authority to grant composers and their works such recognition or promotion as they saw fit.

Considered in this light, the Festival concert series—not unlike the South Bank Exhibition—mark an aesthetic endpoint, rather than a beginning. They mark the culmination of a 45-year process of musical rediscovery and redefinition that began with the Tudor revival, the framing of the ideology of English Musical Renaissance, and the triumph of a largely pre-war consensus about repertory. One would expect the presentation of the universe of contemporary British repertory on such a massive scale to bring forth a burst of oppositional activity: the next wave of redefinitions. In fact, the Festival consensus continued to dominate British concert life for almost a decade, and the real burst of experimentalism arrived in the sixties, with, for instance, the advent of William Glock as Controller of Music at the BBC in 1959.

The timing of the project was opportune and the institutions well suited to the task. By the early fifties, it was possible to confidently take stock of what British composers had accomplished, particularly over the preceding 75 years, as well as what had been rediscovered from earlier eras. The Arts Council of Great Britain was a young organization at the first peak of its influence and resources, with an energetic staff eager to guide the nation's cultural life and display its musical patrimony. The Festival of Britain gave them the opportunity to flex their muscles, exert unprecedented influence on programs, and organize on a grand scale.

Notes

1. Jenny Doctor (1999) thoroughly investigates the dissemination of the music of the Second Viennese School in Britain. While she demonstrates that it was widely known, it cannot be said to have exerted a dominant influence on the mainstream of native composition. Benjamin Wolf (2010) offers a different perspective on the role of this music in Britain.
2. Howkins 1986, Howkins 1989, Harrington 1989 analyze the rise of nationalism and, in particular, pastoralism, in English music in this period.
3. Invited to the first meeting were: the Henry Wood Concert Society, the BBC, the Royal Philharmonic Society, the New Era Concert Society, the Morley College Concert Society, the Exploratory Concert Society, the Robert Mayer Children's Concerts, the Renaissance Society, the London Contemporary Music Centre, the Committee for the Promotion of New Music, the City Music Society, Leonard Smith, David Bicknell, the Thomas Beecham Concert Society, the Calpin Society, the London Philharmonic Orchestra, the London Symphony Orchestra, the Boyd Neel Orchestra, the Jacques String Orchestra, the New London Chamber Orchestra, the Riddick String Orchestra, the National Youth Orchestra, Ibbs and Tilllett, Harold Holt, Lynford-Joel, the Imperial Concert Agency, Van Wyck, the Royal Albert Hall, Chappells, the Wigmore Hall, the Royal Choral Society, the Goldsmiths Choral Union, the Alexandra Choir, the Bach Choir, the London Choral Society, the Workers' Music Association, the London Orpheus Choir, the South London Bach Society, and the Organ Music Society. Invited to the second were: the English Folk Dance Society, the International Society for Contemporary Music, the Music Development Committee, the Rural Music Schools Association, the Royal School of Church Music, the National Brass Band Club, the Free Church Choral Union, the British Federation of Music Festivals, the National Federation of Music Schools, the Composers Guild of Great Britain, the Ministry of Education, the BBC, the Standing Conference of County Music Committees, the Advisory Committee on Amateur Opera, and the British Council.
4. Arts Council Paper 278 (EL4/52) contains notes on ensembles' proposals for the London Season of the Arts.
5. Another unusually thorough source that documents not only programs but also contemporary press reaction to the London Season of the Arts and the Festival of Britain concert, is *Musical Britain 1951* (Howes 1951), a compilation of all the reviews of musical events published in the London *Times* during the Festival.
6. The composers in Appendix 1 whose birth years I have not been able to trace, and who are therefore not represented in Figure 1.1 are Ann Hamerton, Thomas Henderson, Ella Ivirney, and the liturgical composers Hyde and Murray.
7. Wolf (2010), in a similar repertory review, assigns standardized lengths to different genres in order to compare the attention given to different composers. Although his technique is more revealing than a simple count of works, the much greater number of genres in my data renders it unworkable in the present study.
8. This section is based largely on the coverage in *Radio Times* 3/1432 (April 20, 1951). Conekin (2003: 86–87) and Carpenter (1996: 108–109) also discuss the 1851 Week.
9. Among the composers eliminated were Malcolm Arnold, Granville Bantock, Lord Berners, Rutland Boughton, Frank Bridge, George Butterworth, Eric Coates, Edward German, Eugene Goossens, Percy Grainger, Hamilton Harty, Herbert Howells, Elisabeth Lutyens, Humphrey Searle, Ethel Smyth, Charles Villiers Stanford, Bernard Stevens, and Peter Warlock.

2 ... and new
Commissions and premieres

Arranging a comprehensive survey of the nation's art music was not the only way in which the Arts Council of Great Britain sought to define and celebrate national music in the Festival of Britain. Patrons—whether individuals, institutions, or the state—have for centuries marked great occasions with commissions of new musical works. Britain's creative capacities unquestionably deserved demonstration as an essential part of "the British contribution to civilisation" (in the words of the official mission of the Festival). As Duncan Guthrie had envisioned in the memorandum on the Arts Festival reviewed in the Introduction, the Arts Council followed historical precedent by placing commissions in a number of genres and art forms and encouraging the placement of commissions by others, resulting in several high-profile premieres in the Festival.

Taking the initiative and placing commissions for new works with government money was a decisive move beyond the Council's and CEMA's established role of providing subsidies and guarantees against loss, as Eric Walter White pointed out in his later history of the Arts Council:

> Before 1951 the Arts Council had been shy about becoming involved in commissioning schemes. This may have been mainly for reasons of financial caution; but in the background there was perhaps a sneaking suspicion that it was not the job of a body like the Arts Council to run the risks inherent in any policy that involved the diversion of Government money to living artists, who were not wholly reliable characters in the sense that they could not guarantee there would be a commensurate return for the money received. The Festival of Britain, however, provided a golden opportunity to involve the creative artists as well as the performing artists.
>
> (White 1975: 222)

Thus, the Festival, with its imperative to place commissions, drew the Arts Council away from its cautious, results-oriented roots where art policy paralleled social welfare policy, and toward a fuller interpretation of financial support for culture. Having taken this step, of course, the Council had to decide what kinds of art it wanted to bring into being.

On May 11, 1948, the Arts Council Music Panel, chaired by Stanley Marchant, composer and Principal of the Royal Academy of Music, took up the suggestion of placing music commissions for the Festival of Britain. The Panel seized the task with relish, and drafted a recommendation specifying seven works in considerable detail:

a) *A Large Scale Choral and Orchestral Work* to last some 45 minutes, for performance at a special concert to be given by massed choirs assembled from all parts of Great Britain. This work should be suitable for repetition on a smaller scale at provincial centres.
b) *A Festival Psalm*. A Festival setting on broad lines for a large choir and orchestra of a selected psalm for performance at a thanksgiving service at St. Paul's Cathedral or other appropriate occasion of this nature.
c) *Water Music*. In the hope that there will be opportunity to organise concerts on the river Thames, having in mind the precedent of Handel's water music, it is suggested that a work in serenade form be commissioned for military band, designed for performance at a Festival evening "in or about boats".
d) *A Festival Overture* for concert use for normal full orchestra, intended for performance in London and other centres where orchestral music is to be a feature.
e) *A Concerto for Piano and Full Orchestra* for performance at various centres during the Festival.
f) *A Simple Broad Unison Song* with piano accompaniment and possible descant, for use in youth clubs, schools, Women's Institutes, etc., and for rural communities in general.
g) *A Part Song* for male voices and brass band accompaniment intended for use more particularly in mining and other industrial areas where these resources are available.

Note: The texts of (a) (f) (g) above would be commissioned from appropriate writers on themes related to the spirit of the Festival.

(Paper 84, EL4/66, May 28, 1948)

Although this list springs suddenly to life fully formed in the Arts Council minutes, glimmers of the thinking behind it can be discerned. As part of their preparations for the Festival of Britain, the Arts Council conducted research into the musical activities of the 1851 Great Exhibition. The relevant files include excerpts from a biography of Michael Balfe, who wrote an "occasional ode" for that Exhibition, but a report prepared by musicologist Karl Haas (EL6/16, September 1948), confirmed the impression that there was little other original music in 1851.

As some of the organizers would have recalled, the Festival of Britain's more immediate predecessors, the imperial exhibitions of 1911 and 1924, offered better examples. On the basis of the evidence collected by Jeffrey Richards (2001: 177–208), the chief genres of concert music commissioned for these earlier celebrations were patriotic choral-orchestral odes (such as Balfe's from 1851) and works for military band. In 1886, for the Colonial and Indian Exhibition, the

Government commissioned an ode with words by Lord Tennyson and music by Arthur Sullivan. This example was followed in 1911 and 1924 by works of Charles Harriss (*Empire of the Sea* and *England, Land of the Free*) and Percy Fletcher, whose chorus *For Empire and For King* won a competition in 1911. The series of military band concerts in 1924 included a number of major commissions, including Gordon Jacob's *William Byrd Suite*. In addition, the pageants mounted at these exhibitions called forth a spate of new and newly adapted works; Edward Elgar alone contributed numerous works to the Pageant of Empire in 1924, preeminently the *Empire March* (for orchestra) which was used in every section. Finally, over two centuries of royal occasions provided further precedent for state commissions, chiefly occasional odes in a grand line from Purcell to C.H.H. Parry and, later, ceremonial marches such as Elgar's.

Only limited echoes of these earlier exhibition and ceremonial practices remains in the 1951 commissioning program, however. The massed performing forces, which effectively symbolized Britain's imperial scope and might and offered practical solutions to performing outdoors or in vast spaces such as the Crystal Palace, are less in evidence. Furthermore, the tone of the Festival of Britain precluded patriotic and jingoistic outbursts, and at any rate the bureaucrats in charge valued a more elite, "modern" concert culture than that represented in the Empire exhibitions or royal celebrations, one that showcased contemporary performing forces and could be presented as unsullied by politics. The decision to research the Great Exhibition—while motivated chiefly by its centennial—also suggests a desire for more safely historical, academic precedents than the imperial exhibitions and pageants.

While military bands have a role in the Festival of Britain concert program, they no longer take pride of place. In particular, the absence from the initial scheme of a festive march, which would have been the most likely commission 50 years earlier, seems a calculated rejection of past practice. A march may have seemed to some members of the Panel too reminiscent of Empire for the inward-looking modernistic Festival of Britain. (Whatever the reasons for the initial oversight, the Panel reconsidered, and added a march to the scheme a year and a half later.) The Festival Psalm and Water Music were more suitably traditional, leaping as they did over the period of Empire, and reviving Georgian precedent instead. The former corresponded to the Handelian Ode, or Te Deum and Jubilate. With the latter, recalling and reviving the atmosphere of George I's 1717 royal barge excursion, the Panel honored the tradition and musical excellence of military bands while calculatedly erasing their warlike associations. (By contrast, Vaughan Williams unproblematically titled his contribution to the 1924 exhibition *Toccata Marziale*.) Although they could hope that such commissioned works would receive multiple performances, the Panel surely conceived both of these works as occasional, designed for a specific event rather than for concerts in general.

The choral-orchestral work and overture, on the other hand, were probably conceived as contributions to the contemporary concert repertory, likely to attract interest from performers and audiences. The 45-minute length proposed for the first was perhaps intended to differentiate it from the genre of occasional ode in favor of a the more high-minded dramatic or religious oratorio. The piano concerto is similarly standard concert fare, traditionally a lighter and more crowd-pleasing genre than the symphony, but stands out as it has little history of ceremonial commissions. As Stephen Banfield has pointed out (private communication), a boom in concertante piano writing in 1940s British film scores, and the resulting growth in the genre's popularity, may lie behind the Panel's decision to include it in the scheme.[1] The fulfillment of the concerto commission clearly mattered: John Denison, the Arts Council Director of Music, showed dogged persistence in tracking down a composer to write one even though abandoning it would not have publicly damaged the outcome of the commisioning program.

The last two genres on the list sit uncomfortably with the other five. One could argue that the part-song for miners fell beneath the standard of "the fine arts exclusively" set out in the Arts Council's charter. Indeed, this foray into the working-class world of brass bands was rather daring, contrasting with almost every other Arts Council musical project for the Festival and with the spirit of the educated elites who planned them. The composer Thomas Wood, who was serving on the Music Panel when the scheme was approved, probably inserted it into the scheme for himself. Now almost entirely forgotten, Wood was a prolific composer of marches, part-songs and school cantatas, often based on nautical and folk themes. Although the work's inclusion seems in retrospect a shocking conflict of interest, in proposing it Wood could have counted on the support of Ralph Vaughan Williams. Like Wood a vocal advocate for community music-making on the Panel, Vaughan Williams probably saw in the commission an evocation of CEMA's wartime support for amateurs, discontinued by John Maynard Keynes.[2] One can only speculate what the members of the panel more keen on festival psalms thought of the proposal. At the same time, the (admittedly slight) transfer of attention from military bands to brass bands in a way exemplifies the shift in tone from Empire Exhibition to Festival of Britain.

Finally, the unison song was a relatively new genre for serious cultivation, not to mention state commission. British patriotic models from earlier in the century included alternative anthems such as Parry's "Jerusalem," Elgar's "Land of Hope and Glory," and Holst's "I Vow to Thee, My Country" (the latter two consisting of words put to extant instrumental melodies), and earlier exhibition concerts had included unison singing of hymns and, in 1911, Kipling's *Recessional* set to a hymn tune (Richards 2001: 184). The original unison song had gained prominence among the left-wing social movements of the thirties, whose rallies featured mass singing. It is tempting to interpret the creation of a mass song for the Festival as a blending of these different political meanings into a neutral, universal, celebratory national statement, corresponding to the erasure of political difference in the Festival as a whole.

The commissioning scheme as originally put forward thus incorporated carefully selected ideas from the past and modest advances into new territory. With its odd mix of highbrow and lowbrow musical genres it balanced historical awareness or nostalgia with more realistic, even broad-minded assessment of contemporary performance opportunities. The "something for everyone" quality suggests that despite differing historical and cultural interests, not to say prejudices, the individuals that compiled the list were willing to consider and approve one another's pet projects, and that the financial resources were plentiful enough to permit this breadth. This was a model of liberal-minded mandarin cultural planning.

Once approved, the commissioning program, unprecedented as it was in the Arts Council's brief history, generated reflection within the agency on the nature of the uncharted territory it was exploring, and also on the potential long-term results. Although documentation explaining the origins and inconsistencies of the commission list is scarce, two internal memoranda shed light on attitudes within the Arts Council toward the scheme, and on the Council's goals and motivation. Both documents reveal tensions within the agency between grander visions and more humble expectations. The first, an early undated and unsigned memorandum (probably from 1948), addresses both the rationale and the limitations of the scheme:

> The musician is entitled to ask "Will anything of permanent value emerge from the hard work and considerable sum of money spent?" The answer is probably "Consciously,—NO" and "Fortuitously,—PERHAPS". We are, presumably, agreed that a composer, asked to write a work employing conventional resources or cast in a conventional form, for a specific festal occasion, cannot be *expected* to produce anything more than a *piece d'occasion*, which will be listened to, and appraised as such. If it should happen that the work does rise above that level, then we can say we have produced something more permanent—fortuitously.
>
> In a festival of this magnitude, there must be occasions for purely formal pieces, and they should be ordered, and paid for, from the best composers available, whether British or not, purely for the festival. If an established composer were asked to regard the festival as an opportunity to write a "genuine" work on more or less conventional lines, i.e., a symphony or an oratorio, he would say "I shall, or shall not, write that work without the festival, and know that it will get several performances up and down the country within the first year or two of its appearance." He might, however, well say "I want to experiment with unusual resources not normally available, and if you will guarantee an opportunity for such an experiment to be heard, I might be able to prove or disprove something for the benefit of my successors." Berlioz did so, with large resources, and encouragement of this kind might mean that, at least fortuitously, something of more permanent value would emerge.
>
> (EL6/45, n.d. [August 1948?])

Somewhat unexpectedly, the writer of this note concentrates almost entirely on *what* the composers were to write and not at all on *who* they were, other than to insist that they be "the best available." Indeed, only well-established composers seem worthy of notice. The note presents an ordinary state of affairs, reminiscent of Herbert Murrill's comments discussed at the end of the previous chapter, where such composers have major new works performed and broadcast without the aid of Arts Council commissions or publicity campaigns. This optimistic portrayal of

British concert life may have been a realistic assessment of the situation for some of the composers active in Britain at the time, including all the composers to whom the Arts Council eventually offered commissions, but it certainly was not the case for all. The author appears not to recognize or be concerned about the fact that there were composers perpetually excluded from the mainstream.

The writer's argument also emphasizes the conventionality of the commissions. The note makes a case against the commissions placed in established genres in favor of large unusual projects on the Berlioz model ("genuine works"). This is an enticing idea, but in the late forties, standard genres still dominated British composition; composers were eager to show their skill in symphonies, concertos, string quartets, and the like. It would have been visionary indeed for the Music Panel to have offered composers complete freedom in genre and performing forces. But even if they had encouraged experimentation, it is doubtful that many composers would have strayed too far outside comfortable genre boundaries. At the same time, as mentioned above, in its list of otherwise typical occasional genres, the Music Panel exceptionally included a piano concerto, a classical genre but unusual for an occasional work. The writer fails to address this anomaly. As we will see, the issue of conventionalism in genre returned in later criticism of the commissions.

While the memo is supportive of the proposed commissions overall, the limited ambition it expresses and the temporary value predicted for the works produced contrast strikingly with the zeal the Council later brought to the process. For the writer, the Arts Council has a humbler role than the leader of national taste envisioned by other contemporary documents. It is merely purchasing expendable commodities like the bunting decorating the streets, to be thrown away at the end of the festivities, rather than making farsighted investments in the future of national culture. One is reminded of Eric Walter White's quip about securing "commensurate return" through grants to living artists.

This memorandum is an isolated document and probably does not represent a consensus of the Music Panel. Even so, it reveals internal doubts or disagreements that arose early in the commissioning program. In contrast to such internal concerns that the Council had set its standards too low, an Arts Council planning report from May 1950, when the program was well underway, reveals that the public announcement of the commissions on April 23rd had attracted negative mention in the press for its exclusions of lighter genres:

> No great public interest has been taken. There has been some criticism that the commissions should be confined to "highbrow" music. The Council's own Music Panel is quite satisfied that the actual commissions will bring about significant and good contributions, nor do they regard the scheme as being in any way narrow. The whole business of getting light music and works in that kind of *genre* produced for 1951 is outside the Council's normal scope, and it is to be hoped that the commercial opportunities in 1951 will produce their own demand for music of that kind.
>
> (Paper 16, WORKS 25/2/A1/A2/13, May 15, 1950)

The confident tone of this comment is more representative of the Festival papers than the attitude in the 1948 memorandum. More to the point, it addresses the question of genre from the opposite cultural position. Where the anonymous writer of 1948 wanted unconventional and experimental classical music, the press response generated public demand for light and popular music. The Arts Council charter precluded support for dance bands, music hall, and the like, but not every newspaper reader would have known this. A public announcement of special music for a Festival only a year away might reasonably leave some wondering whether the Festival would include the many other kinds of music they enjoyed.

Although there were limits to its jurisdiction, the Arts Council was not deaf to such concerns. The inclusion of the "Simple Broad Unison Song," the "Part Song for male voices and brass band," and, later, the march, although the Arts Council carefully positioned all three squarely in the context of art music, demonstrates a recognition that the commissions had to address a broader audience than that for festival psalms. The popular response to these works and the eventual broadcast of the latter two on the BBC Light and Home services suggest that the effort was successful.

Thus, the initial list of proposed commissions suggests that the Music Panel harbored broad, even contradictory aspirations: to bring forth not merely ceremonial occasional works, but abstract concert works of lasting merit, and to encompass a broad range of British performers and performance occasions, both metropolitan and provincial. In furtherance of the high-art side of this project, along with the seven commissions, the Panel also recommended holding a competition for composers of British nationality under thirty-five years of age for a concerto or concertante work for soloist and chamber orchestra. The other panels of the Arts Council met and produced similar proposals, and in June 1948 the Arts Council's forwarded to the Festival of Britain Executive Committee a full commissioning proposal.[3] Opera commissioning was declared feasible and was looked into, but ballet commissioning was pronounced undesirable, a position which was later overturned. (I examine the results of the opera commissioning schemes in Chapters 3 and 4.) The plans also called for encouraging local and national musical organizations to place their own commissions.

The initial proposal did not list composers for each of the seven musical works, but mentioned that these could be supplied if the proposal was accepted. Even so, perhaps out of a concern that the Festival Executive Committee might want to choose the composers, the Panel's initial report stressed that the Arts Council should have "complete discretion" in such choices. Moreover, it is clear that the Music Panel or music staff privately discussed the composers they wanted for each work, for the meeting report (Executive Note 80, EL6/45, May 11, 1948) has names penciled in next to each work on the list as follows:

1. A Large Scale Choral and Orchestral Work—[William] Walton or [Arthur] Bliss
2. A Festival Psalm—[Gerald] Finzi or [Edmund] Rubbra
3. Water Music [for military band]—Gordon Jacob

4. Festival Overture—[Constant] Lambert or foreign if necessary
5. Concerto for Piano and Full Orchestra—[Arnold] Bax
6. Simple Broad Unison Song—[Ralph] V[aughan] W[illiams]
7. Part Song [for male voices and brass band]—T[homas] Wood

Again, although there is no record of how the Music Panel came up with these individuals, the list itself suggests some criteria other than a perceived willingness to compose to order. With the commissions, the Panel seems to have wanted to generate broad popular interest rather than specialist prestige. The named composers wrote in a variety of styles, but all remained committed to tonality and had musical interests suitable for public, occasional work. Furthermore, with the possible exception of Wood, all were respected contemporary artistic figures whose concert music was widely performed and firmly established with the concert-going public. Vaughan Williams was 75, and Bax 64, but all the rest were in their 40s and 50s with records of significant success before the war. Vaughan Williams's name on this list suggests a conflict of interest like Wood's, although, since he proved uninterested in composing the unison song, he probably had not inserted it in the scheme for his own benefit.

The suggestion that the commission for the overture might have to go to a non-British composer, although it proved unnecessary, is provocative. Particularly in light of the Arts Council's early stipulation that the Festival would feature "the arts of Great Britain only" (Paper 86, EL4/66, n.d. [1948]), the annotation projects some anxiety. Perhaps the committee simply thought that no British composer had the necessary interest or time, but if so, would such a circumstance signal the failure of the whole enterprise? Of course, the term is also ambiguous: "Foreign" could refer either to an actual foreign composer or one of the many émigrés working in Britain, whose status in the Festival was never really clear.

The Festival Executive Committee approved the commissions for the seven Festival musical works on February 3, 1949 (EL4/50, February 15, 1949), along with the initial composers to approach, and John Denison began to notify the composers. Vaughan Williams and Wood were themselves on the Panel, so were aware of their nominations. The Panel passed over Finzi and Walton (then at work on *Troilus and Cressida*) but Bliss, Rubbra, and Jacob expressed interest in the genres offered.

Arnold Bax turned down the commission for the piano concerto, preferring to take on the overture, which, conveniently, Lambert declined, having accepted a Festival commission for the Sadler's Wells Ballet, where he was chief conductor. Lambert did respond to the Arts Council inquiry in jest, offering to write a choral-orchestral setting of Coleridge's early poem "Fire Famine and Slaughter." Perhaps ignorant of the poem's utter unsuitability to the occasion,[4] Council staff took Lambert at his word and examined the poem. (A copy with comment slips remains in the files.) Realizing that it did not address "themes related to the spirit of the Festival," they officially rejected Lambert's offer, which would at any rate have conflicted with the commission offered to Bliss. This bureaucratic response to his *jeu d'esprit* no doubt amused Lambert.

All this activity still left no composer for the piano concerto, so John Denison wrote Benjamin Britten a very solicitous letter ("I would fain do so with the minimum of bother to yourself") to inquire if Britten would take the commission (EL6/45, June 16, 1949). The choice of Britten was daring, as, at the age of thirty-five, he was considerably younger than the other composers, and identified with a more modernist musical aesthetic. But at any rate, facing a very heavy compositional schedule, Britten declined. Denison, going perhaps to the other extreme, turned to the 70-year-old John Ireland, offering a commission for any kind of piece, but suggesting a piano concerto. In broadening the offer this way Denison seems to have stepped outside his mandate, for, when Ireland offered a short orchestral work, Denison had to respond that, in fact, the Music Panel would not accept the change in genre. The panel may have felt that this would conflict with Bax's commission, but Denison gave no explanation, and the matter was dropped.

The commission of the "simple unison song" took an unusual turn when Vaughan Williams, on May 12, 1949, submitted a "Ballad of the Great Exhibition of 1951" to Eric Walter White, but requested that it remain anonymous. Vaughan Williams's cover note suggests that the song did not strike the right tone: "I do not suppose this would be any use to you—I expect you will want something more Old School Tie. In that case I fear you must apply ELSEWHERE" (EL6/45). White passed the song on to John Denison and Thomas Wood, who decided against commissioning anonymous works, and returned the song to Vaughan Williams with their apologies on June 15th (EL6/45, May 12, May 19, and June 15, 1949). Vaughan Williams's song is now lost.

The Council then decided to pass the song commission on to George Dyson, the Director of the Royal College of Music. Dyson, who was on friendly terms with Denison, replied to the commission offer on November 30th in high spirits:

> Since I saw you I have what I think is rather a bright idea: a historical trilogy, lasting about nine hours, for a three-day Festival 'featuring' 1851, 1951 and a prophetic 2051, for brass bands and women's institutes. Alternatively, I will do my best to concoct a unison song, but I think the Arts Council should be allowed to consider the larger scheme. I presume the song should be slightly pink, with a rather 'Jerusalemic' tune.

Denison responded in kind:

> I am thrilled at the idea of your centennial trilogy and suggest that each part should be capable of being played backwards and that all three should also dovetail for performance simultaneously, if required. I am delighted to hear that you will take on the Unison Song if I am unable to persuade the Council to accept the Trilogy. Will you, in due course, let me know which poem or lines you wish to use as I think my masters will want to be sure that they have the exactly right shade of pink. We must settle, too, what your fee is to be. There have been cuts in the budget but I am determined that starving composers shall not suffer.

Denison's final sentence, if flippant, was no jest.[5] The Council paid Dyson handsomely, considering the small amount of work he did on the song: 150 guineas for 65 measures of music consisting of three verses of a strophic melody, with an additional 50 guineas for Cecil Day Lewis, who wrote the poem.

Thus, by October 1949, six composers had accepted commissions: Bliss for the oratorio, Rubbra for a *Te Deum* (a suitably Handelian substitute for the psalm setting), Bax for the overture, Dyson for the song, Gordon Jacob for the military band suite, and Thomas Wood for the work for male choir and brass band. Alan Rawsthorne joined this group in February 1950 when, as the fourth composer approached, he accepted the piano concerto commission. Of these seven composers, Bax and Bliss did not complete works in time for the Festival.[6] Bax, who accepted his commission only hesitantly and after some courting by Denison, seems never even to have started, and apologized to the Council in November 1950. Bliss also wavered over accepting his commission, and although he worked fitfully, he relinquished the commission in December 1950. His *Song of Welcome* to words of Cecil Day Lewis, completed in 1954, may have originated with the Festival commission.

Also in October 1949, with the commissioning scheme well underway, the Arts Council staff finally noticed that their scheme did not include a Festival March, and John Denison approached William Alwyn to write one. In the same month, the Arts Council launched the competition for young composers, handing its management over to the Committee for the Promotion of New Music. The judges were the composers Arthur Bliss, Edric Cundell, John Ireland, Constant Lambert, William Walton, and Thomas Wood (EL4/95, August 10, 1949), all of whom except Wood were honorary Vice Presidents of the CPNM. In February 1951, they awarded the prize of £200 to Peter Racine Fricker for his concerto for violin and small orchestra. At the announcement, there was a flurry of concern within the Arts Council when the staff discovered that the work had already received a performance at Morley College in January, but they decided that this did not constitute a professional premiere at a major venue and it was overlooked.

Including the Fricker concerto, the completed official commissions available to ensembles for performances by the opening of the Festival of Britain were as follows:

1. William Alwyn, *Festival March*, available in Alwyn's original version for orchestra or in a version for military band orchestrated by Denis Wright;
2. George Dyson, "Song for a Festival" to a text by Cecil Day Lewis, available in arrangements for solo voice, unison singing with or without descant, and full choir, with accompaniment by piano, organ, strings, or full orchestra;
3. Peter Racine Fricker, Concerto for Violin and Small Orchestra,
4. Gordon Jacob, *Music for a Festival* for military band and additional ensemble of trumpets;
5. Alan Rawsthorne, Piano Concerto no. 2;
6. Edward Rubbra, *Festival Te Deum* for soprano solo, chorus, and orchestra, op. 71; and

7. Thomas Wood, *The Rainbow, a Tale of Dunkirk*, to a text by Christopher Hassall, for male voices and one or more brass bands (orchestrated by Frank Wright and also available in Welsh translation).

As Becky Conekin has argued, the Festival officially celebrated British culture in a specifically postwar formulation that tried to both encompass and respect, but not highlight, national differences within Britain. But in matters such as musical commissions, the procedures of the Festival did not really encourage national breadth. England housed the bulk of the British population and almost all the centers for professional training in composition at the time, and the Arts Council's focused on composers associated with London teaching and performing institutions. It is therefore not surprising that all seven commissioned composers were English by birth and education. As discussed earlier, the broader repertory of national classical music performed in the Festival was also almost entirely English.

Nevertheless, the commissioning scheme attracted the attention of the Arts Council's regional committees. In March 1950, in response to a proposal by the Welsh committee on music, the Festival Council approved an additional five commissions to honor the musical achievements of the Welsh people (EL4/95, July 6, 1949), of which four were completed, including Arwel Hughes's oratorio *Dewi Sant (Saint David)*. In 1950, the Scottish committee in turn decided to hold competitions for five works by composers of Scottish parentage, birth, or residence (EL6/172). Initiated very late in the Festival planning process, the Scottish scheme is virtually undocumented in the Arts Council archive, which suggests that it was abandoned or not completed on time. Furthermore, in contrast to the thorough, centralized process leading to the "national" commissions, the Arts Council paid minimal attention to the Welsh and Scottish commissions, and devolved all responsibility for them to the local committees. The approval by the Festival Council of the relatively inexpensive schemes can be read as more a conciliatory gesture to these committees than an embrace of national difference in the Festival proper.

The Arts Council also encouraged local governments and private performing organizations to place their own commissions, in two cases funding those commissions through grants. Appendix 2 lists the particulars of the main and Welsh commissioning schemes, along with all the other works privately commissioned for the Festival of Britain or premiered during the Festival. The cost of all the concert-music commissions and related costs came to £2,298. This sum was by no means an enormous outlay of money for the Council; it was only a small fraction of their £400,000 Festival budget, and substantially less than the £5,000 that Mary Glasgow had initially estimated. But it was the first money the Council had ever paid directly to composers for musical works, their first direct contribution to the national musical repertory.

Outside of Wales, a British subject seeking new music in the Festival of Britain either in concerts or BBC broadcasts would have been most likely to encounter the seven main commissions as representative of the nation as a whole. Each of these pieces contributed differently to the Festival and advanced different musical constructions of national identity. Three of them are largely ceremonial: Dyson's song, Alwyn's march, and Rubbra's *Te Deum*. Of these, the "Simple Broad Unison Song" is a charming bit of ephemera precisely crafted to its stated use. Dyson's own term "Jerusalemic" is perfectly apt: In order to strike the same tone of patriotic nobility as Parry's famous tune from the First World War, not only does Dyson's melody unfold in the same stately *alla breve* triple meter, but its opening phrase parrots Parry's final phrase almost exactly. Where Blake's classic text offers opaque and troubling symbols, however, Day Lewis's optimistic Festival hymn provides soothing nature imagery and humane exhortation ("Dear land, whose greatest art has been To graft the new upon the old, Teach us again your patient skill! Help us to heal this angry world!"). On the basis of the melody alone, no one could mistake Dyson's song for anything other than a British national hymn, but the composer's skill at pastiche doomed the work: With *Jerusalem* unshakably established in the British mind, no one needed *Song for a Festival* any more once the Festival ended.

William Alwyn, in his *Festival March*, also knew how to strike exactly the required noble and uplifting tone, as one would expect from such an experienced film composer. Like Dyson's, Alwyn's Festival contribution boldly proclaims its national identity; it is a substantial contribution to the genre of the British ceremonial orchestral march in the tradition of Elgar and Walton, complete with a rising introduction, a vigorous main theme, and a lyrical trio that returns as a rousing peroration. It is hardly a thrown-off piece, however: Alwyn approached his task with characteristic formal logic, unifying the main themes with a web of motivic relationships. If there were more concerts devoted to this kind of music, not to mention more awareness of Alwyn's oeuvre, the *Festival March* would certainly deserve performance, but it was soon lost in a sea of similar works.

The third ceremonial work, Edmund Rubbra's *Festival Te Deum*, op. 71, has vanished with scarcely a trace, overshadowed by the composer's later setting for unaccompanied eight-part choir, op. 115, which is more suitable for liturgical use. The earlier more exuberant setting bears the hallmarks of an occasional work written in haste. But for an eight-bar fugato on the words "Day by day we magnify Thee," the choral writing, while characteristically strenuous, is strictly homophonic and in parallel triads, with the male and female voices often doubled in octaves, thus apparently calculated to be learned in limited rehearsal time. Furthermore, particularly in the accompaniment in the middle sections, the composer relies excessively on his distinctive texture of scales and parallel triads moving in contrary motion at different speeds. In conceiving of this commission as a "Festival Psalm [for] a thanksgiving service at St. Paul's Cathedral or other appropriate occasion of this nature" the Music Panel in its enthusiasm for Georgian precedent may have nostalgically misjudged postwar musical life, in which such ceremonial events no longer had a place. The Arts Council struggled to arrange a performance of the work.

The remaining four commissions are free-standing concert works, less tied to the Festival occasion and more suitable for general programming. Predictably, neither of the two concertos bears any particular stamp of their Festival origins, but "fortuitously" as the writer of the 1948 memorandum had hoped, both are substantial contributions to their genre. Peter Racine Fricker's violin concerto (a competition winner and not a commission *per se*, and thus written on speculation) balances an accessible musical argument with the young composer's penchant for a level of dissonance uncommon in the Britain of 1951. Similarly, Alan Rawsthorne profited by the opportunity his commission provided: The large-scale four-movement virtuosic concerto that he produced, in his appealing extroverted style, remains one of the major works of this under-performed composer.

In contrast to these two concertos, associations with the Festival and a particular sense of occasion are far more apparent in Gordon Jacob's *Music for a Festival*. The Music Panel's original commissioning language, calling for "a work for military band, having in mind a performance in the open air or perhaps on the river," proved overly optimistic, but inspired Jacob. He visited the Royal Military School of Music at Kneller Hall to prepare, and, upon discovering that in addition to a full band they had an ensemble of trumpets (actually, trumpets and trombones, to which Jacob added timpani), decided to integrate them into the work as well. Although no outdoor performance occurred during the Festival, the work has a suitable breadth and clarity of expression, even an "outdoor" quality. Furthermore, it effectively subsumes musical references to the occasional genres evoked by the Festival—marches, fanfares, and the like—into an innovative structural plan: Its 11 movements alternate between the trumpet ensemble and the full band, combining them only for the final "Introduction, Fugue, and Coda". Jacob considered the score one of his finest, and alone among the seven commissioned works, *Music for a Festival* has remained in the repertory of top-quality ensembles, a major contribution to the literature for band rather than merely a sonic backdrop to a regatta on the Thames.

If Jacob's suite is the most lasting work to arise from the commissioning scheme, Thomas Wood's work, *The Rainbow: A Tale of Dunkirk*, was perhaps the most popular during the Festival year. When the work was announced in the press, it attracted attention around the country. This was due in part to performing forces—brass band and men's choir—whose strong ties to northern working-class culture had a broader social appeal than classical genres. Wood's death in November 1950, only months after passing the short score to Frank Wright to be orchestrated, further increased interest. But the work's subject, the Dunkirk Evacuation, undoubtedly also contributed enormously to the work's appeal. This event was very recent history and a source of enormous national pride.

The original language of this commission had called for "a Part Song for male voices and brass band accompaniment." In fact, while conceived for amateur performing forces, the piece that Wood eventually composed is vastly more than a part-song. His initial concept was more like a cantata, and his correspondence with John Denison shows the work growing over the process of composition. The final product, almost 45 minutes long, is practically an oratorio, despite its unusual performing forces.

In Wood's words, *The Rainbow* tells how:

> On Saturday June 1st, 1940 a man in the Treasury left his office, still wearing his bowler hat and carrying his attaché case, and went to Dover where he kept a small boat. During the whole of Saturday and Sunday with help of a volunteer crew he lifted in all 300 men from the Dunkirk beaches, and went back to the office on Monday as though nothing had happened.
>
> (EL6/56)

Christopher Hassall's libretto never names "the Treasury gent", or indeed any individual character. Rather, it presents the story of the evacuation in abstract, collective terms, in keeping with both the beloved British narrative of wartime social unity and the working-class performers' commitment to solidarity.

Wood carefully gauged the demands of such a major work for amateur forces. Other than two gently droll framing scenes, in which the protagonist addresses his secretary at work, the role for speaker is minimized in favor of simple, mostly unaccompanied narration for the soloist with commentary and response by the chorus. The choral writing is largely restricted to homophonic textures and makes significant use of unison (both sung and spoken), at times unaccompanied. Given the unusual constraints both of instrumental color and ability, Wood successfully invokes a tense seascape in the rescue sequence, which is followed by a set of quiet prayers and a peroration on the hymn tune "Nun Danket." As befits the story, this entire central section avoids overt excitement, a mood which is saved for the naval march and alleluias that close the work.

Although Wood composed the work so that it could be performed by a single band and a single choir, he conceived the ideal performance in much larger terms: three bands each with a 40-to-60-voice choir, two additional choirs of 100 voices each, and an offstage choir of 12 to 24 voices. The three bands with their respective choirs each take certain roles in the work and then combine to accompany the massed choir.

The Arts Council staff had committed time and money to placing these commissions and ensuring that the works were composed in time. But bringing music into being was not enough; once the works were available, they then had to arrange performances by professional ensembles at prominent Festival concerts. They announced the works in the press, making it clear that there were no performance restrictions once the Festival opened. In private communications, they encouraged performers to include them in their Festival programs, at times wielding direct influence over concert programs, as Chapter 1 explained.

All seven commissioned works did eventually receive premieres and performances in London during the Festival of Britain. The Arts Council music staff originally hoped to include the ceremonial works in the Festival's opening ceremonies, but this proved impossible. Even so, they succeeded in getting five of the works performed in the first ten days of the Festival. Fricker's violin concerto was first to be heard: The Jacques String Orchestra gave the work its first professional performance on May 3rd, the eve of the opening of the Festival, at the Victoria and Albert Museum. Dyson's song, naturally, was an easy sell: It was published in *Musical Times* in February 1951 (issue 1296) so that groups around the country could learn it, the London Symphony Orchestra and the National Youth Orchestra gave the first official performance at an afternoon concert at the Royal Albert Hall on May 6th, and it was sung at a variety of events throughout the country over the summer.

The Arts Council experienced more trouble getting the two other ceremonial works performed. One early plan called for Rubbra's *Te Deum* to be sung at the Festival's Opening Service at St. Paul's Cathedral on May 3rd. This would have corresponded to the Music Panel's initial conception, but the service was planned for organ and cathedral choir only. The cathedral organist, John Dykes-Bower, made an organ transcription of the score for the occasion, but Rubbra, who had conceived the work for enormous choir and orchestra, fretted that the work was unsuitable for such forces, and it was withdrawn. Much to the annoyance of the Arts Council, the London County Council, who produced the opening week of concerts at the Festival Hall, rejected the Arts Council's suggestion to include the *Te Deum* in the opening concert later the same day. Instead, the London Philharmonic Orchestra gave the first performance (and possibly the only performance to date) on June 30th in the Royal Festival Hall, at the closing concert of the London Season of the Arts.

As with Rubbra's *Te Deum*, the Arts Council proposed that the London Symphony Orchestra play Alwyn's *Festival March* on May 9th during the first week of concerts at the Festival Hall, but again the London County Council rejected this proposal. Nevertheless, audiences first heard the march not much later in the arrangement for band at the finals of the National Brass Band Club Competition in the Royal Albert Hall on May 12th. The London Symphony Orchestra premiered the orchestral version in the Royal Festival Hall on May 20th, and, later in the season, the Hallé Orchestra played it to open the Cheltenham Festival.

Audiences first heard Wood's *Rainbow* in a performance combining bands and choirs from around the country at the same final concert of the National Brass Band Club Competition on May 12th where Alwyn's march was first played. This performance followed Wood's instructions for the disposition of the various performing forces. Other than this London premiere and a performance in Swansea (Conekin 2003: 163), it is not clear how many groups performed this lengthy work in full during the Festival year. Given the letters of interest that the Arts Council received about the work, it is probable that some at least performed excerpts, and that the work was heard at Festival mass band concerts like those held in Bristol and at the National Eisteddfod in Llanrwst. The BBC recognized the appeal of *The Rainbow* and broadcast the premiere on the Light Service, bringing it to a broad public, and repeated the broadcast later in the Festival. A collection of bands and men's choruses gave the work a further London performance at the Royal Festival Hall on December 9, 1951.

The band and trumpeters of the Royal Military School of Music gave the premiere of Jacob's *Music for a Festival* at the Festival Hall on May 14th. Rawsthorne's piano concerto had to wait longer. The London Symphony

70 *Commissions and premieres*

Orchestra, with Clifford Curzon, gave the premiere at the Royal Festival Hall on June 17th, and repeated the work at the Cheltenham Festival. (The four completed Welsh commissions received performances at concerts in St. David's or other Welsh festivals, and the Welsh Festival Choir and London Philharmonic Orchestra also performed the *Festival Overture* of William Hubert Davies at the Royal Festival Hall during the London season.)

Assessment

While the low expectations expressed in the anonymous 1948 memorandum were reasonable, the Festival commissions as whole turned out no worse than similar efforts in history, perhaps slightly better. Ironically, however, where the 1950 press response to the announcement of the commissions faulted their highbrow taste, the limited historical assessment of the scheme has focused on its supposed pandering. Thus, the journalist Barry Turner in his history of the Festival (2011: 204) categorizes the music in the Festival as "predominantly conservative". He goes on to state that the new orchestral works "failed to make their mark" because they were overshadowed by the opening of the Royal Festival Hall, a curious claim that would be hard to prove or even explain. It is more likely that the works were lost in the vast sea of Festival music, old and new, reviewed in Chapter 1.

Paul Kildea, in his 2002 study "Selling Britten" mounts a more sustained critique of the commissions. After relating the rejection of Vaughan Williams's song, Lambert's offer to set the poem "Fire Famine and Slaughter" (which he takes seriously), and Ireland's proposed orchestral work, he writes:

> The Council's desire to control every aspect of the pieces commissioned is obvious; the insecurity of the music department's first years was to be stabilized by a conservative stable of works, each with the Council's imprimatur, and each forwarding the cause of English culture amidst postwar gloom.
>
> (127)

While the Arts Council was certainly controlling, the three rejections do not support such a conclusion. Vaughan Williams insisted that his song, if accepted, remain anonymous, and as a member of the Music Panel was a conscious party to its replacement. Surely the Arts Council was within its rights to reject a proposal as bizarre and insincere as Lambert's for a celebratory national festival. By contrast, the rejection of Ireland's offer of an overture was indeed unfortunate, given his stature, but probably resulted not from a thirst for control but from excessively rigid bureaucratic thinking: Bax had already agreed to write "the" short orchestral work; what would the Arts Council do with two? As for "forwarding the cause of English culture amidst postwar gloom," this was unquestionably one of the goals of the Festival of Britain as a whole; the Arts Council can hardly be faulted for supporting it.

More significantly, Kildea takes the Arts Council to task for its "conservative view of genre" and "regressive view of new music—with its emphasis on familiar forms and genres." Running down the original list of commissions, he sums up:

> With each composer type-cast, and with most suggested genres reflecting England's late-Romantic artistic values—pastoral, industrial, and imperial all vying for attention—the hundredth anniversary of the Great Exhibition was not only to be celebrated, it was to be celebrated in true 1851 style.
>
> (127)

Although it actually would have been impossible to celebrate musically "in true 1851 style"—because hardly any new music was commissioned for the 1851 Exhibition (a fact the Arts Council music staff knew well)—the heart of this complaint echoes that of the Arts Council's 1948 "doubting Thomas," hankering after more experimental commissions. But Kildea does not explain which alternative "forms and genres" would have been less regressive. The string quartet and the song cycle were two non-occasional genres overlooked by the Music Panel but cultivated by progressive British composers, but with their long histories, these genres could hardly be deemed inherently "progressive."

Innovation in genre tends to occur in chamber music and works for small ensembles: Adventurous commissions in the twentieth century often called for unusual forces. Kildea is correct that the Arts Council excluded this possibility from the start. They calculated rightly that the audience for public concerts was more interested in choral and orchestral works, where even today genres remain conservative. Practically speaking, it would have been hard to pass off a commissioned composition for baritone, ondes Martenot, and percussion, or a work of *musique concrète*, as a fitting contribution to the Festival of Britain, however much it delighted enthusiasts of the avant-garde.

As a quick survey of British postwar compositions shows, most of the genres the Music Panel picked were mainstream in the 1940s (and not, in fact, prevalent in Britain in 1851). The institutions of British classical music—and not merely the Arts Council—were conservative in this regard. The Music Panel's call for a "Festival Psalm" admittedly had a Georgian or Victorian air—and the resulting work as a result attracted little attention. But the panel also included the competition for a concertante work and the piano concerto that John Denison had worked so hard to acquire. And the forms that both Jacob's band suite and Wood's cantata took are actually rather innovative. Certainly there is no evidence of that the Music Panel imposed requirements of pastoral, industrial, or imperial expression on the composers, nor is any to be found in the works, unless a piece for brass band and men's chorus is "industrial" by association, or the proposal for music "in or about boats" excessively riparian.[7]

As for type-casting the composers, the genres did indeed match what the Music Panel knew of the composers' proclivities, but this is scarcely a flaw in the planning; they wanted those genres, and they wanted them composed in time for the Festival. (Alwyn, a rapid craftsman, was just the man for a ceremonial march and Dyson could be counted on to dash off a stirring song, while the Arts Council may have passed over William Walton and Gerald Finzi precisely because of their slow pace of work.) Nor were the composers hoary relics of a bygone era; only Dyson, the oldest of the crew at 67, merits the epithet "late Romantic," and that on account of his style rooted in nineteenth century practice rather than his age. Furthermore, awarding the fixed commissions to established composers while making the commission for younger composers competitive avoided playing favorites among the crop of emerging artists; this is exactly the process Duncan Guthrie had proposed in his foundational memorandum.

It is reasonable to object that the Music Panel overlooked exponents of more progressive styles, but there were actually rather few of these in mainstream British musical life in 1948, and would be hard to argue that they were excluded by policy. Britten's music was everywhere evident; the nation's two leading 12-tone composers, Elisabeth Lutyens and Humphrey Searle, both had Festival premieres, although Searle's work was heard in Cheltenham, not London; and the rising modernist Peter Racine Fricker won the young composer's competition. Rather, what the Arts Council appears to have avoided in its commissions were decadence, hermeticism, and intellectualism for its own sake; all the works have a quality of public-spiritedness, an engagement with a real or imagined national audience that matched that of the Festival as a whole, and was compatible with a range of styles and genres.

From the very outset of the commissioning program, a tension, identified in the anonymous 1948 memo, existed between the ambition to create lasting works for the repertory of British music and the ambition to create occasional works simply for the enlivening of the Festival. Both of these outcomes would redound to the Council's credit, of course, but in different ways. At the distance of over half a century, it perhaps seems more praise-worthy to celebrate national excellence in music by calling forth works cutting-edge in style and genre. In this view, only the avant-garde is timely, while everything else is conservative. But such a dichotomy is anachronistic if not disingenuous.[8] It is true that composers such as George Dyson and Thomas Wood hardly worked in idioms that lent the Festival international glamour. Yet their "traditional," even "backward-looking" art was not consequently a less adequate representation of national culture and identity; indeed it ensured their works' broad dissemination. As demonstrated in Chapter 1, in the London Season of the Arts the Arts the Council undertook to curate the nation's entire musical legacy. Presenting new works congruent with that legacy was just as genuine a manner of demonstrating national excellence in art as presenting works that self-consciously rejected or superseded it.

In the late forties, the Arts Council was poised at a moment of enormous opportunity between the past, more demotic cultural provisions of CEMA and the more sophisticated elite postwar cultural role promoted by John Maynard Keynes. The Festival commissioning scheme emboldened the Council, leading it into new realms of support for the arts. Certainly in its decisions it may have overlooked or missed opportunities. Objections can be and were raised against the assignment of particular genres to specific composers, instead of a more open-ended or competitive process, as well as against the composers and genres chosen and the styles of the resulting works. Nevertheless, the results did effectively realize the Arts Council's intentions and broad mission of appealing to a broad national concert-going (and radio-listening) audience, not just to avant-garde elites. Together, the commissions constitute a reasonably catholic overview of mainstream contemporary British art music at mid-century, neither a regressive retread of Victorian conservatism nor a forbiddingly highbrow initiative to advance British modernism.

Notes

1 The most famous example, Richard Addinsell's *Warsaw Concerto*, written for the film *Dangerous Moonlight* (1941), was followed by the use of Rachmaninov's second concerto in *Brief Encounter* (1945) and original works by Bernard Herrmann and Charles Williams in *Hangover Square* (1945) and *Where I Live* (1947). Arnold Bax's score for David Lean's 1948 *Oliver Twist* also makes use of concertante piano.
2 In November 1948, Vaughan Williams continued this campaign for working-class amateurs in a letter to Eric Walter White: "Would it be in order to suggest to you that brass bands should be included in the 1951 Festival? I daresay you know they are the most popular form of music in England and their technique is wonderful; their taste shocking. Perhaps if we admitted them into the fold it would help them in that matter" (EL2/20).
3 The other commissioning schemes were in visual art and poetry. See Hewison 1988: 51–55, Banham and Hillier 1976: 40–51 and 187, and Glendinning 1995: 280–283. On the playwriting competition, see Saunders 2012.
4 The poem is a grotesque attack on the results of the policies of William Pitt the Younger: "I heard a groan, and a peevish squall, / And thro' the chink of a cottage wall, / Can you guess what I saw there?—Whisper it, Sister! in our ear!—A baby beat its dying mother / I had starv'd the one, and was starving the other!"
5 The suggestion that the trilogy be composed to permit simultaneous performance is a reference to the 1848 Triple Oratorio of Pietro Raimondi (1786–1853), a fact Denison undoubtedly expected his fellow aficionado of music-historical trivia to recognize.
6 Curiously, both Andrew Sinclair (1995: 82) and Becky Conekin (2003: 119–120) report *only* Bax and Bliss as recipients of Festival commissions. Perhaps these are now the most familiar names in the list.
7 It is amusing to compare Kildea's dismissal of the supposed pastoral values of the Festival commissions with his enthusiasm for Britten's exactly contemporary *Six Metamorphoses after Ovid*. While Jacob's band suite was never performed on the river, oboist Joy Boughton premiered Britten's work while standing in a boat anchored on Thorpeness Meare at the 1951 Aldeburgh Festival (Kildea 2002: 186). On the other hand, premieres in 1951 included Norman Fuller's *Sinfonia Pastorale*, Cecil Armstrong Gibbs's *Pastoral Suite*, and Hubert Hales's *Pastoral Music*.
8 Christopher Chowrimootoo (2014) has recently called for rehabilitation of the category of the middlebrow in musical scholarship precisely to mediate such dichotomous thinking.

3 On stage...
Festival opera productions

Susana Walton, in her biography of her husband William, reports his comment that in the late forties, "opera was very much in the air in London." (Walton, 1988: 133). Indeed, the immediate postwar climate appeared propitious for opera in every way. The unexpected international success of Britten's *Peter Grimes* in 1945 revived British composers' interest in the genre. The next few years saw the founding of the Covent Garden Opera (now the Royal Opera) as London's second permanent opera company and the English Opera Group, a new professional touring troupe. These developments, along with the postwar expansion of broadcasting and the renewed availability of university and community productions, generated an operatic ferment.

Opera's rise in fortune in postwar Britain was intimately related to the new regime of state art funding, for in this period, governmental funding for opera thrived. The Arts Council from its very beginning regarded opera as the premier art form in Britain requiring state support, and made it the top financial priority (White 1975: 128–129). The leap to prominence of this particular art form is all the more notable for the fact that previously there had been only one very brief state subsidy of any kind for opera, and that had been solely for broadcast performance: In 1931, the government agreed to help pay the costs of broadcasting opera performances over the BBC. That subsidy had lasted only a single year, however, before being eliminated due to a budget crisis (Briggs 1965: 179–181).[1] The postwar policy by contrast called for attention to opera performances on every scale all across the nation.

Officially the Arts Council provided support for both the metropolitan companies and regional needs, but in practice the London companies, and especially Covent Garden, received sizable grants while the small regional and touring companies got only nominal support. (Glyndebourne, uniquely, usually ran without state support in this era, but did receive a substantial grant for the Festival of Britain season.) The large proportion of the Arts Council grant passed on to Covent Garden attracted some public criticism early on, but nevertheless within the Arts Council the commitment to the major opera and ballet companies was increased. While in 1945–1946 Covent Garden received £25,000 (10.6 percent of the Arts Council's £235,000 budget) and Sadler's Wells £10,000 (4.3 percent), these amounts had increased four years later to £145,000 (21.5 percent of the £675,000 budget) and

£47,500 (7.0 percent) respectively (White 1975: 206). Although these proportions seemed large, individuals within both Covent Garden and the Arts Council were fond of pointing out that opera houses on the continent got much larger individual grants. The French government's combined 1946 subsidy to the Opéra and the Opéra comique, £600,000, was set against the comparatively small subsidies that Covent Garden received. And the subsidies did not come close to meeting the expenses of the house. For the 1948–1949 season, the Arts Council grant to Covent Garden was £120,000, but David Webster, the General Administrator of Covent Garden, estimated that the season as a whole cost £400,000.

The substantial support for opera and ballet performances and companies in the budgets of the Arts Council of Great Britain in the late forties was not just the result of that organization's emphasis on civic and national prestige. In the view of the cultural elite, the establishment of international-quality opera and ballet performances was an important step in restoring the city's and the nation's artistic standing in the world. Had this been the only impetus behind the Arts Council's opera policy, however, one would expect to see concern only for the standard continental repertory such as Wagner, Verdi, Puccini, and Bizet. The period 1945–1951 also saw growing interest in new British opera, and the Arts Council had a role to play in this development also. The two sides of the national operatic scene in postwar Britain—establishing high professional standards for native performers and creating a native repertory—were closely related, although they sometimes came into conflict with one another or attracted the support of different groups (Lew 2001, Chapter 2).

1951 was an unusually busy year for English opera in addition to English concert music. This chapter surveys the plans of the Arts Council and performing organizations to encourage and arrange performances of new and old British operas during the Festival year. The Arts Council's commitment to the cause of British opera in preparation for the Festival of Britain was remarkable in its perseverance and eventual success, measured in the number of performances and the breadth of the repertory. In particular, the three major commissions discussed in the first part of the chapter, each challenging in different ways, demonstrate the extent of the Arts Council's determination to bring new operas to performance in the Festival. The range of their efforts in this pursuit resemble those discussed in Chapter 1, and include direct intervention (the long campaigns to bring about commissions), indirect pressure (giving special consideration to ensembles that produced new works), and persuasive lobbying for native repertory. No doubt because of his abiding interest in the history of English opera, Eric Walter White took on the lion's share of this work and deserves the bulk of the credit.

In the original organization of the Arts Council, opera policy was categorized under music and managed by the Music Director, Steuart Wilson, advised by the Music Panel. This arrangement attracted criticism, because it saddled the Music Panel with the affairs not only of all the major orchestras and other performing ensembles, but also of several opera companies, while excluding people with expertise in the dramatic side of opera from policy discussions. Finally, in March 1948, the Arts Council set up a separate Opera and Ballet Panel, which included representatives from each of the five main opera companies at the time (the Covent Garden Opera, Sadler's Wells, The Carl Rosa Opera, Glyndebourne, and the English Opera Group). Unfortunately, the experiment was largely unsuccessful, as this new panel proved too divisive. The representatives from the different companies held widely divergent views on the direction that the Arts Council's opera policy should take. Members realized that what was needed was not specific Arts Council policies and programs, but a working group committee of representatives of the managements of the various opera and ballet companies, to provide coordination and practical cooperation among them (Arts Council Annual Report 1948–1949: 20). After four meetings that accomplished little, the panel was disbanded and responsibility devolved back onto the Music Panel. Although it did not last long as a permanent element of the Arts Council, the Opera and Ballet Panel exerted a considerable influence on the musical plans for the Festival of Britain: Almost the only substantive action in its brief life was the recommendation that the Arts Council commission a number of new operas and ballets for the Festival.

Initial planning

At the May 11, 1948 meeting where the Arts Council Music Panel first discussed Festival commissions for concert works, they noted that several worthy composers were already at work on operatic projects, and that it therefore might be more productive for the Arts Council to aid opera companies in mounting productions of these new operas, rather than to place commissions for yet more new operas. Similarly, the Panel dismissed the need for ballet commissions on the grounds that ballet companies, unlike opera companies, create new works every year (EL6/45, June 14, 1948).

The Opera and Ballet Panel, however, disagreed with the Music Panel's assessment of opera and ballet commissioning and took up the matter itself. The opera subcommittee of the Opera and Ballet Panel met on June 22, 1948 and again on July 19th, and, matching the enthusiasm the Music Panel had shown in their concert-music commissioning plans, proposed to commission three new operas for the Festival of Britain season, one each for the nation's three permanent and established opera companies, Covent Garden, Sadler's Wells, and Carl Rosa (Paper 92, EL4/66, n.d. [December 1948/January 1949]), with payments to the composers of £500 for the commissions for the two major companies, and £300 for the Carl Rosa commission, as well as subsidies to the companies towards the costs of production during the Festival year. No commission was offered to the Welsh National Opera. Founded in 1943, this company had given its first performance in 1946, and by the time of the Festival was receiving a large annual grant from the Arts Council, but in 1948 it probably seemed too new, too remote, and (with miners singing in the chorus) too amateurish for the cosmopolitan opera managers on the panel to take seriously. More to the point, the company had no representative on the Opera and Ballet Panel, who were essentially arranging commissions for themselves.

78 *Festival opera productions*

These three companies were very different. The Carl Rosa Opera, based in Manchester, was a venerable touring troupe, having existed in various guises since 1873 (Martin 2010: 25–30). The company received a short-lived boost from wartime support for touring performers, and in the mid-forties performed a substantial repertory of continental standards in commercial theaters around Britain. But from 1949 the company fell into decline, and for the next few years was held together chiefly by the strong will of its owner and director, Mrs. Annette Phillips. Performance reports from 1949 preserved by the Arts Council express support for touring opera but rate the orchestra and singing as merely adequate and comment on the poor acting and staging. The Arts Council seems never to have taken the Carl Rosa Opera very seriously; certainly it did not merit the consideration afforded to the two metropolitan companies. Although seemingly an opportunity for the company to advance its stature, The Festival of Britain was in fact its last big undertaking; after a decade of increasingly precarious financial health buoyed by Arts Council funds, the company went bankrupt in 1960.

The Sadler's Wells Opera was the older of the two permanent London companies, and the ancestor of today's English National Opera (a name it took in 1974 after it moved to the London Coliseum). Founded by Lillian Baylis after the First World War as part of the Old Vic, from 1925 it performed opera in English at its eponymous North London theater, with a commitment to making opera available to audiences of all income levels. Having survived the crisis brought on by the premiere of Britten's *Peter Grimes* in 1945 (see Crozier 1965 and Carpenter 1992), which saw the resignation of a large number of administrators and singers, in the late forties the company was recovering its footing under the direction of Norman Tucker. Since the Sadler's Wells stage was small and the auditorium seated only 1,650, the company's repertory favored smaller-scale productions of classics and revivals of English repertory. (Arundell 1965 and Gilbert 2011 give a full history of the company.)

Finally, the Covent Garden Opera was the capital's new company, founded in 1946 chiefly by John Maynard Keynes and the publishers Boosey and Hawkes to provide a worthy tenant for the Royal Opera House. Although begun with the stated purpose of developing a national operatic tradition—including native repertory and performances in the vernacular—the company very rapidly (d)evolved into a typical international opera company, offering spectacular productions of continental repertory sung by the biggest stars available from abroad. At the time of the Festival commissions, it was still very much experiencing growing pains. (See Lew 2001, Chapter 2, for a discussion of the history and postwar development of these companies.)

The Arts Council Opera and Ballet Panel included representatives from all these companies, which accelerated communication considerably. The report on opera commissioning therefore not only represents the opinions of the companies themselves but lists the composers that the companies were interested in working with. The representative from the Sadler's Wells Opera expressed a desire to commission a new opera from Ralph Vaughan Williams, and the Carl Rosa Company chose the composer George Lloyd (1913–1998). With Covent Garden the situation was more complicated. Since this company was only in its third season, every single production, not just premieres, had to be created from scratch, the chorus taught its part, and the orchestra rehearsed in a new score. The company anticipated being able to introduce in all only one or two new productions in the 1951 season. They were already aware of a number of projects by British composers which, if ready by 1951, they might want to program: William Walton had just received his BBC commission for *Troilus and Cressida*, and Michael Tippett was at work on *The Midsummer Marriage*. Britten, too, it was reported, was considering a new grand operatic project. (In fact, in June he invited E. M. Forster to write him a libretto, but they did not settle on a subject). With so many possibilities, an additional commissioned opera might be too much for the company to undertake.

Nevertheless, Covent Garden declared Britten to be its choice for a Festival commission. According to his biographer, David Webster, the company's General Administrator, believed *Peter Grimes* to be the cornerstone of the national operatic repertory and wanted to establish a working relationship with Britten at this time (Haltrecht 1975: 122); the request that Britten receive the Covent Garden Festival commission may have been an attempt on Webster's part to bring this about. Moreover, Britten's publisher, Boosey and Hawkes, was closely tied to Covent Garden: The firm held the lease to the theater, and both Ralph Boosey and Leslie Hawkes were trustees of the company. Having failed to secure the premiere of Britten's first grand opera for Covent Garden, there was probably some pressure within the publishing house to secure the premiere of the second.

In fact, even before the Arts Council received authorization to offer Britten the commission, David Webster approached Britten to offer the possibility of writing a new opera for Covent Garden to perform in the Festival year. An October 7, 1948 letter from Webster to Britten asked for an opera with or without official Festival backing (Cooke and Reed 1993: 61–62). Britten clearly had concerns about the artistic quality of the company—he had been unhappy with the way it had staged *Peter Grimes* in 1947—but he responded "I certainly intend to write a big new one which should be ready, if everything goes to plan, by that year" (Carpenter 1992: 270).

With Lloyd, there was a delay in approving the commission. He was a relatively little known figure, and the Arts Council had to explain the choice to the Festival Office. It is not clear who in the Carl Rosa Company first heard Lloyd's music or fixed on him as a suitable composer for commission. A memorandum from Duncan Guthrie to Gerald Barry gives background on Lloyd and his operatic career, and then notes that "the suggestion that he should be commissioned came from the Carl Rosa Opera Company, who are particularly anxious to include a work by George Lloyd in their repertoire" (EL6/23, December 3, 1948). The Council also opted to contact him first and ascertain that he was willing to undertake the commission before putting his name forward. That Britten's and Vaughan Williams's names were advanced without first gaining their assent suggests that the Arts Council was more concerned with the prestige of the commissions than with their viability. Just proposing commissions for Britten and Vaughan Williams looked good, even if they proved unable to accept them. With a lesser figure like Lloyd, it was more important that he actually accept.

On July 26, 1948 the full Opera and Ballet Panel approved the subcommittee's recommendations, including both the three specific commissions for Britten, Vaughan Williams, and Lloyd and the open competition discussed in Chapter 4. These proposals were approved as an official proposal of the Arts Council, and sent up to the Festival Executive Committee. In January 1949, once the full Festival Council had approved the opera commissioning plans, the Arts Council set about approaching the three composers.

When the Festival Executive Committee approved the plans on October 29, 1948, it added an interesting appendix to the plans (EL6/71, n.d.). Besides raising the question of operetta or light opera, which the Opera and Ballet Panel had completely (and deliberately) neglected, the appendix made two main points. First, the Executive Committee suggested that the actual subject of the 1851 Great Exhibition be considered as a topic for operatic treatment, or at least that the theme of the 1951 Festival be included in the term of reference circulated to composers entering the competition. Second, it expressed concern that the results of the commissions be heard in places other than London during the Festival period, stating in particular that the Carl Rosa Company—which was after all a touring company—should perform their new opera in the provinces. The query about light opera was to remain unanswered, whether due to snobbery and prejudice against this genre within the Arts Council—like film, this was a genre that had never been included in the "fine arts exclusively" terms of reference of the Arts Council—or due to a feeling that enough commissioning schemes had already been initiated. Similarly, the Arts Council made no explicit mention of either the 1851 Exhibition or the 1951 Festival as a subject or theme in the competition. As events turned out, however, the Carl Rosa Company did introduce its Festival commission in the provinces.

During the course of Festival planning, the Arts Council considered various additional schemes to provide opera. In April 1949, for instance, Duncan Guthrie suggested that, as another operatic venue and venture for the Festival, operas could be televised from the BBC television studio that was going to be included in the South Bank exhibition (EL6/76, April 13, 1949), but this was judged impractical.

George Lloyd, *John Socman*

Of the three proffered commissions, only George Lloyd's *John Socman* for the Carl Rosa Company materialized as planned. Since the Arts Council had already contacted Lloyd about his willingness to accept a commission for a "full-length opera without spoken dialogue" for the Carl Rosa Company, when they officially offered it to him, he readily accepted (EL6/71, February 4, 1949, Paper 266, EL4/50, February 15, 1949). The Company, on their end, agreed to give the opera a "reasonable" number of times during the season, and the Arts Council guaranteed to subsidize the costs of the production. Lloyd and the Rosa Company jointly worked out the musical forces required, and Lloyd set to work on the opera, *John*

Socman, to a libretto by his father William Lloyd, who had written the librettos for his first two operas as well.

Lloyd is a mostly overlooked figure in English musical history. A contemporary of Britten, he was born in Cornwall in 1913 of mixed Welsh and American extraction, and studied at Trinity College of Music. One of the many British composers of his generation firmly committed to tonal idioms and traditional forms, he was in his twenties something of a phenomenon in London, with a string of successful performances including three symphonies and two operas. However, during the Second World War the cruiser on which Lloyd was serving was torpedoed. Lloyd almost drowned in the resulting oil spill and was one of the few survivors; his physical and psychological injuries required several years of convalescence, and upon his return to the English musical world, he found himself out of fashion.

Lloyd's first two operas, *Iernin* (1934) and *The Serf* (1938), were both very well received in London. Indeed, during 1935, *Iernin* played nightly at the Lyceum, a very rare distinction for a serious opera. The librettos remain firmly within the bounds of nineteenth century operatic dramaturgy, with their romantic medieval plots organized into closed, vocally dominated musical forms. (*Iernin* is set in medieval Cornwall and concerns fairies.)[2] Lloyd was therefore a sensible choice for the Carl Rosa company. His accessible, melodic style and conventional operatic aesthetic matched the conservative tastes of the company's directors and suited the less sophisticated audiences in the provinces presumably more interested in entertainment than aesthetic challenge.

In comparison with the other two commissions, that for the Carl Rosa Opera progressed smoothly. At the same time, the commission forced the Arts Council to keep the Carl Rosa Opera on life support in order to get the work produced, as it became increasingly clear that the badly mismanaged company simply could not survive in its current form. Already in a 1948 memorandum to Mary Glasgow, Eric Walter White predicted that bringing the commission to production would be an expensive undertaking:

> In the course of our discussion, Mrs. Phillips expressed in no uncertain terms her views on opera production and presentation. They are somewhat old-fashioned; but I do not despair of being able to obtain an intelligent production of the commissioned opera, since in the case of the Carl Rosa Opera Company we should presumably have to offer a fairly considerable grant towards the cost of production and this ought to be given on condition that the Arts Council approved the producer and designer.
>
> (ACGB 50/524)

Given the company's endless financial troubles, White's "fairly considerable grant" in the end amounted to £5,000 just for the Festival production. Furthermore, dealing with the administration of the company, and particularly the redoubtable and touchy Mrs. Phillips, proved maddening. In the period from commission to Festival, the company was constantly on the verge of failure, squabbling and fighting with other companies. The orchestra was underpaid, with the Musicians'

Union making demands, audiences were disappointing, and bookings were dropped. At least one singer decamped for Sadler's Wells. Forever crying poverty and their own worthiness, Mrs. Phillips and Frank Gaylor, the Secretary of the Carl Rosa's sister company, Grand Opera Productions, pestered White with incessant queries, demands, and complaints. Phillips was also adept in mustering powerful political allies. In late March 1950, sensing opposition to her demands, she wrote to the papers, announcing that without support the company might have to close down, and even persuaded an MP to raise questions about the Arts Council's (lack of) support for the company, requiring a careful response from Arts Council staff (ACGB 50/524).

The most awkward moment came as a result of an unsigned article in the *Sunday Times* on September 25, 1949. Under the headline "Several British Operas on the Stocks", the article discussed the forthcoming premiere of Bliss's *Olympians* at Covent Garden and the Arts Council's commissioning schemes, and then listed several prominent British operatic projects in progress or recently completed, including works by Lennox Berkeley, Britten, Alan Bush, Edmund Rubbra, Tippett, Vaughan Williams, and Walton (EL6/71, September 25, 1949). The article, for which the Arts Council had not supplied any information, neglected to mention Lloyd's work, and Phillips, taking the omission to be a deliberate snub, wrote to the Arts Council to request more publicity for the company and *John Socman*. After some internal scrambling, further complicated by the publicity ban imposed by the government during the currency crisis in October and early November, the Arts Council drafted a press release for issue by the Carl Rosa Company giving particulars of the commission and the upcoming premiere (EL6/71, September 24 to November 12, 1949).

While these petty dramas unfolded, Lloyd completed *John Socman* and delivered the completed score on April 4, 1951. Not surprisingly, given the self-defeating level of distrust and suspicion in the company, the period of preparation was marred by backstage intrigues. Eric Walter White's report on the premiere hints at the dysfunction:

> Dennis Arundell [the producer/stage director] felt that a considerable amount of time had been wasted at rehearsals ... particularly at the dress rehearsal stage when Hammond [the conductor] was apt to stop the rehearsal to correct the orchestra and/or singers. (Sir Steuart Wilson thought the rehearsal schedule would compare not unfavourably with Covent Garden's for *The Pilgrim's Progress*). Arundell has asked for his name to be removed from the billing as producer.
>
> In addition, Arundell was very annoyed because at the end of Act 2 Mrs. Phillips countermanded his order that the tableau curtain should be taken as a tableau, and the principals' calls should be taken in front of the drop curtain. The first curtain was taken with the chorus in character and the principals frankly acknowledging the applause. (Words were exchanged about this by Arundell and Mrs. Phillips on the stage in the interval between Acts II and III).
>
> (EL6/71, 16 May 1951)

The company premiered the work at the Hippodrome in Bristol on May 15, 1951 at the start of the Festival season. They then took it to various other cities, and repeated it the following year in Edinburgh.

The synopsis of *John Socman* included with the press release reads as follows:

> The scene is laid on the Great Plain, Wiltshire, the action taking place in A.D. 1415 shortly after Agincourt.
>
> The tale concerns two sets of people whose lives cross each other's. On the one hand two young lovers—Richard, an archer returning from Agincourt, and Sybil; on the other—John Socman, a local justice, and a Glee-maiden he had married while serving at Bordeaux, whom he had subsequently abandoned to some cut-throats to get rid of, but who actually had, unknown to him, been saved from her fate by a dumb tumbler.
>
> At the opening of the action, John Socman is pursuing Sybil whom he wishes to marry, hoping in her to find forgetfulness. She is saved from him by Richard, but Socman has Sybil's father, a lollard, arrested for heresy: and to save her father from the stake Sybil despairingly agrees to Socman's wishes.
>
> Meanwhile the Glee-maiden—sometimes gay, at other times an almost distraught creature who has partially lost her memory, but who vaguely knows she is looking for someone that has gone from her life—is wandering the country-side singing her songs and accompanied by her Tumbler.
>
> At a triumphal procession of soldiers returning from Agincourt she hears Richard ask for aid from Sir Hugh Mannay, their commander, saying that he has had Sybil taken from him by John Socman. Hearing this name, the Glee-maiden becomes violently agitated, her memory suddenly clears and she realises for whom she is searching. It is the name forgotten. At last the lost is found.
>
> Richard goes to Socman's house, with him the help given by Sir Hugh Mannay. He finds that Sybil has already been forced to marry. He and Socman fight but are interrupted as Sir Hugh enters accompanied by the Glee-maiden. She has told her story and Sir Hugh has accepted her as John Socman's wife. Sir Hugh explains to everyone the crime John Socman would have done, adding that it is left for the Glee-maiden to judge the Husband who had abandoned her. Amazed and penitent, John Socman begs forgiveness, which the Glee-maiden still loving him grants; and nothing now stands between the union of Richard and Sybil. The scene closes with rejoicing.

As with his earlier two operas, Lloyd planned the score as a number opera in the Italian tradition, with an alternation of self-revelatory arias for the principals, impressive dramatic ensembles bringing the characters into conflict (some with chorus), and genre numbers such as dances, carols, choruses, and songs for the Gleemaiden. (There is a small divertissement in Act 2, Scene 2 before the regiment arrives.) Lloyd's idiom is certainly conservative for its day, as Matthew Rye (1995: 348–349) points out, but not excessively so. Although based on the best models from the *bel canto* era and Verdi—Lloyd was in a sense the heir to Michael Balfe—

his music makes effective if subdued use of dissonance, bitonality, and rhythmic variety. Nevertheless, the melodies in *John Socman*, if fluent, often fail to take flight, the numbers run long, and the orchestration tends to be monotonous.

In contrast to other operas of the period, the chorus in *John Socman* plays a completely conventional role. Recognizing the power of the opera chorus to stir the emotions (especially patriotic ones), the Lloyds provided a drinking song, a martial song, a welcome for the troops, and the jolly final ensemble: "Shout for the heroic years gone by, though in the far dim past they lie, for courage that can never die." But the chorus never steps beyond observing and commenting on the action in the manner of conventional nineteenth century opera. It has no stake in the struggle between Richard and Socman for Sybil.

The opera also has dramatic flaws. The plot is constructed to provide various stock operatic characters and situations while the largely irrelevant genre numbers, including the substantial final chorus, detract from the sense that anything serious is at stake, and mute the score's emotional charge. Anthony Payne (1951: 318) branded the work "a Wardour Street 'Trovatore'," although the plot more closely resembles that of *Luisa Miller*. If we take the plot seriously, the circumstances reveal themselves to be dark and the title character shows psychological depth and complexity. (One reviewer compared him to Scarpia, although Socman is actually more conflicted than Puccini's monochromatic villain.) But Socman's repentance and transformation at the climax is sudden and insufficiently motivated, even out of character, snatching a happy ending unconvincingly from the jaws of tragedy. Although entertaining enough, to audience members expecting a new opera to grapple with sophisticated, modern issues, *John Socman* was a disappointment, neither musically nor dramatically challenging.

Not surprisingly given the Carl Rosa Opera's difficulties, the performance did not achieve a very high standard either. While Eric Walter White, in his report, praised the sets, costumes, and staging, as well as the singers, he noted that "at times the playing of the (enlarged) orchestra suffered from faulty intonation; certain tempi were too quick (the friar's buffo part suffered badly in consequence); and the singer's words were often inaudible, not necessarily through any fault of their own, but because the band was too loud or the scoring too thick."

Given the high profile of its commission, *John Socman* attracted notice and important critics such as Frank Howes of the *Times*, Martin Cooper of the *Telegraph*, and Desmond Shawe-Taylor attended the premiere. But due to the piece's hackneyed subject matter and unchallenging musical setting, no one took it very seriously, criticized it deeply, or made any great claims on its behalf, although Anthony Payne (1951: 318) did express disappointment that the work was so "deeply conventional": "We would hardly have suspected anything if we had been told that this was a revival of one of those forgotten romantic operas by Goring Thomas or Mackenzie which the Carl Rosa Company used to commission towards the end of the last century." Like White, Frank Howes noted the poor performance by the orchestra and conductor, but found the work pleasantly entertaining: "Lloyd has abundant invention and his opera is continually melodious, though his idiom is eclectic. . . . [T]he medievalism which so easily becomes a bore is not obtruded and does in fact set the theme of unchanging England . . . which has been the composer's chief inspiration" (Howes 1951: 56).

A more searching analysis of the opera's virtues and failings was that of Eric Walter White, who wrote a substantial assessment of the work and the production for the Arts Council. White praised the sets, costumes, production, and performance, but expressed reservations about the score and libretto:

> George Lloyd shows the same promise as a dramatic composer that he did in *Iernin* (1934), but that promise still remains unfulfilled. Whereas the influence of Wagner was particularly dominant in *Iernin*, there is now a stronger Italian feeling (Verdi) enlivened by flashes of twentieth century rococo (Richard Strauss in *Der Rosenkavalier*). So long as the score is clear, it is often extremely successful—e.g. the first glee maiden's song, some of the duets, the opening chorus in the inn (Act 1, Scene 2), the tumbler's number (Act 2, Scene 2), the music that accompanies the duel, occasional patches of recitative quite lightly accompanied. But as a whole the work is too much cluttered with junk; and unskillful orchestration sometimes reveals other crudities. Act 2, Scene 2 is very disappointing. Its effectiveness is blurred by messy episodes; and when the soldiers return from Agincourt, Lloyd fails to rise to the occasion. His 'Agincourt' chorus is extremely banal.
>
> Many of these difficulties might be overcome if George Lloyd had continued opportunities for working as a composer. (There has been to great a gap between *The Serf* (1938) and *John Socman* (1951) because of the war). I feel sure, however, he needs a better libretto if he is to make a success of his next music drama.
>
> (EL6/71, 16 May 1951)

Ever the crusader for English Opera, White was at pains to lay some of the blame for the weaknesses of the work and Lloyd's failure to develop fully as an operatic composer on history and circumstance (and, implicitly, the limited operatic opportunities for British composers).

Stephen Banfield (1997) agrees that the music is not as fresh as that of Lloyd's two earlier operas, and suggests that the rapid work on the opera necessary to have it ready for the Festival season told on Lloyd's health. Indeed, Lloyd, still in a weakened state from his wartime ordeal, pushed himself to complete *John Socman* in time, and his contention that the premiere had been botched triggered the first of several nervous break-downs. The liner notes of the 1994 recording of excerpts claims that he did not set foot in an opera house for the next 18 years, although he composed into the 1990s.

On balance, then, the Festival commission for the Carl Rosa Opera Company resembles some of the concert music commissions reviewed in Chapter 2. The process unfolded smoothly enough, with the work completed on time and according to the commission's specifications, and the performances, if not of the highest standard, met the Festival's requirements. The episode was therefore, so to speak, an administrative success. Furthermore, if the work was artistically inconsequential as a contribution to a national operatic repertory, it had value as an occasional work. Indeed, with its similarities to a jolly historical pageant ("O cry Agincourt! Harry for England! Hurrah!"), it matched the mood of the Festival in the provincial centers where it played quite well. (The same cannot be said of all the operas premiered during the Festival.)

Ralph Vaughan Williams, *The Pilgrim's Progress*

In comparison with Lloyd's, the remaining two Festival opera commissions ran into difficulties almost immediately. Ralph Vaughan Williams, as the Arts Council staff well knew, had recently completed an opera on John Bunyan's Puritan allegory *The Pilgrim's Progress*. In November, 1948, while the Festival Council was still considering the commissioning plans, Vaughan Williams approached Eric Walter White about arranging a private run-through of *The Pilgrim's Progress* at the Arts Council building. Hoping to receive an offer to stage or broadcast the work, Vaughan Williams made it clear that he especially wanted representatives from the Covent Garden and Sadler's Wells present, as well as Steuart Wilson, the BBC's Director of Music.

The run-through took place at the Arts Council Offices on December 2, 1948, in the presence of, among others, David Webster and Karl Rankl of the Royal Opera House, Norman Tucker of Sadler's Wells, Steuart Wilson from the BBC, and several of the Arts Council staff (ACGB EL2/20, November 11–30, 1948). According to a later Arts Council memorandum the representatives from Sadler's Wells and Covent Garden were "favourably impressed" but did not express interest in performing the work (ACGB EL6/55, January 25, 1949). In particular, the management of the Sadler's Wells Company did not find the work, which required a spectacular production, suitable for their theater.

This same period (the end of 1948) saw the planning of the Festival opera commissions.[3] A January 1949 memo from Eric Walter White suggests that, for the Sadler's Wells Opera, Vaughan Williams should write an entirely new opera based on Thomas Hardy, but recognized that before the composer agreed to such a commission, he would want a guarantee of a performance of *The Pilgrim's Progress*. (Sadly, the Hardy novel suggested to Vaughan Williams on this occasion is not specified in the correspondence.) So the Arts Council suggested a cathedral performance, first internally suggesting Canterbury, but then to Vaughan Williams either Chichester or Liverpool. Vaughan Williams was unenthusiastic about a cathedral performance of *The Pilgrim's Progress* (a feeling that he would reiterate many times). He explained that if the premiere were held in a cathedral the work would be limited to cathedral performance thereafter, while he had imagined the work for the operatic stage. Nevertheless in a letter to Eric Walter White of February 9, 1949 he agreed to accept such a performance if there was no other option. He preferred Chichester, as being closer to London and to his home in Dorking, Surrey.

In late March 1949 John Denison and White went down to Dorking to talk about arranging a production of *The Pilgrim's Progress*. There, they broached another performance venue: Instead of a theatrical performance, they asked, would Vaughan Williams consider allowing the BBC to *televise* the premiere of the opera from the studio they were planning to put up on the South Bank Festival site. As John Denison wrote in a later memorandum, "It occurred to me that perhaps Vaughan Williams' "Pilgrim's Progress", which seems to be homeless at the moment, might fit in here" (AACGB EL6/76, April 13, 1949). Nothing came of this idea, but it would have constituted one of the BBC's first experiments in broadcast opera. At the same meeting, Denison and White offered the Hardy opera commission for Sadler's Wells, but Vaughan Williams declined, unwilling to undertake another operatic project without first seeing the current one through to production. This would appear to have left Sadler's Wells without an opera commission, but, as we shall see, only two months later Benjamin Britten expressed his preference for Sadler's Wells for the production *Billy Budd*.

With the possibility of a new work dismissed, the Arts Council became deeply involved in arranging the performance of *The Pilgrim's Progress* as part of the Festival, even if it was not a Festival commission. The path leading to the Covent Garden premiere on April 26, 1951, a gala prelude to the Festival, proved to be a circuitous one. By the time of the March 1949 meeting, having received no offers from either major London opera house or the BBC, Vaughan Williams had on his own contacted Patrick Hadley, the Professor of Music at Cambridge and a director of the Cambridge Arts Theatre, and proposed that the University stage *The Pilgrim's Progress* (EL6/55, March 23, 1949). The Arts Theatre board took the possibility seriously, and by May, the Cambridge Festival committee was considering making the opera the centerpiece of the Festival events in the city, alongside the kinds of summertime entertainment that Cambridge had offered in the past, such as serenade concerts in a college courtyard, madrigals on the river, and student productions of plays.

Upon learning of this, White wrote to Hadley, inquiring about what sort of production they might be considering. The Arts Theatre board arranged an audition of the opera in early June 1949 with Vaughan Williams and William Fell, the local Arts Council representative, present. They decided, given Vaughan Williams's ties with Cambridge, and Bunyan's own regional ties, to present the opera as part in the summer of 1951. Since at this point in the planning of the Festival of Britain 1951, Cambridge was not an official Festival site, the performance could not be designated an official Festival of Britain event. Although plans were made to use student singers (the orchestra would be professional), the production of a full-length opera, with numerous sets and a large cast, promised to be expensive. Vaughan Williams insisted that the original orchestration not be reduced for the production. This would require both hiring a great number of musicians and enlarging the orchestra pit in the theater. The management of the Cambridge Arts Theatre hoped to be able to make some money towards the production available from other, less expensive festival events, or even from a BBC broadcast, but they realized that they would need a financial guarantee from the Arts Council. At first they believed that the shortfall would not be too great an amount, and the Arts Council similarly believed that they could supply the necessary guarantee.

Either the Covent Garden management were slow in making decisions, or else they had had a change of heart from the previous year, but on June 23, 1949, with planning progressing in Cambridge, David Webster wrote unexpectedly to Vaughan Williams expressing new interest in the opera and requesting to borrow the score. The reasons for Webster's turnaround are unclear. Tracing the early history of the company is difficult because, as Norman Lebrecht (2000: 9–10) has revealed, the Royal Opera House largely denuded its archive in an effort to cover up financial mismanagement. However, the apparent transfer of Britten's commission from Covent Garden to Sadler's Wells, discussed in the next section, may have left Webster feeling the need for a British premiere as the Festival grew closer. (After this dalliance with Sadler Well's, *Billy Budd* eventually returned to Covent Garden.) It cannot have escaped Webster's notice that Vaughan Williams's work was paradigmatically national in subject matter and musical treatment: The source is a book central to the English literary canon and the landscapes and characters are historically English types.

Vaughan Williams sent the score along, but reminded Webster in a note that, because Covent Garden had shown no interest for six months, other performance plans were underway: "You will remember that I had the pleasure of seeing you at the Arts Council when Mr. Mullinar played through the opera, and as you made no sign, then or since, I rather naturally came to the conclusion that you were not interested, and I began to make other negotiations" (AROHCG, "The Pilgrim's Progress"). Both the Arts Council and Vaughan Williams took the position that the Cambridge Arts Theatre had first performance rights. (In August, 1949, in the midst of all this negotiation, Vaughan Williams tried unsuccessfully to retire from the Music Panel of the Arts Council, citing the ongoing decision-making about the performance of his own work in Cambridge. He was persuaded to stay on for several more months (EL2/20, August 3–17, 1949).)

In September, David Webster again wrote to Vaughan Williams to inquire about staging *The Pilgrim's Progress* at Covent Garden. Despite this interest, as late as November 1949 Vaughan Williams still remained loyal to Cambridge. He asked Webster not to request Cambridge to give up the premiere in favor of Covent Garden, since the opera was promised to Cambridge, and such a request would put Vaughan Williams's honor into doubt. Vaughan Williams was adamant on this issue, writing to the Arts Council: "I told [Webster] that there is honour even among musicians." An Arts Council report mentioning even the possibility of opening *The Pilgrim's Progress* at Covent Garden drew an angry protest on November 9, 1949 from Vaughan Williams.

From the internal correspondence it is clear that the Arts Council was (understandably) more enthusiastic about a Covent Garden production than Vaughan Williams was, but were worried about offending him. They therefore set about playing a double game, encouraging Webster while at the same time assuring Vaughan Williams that Cambridge did indeed retain the rights to first performance. Before the situation became too fraught, a solution presented itself: The Cambridge Arts Theatre, having looked more carefully at their budget, declared in mid-November 1949 that they could not afford to do *The Pilgrim's Progress* unless the Arts Council could finance the entire £4,000 production, which was out of the question. This meant that Covent Garden was again a possible venue so long as

Vaughan Williams did not feel that the Arts Council people had manipulated him. Noting the delicacy of the situation, John Denison wrote in an internal memorandum, "Provided V.W. gets a proper 'NO' from *Cambridge* (and that we stay very much in the background,) I have a pretty good idea that he will be delighted for Covent Garden to do it!" (EL6/55, November 14, 1949). Later, he wrote, "Care will be needed in handling this matter if we are to avoid giving offence to the composer, though I am sure that, once the decision to present 'Pilgrim's Progress' at Covent Garden has been taken, he will be more than happy. His real anxiety is to avoid any feeling that he has broken his word with Cambridge" (EL6/36, November 29, 1949).

This in the end was the solution. On February 17, 1950, the Arts Council officially informed the Arts Theatre that it could not approve their request for *The Pilgrim's Progress*. A few days later, the Arts Theatre Trust regretfully informed Vaughan Williams that they were unable to stage his opera in 1951, and Covent Garden stepped in to take over the premiere. The producers in Cambridge remained interested in the work, however, and staged the opera in 1954; this revival pleased Vaughan Williams much more than the Covent Garden premiere.

On Thursday April 26, 1951, exactly a week before the official opening of the Festival of Britain 1951, the Covent Garden Opera Company presented the first performance of *The Pilgrim's Progress*, followed by six more performances during the Festival. Since the work was not an official Festival commission, and thus did not receive a special Festival grant from the Arts Council, in the view of many observers (Vaughan Williams himself among them), the company skimped on the production. But even in an underfunded and amateurish production, a work by the 78-year-old Vaughan Williams, then regarded as the dean of English composers, constituted a major national musical event. The national and international spotlight provided by the Festival context lent it even greater importance. And with the delay in the production of Britten's *Billy Budd*, *The Pilgrim's Progress* was not only the first operatic premiere of the Festival season but the only English work presented in Covent Garden's Festival season.

Furthermore, because of the opera's subject, the premiere was religious event as well. Christian periodicals announced and reviewed it and a distinguished audience containing numerous prominent clergymen from both the Established and Nonconformist Churches, including the Archbishops of both Canterbury and York, attended the premiere. Both the first performance and the second one, on Sunday, April 30th, were broadcast live over the BBC. In the theater, the work was greeted with sustained attention and rapturous applause, Vaughan Williams receiving a lengthy ovation. In a "post-mortem" letter to Vaughan Williams the next day, Edward J. Dent commented on the rapt attention that both the audience and the performers had shown (Kennedy 1980: 196).

As this reception reveals, *The Pilgrim's Progress* was in one sense an ideal operatic contribution to the Festival of Britain. This was emphatically "English opera," its national *bona fides* unassailable, and although press reaction was mixed, it captured the attention of the operatic audience and granted Covent Garden the Festival prominence that Webster surely desired. From another perspective, however, the work fits awkwardly into its historical context. Vaughan Williams had not conceived of the opera for the Festival; he began work on it in 1925, and its origins lie twenty years before that. The work suffers from an excess of static choral tableaux, elaborate rituals, and impersonal religious texts that lay out a conflict-free path to universal salvation. In contrast to the forward-looking, industrial, classless Britain celebrated by the Festival, and particularly in London, the opera is permeated by nostalgia for a rosy prelapsarian England irretrievably at odds with postwar social and economic reality. (Lew 2002 gives a full analysis and interpretation of the genealogy and production of the opera, and the critical reaction to it.)

Benjamin Britten, *Billy Budd*

However fundamentally unsuited *The Pilgrim's Progress* was to be the paradigmatic Festival opera—a standard which no one at the time would have applied to any work—the Arts Council had reason to congratulate itself on the dexterity with which they managed its circuitous progress. Balancing the wishes and sensitivities of a number of individuals, they brought about a modestly successful operatic premiere, even after the planned commission vanished. Arranging the Covent Garden commission with Britten would prove even more troublesome.[4] From the moment when Britten's name was first mentioned, the Arts Council found itself faced with a seemingly unending series of obstacles and engaged in complicated and often frustrating bargaining, not only with Britten himself, but with members of his entourage and with several major opera producers. One factor complicating the negotiations with Britten was the fact that, uniquely among contemporary composers, he controlled his own opera company, the English Opera Group. Britten had founded this company in 1947 along with former members of the Sadler's Wells Opera ejected by the crisis attending the 1945 premiere of *Peter Grimes*. Eric Crozier, who was one of Britten's closest collaborators at the time—he had directed the first production of *Peter Grimes*, helped found the English Opera Group, and written the libretto for *Albert Herring*—was also closely involved in the activities of the Arts Council Opera and Ballet Panel. When Crozier saw the subcommittee report recommending a "grand opera" commission for Britten and Covent Garden, he wrote immediately to Eric Walter White, setting out some of the personal and administrative difficulties such a commission might entail:

> The unhappy experience of *Peter Grimes* at Covent Garden [1947], together with other experiences of staging opera in large opera-houses abroad, have convinced Ben and myself that a large-scale contemporary opera can only be properly rehearsed and performed by an extension of the method of work we have evolved in The English Opera Group. Ben is determined that he will *not* write a large opera for Covent Garden: he will only write one on the understanding that it will be staged by the English Opera Group in association with the chorus and orchestra of Covent Garden, and under the direct artistic

control of the E.O.G. The new opera will be planned to make this way of working possible. In plain terms, the nucleus of the production—principal action and singing—will be made so that we can rehearse it thoroughly and seriously before adding the chorus to it—and the chorus part will be restricted to broad, simple scenes suitable for a chorus like that of Covent Garden.

You will realise that what Ben is aiming at is the best possible standard of rehearsal and performance, and to avoid the complexities of a work like *Grimes*, which make it difficult to attain a good performance in any but the best-organised opera-houses. I think you will agree that this is reasonable, for opera-production is such a complex affair that any composer must demand the conditions of work that his opera needs.

Secondly—I believe it may be possible to obtain a private commission for Ben's next opera that would be considerably greater than any commission the Festival of Britain could offer. If this should materialise, would it cause any embarrassment to the Arts Council or the 1951 Festival should Ben accept? This idea may come to nothing—but I think you should be warned of the possibility.

(EL6/71, July 5, 1948)

Although in the end neither the kind of opera and rehearsal process that Crozier outlined in this letter in Britten's name, nor a private commission materialized, the letter gives a good idea of how independent-minded and suspicious of existing operatic authority the English Opera Group and Britten were, and gives a hint of the kind of difficulties they would present both to the Arts Council and to companies in the following months.

When the Arts Council first approached Britten, in the autumn of 1948, he claimed to be "uncertain whether he could find a suitable subject and librettist" according to Eric Walter White (EL6/71, May 23, 1949). This was not strictly true, for Britten and E. M. Forster had spent a week in August actively searching for a topic for a libretto. The subject of the work and the official commission offer arrived in tandem: The first mention of Herman Melville's *Billy Budd* occurred in a letter from Britten to Forster on 6 November 1948, and White wrote to Britten to offer the commission for Covent Garden on November 24 (Cooke and Reed 1993: 62).

By the time the commissions had been approved by all the granting bodies, however, in December 1948, Britten had taken ill, and his convalescence in Venice over the winter both made him difficult to reach and delayed his composition schedule in the spring—he was working on the *Spring Symphony* and then had to compose *The Little Sweep* for the 1949 Aldeburgh Festival—leaving the commission open to doubt. To secure the commission, The Arts Council, and Eric Walter White in particular, assiduously courted Britten for the next two years, up to the very threshold of the Festival itself. A series of status reports and internal memoranda over this prolonged period of bargaining reveal a Britten torn by ambivalence about the commission and trying to retain as much control as possible over its terms. At the same time, however, work on the opera proceeded; Britten did not hold up his work on account of uncertainty about the status of the premiere. In January 1949 Britten and Forster settled definitely on Melville's novel (Crozier 1986: 12), and Forster and Eric Crozier worked together to produce the first complete draft of the libretto in the first two weeks of March.

Also in March 1949 White wrote to Britten to explain the financial terms of the proposed commission, and asking politely for a response. He wrote again in May to request a meeting to discuss the still-unresolved matter, and further explained the details—that the subject and librettist were up to Britten, but that the scoring and *mise-en-scène* had to suit Covent Garden, which would have the rights to the world premiere during the Festival, or in the season starting in the fall of 1951. When the two met on May 20, Britten announced that he had chosen *Billy Budd* as his subject, that Crozier and E. M. Forster were writing the libretto, and that the opera would indeed be ready by the Festival. The Melville novel, with its setting on a British man-o'-war during the Napoleonic wars, conveniently provided a subject suitable both to the spirit of the Festival commission and to Britten's pacifist preoccupations. The nature of the opera, however, raised potential problems in Britten's mind for Covent Garden. There were to be no female voices, and Britten imagined that the work was going to be "definitely intimate in scale". It therefore was probably unsuited to the flashy productions then typical of Covent Garden, and Britten suggested that it be staged by Sadler's Wells at their home theater. Either Britten himself or the Arts Council staff (Carpenter 1992: 286) suggested that Sadler's Wells present the opera as part of the Edinburgh Festival.

Britten's preference in 1949 for Sadler's Wells over Covent Garden as the company to produce his second full-scale opera may seem odd after the vicious treatment afforded him, Pears, and Crozier by much of the company in 1945 during the preparation of *Peter Grimes* (see Crozier 1965: 414–415; Carpenter 1992: 217–220). Given the directorial excesses and artistic weaknesses of Covent Garden, however, he may have believed that he could exert more control over the production and more successfully use his own English Opera Group as its nucleus at Sadler's Wells. Like the Cambridge Arts Theatre, which was at that point considering staging *The Pilgrim's Progress* for the Festival, the Sadler's Wells Theatre, envisioned for the *Billy Budd* premiere, was not adequately set up to accommodate a full orchestra in the pit, and Britten made it clear that the pit would have to be enlarged by 1951 in order for Sadler's Wells to mount the production. At the end of his official report on the May 20th meeting, White added a somewhat disconsolate handwritten postscript, "It is clear, I think, from what I have said above, that he finds it difficult to accept our commission in its present form" (EL6/71, May 23, 1949).

At the end of May 1949, the Arts Council Executive Committee proposed offering Britten an open commission, with the premiere reserved for the Festival but the company to be decided on at a later date. This was chancy; without prearrangement, Britten might write an opera unsuitable for any company, or all the available companies might turn the opera down. Yet the proposal found support within the Arts Council; perhaps it was noted that without a definite Vaughan Williams production, and with the outcome of the opera competition (reviewed in the next chapter) necessarily uncertain, the Arts Council needed a Britten opera lest the entire new operatic output of the Festival consist solely of George Lloyd's work for the Carl Rosa Company. Such a circumstance would be unsatisfactory with so much energy going into British art, both old and new, for the Festival, so the Council approved the idea of an open commission.

White quickly wrote to Britten to inform him of the new terms on offer, and to assure him that the orchestra pit at Sadler's Wells was being expanded that very summer, yet Britten still did not respond. That summer, he departed for a concert tour of Scandinavia, again cutting off communication. In August 1949, after his return, he invited Crozier and Forster to his home in Aldeburgh to revise the libretto. Shortly thereafter, with a final draft of the libretto ready for composition, it was discovered that the rights to Melville's novel might not in fact be available. This would have meant that, should Britten set the libretto to music, no performance at all would be possible for many years until the work entered the public domain. Hopes for the commission foundered until Britten's publishers, Boosey and Hawkes, managed to procure the rights. (One potential problem with the rights may have been that the Italian composer Giorgio Ghedini had recently composed a one-act opera on the same story.)

In an October 1949 letter to White, Britten expressed the concern that, with all these delays and uncertainties, he would not be able to finish the score in time for a Festival performance. He played this concern to his own advantage, however, remarking that if he did accept the commission, he would feel bound to complete the work in time and have the first performance in Britain, but that in the absence of a commission, he felt no such duty. At the same time he reiterated the condition that he supervise the casting and size of the orchestra in the case of a performance at Sadler's Wells. Unsurprisingly, the day after receiving this letter, White despairingly suggested to Ernest Pooley, the chair of the Arts Council, that the entire commission be dropped.

Commission for the Festival or no, Britten had obviously decided by this time to compose *Billy Budd*. The libretto was in its final stages of revision, which meant that Britten had already done substantial precompositional work on the opera. Enough hope still remained in the Arts Council for the commissioning process to continue, even though, in the continuing absence of a settlement, it was feared that Britten would assign the rights to another country. In the wake of Britten and Pear's tour of the United States from October to December 1949, a December 31st Arts Council memorandum suggests that the Metropolitan Opera in New York was interested. This may have been merely a paranoid imagining on the part of the memorandum's drafter, for there is no other evidence of such an offer, and, in fact, the February 1948 production of *Peter Grimes* at the Met had been a financial disaster for the company (ACGB 51/75).

Pooley, as the highest authority in the Arts Council, therefore decided in early January 1950 to offer Britten everything he now said he wanted: a commission for Sadler's Wells guaranteeing him as much control over the production as he needed. When this decision was communicated a few days later to Britten, however, he complained that the terms described in the letter were still ambiguous, and demanded another six to eight weeks to make up his mind. According to White, he was now envisaging a premiere by his own hand-picked principals and the Sadler's Wells chorus, with the Royal Philharmonic in the pit, at the 1951 Edinburgh Festival, but he continued to express sometimes contradictory doubts and fears: whether Sadler's Wells could afford the production, whether the Edinburgh authorities would agree to it, and even whether the Edinburgh "international snob audience" was the right public before which to launch a new opera.

White visited Britten in Aldeburgh on February 1 and 2, 1950 and found that Britten's ideas on the production were advancing, and that he was just beginning composition of the score. White's confidential "(Lack of) Progress Report" arising from the meeting describes Britten as demanding for the work an orchestra of 70 or more, three guest artists in the lead roles, a 60-voice male chorus, Carl Ebert as producer (stage director) and John Piper as designer. White urged Britten to get in touch with the directors of Sadler's Wells and the Edinburgh Festival, whom no one had yet completely apprised of the situation despite the months of discussion with the composer.

Events finally seemed to be moving forward, but before Britten could contact the companies, on February 9, 1950, he attended a performance of Giuseppe Verdi's *Falstaff* at Sadler's Wells, and was "distressed" and "dismayed" by the lack of artistry that he saw. By mid-month, according to White, "whereas formerly Britten was hostile to the idea of Covent Garden mounting *Billy Budd*, he is now dismayed at the idea of either Covent Garden or Sadler's Wells mounting it" (EL6/71, February 15, 1950). The commission seemed as remote as ever. White, however, hoping that Britten's fears would diminish while work on the score stimulated his desire for a production, advised the Arts Council not press for acceptance, but to delay yet again, leaving the commission offer open.

Britten soon wrote to White, "I do want to have an opera ready for the 1951 Festival, and I hope everyone realises that. But the reason I'm 'sitting on the fence' (!) comes from a reluctance to promise a work, terribly difficult to write, at a date, uncomfortably close, in theatres, which alas I have no great confidence in!" (EL6/71, February 18, 1950). He still hoped at this point that somehow an arrangement with the Edinburgh Festival might be the best solution, but now estimated that the score would not be ready until autumn of 1951. White responded that if the score was not available until autumn, it would be hard to fit into the Festival, which was scheduled to end September 30th. Furthermore, at this point, White believed (wrongly, as it turned out) that the Edinburgh Festival was planning to stage the premiere of Stravinsky's *Rake's Progress*, which would make an additional operatic premiere unlikely. To entice Britten to accept the commission, he again pointed out that there would be extra money available from the Arts Council for the production of a commissioned opera, whereas without a commission, the production would have to be mounted within the opera company's regular budget, as in the case of *The Pilgrim's Progress*.

The impasse held for another six months. Britten, now finally composing *Billy Budd*, remained unable to make a decision about the commission, while the Arts

Council hopefully bided its time. As White had hoped, work on the opera gradually overcame some of Britten's concerns. He finally made overtures to Sadler's Wells and Edinburgh but nothing was decided. In August 1950, in response to a query from White, Britten at last seemed ready to accept the commission. He wrote that the most likely scenario was still a premiere by the Sadler's Wells company during their visit to the Edinburgh Festival followed by performances in London. Sadler's Wells still had to consider and approve the terms, and then there arose further questions on Britten's part about the librettists' portion of the payment. Britten finally accepted the commission in October, over two years after it was first offered. Britten received the whole £500 commission, but passed on one sixth of it to each librettist.

Almost immediately new problems arose. The press release announcing the commission and performance plans was held up while Sadler's Wells haggled with the Edinburgh Festival over the budget for the premiere. At the same time the full scale of Britten's opera—hardly "intimate" as he had first imagined it—came to light: The score demanded a huge male chorus and an orchestra with triple woodwinds, four trumpets, solo saxophone, and six percussionists. Sadler's Wells' negotiations with Edinburgh proved unsuccessful, and in November 1950, five months before the start of the Festival, the Sadler's Wells Opera Company stated that they were unable to undertake the production. As Norman Tucker, the company's Artistic Director, described: "As the composition of the work proceeded it became clear that this all-male opera called for more than the normal resources of Sadler's Wells. A heavy extra financial burden was thus involved and unfortunately neither Edinburgh nor Sadler's Wells with the assistance of the Arts Council was able to bridge the gap" (EL6/71, January 24, 1951). According to Philip Reed, the officials at the Edinburgh Festival now approached John Christie and the Glyndebourne Opera in the hopes of convincing them to take on the project, but to no avail (Cooke and Reed 1993: 61).

The Arts Council, hoping to salvage the commission for the opera, almost half complete in short score, immediately approached Covent Garden, for whom, after all, the commission had first been proposed over two years before. David Webster, who had particularly wanted a Britten premiere in the first place, expressed willingness to produce the opera. With the 1950–1951 season already underway, the soonest he could schedule the work was October 1951, the start of the next season, after the official end of the Festival (EL4/95, December 6, 1950).

Britten, of course, had to be reconciled to the new arrangements. According to Humphrey Carpenter, Britten's "expectations of Covent Garden were not high —to Forster he mentioned worries about 'the size of the house, state of company, lack of co-operation'" (Carpenter 1992: 298), yet he agreed to have Covent Garden take over the premiere. Britten's acceptance of the transfer to Covent Garden, after all the trouble he had given the Arts Council over the choice of company, indicates his practicality; if Covent Garden was the only available option, he would take it, especially when, as White had hoped, work on the opera was fostering his eagerness to see it produced. Also, within the Covent Garden Opera Company, Britten found a sympathetic ear: When David Webster eventually traveled down to Aldeburgh in February 1951 to hear some of the music, parts of the score left him in tears (Cooke and Reed 1993: 63). Britten's acceptance of the transfer may also suggest that the changes in the company over the intervening two years had raised Britten's opinion of its abilities somewhat. Steuart Wilson had come on as Assistant Manager, and the company was beginning to rise above some of the aesthetic defects and growing pains of its earliest years. So the opera ended up back at the company for which it had originally been proposed.

Even after Covent Garden accepted the opera for the 1951–1952 season in November 1950, the two opera companies and the Arts Council bickered for two months over the exact wording of the press release to announce this shift in plans. Sadler's Wells wanted to avoid statements in the press that the opera was "beyond the resources" of the company, with the suggestion that the company was limited in its artistic abilities, preferring "beyond the financial resources". Eric Walter White, who had worked so hard to see the opera to production, was clearly angered by the turnaround at Sadler's Wells, and objected to this formulation: "In view of the discussion that took place when representatives of the Royal Opera House and Sadler's Wells met members of the [Arts Council] Executive Committee, I am sure you will understand that I am unable to accept a statement that implies that the sole reason for the decision by Sadler's Wells not to produce the opera is a financial one" (EL6/71, January 23, 1951). In the end, Covent Garden and Sadler's Wells issued separate press releases, a circumstance that was noted by the press and that generated a small stir of negative publicity vaguely reminiscent of the brouhaha that had preceded the premiere of *Peter Grimes* in 1945. Britten wrote to White in a tone of combined frustration and resignation:

> After a week of telephone conversations, carbon copies and Press announcements all to do with "Billy Budd", and the general operatic situation in England, there seems to have fallen a blissful silence. I hope this means that the situation is now settled and that one can get on writing the work. I was grieved, when over the telephone, the Daily Express was inclined to credit me with having anti-Festival of Britain feelings and that many correspondents have credited me with abandoning the idea of "Budd" altogether. Also, the general tone of the Press announcements have [*sic*] been that the work has gained in elaborateness and extravagant demands since I started writing it. This is of course, in spite of what Norman Tucker may say, entirely untrue. Nor can the letter that Tucker wrote to the Edinburgh Festival, which squeaks about lack of financial resources, be taken too seriously. The situation seems mad. What the truth is I have no idea, but as I said before, I hope the matter is now closed and I can get on with writing the work itself.
> (EL6/71, February 1, 1951)

Britten was guilty of some self-delusion in his claim that the opera had not "gained in elaborateness" since he started working on it. *Billy Budd* is hardly the opera, "definitely intimate in scale", that Britten had imagined for Sadler's Wells in 1949. Still, whatever confusion it may have caused, the transfer and postponement of the premiere to Covent Garden in the autumn was fortunate for Britten, for composition of the opera took longer than he originally foresaw. The short score was not complete until August 1951. Finding singers and a conductor then presented new challenges, and the premiere was pushed back from October to November 22, 1951 (Britten's 38th birthday), and then again, at the request of Josef Krips, who was to conduct, to December 1st. This was two months past the close of the Festival of Britain and into the new Conservative government, and was a period shadowed by the final illness of George VI. Britten finished the orchestration on November 2nd, barely in time to get the parts copied and the orchestra rehearsed. Then, at the last minute, claiming difficulty in reading the photostat copies of the manuscript score, Krips pulled out, leaving Britten to conduct the first performances himself. (Peter Gellhorn, the house assistant conductor, took the later performances.)

In comparison to the slapdash production Covent Garden had thrown together for *The Pilgrim's Progress*, its first, more timely contribution to the Festival year, *Billy Budd* received a painstaking production. This difference was surely due to the tight control Britten demanded over the production, the greater seriousness with which David Webster attached to the work, and the additional money that the Arts Council supplied for a commissioned work. Directed by Basil Coleman and designed by John Piper, the opening was attended by an audience including major musical figures such as Krips, Malcolm Sargent, Joan Cross, and Margot Fonteyn, and was broadcast live on the BBC Third Programme.

After the premiere, Britten wrote William Emrys Williams, who had taken over from Mary Glasgow as Secretary-General of the Arts Council, "We all felt disappointed that the original plan of doing it in the Festival period was not possible—but I hope that you and your Council feel that the current production at Covent Garden is as fine as I do, and worthy of the Festival" (EL6/71, December 5, 1951). But as Britten probably recognized, though he never would have admitted it, the opera probably benefited from its temporal removal from the Festival.

Britten's institutional supporters mounted a publicity drive for the work that overlapped with the Festival's end and associated it retrospectively with the Festival, but the opera itself was not tested against the Festival backdrop. Although Vaughan Williams's opera never commanded the respect afforded to *Billy Budd*, critics went overboard in their estimations of the *Englishness* of *The Pilgrim's Progress*, a reaction with no parallel in the reception of *Billy Budd*. This difference cannot be explained merely by the timing of Britten's work after the close of the Festival. More than either Vaughan Williams's or George Lloyd's operas, Britten's casts a critical eye on the myths of national grandeur, striking a tone which could easily have raised hackles during the Festival. True, congruence with the Festival's celebratory tone was hardly the chief yardstick for judging new operas even in 1951, and the work's historical English setting were superficially suited to the Festival context. Still, one wonders what Festival audiences and critics would have made of its disturbing moral ambiguities, problematizing of honor and military heroism, and thinly veiled homosexual subtext.

For their parts, Eric Walter White and his Arts Council colleagues must have felt a surge of pride on the occasion of the *Billy Budd* premiere. This, after all, was what the Arts Council had hoped to accomplish with its Festival music programs. The road leading there had been agonizing, but it had produced a fine production of a work of considerable sophistication.

Brian Easdale, *The Sleeping Children*

The three operas ushered into production by the Arts Council were not the only premieres of the Festival Season. Also receiving first performances were Brian Easdale's commission for the English Opera Group, *The Sleeping Children*, first performed in mid-July at the Cheltenham Festival of Contemporary British Music and later broadcast by the BBC, and *The Mayor of Casterbridge*, by Peter Tranchell, performed at Cambridge in late July. In 1949 the Council's opera competition scheme discussed in Chapter 4 had judged both of these works unworthy of commissions. While welcome contributions to the cause of national opera, then, these performances at a time when the works that had won the competition were not attracting performer interest generated some embarrassment for the Arts Council.

Easdale's commission arose from the awkward fact that the English Opera Group's first three productions after their founding in 1947 had been written by Benjamin Britten, and the company's managers saw the artistic (or at least public-relations) benefits of expanding the repertory to include works by other composers. Britten had come to know Easdale when they were both working at the GPO Film Unit in the thirties. Although there is no record of why the EOG approached Easdale, the choice was undoubtedly Britten's. If Easdale had settled on a project before the EOG approached him, the opera's milieu and subject—an English preparatory school and the influence of the adults' actions on the children there— may have also attracted Britten, for whom such topics exerted a life-long fascination. The EOG initially wanted a work for the 1950 Aldeburgh Festival, but when it became clear that Easdale's score would not be available in time, Britten prepared his edition of Purcell's *Dido and Aeneas* instead, and *The Sleeping Children* became a Festival of Britain premiere by default. In 1951, although the EOG mounted a "Festival of Britten" at the Lyric Theatre, Hammersmith, featuring the composer's three original scores (*The Rape of Lucretia*, *Albert Herring*, and *Let's Make an Opera*), they could also counter the impression of being a one-composer company with *Dido*, works by Monteverdi and Holst, and Easdale's score, at their other performances in Cheltenham, Aldeburgh, and on tour. The EOG further diversified its repertory the next year with an arrangement of Thomas Arne's ballad opera *Love in a Village* by Britten's protégé Arthur Oldham.[5]

Easdale (1909–1995) is chiefly remembered today for his film music, particularly the extensive score for the ballet film *The Red Shoes* (1948), which brought him renown as an approachable modernist composer. *The Sleeping Children*, with a libretto by the famous stage director Tyrone Guthrie, was Easdale's third opera, following a youthful effort, *Rapunzel* (1927), and a "ritual opera" entitled *The Corn King*, composed in 1935 but only produced in 1950 after the success of *The Red Shoes*.

The synopsis of *The Sleeping Children* in the Cheltenham program reads:

> The scene of the Sleeping Children is a small school in the country and represents the Headmaster's Study, Matron's Room, and the Dormitory. In the opening Nocturne the five principal characters and the Children are introduced. The Children represent the sleeping, dreaming part of creation, unconscious, but none the less vital. The School is a world through which one passes, but where one does not remain, and where lessons are supposed to be learnt.
>
> Act I: It is night and the Children are asleep. The Headmaster has not long returned from the war, and his new plan for the running of the School is uppermost in his mind. Matron is sewing the new school flag, which to her stands for the pride and the regeneration of the School. The Janitor is locking up. The Assistant Master and the Wife of the Headmaster are going to the Study to tell the Head that, while he was away, they became lovers. Matron rouses the souls of the Children to sing, so that they can hear, and feel. The Assistant Master and the Wife try to tell the Headmaster what has happened. At first he is absorbed in explaining his Chart and does not hear them; then at last he understands that his wife is with child. In the next scene the Assistant Master and the Wife realize how strongly they love each other. The Wife sings to her unborn Child. Matron and the Janitor hear a storm rising, which is also felt by the Headmaster, and the Sleeping Children. At its climax the Headmaster tears his plan in pieces; he is drowned in a passion to kill. The Children implore him not to wound them by his violence.
>
> Act II: After the storm the country was gripped in an iron frost. Now it is night again and the Children are sleeping; the thaw has set in and it is heavy and windless. Matron is thinking of the past weeks of frost, fear, suspicions and gossip in the school. Both she and the Janitor are full of foreboding. The Wife opens her heart to Matron—why must so much complex emotion be her lot, when she herself is so simple and hum-drum? In the study it is dead of night. The Assistant Master visits the Headmaster, who has made a new plan. The Children's voices are heard, feeling the tension and the growing nightmare. The rain has started and is now streaming down in torrents as the Headmaster puts his plan into execution. Matron and the Wife hear cries from the Study. The souls of the Children are awakened by danger, and their chorale accompanies the struggle, in which the Assistant Master finally overcomes the Headmaster. Broken by his own violence, the Headmaster longs for death. Matron persuades him to accept the inevitable—"The storm is over. Winter is passing. Soon it will be spring."
>
> Act III: It is Founders' Day, and a sunny morning, but the Janitor is gloomy. The Wife and Assistant Master are going away together. He will take her to a new life, a new world, but she feels that the wrench from her old life will cause a wound. Their love is strong, however, and even a wound is better

than death. Matron and Headmaster are left alone to face the scandal. She thinks the School cannot survive unless the Headmaster also leaves. He will not listen to her—he knows now that the School is his life. Matron declares that she will stay, and calls the Janitor to ring his Great Bell, in defiance of scandal, fear and shame. The Children hear, and every voice proclaims that love is the seed of life. But although the Great Bell rings out and Matron hoists her flag, the Children reiterate the words of the opening Nocturne: "We Children are asleep, asleep and dreaming. You are not alone." Their voices continue after the others as the unbroken thread of sleeping a universal life.
(BPF RC/79/D)

Unfortunately, the plot and the libretto, and even to an extent the music of *The Sleeping Children* appear chiefly to have confused and distressed its spectators. Certainly, the provincial opera-goers for whom the Carl Rosa Opera mounted conventional entertainments like *John Socman* and the London audience grateful for the nostalgic affirmation of *The Pilgrim's Progress* had little experience with or patience for symbolic psychodrama. Easdale and Guthrie's concoction probably went too far scenically and textually even for some of the experienced public who appreciated the ambiguities and sophistication of *Billy Budd* and the novelty-seekers at the Cheltenham Festival. To begin with, the summary in the program only hints at the bizarreness of the libretto, particularly the confrontation scene in Act 2. The Headmaster's "new school plan" is in fact a giant blank piece of paper fixed to the wall. As he banally plies his assistant with drinks, the Headmaster locks the door to his study, snaps the assistant into pillory, and repeatedly stabs him with giant pen, writing names on the huge chart in blood. All the while, the chorus and other characters intone ominously offstage.

The libretto is mostly in prose. One would expect Tyrone Guthrie to have known about theatrical effectiveness, but he rarely gives characters lines that they might actually say or even think; there is no indirection, no subtlety, no revealing of character through dialogue and soliloquy. Instead, the characters telegraph their emotions baldly, in a kind of theater director's shorthand. In Act 2, the Wife bemoans her fate by describing her feelings where any decent librettist would have given her a Willow Song. The third act consists almost entirely of sententious platitudes referring to no one in particular, at times tipping over into Gertrude-Stein-like nonsense: "Our acts are the fruits of past selves," "Hatred destroys life. Love creates and loves the seed of other lives and others and others" [sic].

As a replacement for characterization, Guthrie indulges in a torrent of blatant symbolism: the flag needing mending, the bell that will not ring, the Sleeping Children themselves. Too often the symbolism becomes puerile in the characters' mouths, as when the Assistant asks for the key and the Headmaster replies "You have already unlocked my door . . . my precious treasure, you have picked the lock, you thrust your key into my . . . your key, your pen . . . you have dipped your pen and scrawled your name." Furthermore, the constant recourse to the pathetic fallacy, with the weather unerringly mirroring the characters' inner states, becomes unintentionally comic. Such reliance on symbolism participates in a movement fashionable with the postwar intelligentsia, among whom psychoanalytic theories were just beginning to spread. But the resulting dramatic and textual bizarreries appear to have bewildered and dismayed most audiences and critics.

Whether Easdale himself had concerns about the libretto is not clear. Given the ritual action of *The Corn King*, he may have shared Guthrie's enthusiasm for a new sort of symbolic opera. At any rate, he gamely set Guthrie's words in his flexible and approachably modern style. The dramatic model is post-Wagnerian, rather than number opera: Each act flows continuously, organizing itself into coherent passages connected by transitions and transformations. The harmony is usually grounded in a key or pitch-center, and uses an extended triadic vocabulary, not heavily chromatic but with bitonal and added-pitch touches, rapidly-changing key areas, and many augmented triads; the frequent use of unison and unaccompanied lines in the orchestra is a technique probably derived from film scoring. A study of the score shows Easdale's awareness of the dramatic possibilities of tempo, dynamics, and texture. The heightened climaxes (where musical excitement can overpower the risible text) are effective musically, as are some of the extended quiet passages such as the score's opening and closing "nocturnes". The choral passages, restricted to unison and thirds and building only to occasional fuller chords at well-placed moments, are some of the highlights of the score.

Given Guthrie's wordy and expository libretto, the score contains a great deal of recitative and parlando. To organize these long passages musically, Easdale often created accompaniments out of repeating motives, complex and harmonically interesting, but rhythmically static. Of course the vamp accompaniment is a time-tested Italian operatic technique, but where the melodic ideas are not strong, and the component sections don't create a sense of form, the scene can fail to come to life. In *The Sleeping Children*, the passages of lyrical melody vary in quality. In part this is due to the difficulties of setting a prose libretto. The vocal parts too often sound like instrumental lines, rather than vocal melody, because Easdale forces the awkward phrases of the libretto into his tunes' repeating rhythmic and pitch patterns. This severs the connection between melody and emotional meaning, even as Guthrie weighs the words down with symbolic meaning. One feels sorry for Easdale, setting such resolutely unpoetic lines as "I found I had made a disastrous omission. I ignored the existence of human nature, of flesh and blood. A plan must be made of more than paper." The words offer him little melodically; indeed, his rhythmic inspiration falters most when the text becomes most egregiously banal.

The English Opera Group performed the work in Cheltenham, Liverpool, and Aldeburgh. (They did not include it in their London repertory.) Given the profile of the company and the context, the work attracted much press, and got mixed notices. In general, reviewers from more sophisticated journals—Frank Howes at the *Times*, Dynely Hussey at the *Listener*, and Desmond Shawe-Taylor at the *New Stateman and Nation*—panned the work, with more appreciative comments coming from local papers.[6] The *Birmingham Post* review of the broadcast found a middle ground, pointing out the work's "curious mix of genuine inventive and imaginative power with a certain pseudo-psychological pretentiousness, even phoniness" that evoked simultaneously embarrassment and enthusiasm. Most reviewers had little positive to say about the libretto, either in total conception or in literary detail. But the brooding quality—the "dark colors" (*Birmingham Post*) and "constant surge of unrest" (*Gloucestershire Echo*)—of Easdale's score attracted praise, as did the choral episodes. More negative reviewers such as Shawe-Taylor, did however object to the "monotony of pace and the constant obscuring of the words by the orchestra" (a problem corrected in the radio broadcast). Both the lighting and the single expressionist set, reminiscent of *The Cabinet of Dr. Caligari*, with architectural fragments set at odd angles that could be obscured by scrims and lighting changes, attracted some praise for simplicity and versatility.

In contrast to all of this, Paul Hamburger, the reviewer for Lord Harewood's journal *Opera*, gave the work a lengthy and glowingly positive review that is however so strangely argued and so fulsome in its praise that it leaves the reader doubting the reviewer's standards. Hamburger (1951: 505) found the symbolic drama profound, "eternal in its essentials, topical in their application," pronounced Guthrie's text "musical" and Easdale's contribution nothing short of brilliant in almost every respect. While there is no reason to doubt Hamburger's sincerity, one would scarcely have expected to find a poor review of an undertaking by Britten in Lord Harewood's journal; Harewood was one of Britten's closest friends.

Hamburger's opinion clearly represented the minority view. Whatever positive aspects reviewers could find in the music on its own, the piece as a whole seems to have been crippled from the start. Not only was the work profoundly out of step with the expectations and tastes of British opera- and concert-goers, but, more significantly, the English Opera Group itself seems to have been ambivalent about it. After 1952, the English Opera Group never revived the work, and it quickly sank out of sight.

Peter Tranchell, *The Mayor of Casterbridge*

The last high-profile operatic premiere of the Festival year came about in spite of the initial discouragement of the Arts Council.[7] The medieval university towns, Oxford and Cambridge, were not listed as Festival Centers in the Arts Council's first plans, although the Council actively promoted the universities' contributions to the national celebration and made it clear that some financial assistance could be made available. Nevertheless, the Arts Council proposal submitted to the Festival Executive Committee mentioned the desirability of having the universities offer special summer courses or conferences in the arts, music, or drama. Cambridge in particular, an Arts Council memorandum said, "with its strong Theatre and musical tradition and resources, has much to offer, and it is now a question as to how Music and Drama can be strongly represented in 1951 in Cambridge and who is to provide the necessary financial backing" (EL6/36). Ernest Pooley, the chairman of the Arts Council, wrote to the Vice Chancellor of the University of Cambridge as early as July 5, 1948, and met with the Vice Chancellor the following February to further motivate the University's participation. In May 1949, the University, along with the local Arts Council representative, formed a provisional committee to explore the matter.

As recounted above, in early and mid-1949, Vaughan Williams and the Arts Council attempted to arrange the premiere of *The Pilgrim's Progress* as the university's main offering in the Festival. When this plan was abandoned, in November 1949, several anxious months ensued; in January 1950, the Arts Council first began seriously to consider the proposal that Cambridge and Oxford be included as official festival centers, but Cambridge failed to come up with adequate substitute performances to justify such a designation. In February 1950, as the designation was going ahead anyway, John Denison at the Arts Council suggested to the Cambridge committee that they remount a recent local staging of Purcell's *Fairy Queen* or another of that composer's stage works. Later that month, William Fell, the Arts Council's regional director in Cambridge, wrote to inform Denison unenthusiastically of another project that had arisen: Patrick Hadley had suggested a performance of the newly-composed opera *The Mayor of Casterbridge* by his student Peter Tranchell (1922–1993).

> [Hadley] brought up the possibility of an opera based on Hardy's 'The Mayor of Casterbridge', the music to be written by a boy named Tranchell who went down from Cambridge last year.
>
> He did the music for the Footlights Revue, but I understand that the music for the opera is still only in his head; and I did gather that the libretto, or whatever you people wanted towards a libretto when considering opera commissions for 1951, has been before the appropriate committee and turned down.
>
> It all seems so delightfully vague and so typically Cambridge, and I was glad to have your copy-letter about the Purcell idea this morning, because I did touch on this point yesterday at the meeting, and roughly said that a Purcell contribution on the lines of what they had done in former years was really what was wanted.
>
> The typical university answer I got back was that we can do Purcell in 1952, 53, 54, 55, 56 and so on!
>
> I was determined to have another go at wiping out this Tranchell business, and your letter this morning makes the position easier for me; and as you have sent it out really almost as a point of policy, I think they will play.
>
> (EL6/36, February 25, 1950)

Tranchell had submitted the opera project to the Arts Council's competitive opera commissioning scheme reviewed in the next chapter, and the judges had rejected it in September 1949. Therefore, Denison asked Eric Walter White, who was running the opera competition about it in early March. Knowing that decisions in the commissioning scheme were imminent, White replied with a measure of frustration:

> The Mayor of Casterbridge was (as far as I remember) quite intelligently planned as an opera; but both composer and librettist were extremely young and inexperienced. If Cambridge want to put on a new English opera in 1951

as well as (or instead of) a Purcell revival, I should be happier if they would wait to see if one of the commissioned operas under the open scheme would suit them.

(EL6/36, March 3, 1950)

Although, as this correspondence shows, the Arts Council staff was unenthusiastic about this proposal it nonetheless gathered steam. Tranchell and his librettist Peter Bentley had thoroughly revised the libretto that they had submitted to the Arts Council,[8] and a committee of Cambridge University musicians decided to review the music and make a decision; if favorable, they would mount the work with a small orchestra using their own resources. In March, Denison attended a meeting of the Cambridge Arts Theatre Trust to discuss Festival planning, where he explained that while the Council supported the university's impulse to recognize their own young composers, but they should not expect financial assistance for the production.

At the same time, other plans for the Cambridge festival developed, including a staging of the John Dryden/William Davenant/Henry Purcell *Tempest* (rather than *The Fairy Queen*) and "a Pageant written around famous English composers, with particular emphasis on those who had associations with Cambridge in the year 1851, to be given by members of the Marlowe Society and the Cambridge University Musical Society with a professional orchestra and soloists" (EL6/36, May 16, 1950). (Howes 1951: 212, gives an amusing description of this pageant.)

In its final form, the Cambridge Festival of 1951 included all three productions, as well as a large number of orchestral and choral performances. The Cambridge Philharmonic and several London orchestras visiting the city played during the festival period, joining with the University Chorus to perform a considerable amount of English music including Elgar's *Dream of Gerontius*, Vaughan Williams's *Sea Symphony*, and Howells's *Hymnus Paradisi*. One choral concert featured Robert Fayrfax's *O bone Jesu* mass. The Lady Margaret Singers gave the premiere of a *Festival Te Deum* specially commissioned from Robin Orr, and a visiting military band played a concert entirely of British music.

The synopsis of *The Mayor of Casterbridge* printed in the program reads as follows:

Act I: *Weydon Fair on a spring evening, 1805.* Michael Henchard buys rum-laced furmity. He gets drunk and sells his wife and baby daughter to a sailor.

Act II, Scene I. *The Parlour of the King's Arms, Casterbridge, 1825.* Henchard, now a leading corn merchant and Mayor of Casterbridge, meets Farfrae and persuades him to become foreman of his yard. The same evening, Susan, deserted, apparently, by the sailor, arrives in search of her former husband. Henchard, mainly for the sake of the grown-up Elizabeth-Jane, resolves to re-marry her secretly.

Act II, Scene II. *The back of the house and yard of Henchard's establishment.* It is an early morning in spring, next year. Susan has died. Henchard reveals to Elizabeth-Jane that he is her father but later discovers from a letter of Susan's that this is not so: Elizabeth-Jane is the sailor's daughter, the baby child having died after the sale twenty years ago. Henchard angered by this bitter knowledge and by the realization that Farfrae, now more popular than his master, is in love with Elizabeth-Jane, quarrels with Farfrae over a trifling matter and dismisses him from the post of foreman.

Act III, Scene I. *The Court of Petty Sessions, Casterbridge, March, 1827.* The furmity seller of Weydon Fair is brought up for trial before Henchard, the chairman of the magistrates, and, in self-defence, reveals the story of the wife-selling.

Act III, Scene II. *Casterbridge Market Square, August 1827.* The sailor arrives, looking for his wife and daughter. Henchard, now on the decline, meets him and in a last attempt to silence the past and keep Elizabeth-Jane, tries to be rid of the sailor by claiming that Elizabeth-Jane is dead. Elizabeth-Jane appears and Henchard is confounded publicly when the sailor recognizes his daughter.

Act III, Scene III. *The yard of what was Henchard's and now is Farfrae's establishment: a night in early summer, 1828.* Elizabeth-Jane and Farfrae have been married. Henchard, cast out from society, returns to ask for Elizabeth-Jane's forgiveness. This is refused. There is now nothing left. Outside the house where once he was master, Henchard recites his last bitter testament: "Let them not bury me in consecrated ground; Nor let a sexton toll the bell; Let nobody be wished to see my dead body; Let no mourners walk behind me at my funeral; And let no flowers be planted on my grave; And let no man remember me."

(CUL Tranchell 10/1/1/8-10/1/1/9)

Tranchell's correspondence with Peter Bentley in December 1950 shows just how quickly the entire production was put together. Tranchell sketched out a draft libretto by himself earlier in the year and began setting it to music, even as he was awaiting critiques, revisions, and additions from Bentley. This process naturally created the need for extensive musical revisions once Bentley started changing the words and dramatic structure. As if this were not challenging enough, by December, Tranchell was composing, recomposing, and at the same time making performance arrangements, casting singers, and engaging the orchestra. It is not surprising that, under such time pressure, elements of the final product were uneven.

The libretto as set, which we must assume was a joint product of Bentley and Tranchell, is well constructed dramatically, and even poetic where necessary. Tranchell and Bentley succeed most notably in framing Henchard as a tragic hero, concentrating on the process by which all the inhabitants of the town gradual turn against Henchard, who has violated both family decency and business ethics. They use the chorus effectively as a foil to Henchard. The chorus begins in a conventional manner, commenting on the action and singing decorative folksongs in the manner of *John Socman* or any number of nineteenth century operas. Then, at first briefly in Act 3, Scene 1 and with full force in the enormous ensemble of rejection in Act 3, Scene 2, the chorus takes on a more active role, joining the principals in the condemnation of Henchard and bringing the full weight of community rejection against him. The example of *Peter Grimes* lies behind the chorus of hostile townsfolk that ends this scene. Henchard like Grimes commits great errors but remains sympathetic to the end of the opera. Elizabeth-Jane's outright hostility in the face of his genuine contrition in the closing scene makes his end tragic rather than merely pathetic.

As the reviewer for the journal *Opera* noted, however, the great flaw in the scenario is the courtroom scene (Act 3, Scene 1), and in particular, the usher's lengthy exposition. This passage, while it informs the audience what has happened, fails to develop the characters. Indeed, of the principals, only Henchard appears in the scene; forces separate from the family and professional matters that dominate the rest of the opera bring about his initial downfall. The audience never sees Farfrae's, or more importantly, Elizabeth-Jane's initial reaction to learning that Henchard sold Susan at Weydon Fair. (It is therefore strange that Bentley, reviewing the libretto a decade later, singled this scene out for particular praise.)

Tranchell's chromatic idiom in *The Mayor of Casterbridge* is similar to that in his later works. Chromaticism, added pitches, and contrapuntal inner parts blur the triadic and tonal harmonic motion under even the simplest vocal textures. The melodic writing is lyrical but chromatically complex, with the frequent intrusion of tritones, minor thirds in major contexts, and similar techniques. The dramaturgy falls somewhere between the Italianate number-opera favored by Lloyd and the fluent post-Wagnerian continuity of Easdale. As in late Verdi, or, more proximately, Britten, each scene is a continuous whole, but the music flows into and out of clearly formed (if often through-composed) lyrical episodes that avoid strong terminal cadences, so as not to interrupt the continuity.

One example is the brief and touching duet in Act 2 for Henchard and Susan, a passage of a mere twenty measures. Tranchell knew he had a good thing, for he recalled it instrumentally to underscore the pathos of Elizabeth-Jane's final rejection of Henchard in the closing scene. But the moments of character-illuminating musical repose in the score are insufficient, a fact noted by Harold Rosenthal in *Opera*:

> Both librettist and composer have, presumably in the interests of keeping the action moving, rather overdone this short-circuiting of events, so that we get some rather abrupt scenes and curtains. The first meeting of Henchard and Farfrae is one example of this, and the reunion between Henchard and Susan is another, for both musically and dramatically they peter out, just when we are getting ready for a good duet.
>
> (Rosenthal 1951)

The scarcity and short duration of lyrical passages, even the avoidance of aria when a scene seems to be building to one, was a deliberate choice of Tranchell's. At this early stage in his career, he was very opinionated about opera and harbored a deep fear of stopping the narrative flow for moments of lyrical stasis. In a long December 1950 letter to Bentley, in the midst of his most intense work on the opera, he outlined his operatic manifesto in terms reminiscent of the Russian realist operatic reformers of a century earlier:

I want the thing to be dramatic. Therefore the only possible ingredients are: (1) events in dumbshow . . . (2) information as to the progress of the story mostly in recitative obviously, but still dramatic . . . (3) points where the interest or tension is so great that one can afford to waste time on a "tune" for someone to expatiate on the situation or their prospects, more or less stationary for a bit. . . . My concern is more for a dramatic intensity than a concert of arias in loosely connected sequence. I hope that no-one will notice any music except at that point where I've put a tune, (which is where the tune not the drama must have the required effect of moving the audience).

(CUL Tranchell 10/1/1/1/11)

Despite Tranchell's desire that the plot should continue moving forward at all times, the score is rather tuneful. Almost every scene contains one genre number, usually an ersatz folksong sung by a principal or the chorus: the chorus's drinking song, Farfrae's Scottish song, the farm laborers' folksong after the death of Susan, the choral interlude in Act 3, and Newsom's sailor song. These melodic passages provide welcome respite from the unfolding plot and more complex music.

Elsewhere, the tendency of the score is toward dialogue. Even in the large-scale ensembles, the voice parts often remain in counterpoint rather than joining in a single melodic impulse; similarly, when more than one character is singing they almost always have different words. The impressively organized quartet with chorus in Act 3, Scene 2 is a good example of this technique: Over the course of the movement, as Henchard tries to justify himself in various ways, becoming increasingly overwrought, Elizabeth-Jane gradually rejects Henchard in favor of Newsom, and everyone finally unites against Henchard, who strikes Farfrae at the climax. Given the large amount of incident the opera needed to cover, this approach to ensembles may also have been a necessity if the opera was not to run too long.

The production, combining amateur and professional performers, ran from July 30th through August 5th at the Cambridge Arts Theatre and formed the centerpiece of the Cambridge Festival. Although the Arts Council did not officially fund the production, in March 1951 the Cambridge Festival Committee requested a grant of £250 for copying parts and printing vocal scores, which the Arts Council supplied. The singers were largely amateurs drawn from music and drama societies in the city and university. Tranchell himself conducted some of the performances, which were accompanied by a chamber orchestra, including piano and electric organ, composed mainly of students from the Royal College of Music. Peter Bentley, the librettist, directed the production.

Critical reaction was mostly positive. Tranchell's idiom mostly attracted praise, although it was also described as thick, fussy, or "adding wrong notes to right chords" (Jacobs 1951b: 421). Although there are only a small number of folk-like numbers in the score, their inclusion sparked different reactions. On one hand, the *Times* suggested that a more diatonic folk-like style might better suit the opera's country-life subject, while on the other hand, Harold Rosenthal found just what the Times reviewer suggested:

There is much of the ballad opera in it, and the inclusion of authentic Scottish folk-tunes reminded at least one listener of *Hugh the Drover*. The choral writing was noteworthy. . . . The whole experiment was eminently worthwhile and certainly was a far more important contribution both to the Festival of Britain and British opera than was *John Socman*.

(Rosenthal 1951)

The work also received particular notice as a rare operatic adaptation of a classic English novel, although the elimination of the Lucetta plot, another source of tension between Henchard and Farfare, provoked complaint. Indeed, despite this radical compression of the source material, the work's literary pedigree drew from the enthusiastic reviewer for the *Times* an established national metaphor to explain the work's appeal:

Tranchell has seized the mood of Hardy's novel with a precision uncanny in a composer whose idiom seems naturally so sophisticated. . . . [T]he accents with which he clothes the melodic bones of his melody give the piece a freshness that belongs to the English countryside. . . . If not a total success, then, *The Mayor of Casterbridge* offered promise and much of compelling interest for anyone concerned with the development of an English operatic tradition.

(Howes 1951: 210–211)

This was significant praise, but not enough to launch Tranchell's career as he had hoped. *The Mayor of Casterbridge* was a semi-amateur production of a work by an unknown composer in a regional venue, and the fourth premiere in a summer of new operas and almost constant music-making throughout the nation, all of which contributed to a lack of sustained attention.

For a student revival in 1959, Tranchell planned thorough revisions but in the end, other than a major reworking of the opening choral scene, he made only small changes. The BBC broadcast the revival, but it received poor reviews. The performance was inadequate and music such as Tranchell's was moving out of fashion. Tranchell tried to get Bentley to work with him on further revisions, but Bentley had soured on the project. He wrote Tranchell several extremely critical analyses of the opera in 1960 and 1963, and they both dropped the project. The work has never again been performed.

Opera revivals

Two more new works supplemented the five high-profile operatic premieres discussed above. Late in the year, students at Oxford University mounted the first production of *Incognita*, the fifth and final opera by the Austrian immigrant composer and musicologist Egon Wellesz (1885–1974), and his only one with an English libretto. Like Tranchell and Easdale, Wellesz had submitted this work to the open commissioning scheme but the judges had rejected it. The libretto, based on the only novel by Restoration playwright William Congreve, traces the romantic misadventures of a number of Florentine youths during a masked ball. Not surprisingly, given the material and the composer's background, Matthew Rye (1995: 372) describes the opera as "Straussian." Then, for their local festival, the Canterbury Cathedral Choir School commissioned composer Antony Hopkins to write *The Man from Tuscany*, a choirboy opera on an invented episode in the life of Johann Sebastian Bach in "a musical style that is more pastiche than originality" (Rye 1995: 371–372). Neither work attracted much notice or constitutes a contribution either to the Festival or to the development of English opera.[9]

Naturally, *John Socman, The Pilgrim's Progress, The Sleeping Children, The Mayor of Casterbridge*, and *The Man from Tuscany* were hardly the only British operas performed in the Festival season. While the Arts Council was trying, with its various commissioning schemes, to get a record number of *new* British operas produced for the Festival, there was also the matter of stimulating revivals of older British operas, and of expanding the availability of opera in general. In April, 1949, a letter was brought to the Arts Council's attention commending the agency's just-announced plans to commission new operas for the Festival of Britain, but advancing in addition the cause of older works (EL6/71, April 10, 1949). The letter, from a Mr. Bunce, mentioned in particular Charles Villiers Stanford's *Travelling Companion*, Frederic Delius's *Village Romeo and Juliet*, and Vaughan Williams's *Sir John in Love* as deserving revival. Eric Walter White was not surprisingly the most outspoken supporter of this repertory at the Arts Council. His comment on the routing slip attached to the letter reads, "We must certainly bear this in mind as part of, not only 1951 [i.e., Festival of Britain] policy, but also long-term policy for English Opera. Place must be found in the repertories of our national opera companies for *Dido, Beggar's Opera, Bohemian Girl, Maritana, Lily of Killarney, the Wreckers, Shamus O'Brien, Hugh the Drover*, and doubtless other, including those mentioned by Mr Bunce." Although not all of these works received revivals, White had considerable success in spreading his enthusiasm, at least for duration of the Festival year. To exert influence over operatic ensembles, the Arts Council used the same methods described in Chapter 1 with regard to instrumental and choral groups.

The Arts Council Festival grants to opera companies underscore how high a priority opera and ballet performances were for the Arts Council in the Festival year. The breakdown of expenditures for the Festival of Britain (Paper 299, EL4/54, February 28, 1951) shows that the Arts Council spent £3075 on six opera commissions and their related expenses—*John Socman, Billy Budd*, and the four winners of the opera competition discussed in Chapter 4—and £475 on three ballet commissions. Glyndebourne, which had been struggling since the end of the war to revive its summer opera festival, received a huge £25,000 guarantee (one sixteenth of the total Festival allocation to the Arts Council). The English Opera Group received £5,000 (double their usual grant), Covent Garden £7,000, Sadler's Wells £18,000, the Welsh National Opera £6,000, Carl Rosa £5,000, and Intimate Opera, a tiny touring troupe, £500. In addition, the Riddick String Orchestra received £800 to finance a production of two stage works, and the Cambridge and Oxford Festivals received £1,500 and £1,200 respectively (although not all of these amounts went to opera productions of course). With the £3,075 spent on opera commission added to these sums, the £70,375 spend on opera constitutes 17.6 percent of the Arts Council's total allocation for the Festival.

Not all of this money advanced the cause of national opera. Glyndebourne, for instance, in keeping with its continental pretensions, mounted an all-Mozart season. The only British opera Covent Garden offered during its regular season was *The Pilgrim's Progress;* the rest of its repertory was thoroughly continental and conventional: Beethoven, Wagner, Verdi, Strauss, and Puccini. After the conclusion of the regular summer season, however, the company expanded its British offerings with 13 performances of the joint opera-ballet production of Henry Purcell's *Fairy Queen* directed (and adapted) by Constant Lambert that had inaugurated the company in 1946. The repertory of the Sadler's Wells Opera for the Festival season both in London and on tour included two revivals of British works—a new production of Purcell's *Dido and Aeneas* and Vaughan Williams's *Hugh the Drover*—along with works of Gounod, Mozart, Puccini, Verdi, Wolf-Ferrari, and the first British production of Janáček's *Káťa Kabanová*. A proposed production of Ethel Smyth's *Wreckers* never materialized.

For its Festival season, the English Opera Group mounted the most elaborate season in its short history and, in keeping with the Group's name, the entire repertory but for one work was English. Over the course of the summer, in a number of cities, in addition to *The Sleeping Children*, the EOG performed all three of Britten's extant chamber operas—*The Rape of Lucretia*, *Albert Herring*, and *Let's Make an Opera*—and a double bill of Purcell's *Dido and Aeneas* and Claudio Monteverdi's *Combattimento di Tancredi e Clorinda*. They also offered first public performances of Holst's *Wandering Scholar* since the composer's death in 1934. However, the run of performances in May at the Lyric Theatre, Hammersmith, during the London Season of the Arts was one of the summer's least successful ventures (Arts Council Annual Report 1950–1951: 6; Kildea 2002: 102–107).

The D'Oyly Carte company, firmly and successfully for profit and not in any need of government handouts, offered no less than eight of W. S. Gilbert and Arthur Sullivan's operettas in London over the course of the summer. Thomas Beecham mounted a production of Michael Balfe's *Bohemian Girl* in Liverpool and London (EL6/172). There were also various performances of shorter or more minor British operatic and musical stage works (such as masques) by small companies and amateur groups, as listed in Appendix 2. Intimate Opera in particular entered into the spirit of the Festival by offering virtually all of its homegrown repertory.

Mr. Tranchell's regret

Despite the respectful reviews it garnered, the Cambridge Festival production of *The Mayor of Casterbridge* failed to spark the operatic career that Peter Tranchell hoped for. Tranchell went on to become Director of Music at Gonville and Caius

College, and, according to a story long disseminated in Cambridge combination rooms, in later years he laid the blame for his opera's limited success on the Covent Garden production of Benjamin Britten's *Billy Budd*, which, he supposedly complained to his colleagues, absorbed all the available attention for new British opera in the year 1951. Lewis Foreman (2003: 75) repeats this claim:

> Peter Tranchell's competing opera *The Mayor of Casterbridge*, rejected by the competition at an earlier stage, was produced at Cambridge in 1951.... Unfortunately it was side-lined by the simultaneous production of *Billy Budd* at Covent Garden.

There is a grain of truth in this otherwise inaccurate account. In retrospect, we can recognize *Billy Budd* as the most significant and widely performed work to result from a Festival of Britain commission. Nevertheless, it was hardly the only operatic work competing with Tranchell's score for attention in 1951. For Tranchell, as for many British composers working between 1945 and 1975, it was always easy to envy and blame Britten's success. But the bustle of the Festival of Britain itself, and not the premiere of *Billy Budd*, obscured Tranchell's achievement.

Clearly, if Tranchell ever really claimed that the success of *Billy Budd* doomed *The Mayor of Casterbridge* (as his colleagues in Cambridge are wont to recall), this represents a distortion of memory on his part. *John Socman* and *The Sleeping Children*, both of which, unlike *The Mayor of Casterbridge*, received fully professional productions, equally failed to attract more attention and further performance. But *Billy Budd* cannot be blamed for the fate of any of the other operas first staged in 1951. Contrary to Lewis Foreman's claim, the performances of *Billy Budd* were not simultaneous with *The Mayor of Casterbridge*, or indeed with any of the Festival operas. Rather, they came at the very end of the year, and in a completely different artistic atmosphere from the creative explosion of the Festival of Britain that formed the context for the other operatic ventures. When Britten's opera finally arrived, the press scarcely compared it with the earlier premieres of the year. In part this lack of critical comparison was due to the privileged place in the British operatic pantheon, above and apart, that both Britten and Covent Garden had created for themselves.

More to the point, and contrary to the way Tranchell's complaint is reported, *Billy Budd* was not an instant success that swept away the memory of all that had come before. The work was indeed preceded by a blaze of publicity; by 1951, Britten's coterie of supporters exercised considerable power in operatic circles. In advance of the premiere, his publisher Boosey and Hawkes devoted a substantial portion of the Autumn 1951 edition of *Tempo*, their house journal, to the opera, and the journal *Opera*, run by Britten's friend Lord Harewood, gave the upcoming premiere similarly prominent coverage. (Both of these were published well after the run of *The Mayor of Casterbridge* and indeed after the end of the Festival of Britain.) Such activity generated widespread anticipation, but equally attracted negative comment: "[Britten] has an astute and enterprising publisher who blazes his trail with blinding and deafening advance publicity" (Williams 1951). And, when *Billy Budd* was finally performed, reviews were respectful but mixed. While some historians (Carpenter 1992; Kennedy 1993) read the critics' overall tone as positive, others (Cooke and Reed 1993) stress the negative reactions that often compared the new opera unfavorably with *Peter Grimes*, which is more tuneful and more easily appreciated at first hearing. With so many critics expressing severe reservations this time around, *Billy Budd* could not repeat the sensational success and spread of *Peter Grimes*.

Covent Garden gave the opera six performances in London in December 1951, took it on tour around Britain, performing it in Cardiff, Manchester, Glasgow, and Birmingham, and then, in May 1952, performed it to famous bewilderment in Paris. In 1953, *Billy Budd* received a production in Wiesbaden, tremendously successful but marred with many disfiguring cuts, an even more severely abridged NBC television production in the United States, and a student production at Indiana University. It then fell out of the repertory until Britten revised the work, condensing the four original acts into two, for a 1961 BBC broadcast, but even the revised version was first staged (at Covent Garden) only in 1964. Obviously, Lloyd, Easdale, and Tranchell would have been overjoyed with such a run for their works, but it hardly represents a runaway success. *Billy Budd* did not become a standard repertory work until the seventies (Cooke and Reed 1993: 135–149).

Contrary to "Mr. Tranchell's regret", then, neither *Billy Budd* nor any other single production could be said to have absorbed all the publicity for new British opera in 1951, freezing out its rivals. Indeed, if anything, there was too much British opera, both new and old during, the summer of 1951 for any production to dominate the news. By any reckoning, 1951 was an extraordinary year for British opera. The satisfaction with which boosters of native opera viewed this burgeoning list of premieres and revivals in 1951 is apparent in the grander pronouncements of the period. In his *Radio Times* Autumn 1951 season preview quoted at the end of Chapter 1, Herbert Murrill included opera as one of the genres that British composers could confidently launch into the local repertory. Also in the Festival year, Eric Walter White published a survey of the British operatic scene. He admitted that progress towards the creation of a "national opera", encompassing works, performers, and institutions, had been slow: The companies were still young, and more opera was needed outside London. He also called for an increased investment in operatic training. But on the heels of a summer of unprecedented operatic activity, in the run-up to an internationally important premiere, White waxed optimistic on the subject of repertory:

> The fact that only now is this country starting to establish what nearly all other European countries have had for years, if not centuries—namely, a national opera—should not necessarily prove a disadvantage. If our composers, librettists, producers, performers and audiences are unfettered by tradition, they should be all the better able to tackle this new job without hard and fast preconceptions. English opera is emerging from the difficulties and tribulations of the last three centuries with fresh vigour and confidence.

Composer, poet, interpreter, listener—all now have the chance to help create a new and glorious age of opera.

(White 1972: 209–210)

The Festival of Britain represents a real, if modest moment of arrival and maturity for the genre. The Arts Council's efforts helped establish opera as a normal, indeed a prominent, part of English artistic life, securing for it a status that had only barely begun to develop before the war. At least an elite class of British composers could reasonably aspire to have their operas performed in the most prestigious operatic venues in the nation before international audiences.

Still, more than a half-century later, much of Murrill and White's confidence seems misplaced; certainly, as Chapter 4 demonstrates, the outcome of the Arts Council's opera competition, an unprecedented and unrepeated attempt to directly stimulate new national repertory, was unsatisfactory. *Pace* Murrill, British opera in 1951 still had a long way to go before it could match the acceptance of symphonies and concertos.

Furthermore, the Festival signals a failure for dreams of *popular* national opera. Critical responses to Festival operas reveal that the maturing of operatic institutions and audiences accompanied a retreat toward a more elite attitude toward the genre. As Irene Morra (2007) traces, this was a gradual trend, not a sudden cultural paradigm shift toward a challenging modernist aesthetic. Much of the Covent Garden audience for *Billy Budd* in 1951 was capable of appreciating its ambiguities, accustomed as they were to Britten's "psychologically explorative" earlier works (to use the term in Morra 2007: 114). And the charges of traditionalism in style and construction aimed at *John Socman* by critics beginning to demand more contemporary plots and treatments also apply to an extent to *The Pilgrim's Progress* and *The Mayor of Casterbridge*, and to *Wat Tyler* and *A Tale of Two Cities* among the competition winners surveyed in the next chapter.

But such attitudes did not represent the nation's only opera audience in 1951; there was a public for lighter fare as well. Works like *John Socman* had the potential to please large numbers who still liked traditional tonal and tuneful nationalist spectacles. For this reason, knowing that their audience lay in the provinces, not in the metropolis, the Carl Rosa Opera Company perhaps chose the composer for their commission well despite their limited success with the work. Taken as a repertory, the Festival of Britain operas seem to resist the trend toward sophistication even if they succumbed to it historically, and signal a moment in British operatic culture that balanced modernist ambitions with broad public understanding and appeal. These mixed motives, the attempts to retain popular and accessible elements in the face of pressure to become increasingly elite and esoteric, were also apparent in the Arts Council's plans for concert music surveyed in Chapters 1 and 2, and offer another instance of the aesthetic category of the middlebrow (Chowrimootoo 2014).

In the late 40s, parties debating national opera policy were still talking of the founding of an English *Volksoper* (Donaldson 1988: 47). However, dreams of establishing a broad-based opera tradition that attracted and spoke to people

114 *Festival opera productions*

of different social classes and backgrounds, like most such projects in the mid-twentieth century, were doomed to failure. In addition to romanticizing the history of opera in Europe, such ambitions were out of step with the direction of modern British, indeed Western culture, and withered fast. The professionalization and internationalization of opera companies—not just in London—and their integration into the classical music industry gradually marginalized all new works but those with the most contemporary credentials. Classical music could never hope to compete with popular music for audience appeal, or with television as a dramatic genre of broad interest.[10] It is surely a significant mark of the changing expectations for British opera that most of the works commissioned and produced in the Festival were never taken into professional repertory. To the extent that they survived oblivion at all, along with a number of additional works discussed in Chapters 4 and 5, this was thanks to amateur and conservatory performances.

Notes

1 Martin 2010 provides a very thorough survey of opera companies and troupes in England beginning in the later nineteenth century.
2 Martin (2010: 222–223, 231–234) gives a brief summary of the creation of Lloyd's first two operas.
3 This account of the negotiations over the premiere is derived largely from ACGB EL6/55 and ACGB EL6/36.
4 The detailed account that follows is based on Eric Crozier's first-person account of the creation of the opera (Crozier 1986), Philip Reed's chronicle in Cooke and Reed 1993, and the documents relating to the *Billy Budd* commission in EL6/71. See also Britten 1969: 85–86, Furbank 1978: 283–286, and Kildea 2002:117–131. Kildea also traces Britten's tense relationship with the Arts Council over a longer period.
5 In 1951, several reviews of Easdale's opera, including that in the London *Times* opined that the constitution of the chamber orchestra Britten had established for EOG productions was unbalanced and covered the voices. In response, Oldham wrote a letter to the *Times* defending the ensemble, for which he was composing at that moment (Oldham 1951).
6 Howes wrote two reviews, first calling the work "an embarrassing opera which evoked sympathy for the singers who had to go through with it" and declaring that "[t]he music is an encumbrance on the plot and the text is prohibitive of independent music" and later reasserting that "the total result is appalling" and condemning not only Easdale and Guthrie but Britten for supporting an opera which "encompasses error on such a scale that an inquest is expedient" (Howes 1951: 46–47).
7 The account that follows is largely based on documents in EL6/36 and the Tranchell Collection of the Cambridge University Library.
8 The version submitted to the Arts Council included the Lucetta plot and the Skimmity Ride, the climactic scene of Hardy's novel, which Tranchell and Bentley completely eliminated in the final version.
9 One other commissioned musical-dramatic work, not an opera but rather incidental music, stands out as possibly the most challenging compositional assignment of the year. The Festival of Britain Catholic Committee mounted a dramatized version of Newman's *Dream of Gerontius* and commissioned Fernand Laloux, the organist at Farm Street Jesuit Church in London, to write the score.
10 On the decline of the hopes for nationally significant opera in Britain in this period, see Lew 2001, Epilogue.

4   ... and off
The opera commissioning scheme

The ill-fated scheme to commission new operas on the basis of an open competition was the most ambitious of all the commissions, grants, concert series, and other cultural events sponsored or produced by the Arts Council for the Festival of Britain. With this high-profile plan, the Arts Council confidently aimed to tap into the new postwar enthusiasm for opera and coax into being a decisive contribution to the national repertory. Furthermore, while far from the most expensive of the Arts Council's undertakings for the Festival, it was the most extended; from conception through final judgments the meetings and decision-making went on for almost four years.

But, while not exactly a fiasco, the opera commissioning scheme ended up revealing the limits of the Arts Council's sway and the institutional challenges facing those who would direct repertory. The Arts Council took a different approach from that which they had adopted for the relatively successful concert music and direct operatic commissions. With hindsight, the Arts Council's confidence in their ability to predict and manage the outcome and to cajole companies to perform works was misplaced. Rather than selecting specific composers in advance, as they had for the concert music, the Council ceded control of the commissions to an anonymous competitive process. As vast numbers of poor quality proposals poured in, and then the judges themselves failed to reach unanimity, it became clear that the scheme's architects had misjudged the state of operatic composition in Britain. And as the process dragged on, it also became evident that they had misjudged their chance of securing performances at the end; the Council and the winning composers essayed every means to bring about performance in the face of indifference, resistance, and procedural obstructions from potential performers.

The competition had its roots in the same meetings of the opera subcommittee of the Opera and Ballet Panel in June and July 1948 that led to the three commissions surveyed in the previous chapter. Recognizing that, at that early date, none of these commissions was certain to produce a successful result, and that there were sure to be other less prominent composers ready to tackle the operatic genre if a suitable commission were available, the subcommittee reported:

> It would seem appropriate . . . that there should be some opportunity for other composers; and, in this connection, it is suggested that there should be a

competition for new operas. Although no special restrictions would be laid down about the scale of the operas (size of orchestra and chorus, number of principals, number of sets, etc.) to be submitted, it would be pointed out that composers would be wise to plan their works with due regard to the capacities of the various theatres where operas are performed and of the companies that produce them. It should also be borne in mind that there may be certain companies not mentioned ... above—e.g., Glyndebourne, New London Opera Company, English Opera Group, Intimate Opera—which could mount such an opera during the Festival period. Even so, it is clear that stage production of the winning opera or operas could not be guaranteed.

The competition would be open to all British composers; and a special jury of about five persons would be appointed by the Arts Council to judge the entrants. There would be the following stages in the competition:-

(i) The entrants would be judged on submission of a synopsis of the libretto;
(ii) Each successful entrant would receive an instalment of, say, £100 and would be asked to submit the score of the first act;
(iii) Each entrant, whose first act was approved by the jury, would receive a further instalment of, say, £200 to enable him/her to complete the opera;
(iv) The final judgment would be given on the completed opera.

(Paper 92, EL4/66, n.d. [December 1948/January 1949])

Although the minutes of the subcommittee meetings are not preserved, it is likely that Eric Walter White was one of the originators of the Council's opera commissioning program. White was very knowledgeable about British operatic history and deeply committed to the cause of opera in Britain. At this very period he had just started or was soon to start work on the first edition of his book *The Rise of English Opera* (White 1972), which surveyed past achievements in copious detail and made a strong case for the continuation and strengthening of the native operatic tradition. After the commissioning scheme was launched, he drafted an article for the journal *Opera* in which he provided the project with a lengthy justification:

Virginia Woolf once postulated a standard income of £500 a year—nearer £1000 a year by present day standards—and a room of one's own as the minimum without which an artist could not be expected to feel fully free and secure in the exercise of his or her art. This is not dissimilar from the needs of a composer setting out to compose his first opera. Where is the patron with sufficient faith to give him the support he wants? As Rupert Brooke said in his address on Democracy and the Arts to the Cambridge University Fabian Society in 1910, "It is no use paying a man to learn the intricacies of musical composition for seven or eight years and then leaving him stranded. It is just the greatest who would suffer."

In the days when opera was a dynastic entertainment, the composer was generally a servant of the Royal Household. Those days have passed, but in almost every country where opera is a flourishing concern the State has now taken over the duty of financing this beautiful but complex and expensive art-form. If opera houses and opera companies were in a sufficiently secure financial position, they ought themselves to take the initiative in commissioning new works for their repertories; but few appear to have the means or inclination to do so today.

(EL6/71, July 17, 1950)

The conclusion White drew was that the State should equally take over the patronage of the opera composers, at least in the commissioning of works by unknown composers, so that they might have a chance to have their works heard and develop their skills in this genre.

The subcommittee report and White's article suggest the high ideals behind the opera commissioning concept. While ambitions for the commissioned concert works varied, with some viewing them as little more than appropriately festive occasional music, the opera commissions aimed for quality works and for the discovery and development of fresh talent. The Arts Council was sure that there were talented composers in Britain, who if given the opportunity would produce operatic contributions worthy of the country's companies. Furthermore, and crucially, the Arts Council at this period saw itself as having the clout to get those companies to take up the new operas.

The very idea that a panel of judges would be able to sift through projects in the complex and varied realm of opera and pick out works of exceptional promise was idealistic, or at least optimistic. As we have seen in Chapter 1, the opera competition was not the only arts competition engendered by the Festival of Britain, but in no case was the work being judged as large as a full-length opera. The expectations of the committees that initiated the other Festival competitions were lower, and the "prize" far less prominent than performance by a major company.

There are precedents for the idea of an opera competition—Pietro Mascagni's *Cavalleria Rusticana* won a competition for one-act operas sponsored by the publisher E. Sconzogno in 1888, and the prize catapulted the opera and its composer to overnight fame. An earlier competition by Sconzogno had spurred Giacomo Puccini to write *Le villi*, which similarly began that composer's career. But the Arts Council's competition was a far cry from these competitions in Italy, where opera was the national theatrical art form and there were literally dozens of companies with the will and resources to produce new works. While placing faith in their (as yet unchosen) judges to select deserving works, the Arts Council had to inspire composers to enter the competition, generate interest in the winning scores among the tiny number of opera producers, and then hope that the imprimatur of the competition would generate audience interest as well.

Given these challenges, and, admittedly, with hindsight, it is surprising that the Arts Council undertook the project at all. Nevertheless, the project was approved with almost precisely the same language as the subcommittee's original proposal. The full Opera and Ballet Panel met on July 26, 1948, and, noting that the monetary amounts given "were only approximate and might be less" (EL4/95, July 28, 1948), accepted the subcommittee's proposal, and passed up to the full Arts Council a recommendation using almost precisely the same language, along

118 *The opera commissioning scheme*

with the three opera commissions for Britten, Vaughan Williams, and Lloyd. The Arts Council Executive Committee accepted both proposals two days later, and forwarded them to the Festival of Britain Executive, which approved them in late October (EL4/50).

The standing opera subcommittee formulated the conditions for the commissioning project in more detail in December 1948, and at that time made the further recommendation that the word "competition" be dropped from its designation. This was because there was no prize as such to be awarded: Incomplete operatic projects were to be judged and the composers of the chosen opera were to receive commissions to complete the works, but nothing further was explicitly promised. (This was in contrast to the three named commissions, which were to be performed by the three major opera companies during the Festival season.) Furthermore, according to White, who ran the scheme, the committee wanted to downplay the competitive aspect: The members of the committee, he wrote, felt that "certain entrants might be discouraged from submitting works if they thought it was to be a competition" (EL6/71, December 10, 1948). As later events proved, avoiding the term "competition", with the implication that all entries would be considered equally by the judges, also enabled the Arts Council to justify the need to be selective in choosing the applications that received full consideration.

The project was to unfold as follows: Only full-length English-language operatic works—including light operas with some spoken dialogue—by composers of British nationality or foreigners permanently resident in the United Kingdom would be eligible. (This provision excluded citizens of former colonies, but British subjects living abroad remained eligible.) After submitting a preliminary application to the Arts Council, each composer would be asked to provide the panel of judges with an "outline" of his or her project, described in the draft of the application as consisting of:

(a) The story of the opera, told not as a programme synopsis but in the form of a short story of about 2,500–3,500 words.
(b) A synopsis of the dramatic action and musical treatment by scenes and acts, with or without musical examples in notation.
(c) One scene at least of the libretto as passed by the composer.
(EL4/95, January 12, 1949)

To ensure the impartiality of the judges, composers would submit these outlines under pseudonyms given in their preliminary application. Only the Arts Council staff would see the initial application forms, which enabled them to keep track of the identities of all the composers, and they would act as intermediary for all materials passed to the judges. In response to an early query, White defined the vague term "synopsis of musical treatment" as a description of "whether you are proposing to construct your opera as a sequence of closed numbers, or as a music drama; what part is likely to be played by recitative; what are the operatic forces you propose to employ, soloists, principals, and chorus, and any indication of the musical style that can be given by short excerpts or illustrations" (EL6/69, n.d. [mid-1949]).

Composers whose outlines the judges deemed to have potential would then be asked to provide a full act or one quarter of the opera in piano score, or in full score if the judges required. Only the composers passing this second round would be awarded commissions for the completion of the entire work. The £5,250 budget for the entire scheme (EL4/95, January 12, 1949) shows that the Arts Council was imagining that, at the most, 20 projects would pass round one and of these ten at the most would pass round two and receive commissions. Even recognizing that this was an upper limit, these numbers represent a very sanguine projection of the project's outcome.

The application form was necessarily more ambiguous on the possibility of arranging performances of the winning works than was the original internal memorandum. The form warned that "although eventual stage productions will be the aim of these commissioned operas, the Arts Council cannot guarantee that the successful opera or operas will actually be produced during or after the Festival of Britain, 1951." But it went on a bit more confidently: "The Arts Council, however, will reserve for a period of two years as from the delivery of the completed works the right to nominate the first production of the accepted operas" (EL6/45, March 1949). It also repeated the suggestion that composers "bear in mind the existing operatic resources of the country in the way of opera houses and opera companies" (EL4/95, January 12, 1949). Still, although performances of the winning scores were not promised, given the backing of the government and the publicity of the competition, they appeared likely.

In January 1949, the standing opera committee, with the help of the organist and composer Stanley Marchant, put together a proposed list of judges representing a variety of different areas of operatic expertise. On their behalf, John Denison, the Arts Council Music Director, wrote to David Webster of the Royal Opera House for suggestions. In his response (EL6/45, January 11, 1949), Webster recommended as judges of "the libretto and dramatic side" the distinguished music critic Ernest Newman and the musicologist and critic Edward Dent, a former Professor of Music at Cambridge who was an authority on operatic history, had translated Da Ponte's librettos for the Sadler's Wells Company, and had directed several English baroque operas (notably *Dido and Aeneas*). Webster further proposed composer and conductor Constant Lambert, Musical Director of the Sadler's Wells Ballet, composer Arthur Bliss, and the active opera singer Joan Cross.

The list forwarded to Marchant omitted Cross, but also included Frederick Austin, an eminent retired singer, occasional composer, and Artistic Director of the short-lived British National Opera Company (1924–1929), Lawrance Collingwood, the retired principal conductor of the Sadler's Wells Opera and occasional composer, and retired oratorio and opera singer Steuart Wilson, the former Arts Council Music Director who had sung with the British National Opera Company, the Old Vic (the predecessor to the Sadler's Wells Company), and Rutland Boughton's Glastonbury Festival and was by this time primarily a musical administrator serving as the Music Director of the BBC. Other significant names on the list were Aylmer Buesst, Mosco Carner, Tyrone Guthrie, Julius Harrison, Hans Oppenheimer, and Norman Tucker.

According to the correspondence of Eric Walter White, there was some resistance in the Opera Panel, presumably on the grounds of conflict of interest, to inviting figures such as Tucker who were actively engaged in running opera companies (EL6/71, January 28, 1949). (Tucker was the Artistic Director of the Sadler's Wells Opera Company.) Nevertheless, Wilson and Dent were both trustees of the Covent Garden Opera; Dent had also served on the Board of Directors of Sadler's Wells. As for Cross, Denison wrote to Webster that there was no room for a separate performing singer, and both Austin and Wilson had backgrounds as singers (EL6/45, January 13, 1949).

Invitations to sit on the panel, along with drafts of the rules and applications for the project, were extended to Wilson, Dent, Newman, Collingwood, and Lambert. Wilson was asked to chair the panel. When Newman declined a spot, his place was offered to Austin. In his letter accepting a position on the panel, Dent objected to his own selection along with Newman. Referring to himself and Newman as "ancient monuments", he opined that the Arts Council should really have asked younger people (EL6/61, January 20, 1949). In January 1949, Dent was 72 and Newman 81. Austin (Newman's replacement) was 76 years old. Collingwood was 61, Wilson 59 and Lambert only 43.

Wilson, Dent, and Austin met with Arts Council staff on February 18, 1949 to approve the conditions and timetable and their own fees and procedures. Collingwood and Lambert were unavailable for this meeting; but Gerald Barry may have sat in on part of it (EL4/50). Arising from this session was one important change. The original draft terms had read:

6. Each composer whose outline libretto is approved by the Judges will receive an advance payment of £100 by the Arts Council and a request for the submission . . . of the piano score of an act, or alternatively, of a section of the opera which is calculated to be not less than one quarter of the whole. . . .
7. Composers who satisfy the Judges at this stage will receive a payment of £200, £100 of which will be paid over at once and the remaining £100 of which on delivery of the completed score.

(EL4/95, January 12, 1949)

Collingwood objected to paying out on the basis of a libretto alone (actually, the initial submission consisted of a synopsis, a portion of the libretto, and a description with examples of the style of musical treatment). Those present at the meeting agreed with this objection, and the initial payment was therefore dropped, leaving a £100 payment upon approval of the first section of the score, and the remaining £200 upon delivery of the completed score. Composers were to submit their applications and "outlines" for round one of the judging by June 30, 1949, and the partial piano scores of those projects that the judges deemed worthy for round two by December 31, 1949. The deadline for submission of the full scores of the works actually commissioned was set for September 30, 1950. The first stages of the process thus were quite short, and the panel envisioned considering the submissions on a rolling basis. As the information sheet pointed out, "Composers are reminded that *the earlier* their opera outline and sample of work in progress are submitted, *the sooner* they will receive the Judges' verdict and *the longer* they will have to complete the composition" (EL4/95, January 12, 1949, emphasis in original).

The participants in the February 18th meeting also addressed the pay for the judges. The judges suggested an hourly rate for their work, but when the Arts Council Executive Committee balked, some negotiation ensued, and at the end of March the judges agreed to a fixed sum of £175, paid in installments as they completed various stages (EL6/71).

Implementation

The Arts Council publicized the scheme in late February through the press, music publishers, the Composers' Guild, the Committee for the Promotion of New Music, the London Contemporary Music Centre, and the British Council. By March 8, 1949, the Arts Council had received nearly 40 inquiries, and several procedural questions had come up. The judges decided to disallow already printed works. They did allow composers to submit more than one proposal, but the composer had to submit them all under the same pseudonym with the understanding that only one could be commissioned. In the case of already substantially completed works, the judges allowed the submission, along with the "outline", of a completed section of the music, to speed up the judging.

The competition sparked more interest than the Arts Council planners or the panel of judges had expected. The encouraging tone of the announcement, and its broad dissemination, implied that scheme was open to all applicants, regardless of education and experience. Britain teemed with amateur musicians and composers who, regardless of their limited professional training and abilities, saw the competition as their chance to have their creations recommended to the nation's lyric stages. By the deadline at the end of June 1949, the Arts Council had received 182 inquiries and 117 applications. This tremendous response—the Arts Council had expected a preliminary response in the range of 50—necessitated a slight change in the rules: an initial review and cut of the applications so as not to deluge the judges with outlines. This task fell to Eric Walter White and John Denison, the Arts Council Music Director. These two made their selection on the basis of the application forms. Along with the applicant's name, sex, nationality, address, date of birth, and chosen pseudonym, these forms called for the particulars of the composer's training and compositions: "Please mention which of your works have been published. If no work of yours has been published in orchestral score, mention which works (if any) you can submit in MS orchestral score if asked" (EL4/95, January 12, 1949). This information enabled White and Denison to judge whether the applicant was eligible under the rules by nationality or residence, and whether he or she had the necessary educational background and professional experience to warrant serious consideration. In this preliminary division, they accepted 36 applicants and immediately rejected 44. They went through the remaining 37 again, recording their impressions ("accept," "doubtful," or "reject"), and passed all except the 12 proposals that they both marked for rejection (EL6/71).

Unsurprisingly, this first review proved controversial. Nine of the rejected applicants objected to the fact that their projects had been eliminated by bureaucrats at the Arts Council and never even reviewed by the judges. In mid-June 1949, these complaints had reached the ears of Ernest Pooley, the Chairman of the Arts Council, who expressed some dissatisfaction. In response, White wrote up a justification of his and Denison's actions:

> 1. It was always intended that the Arts Council should reserve discretionary powers in connection with the scheme and provision was made for this in . . . the published conditions. 2. Reasons for rejection by the Arts Council could be (a) because applicants were not of British nationality or of bona fide residence in this country; or (b) lack of sufficient music training or experience to justify our inviting them to take part in the scheme. 3. John Denison and myself have also borne in mind the facts that over 100 persons have applied, and Sir Steuart Wilson on behalf of the Judges has expressed the opinion that the optimum number for the next stage of the scheme (i.e. libretto judging) would be about 50.
>
> (EL6/71, June 23, 1949)

To this memorandum, Denison added a postscript:

> In my own view, we may have been at fault in drafting the publicity for the scheme too simply. The point which should have perhaps been underlined is that it is not a competition but a scheme where people can apply to be commissioned. Apart from the general principle that a patron who is prepared to commission must obviously have discretion in his choice, there are the very practical reasons given by Mr. White at §2 and §3 of his note. For the purposes of the scheme—which is not to catch entirely unknown talent—I think that justice has been done, and everyone with prima facie qualifications for writing a reasonable opera has been accepted. If the entirely unknown was to be catered for, a competition would have been the right answer. We have, I think, considerably exceeded Sir Steuart Wilson's figure of 50!
>
> (EL6/71, June 23, 1949)

In Denison's comments in particular, we can see the face of the scheme changing as it came in contact with practical realities. In its original motivation, the scheme had in fact resembled an open opera competition, but Denison could conveniently hide behind the revised language, and argue for the less purely merit-based system of commissions chosen at the patron's pleasure. In addition to offering these explanations, on July 12, 1949 White asked the composer Thomas Wood, the Chair of the Music Panel, to review the rejected applications, so as to give the preliminary rejections the weight of professional authority outside the Arts Council bureaucracy. Wood reviewed the applications and responded that he supported White and Denison's decisions, and the matter was laid to rest (EL6/71, July 12–14, 1949).

Meanwhile, as the remaining 61 composers were accepted into the scheme, the Arts Council invited them to submit outlines of their operatic projects. (Some applications had come in so late that the Arts Council had to grant the composers extensions because the outlines too were supposed to be submitted by the end of June.) Four composers withdrew at this stage, and two submitted two outlines, for a total of 59 outlines to be considered by the judges. From the correspondence, it is clear that in cases where composers had already embarked on their projects before the announcement of the scheme, they often enclosed segments of short score or even full score along with the requested outline materials. As the outlines came in, White forwarded them to the judges for consideration.

The list of composers who submitted works to the scheme is impressive, including prominent figures from the worlds of film music, light music, and academia: Malcolm Arnold, Lennox Berkeley, Christian Darnton, Norman Demuth, Arwel Hughes, Maurice Johnstone, Clifton Parker, Ian Parrott, Cyril Scott, Humphrey Searle, Bernard Stevens, and Egon Wellesz all submitted projects. The scheme did not, however, attract all the operatic talents of the period. Obviously, Britten, Vaughan Williams, and George Lloyd, who had received or were being courted for separate Festival of Britain opera commissions, had no need of the scheme—in any case Britten and Vaughan Williams were far too well established, and their incomes too secure, to complete in an Arts Council scheme for £300. Michael Tippett was a different matter, and conspicuous in his absence. His works of the 40s—the oratorio *A Child of Our Time* (1941), the song cycle *Boyhood's End* (1943), the second and third string quartets (1943, 1946), and the first symphony (1945)—had brought him increasing renown both in Britain and abroad. Still, he was by no means assured the kind of reception that Britten or Vaughan Williams could command. At the time the scheme was announced he had recently started composing his first opera, *The Midsummer Marriage*. A note between Eric Walter White and John Denison preserved in the Arts Council archives sheds some light on Tippett's decision not to submit his work:

> Mr Denison—I need your advice on this exchange of letters with Michael Tippett. Personally I think the crux of the matter is contained in the last of his last letter. Schotts are his publishers; Schotts help to finance him; Schotts will have to take over a considerable liability for *The Midsummer Marriage*. If I were in Michael's position, I think it is Schott's advice I should follow in this matter of commissioning. If they feel it is *infra dignitatem* for him to enter the work under a pseudonym for this type of scheme merely for the sake of possibly winning £300, then he had better not do so. After all, he will probably find little difficulty in getting his opera produced abroad as soon as it's ready, whether any company in this country is interested or not.

> I agree—we have spoken and I think Michael has decided definitely against entering. Let him finish the work! J[ohn] D[enison].
>
> (EL6/71, March 26, 1949)

Tippett's reputation abroad, as well as his financial relationship with his eminent foreign publisher, made the scheme seem unnecessarily parochial for him and militated against his entering. No similar considerations, however, dissuaded Wellesz, who enjoyed a reputation in Europe and Britain extending back over 30 years, or the Australian composer Arthur Benjamin, whose publisher, Boosey and Hawkes, was very actively promoting his music.

In July and August the judges began the slow process of reviewing the outlines, librettos, and eventually, the music, of the submissions. Appendix 3 lists all the applicants and submissions to the scheme, and the stages at which they were accepted or rejected. For the first stage of review, each outline was sent to a single judge. The quantity of material was so great that the judges decided to allow each judge a veto; that is, any project that the first reviewing judge considered worthless would not be considered further. On August 5, 1949 Steuart Wilson reported this procedure to White, who assented. The first judges' meeting was set for September 9, 1949. At this meeting, the 59 projects were dealt with in several different ways. Two were disqualified under the rules of the scheme. The Arts Council records state that the first of these, Brian Easdale's *Sleeping Children*, was disqualified because it was in a single act. Although it is possible that in an early stage of planning this was the case, the explanation may also have been entered in error, because in its final form the work is a full-length opera in three acts, and it is hard to see how its material could be presented in a single act. It is therefore more likely that the judges disqualified the work when they discovered that the English Opera Group had already commissioned it for performance in 1950. The records state no reason for disqualifying Cecil Armstrong Gibbs's *Twelfth Night*, but this was probably because it too was not a new project; Gibbs had completed the work in 1946–1947.

The judges rejected 22 proposals outright. With these, they decided not to offer composers any reasons for rejection, but Wilson agreed to give the composers spoken summaries of the judges' reports if they came to see him in person. The judges allowed an exception to this ruling in the case of Albert H. Coates (not to be confused with the light music composer Eric Coates), whose opera *Pickwick* had been performed at Covent Garden in 1936. Although the judges rejected the outline for Coates' opera project, *The Boy David*, on October 25, 1949, the notes for the January 20, 1950 meeting call for a report to be made on the work, and it is listed again as rejected along with specific reasons for rejection in the notes to the April 20, 1950 meeting (EL6/71, October 27, 1949, January 24 and April 25, 1950). Wilson then specifically instructed White to include these reasons in the rejection letter to Coates (EL6/71, May 2, 1950). Two possible explanations for this double consideration and special treatment offer themselves: Either Coates, who was in South Africa and therefore unable to come to the Arts Council office, requested a written explanation, which the judges discussed and prepared in early

1950, or else he sent additional musical materials which crossed in the mail with notice of his October rejection, and the judges magnanimously decided to consider the work again in light of the newly received materials. There is no direct evidence of either of these circumstances in the Arts Council archive.

This left 27 outlines still undecided, to be passed to another judge for consideration. For seven of these, the judges directed White to ask the composers to send in more examples of the music. This request marked another slight change in the scheme's procedures. Since some composers already embarked on their work had submitted partial scores at the outset, the judges understandably had difficulty judging other projects on the basis of the largely verbal descriptions called for in the "outline". As round one of the scheme progressed, therefore, the judges considered more and more of the music of the operatic projects, increasingly calling for sections of score. In effect, they ran round one (the "outlines") and round two (the sections of score) together. Thus by the time the judges had considered all the projects to their satisfaction, they were ready in most cases to proceed directly to commissions.

At the first meeting, only one project, Karl Rankl's *Deirdre of the Sorrows*, a setting of the play by the Irish writer John Millington Synge, was passed directly to the next round. Given the measure of indecision about so many other projects, and the frequent requests for more music, the rapid decision about Rankl's opera suggests that he had already completed substantial work on it and had submitted a large portion of the completed music. Curiously, another composer, Leonard Salzedo, also submitted a project based on the same Synge play. This raised the question of which composer had the rights to the text. White took up the matter with Samuel French, Synge's publisher, in December 1949, when it looked like an announcement of the results of round one was imminent. French responded that Salzedo had held an option on the text only through October 1949, so Rankl was free to negotiate with them for the rights (EL6/71 14 December 1949, EL6/73).

At the same meeting, a 60th project, *Orestes*, by a composer who took the pseudonym "Richard Jones", was accepted into the scheme. The composer's application and outline must have arrived late, and White apparently forgot to enter it, with its composer and pseudonym, in the complete table of submissions, so the identity of its composer cannot be determined.

The judges next met on October 25, 1949, when they rejected a further 13 projects, leaving 22 to be passed to a third or fourth judge. They also asked White to request additional music for 10 more of the projects still under consideration. One of the works the judges rejected at this meeting was Clifton Parker's *Aucassin and Nicolette*.[1] Other than the operas of the four winners and two other finalists, on which the decision took many months, Parker's was the only work which seems to have earned the judges' sincere approval. Later, in his May 5, 1950 interim report, Wilson revealed that the judges had ruled it out "with regret" only because, unlike a work suitable for Covent Garden or Sadler's Wells, it "could only be effective on more intimate terms" (EL 6/71, May 5, 1950). In Parker's own description, "it is cast so that the stronger acting parts contain little or no singing, while the principal singers have little or no acting, and the central female figure is mute. The music is not continuous but predominates throughout in various forms—a good deal of chorus on and off stage, music behind speech and action, in addition to the normal solos, duets, and ensembles" (EL 6/71, August 17, 1950).

At the third meeting, on December 9, 1949, the judges rejected 11 more projects, leaving just 11 to be considered further plus Rankl's *Deirdre*, already passed. By this time it was no longer possible to abide by the original timetable, which called for substantial excerpts from scores of approved outlines to be submitted by December 30th. The judges, however, by requesting the music they needed when they wanted it, had rendered that separate formal step largely unnecessary. A meeting was set for January 20, 1950, at which they expected to make the final decisions on the combined round one and round two. Believing that the judges' work was almost at an end, the Arts Council authorized payment of the first £100 of their fee, with the remainder to be paid upon the successful completion of the scheme.

Composers had been permitted to submit more than one outline, so long as they used the same pseudonym. It was noticed at the December meeting that two of the projects still in the running, *The Sleeping Beauty* and *The Tinners of Cornwall*, were by the same composer (Inglis Gundry, although the judges only had access to pseudonyms). Since the ranks were thinning, and no composer could be offered more than one commission, the judges directed White to ask the composer to concentrate on the latter project. As requested, Gundry withdrew *The Sleeping Beauty* from the scheme in December 1949. Unfortunately, *The Tinners of Cornwall* too was eliminated along with four other projects at the January 20, 1950 meeting. This left only six projects: Rankl's *Deirdre of the Sorrows*, Arthur Benjamin's *Tale of Two Cities*, based on the Dickens novel, Alan Bush's *Wat Tyler*, about the 1381 English Peasants' Revolt, Berthold Goldschmidt's *Beatrice Cenci*, after Shelley's verse drama set in Renaissance Italy, and two biographical operas, Lennox Berkeley's *Nelson*, which focuses on the admiral's affair with Emma Hamilton, and Wilfred Mellers's *Tragicall History of Christopher Marlowe.* From Bush and Berkeley, the judges requested more music. The judges appear to have had particular difficulty with Bush's operatic technique or with the musical style of his opera because after inspecting the first part of the score that Bush sent, they requested four more sections of full score over the following nine months before making their final decision.[2] With regard to the other four projects, they found themselves not quite ready to make their commissioning decisions yet. Presumably all the judges had to consider all the materials for all the remaining operas, which took some time.

At some point in the judging process, especially in these late stages when there were so few scores being considered so carefully, the anonymity of the composers must have eroded. This was in a way inevitable; the musical world in Great Britain was small and it was unlikely that prominent figures like the judges would not know what kind of operatic projects the major composers in the land were working on. Rankl, for instance, was the Musical Director of the Covent Garden Opera, where Dent served as a member of the Trust, and which hired Wilson as Assistant

General Administrator in March 1950. Unless Rankl had toiled away on *Deirdre of the Sorrows* in complete secrecy, never mentioning it to David Webster or anyone else, word of its existence could easily have reached the judges' ears independently of the Arts Council scheme. Similarly, in this period Benjamin was being actively promoted by Boosey and Hawkes; in spring 1950, on the eve of his receiving a commission, the publisher's house journal *Tempo* published an issue dedicated largely to Benjamin including an article by Dennis Arundell, "Arthur Benjamin's Operas", which included a glowing report of the new "Romantic Melodrama", *A Tale of Two Cities*; again, it is likely that at some point before this one or more of the judges may have heard tell of Benjamin's current operatic project. Goldschmidt's *Beatrice Cenci* took its subject and some of its musical material from his 1948 incidental music for a BBC radio production of Shelley's play, which any of the judges might have heard, and which Wilson in his capacity as Music Director of the BBC almost certainly reviewed in some form before broadcast. And Bush was Professor of Composition at the Royal Academy of Music, as well as an active composer and conductor in the field of worker's music; his work on *Wat Tyler* was probably known by some of his associates in those fields.

The anonymity of some of the composers was further breached by the unsigned September 25, 1949 article in the *Sunday Times*, mentioned in Chapter 3, which included Bush's *Wat Tyler* and Berkeley's *Nelson* in its list of operatic projects then underway (EL6/71, September 25, 1949). According to a letter written by Eric Walter White two days later, the Arts Council did not supply information to the newspaper for the article, and was embarrassed that it mentioned two of the projects being considered anonymously (EL6/61, September 27, 1949).

Beyond the spread of rumors of composers' activities, the judges' close study of the scores of the works probably afforded them considerable stylistic clues; perhaps not in the case of Rankl, who was completely unknown as a composer, but likely in the cases of Goldschmidt, Benjamin, Berkeley, and Bush, who were all published and performed composers with distinct stylistic features that one or more of the judges could easily have recognized. Steuart Wilson admitted as much in his May 5, 1950 interim report to Ernest Pooley, chairman of the Arts Council, but he assured Pooley that such information had not been shared:

> I should mention that, owing to various circumstances, notices in the Press, recognition of handwriting, etc., it has been impossible for some of the Panel not to be aware of the identity of some of the composers. But at no time has all the Panel been aware of this until after a decisive judgment had been passed.
> (EL6/71, May 5, 1950)

Even if, as Wilson implied, the judges did not share the names of the composers whom they recognized with one another, once the decision was made to commission a work and the composer's name could be officially "unsealed", its revelation probably did not particularly surprise any of the judges.

After the January 20, 1949 meeting there was a three-month gap in the proceedings. When the judges met again on April 20, 1950, the score of *Christopher*

Marlowe was still circulating, so the judges could not yet reach a decision on it. They also remained uncertain about *Wat Tyler*, and asked for more musical material from its composer. The discussion of *Nelson* was more contentious: With Wilson not voting because he was chairman, all the judges except Lambert agreed to reject it, but Lambert, who could not be present at the meeting, was a strong supporter of the work. The judges therefore rejected it pending Lambert's consent, which amounted to postponing final judgment.

At this April meeting, however, the judges decided to offer commissions for the three other projects: *Deirdre of the Sorrows*, *A Tale of Two Cities*, and *Beatrice Cenci*. Wilson's May 2, 1950 report to White announced the decisions on these three scores, and listed only *Wat Tyler* and *Christopher Marlowe* as still under consideration, apparently assuming that *Nelson* was as good as rejected. Significantly, he stated that of the remaining two only one would probably pass.

When White revealed the three chosen composers' names, the Arts Council found itself facing a bizarre and completely unexpected problem: Arguably, not one was British. Rankl and Goldschmidt were both refugees working as conductors in London: Rankl a liberal Austrian with a Jewish wife, Goldschmidt himself a German Jew. Benjamin, although British-trained, was by birth Australian. Although the terms of the scheme had explicitly opened it to foreign composers who had established permanent residence in Britain, these results could constitute an embarrassment to the Arts Council. The scheme was part of the plans for the Festival of *Britain*, after all, a fairly parochial festival celebrating British achievement and the British way of life. If the Arts Council announced festival opera commissions not one of which was awarded to a British composer, critics and the press could take it as a unwitting demonstration of British ineptitude in the field of opera rather than the artistic triumph intended. The entire scheme risked becoming a publicity disaster.

White's April 24, 1950 note to Wilson, which officially revealed the composers' identities to the panel of judges, demonstrates that these worries were on the minds of people at the Arts Council. The three operas remaining under consideration were all by "properly" English composers: Bush, Berkeley, and Mellers. Officially, Wilson could not know this, but White wrote to ask whether the Arts Council should announce the winners or wait for the last decisions, commenting:

> In some ways I think it may be desirable for us to give publicity to the commissioned operas as soon as possible; but I realize that if there is to be a fourth commissioned opera *and its composer happens to have an English name*, it may be preferable to hold up press publicity until we can include him as well as the three composers mentioned above.
> (EL6/71, April 24, 1950, emphasis added)

White's concern, unjust as it may appear to us today, was not without basis. In the years after the Second World War, British musical organizations' attempts to incorporate immigrants generated occasional bursts of public disapproval. Karl Rankl himself suffered press attacks, although when he was appointed in 1947, the Covent Garden Opera did not yet hold a position of great importance in British musical culture. The same year, however, the appointment of Rudolf Schwarz as conductor of the Bournemouth Municipal Orchestra—an established English provincial institution—sparked a firestorm of criticism. With the Britishness of such figures an undecided question in the musical culture, White had every reason to fear a similar uproar over "English" opera commissions.

John Denison registered his agreement with White's caution on a routing slip attached to the note, and it is clear that Wilson concurred as well. His May 5, 1950 Interim Report to Ernest Pooley summarized the progress of the scheme up to that point. Wilson briefly described the panel's working procedures and then recommended the three passed scores for official Arts Council commissions. He also listed two of the other three pieces—now, strangely, *Wat Tyler* and *Nelson*—as "operas which require more scrutiny". (It is not clear why he left out *Christopher Marlowe* this time, when he had left out *Nelson* in his note to White three days earlier; the switch may have been simply a slip.) Finally, he recommended "that the composers of the first three operas be informed in confidence that they may proceed; but that no public announcement be made until the whole list be made public. It is likely that the total number will be four only" (EL6/71, May 5, 1950).

On May 23, 1950, the Arts Council sent letters to Benjamin, Goldschmidt, and Rankl, informing them of the offer to commission their operas. Since the entire scheme was running late, the date by which the full score was due to be delivered was extended to December 31, 1950. The first £100 of the £300 commissioning fee would be paid upon the composers' acceptance of their commissions, with the remainder paid upon delivery of the completed full score. Although the composer would retain copyright, performing, and all ancillary rights, the Arts Council reserved the right, as stated in the announcement, to nominate the first performance for a period of two years after the delivery date. The Arts Council could not guarantee such performances, but would "naturally do their best to bring about such a production" (EL6/71, May 8, 1950).

All three composers accepted their commissions. Goldschmidt, who had continued his work, had already completed the full score of *Beatrice Cenci* in April, and, with the support of the commission, set about arranging a read-through of the work with piano and a few singers at the Arts Council. (The Arts Council from time to time made its salon available, and even helped arrange and pay for such auditions of new works for conductors or other individuals who might choose to program them.) Rankl wrote that he expected to complete the score to *Deirde of the Sorrows* over the summer, before the new opera season at Covent Garden began. Benjamin, however, was leaving for Australia and wrote that he would not have time to complete *A Tale of Two Cities* by the end of the year. He therefore asked for an extension into the following year. He also wrote that he had already played the score first to Rankl alone (in the latter's capacity as Musical Director of the Covent Garden Opera) and later to Rankl and David Webster (the General Administrator of the Covent Garden Opera, and Rankl's boss), both of whom had expressed interest in the work.

130 *The opera commissioning scheme*

Meanwhile, the three last scores were still under consideration by the judges. The judges met on June 22, 1950 to review the new portions of music received from Bush, and as a result recommended *Wat Tyler* also for a fourth commission. Apparently believing that the remaining two scores would not result in positive decisions, or simply recognizing the lateness of the season, the judges urged the Arts Council to make a formal statement of the four winners at this point. The press release on Saturday July 1, 1950 (in time to be picked up by the widely read Sunday papers) listed the composers and librettists of the four commissioned operas as well as the members of the panel of judges. It mentioned the terms of the commissions offered to the composers, and revealed that two other works were under consideration without giving any further detail.

The judges met again on November 22, 1950 to consider the status of the various outstanding projects. They accepted Goldschmidt's full score and authorized the final payment to him. Rankl had submitted the complete vocal score, and the judges granted him an extension until the end of February 1951 to deliver the orchestral score. At the next meeting, in early March 1951, the judges accepted the final score of *Deirdre of the Sorrows*. Benjamin and Bush also delivered their full scores during the course of the year.

Additional outcomes

After the public announcement of the four commissions in July 1950, the two remaining works, *Christopher Marlowe* and *Nelson*, continued to cause disagreement among the judges for 20 months. The judges asked for revisions to *Christopher Marlowe*, and gave Mellers until September 30th to produce a new version of the portion he had submitted. Mellers, whose summer school teaching plans would have to be rearranged to meet this deadline, wrote to White on June 30th asking for reassurance that the judges were not just stringing him along, that there was still a genuine chance of his receiving a commission (EL6/71, June 30, 1950). White replied reassuringly on July 3rd and agreed to meet with Mellers at the Arts Council offices to talk over the situation in person. When the judges met again on November 22, 1950 no final decision could be made, because two judges still had to consider the revised score. After a long delay, the judges met in early March 1951, and rejected the work.

As for *Nelson*, Lambert succeeded in convincing the other judges not to reject the work right away. It was not accidental that he was the champion of Berkeley's opera. Berkeley was a student of Nadia Boulanger and was influenced by and friendly with Ravel and Poulenc. The only active composer on the panel, and the youngest member by 16 years, Lambert admired French music as well as elements of the neoclassicism of composers such as Stravinsky. He was thus in sympathy with Berkeley's musical style, where the other judges simply disliked it or found it unsuitably light for the life of Britain's great Admiral. Despite Lambert's advocacy, the other judges remained dubious that *Nelson* could be adapted sufficiently to overcome their objections to Berkeley's music and dramaturgy.

On June 26, 1950 Wilson sent White a letter, the substance of which was to be passed on to Berkeley, explaining the judges' concerns (EL6/71, June 26, 1951). If the composer was willing to undertake major revisions, Wilson wrote, then the judges would extend the time limit and give him very detailed criticism. Wilson described the changes to be called for as "radical", but gave no indications of their scope and nature. If, he said, the composer and librettist were satisfied with what they were working with now, there was no point in proceeding. Berkeley wrote back to White on July 2nd expressing a keen interest in the judges' advice, but not promising to change everything according to the judges' demands. Therefore, dropping the pretense of anonymity, Berkeley met with Wilson on July 30th to review the judges' detailed criticisms. On August 23rd, Berkeley submitted a revised portion of Act 1 of *Nelson*, along with a letter thanking Wilson for the criticisms, but taking exception to some of them. Unfortunately, the archival correspondence about these revisions contain no musical detail.

At the November 22, 1950 meeting it was reported that Berkeley was considering the criticisms further and would resubmit the opera at the end of the year. Either Berkeley worked more slowly than he had originally projected or else the judges demanded still more from him, for at the meeting in early March 1951 when they rejected *Christopher Marlowe* the judges did not come to a consensus on *Nelson*. The possibility of a commission was kept open, with the promised revised version due by June 25, 1951. In May, Berkeley responded that he could not have the revisions done until the end of August, and Wilson, acting on behalf of the judges' panel, granted him a further extension, to September 1, 1951.

Since the scheme had not officially been wrapped up, the judges had never received their final payment of £75. In August 1951, with only *Nelson* left to decide on, the Arts Council authorized payment of £65 of this amount, with the last £10 payable when the final decision was made. Then, on August 29, 1951, Constant Lambert, who had been Berkeley's most ardent supporter on the panel, died suddenly. Berkeley finally delivered the complete first act of the revised score in November 1951, and it began to circulate among the remaining judges. They did not review the work in full and report on it until February 13, 1952. Wilson was inclined to favor it, but as the chairman of the panel, he did not cast a vote. The remaining three judges, Austin, Collingwood, and Dent, remained opposed to commissioning the opera, and without Lambert to champion it, they rejected it. Berkeley had labored on it for almost three years.

In addition to the four completed commissions and the two runners-up, the opera commissioning scheme had a curious additional outcome. In mid-July 1950, Eric Walter White wrote to Anne Wood, the secretary of the English Opera Group, to ask if the EOG would be able to help the Arts Council organize play-throughs of the four winning operas. This idea went nowhere, since Britten didn't like it, Benjamin feared that it might put off serious offers from other companies, and Bush could probably get his opera read without such help. But since the announcement of the winners had mentioned that the scores were chosen from "over 60 submissions," Benjamin Britten and the administration of the English Opera Group became curious about the rejected works. Doubting the wisdom of

132 The opera commissioning scheme

the panel of judges, and suspecting that a reasonable work for the English Opera Group might lie among the rejects, Britten had Wood request a list of the submissions from the Arts Council. White and Wilson agreed that to release the list of rejected projects would be unwise, since to do so might suggest that the panel of judges was incompetent and that the money for the scheme had been wasted. (This was probably precisely what Britten meant to suggest.) White demurred, using the anonymous submission process as a pretext, and in a July 27, 1950 memo to White, Wilson wryly proposed that the English Opera Group should advertise their own competition "and await the 50 operas that would descend on them". He did however suggest that White cautiously mention Clifton Parker's *Aucassin and Nicolette*—which had so impressed the judges—to the English Opera Group, without revealing the composer at first. White did so, describing but not identifying the work, and on September 11, 1950 Anne Wood wrote back to White, turning down the work, but mentioning that Britten was "on the track of one or two operas". The English Opera Group had in fact commissioned Brian Easdale's one-act opera *The Sleeping Children*, which the judges had disqualified. The EOG scheduled it for their 1950 summer season, but the plans to produce it that year fell through as it was not ready in time (EL4/95, March 29, 1950). The English Opera Group gave the premiere during the Festival season.

White's final report on the scheme, submitted to the Arts Council as Paper 322, contained a number of general final comments. He defended the process of elimination and its results, even though some of the rejected projects had received productions—as we have seen, Peter Tranchell's *Mayor of Casterbridge* had received its premiere in an amateur production in Cambridge during the Festival of Britain, and Egon Wellesz's *Incognita*, based on a novel by Congreve, had been similarly mounted by the amateurs of the Oxford University Opera Club in December 1951 (Routh 1972: 166n). White also opined that, given the rectitude of the judges, the provision of anonymity had been unnecessary, especially since it had been impossible to preserve in any case. White's final comments were the most significant:

> I think that experience shows that we were wrong to launch this scheme when we were unable to guarantee production of any of the winning operas. This vital defect has cast a slight air of gloom over the proceedings. The composers of the four commissioned operas have, it is true, each received £300; but it has certainly cost them more than this in time, material, etc., to compose their operas, and in no case at the present moment is a production probable.
> (EL4/55, March 19, 1952)

Denison, in a February 18, 1953 letter to Rudolf Bing (by then the General Manager of the Metropolitan Opera), echoed White's sentiments:

> My own personal criticisms of our Festival scheme centre round the fact that we were unable, in the event, to guarantee stage production of any of the four works which received awards. While it was made quite clear in the

announcements and conditions that we could offer no such guarantee, the disappointment of composers and the interested public was most marked because even though they received their fees for composition, this was, comparatively speaking, cold comfort compared with the satisfaction of seeing a production staged. Indeed, I would recommend to anyone contemplating a similar scheme that money should be set aside to cover costs of production of the chosen work as an integral part of the scheme.

(ACGB 51/75)

As it turned out, the "gloom" White wrote of lasted far beyond 1952. For operas chosen in such a high-profile campaign, at such an apparently auspicious time, the four winning works had notably unsuccessful careers.

Criteria of judgment

Before turning to the operas chosen by the Festival of Britain opera commissioning scheme and their unfortunate histories, it is worthwhile to consider the aesthetic and formal criteria that the judges brought to their deliberations. Archival documents provide only limited evidence of the kinds of projects that they valued. Their working procedure seems to have been to bring written or mental notes to the meetings, discuss the projects, and make decisions by consensus, which Wilson then reported in the simplest form to White. Other than the overall positive or negative judgments, no minutes appear to have been taken at the meetings, and any extant handwritten notes and final reports of the judges may remain only among their own, or Steuart Wilson's private papers. Some generalizations can be made, however, from the anomalous cases in which judges' reports remain in the Arts Council files and from the characteristics of the winners and runners-up.

A few surviving memoranda detailing the judges' opinions of a work give us a closer look at the kind of reasoning they employed. The letter from Steuart Wilson to Eric Walter White reporting the results of the April 1950 judges meeting contained the following addendum concerning the submission of Albert H. Coates:

> *The Boy David* is rejected because the Panel felt that the nature of the operatic handling was incompatible from the beginning with the material of the story, i.e., that the boyish figure of David could not be represented successfully with the quality of music and the weight of scoring which the composer has put into it.
>
> (EL6/71, April 25, 1950)

Without examining Coates's score, there is no way to determine specifically what the judges deemed objectionable, and this comment is very brief and can only represent a part of the judges' thinking. Still, it is notable that Wilson does not impugn the inherent quality of Coates's music; rather he reports the judges to have found it too heavy and inappropriate for J. M. Barrie's tale of a biblical shepherd boy. The comment implies that the judges were not necessarily prejudiced in favor of massive or profound works, as one might expect given the national stature of the competition. In their work they took care to consider the suitability of musical style to the operatic subject. A lighter treatment of Coates's subject might have done better.

The final report on Berkeley's *Nelson* provides a more detailed look at the judges' preoccupations. This document, which is filed along with White's draft of the final report on the entire scheme, is the only substantial report on any project. It reads in part:

Austin:

1. The portrayal of Nelson's character tends to weaken the work as a whole in weakening the central character. The work lacks distinction.
2. Musical types generally apt—musical working out often casual and inconclusive. Some fluctuations in literary level and some imperfect word-settings and accentuation.
3. In spite of work done on it, the main features remain as before. Characters do not come to life. Music more varied and singable: modern in style but casual and rambling, lacking in strength and originality.

Collingwood:

1. Although he seems to have the right ideas in setting words to notes and displays interesting rhythms occasionally, he has no sense of harmony and the whole in my mind is horrible.
2. Not in sympathy with this kind of music. Harsh and dissonant, or commonplace. Dramatic situations are treated well, recitatives always to the point. Words—though sometimes awkward for setting—are nearly always treated effectively.
3. In all honesty—with the disadvantage of knowing who the composer is—I cannot recommend this work for selection.

Dent:

1. Author counts too much on general familiarity with the story. Result is a series of operatic conventions which would produce the same sort of music whoever the characters were. The real historical persons are reduced to mere opera singers.
2. The music sometimes fits the words so badly that I should suspect the composer of not being an Englishman. Dull in itself, what is meant for recitative is incorrectly declaimed, what is meant for aria is unattractive in melody.
3. I have tried to reconsider this opera in view of Lambert's very divergent criticism, but I am still not very favourably impressed with either the libretto or the music. (recommendations follow which were passed on to the composer).
4. This act has been very thoroughly reconstructed, to its great improvement.

The composer seems to have a keen eye for what is "operatic" and conventionally effective, and to be rather indifferent to character drawing. The best parts of the opera are generally those which show evidence of hard labour.

(In the covering letter Dent says: "I don't like it myself but I suppose we ought to accept the opera for an award and the improvement of this Act I is so remarkable that we may hope for more improvement in the following Acts.")

Lambert:

1. I am quite at a loss to understand why the other Judges have dismissed "Nelson" in so summary a fashion. It has freshness, invention and a genuine musicality. I feel most strongly that the other Judges should look at this work again. In my opinion it has great potentialities.

N.B. The following paragraphs refer to the un-revised version of Nelson:- Austin—1 and 2; Collingwood—1; Dent—1, 2, and 3; Lambert—1. The following paragraphs refer to the revised version:- Austin—3; Collingwood—2; Dent—4.

(EL6/71, February 20, 1952)

It is a shame that Dent's detailed recommendations and Lambert's vigorous defense of the piece (most probably never written down) are not preserved. Yet what we have brings to light some of the issues and criteria that concerned the judges. Musical style was understandably a central concern. As one might expect, the judges reacted to Berkeley's music on the level of personal taste, but in general—and ironically given their rejection of Coates's score—they seem to have applied operatic norms derived from the romantic repertory, with its larger forms and full-bodied expression. Thus, while they could countenance the density and intensity of Goldschmidt's musical style, the relative sparseness and occasional emotional distancing of Berkeley's, betraying the influence of Stravinsky and neoclassicism, bewildered them. Austin judged it indifferently modern, "casual and rambling"; Collingwood found it horrible. Lambert, of course, the only serious composer on the panel, and himself a devotee of Stravinsky, deemed Berkeley's score fresh and genuinely musical.

Beyond this, two overall dramatic questions arose: Austin and Dent observed general deficiencies in the musical depiction and differentiation of character. They may have found the absence of Germanic markers of profundity in Berkeley's style incommensurate with the plot's potential for heroic action. Indeed, Dent's comment that "the real historical persons are reduced to mere opera singers" suggests that he may have taken mild offense at the ironic deflation of the mythic Admiral into a conventional operatic lover, mooning over his Emma as he dies on board the *Victory*. On the other hand, Collingwood along with Dent noted Berkeley's skill in handling larger situations. Presumably they were referring to the choral scenes and moments of high drama, where individual characterizations was less important.

Almost all the judges addressed word-setting, and noted lapses in prosody. But since they had reviewed and advanced a portion of the libretto earlier, when they judged the librettos of dozens of other projects unfit, Austin and Dent's reservations about the quality of the libretto have only limited relevance. Even so, Collingwood ("right ideas . . . and . . . interesting rhythms", "recitatives always to the point") and Austin ("singable") equivocated where Dent condemned completely.

This heavy attention on word-setting seems to signal real lapses on Berkeley's part, but, given the limited and idiosyncratic repertory of English opera, there really was no firm tradition of English operatic prosody for composers to draw on or for critics to use as a basis of comparison. There certainly were no flexible rules of word-setting, of the type developed in the Italian language, with its vastly longer and fuller operatic history. By the forties there was a long tradition of English song, oratorio, choral symphony, and cantata, but, in the words of Philip Brett (1983: 149), "English writing for the voice has been dominated by strict subservience to logical speech-rhythms, despite the fact that accentuation according to sense often contradicts the accentuation demanded by emotional content." In reviewing Berkeley's score, Dent in particular seems to have applied rigidly academic standards of English prosody rooted in the 19th and early 20th centuries.

The model for Berkeley's word-setting that the judges did not perceive or refused to acknowledge was Benjamin Britten. In his vocal works, Britten had abandoned the meticulous if often dull English adherence to word stress and vowel length, and turned to Purcell's and Dowland's songs, with their individual approach to word-setting and sometimes florid melismas. Berkeley, a friend and musical associate of Britten's, held similar opinions and joined him in thoughtful experimentation in this area.

Revealing as this limited document is, we should not assume that it represents the judges' working methods in totality. The comments on *Nelson* necessarily focus on those elements of the work that struck the judges as problematic; other works no doubt prompted different kinds of critiques. Furthermore, their prolonged disagreement and discussion about Berkeley's opera may have produced a lengthier and more articulate response than the relatively quick decisions on other works.

Of the six winners and runners-up, the Rankl and Mellers scores are unpublished. According to Lewis Foreman (personal communication, 2000), who recovered the score from a BBC rubbish bin and arranged broadcast of several excerpts, Karl Rankl's *Deirdre of the Sorrows* moves fluidly among a number of different styles, encompassing both lyrical tonal passages and 12-tone writing in the manner of Rankl's teachers, Schoenberg and Webern.

The truly mysterious score is Mellers's *Tragicall History of Christopher Marlowe*, which has never been performed. It obviously concerned the life of the Elizabethan playwright, and probably ended with his murder, but Mellers withdrew the work and appears later to have destroyed the manuscript, so questions of how it presented this material must remain unanswered.[3] Mellers's one published comment on the score reveals that, logically enough given the period of the drama, his musical idiom derived in part from Tudor models, but nothing else is known about the work:

> I chose as the theme the life of Christopher Marlowe, closely relating him to his own Faustus, and treating his story as a parable of the conflict between the Middle Ages and the modern world—a conflict in the wake of which we still live. This seemed to me to be a subject that had its roots in our past and was relevant to our present; to be a violently dramatic theme based on a physical and moral tension, giving opportunities for both a realistic and an allegorical treatment; and to be nothing if not rhetorical. For better or worse, I think this has come out in the music which, whatever its value as music, is certainly theatrically "effective." Yet although theatrically sophisticated and rhetorical, the idiom has, I think, a relation to the Elizabethan tradition in that it depends on a kind of multiple modality—an extension of the device of false relation. This was not a conscious contrivance—I noticed it only in retrospect.
> (Mellers 1952: 195)

This leaves four scores for scrutiny: those of Benjamin, Berkeley, Bush, and Goldschmidt. It is clear that disagreements between judges with very different tastes and strongly-held beliefs about operatic propriety made the opera scheme more contentious than the guiding of London concert programs or commissioning of concert works, and in any case four such varied large-scale works provide limited evidence for broad generalization. Nevertheless, they share certain stylistic and structural traits; as with other Festival musical projects, the opera commissioning scheme staked out a broad aesthetic middle-ground. All adhere to mid-century stylistic norms, fundamentally tonal and triadic at base, but loosed from the strictures of functional common-practice harmony and with large admixtures of polytonalism or free chromaticism. This is still a very broad field. Bush's style in *Wat Tyler* tends to be heavily modal—locally diatonic but shifting rapidly among key areas. Benjamin wrote in a popular and tuneful idiom on the borders of what the BBC classed as "light music"; *A Tale of Two Cities* is more polytonal than *Wat Tyler* but with clearer functional harmonies for the lyrical moments. Goldschmidt wrote *Beatrice Cenci* in a chromatic style with considerable contrapuntal and motivic development, as befit his German conservatory training—he had been a student of Schreker in Berlin. Berkeley largely maintained his French-derived harmonic clarity and lightness of melodic touch and orchestral color in *Nelson*. Although all the operas have self-contained lyrical passages (such as arias, strophic songs, and choruses), in every case entire scenes or acts are through-composed, the numbers flowing one into another, and all four composers bind their scores together with a system of motives which represent characters or ideas. It is likely that other submissions from conservatory-trained composers fell within a similar stylistic universe.

Although arguably the judges did not represent the foremost trends in contemporary British music of the day, the overall level of professionalism and sophistication of style in the finalists shows the panel's commitment to a certain modernity of style and musical construction. Given the traditionalism of much British musical taste and the huge number of submissions from composers who had not benefitted from study of more complex practices, the judges undoubtedly rejected many far more conservative submissions. Not a single score in a strictly functional, common-practice style organized into individual numbers with distinct melodies and keys—not even a relatively sophisticated version of this style such as is found in George Lloyd's *John Socman*—survived the initial stages of the scheme.

Still, much like the Arts Council functionaries who organized the London Season of the Arts and placed the commissions for concert music, the opera judging panel had its limits when it came to stylistic open-mindedness. They were most impressed by moderately contemporary idioms that could still be appreciated by an audience untutored in the more extreme modernisms. If its 12-tone passages are substantial, Rankl's *Deirdre of the Sorrows* would be evidence of significant breadth: the only 12-tone work commissioned by the Arts Council in the Festival. But Rankl's score is not readily available, and the judges rejected *The Life of the Insects*, the proposal submitted by Humphrey Searle, who was beginning to write in a 12-tone style in the late forties.

The judges seem to have been more comfortable with odd harmonies than with odd plots. Without access to the judges' notes it is impossible to ascertain whether they objected chiefly to the musical style of Searle's project, but its rather peculiar title highlights another element shared by the winners and runners-up: They all treat a traditionally narrative subject—there are no modernistic dramatic experiments. The range of subjects, to be sure, is fairly wide: Bush's opera treats a historical, medieval peasant uprising, while Benjamin's condenses Dickens's classic novel of an English family caught up in the French revolution. Berkeley and Mellers worked with their librettists to craft operas out of the lives of famous Englishmen, one a military leader (portrayed equally as a romantic lover) and the other a playwright and spy. Rankl and Goldschmidt adapted existing plays, the one a somber Irish family drama, the other a gruesome tale of incest and revenge set in the Italian Renaissance. But none of these subjects, not even the potentially shocking subject of *Beatrice Cenci*, is out of place on the opera stage, which regularly features violent conflict, murder, and suicide. Decades after works like Arnold Schoenberg's *Erwartung* or Paul Hindemith's *Hin und zurück*, and countless other operatic experiments on the continent, no project featuring modernist dramaturgical hijinks or surrealist, absurdist, symbolist, or other non-realist narrative techniques made it through to the final rounds. This fact probably bespeaks both the judges' dramaturgical traditionalism and the applicants' lack of theatrical sophistication, although details of most of the proposed operas are unavailable. As discussed in Chapter 3, the libretto of at least one disqualified work, Brian Easdale's *Sleeping Children*, does not follow ordinary realistic dramatic logic, but rather operates on the level of psychological symbolism.

More complicated is the question of the judges' expectations for, and reactions to, the scores' English qualities. One contemporary point of view might have held that a competition for British composers (however defined) mounted for the Festival of Britain should honor operas that were in an appreciable sense British. It would appear that the judges did not apply this standard in a superficial way, with respect either to subject matter or musical style. It is likely that, if queried on the topic, they all would have claimed to have set aside such parochial considerations. But it seems that two different sets of positive qualities led the judges to their final decisions, as revealed by two brief comments in other notes of Steuart Wilson's, on the occasion of the first three commissions:

> [W]e thought it necessary to distinguish between works of very high musical merit which would possibly not find a ready market in the Opera House, and works whose chief merit lay in their "sense of the theatre."
>
> (EL6/71, May 5, 1950)

> [*Deirdre of the Sorrows*] and [*Beatrice Cenci*] have been accepted as much on their intellectual value as for their music; as [*A Tale of Two Cities*] is accepted on its potential stage value.
>
> (EL6/71, April 25, 1950)

The judges could not have failed to deduce that the scores of *Deirdre of the Sorrows* and *Beatrice Cenci* were written not by British-trained composers, but by immigrants armed with full modernist German training. The speed with which the judges came to consensus on these two works suggest that they applied a different standard to them, impressed by their sophisticated continental styles, harmonic and contrapuntal mastery, and perhaps by their engagement with psychologically complex plots. Although the judges deemed them stageworthy, it may not be excessive to read into Wilson's comment doubts as to their viability with English audiences.

By contrast, the bitter stylistic disagreements over the remaining "properly English" works suggest that there the stakes were higher, even if the judges were not consciously aware of applying a double standard. Wilson's note seems to cast Benjamin's opera as a lightweight, at least by comparison to German sophistication. No doubt the panel judged the work competently crafted, but it is also a more guaranteed crowd-pleaser, based after all on the perennially popular and sentimentally sensational Dickens novel. Bush's *Wat Tyler* although not specifically mentioned in Wilson's note (it had not yet been commissioned), is of a similarly popular cast.

Not wanting to be accused of either pandering or picking involved scores that only musicians could appreciate, the panel may have hedged its bets with its final selections; this amounted to passing the problem up to White and Denison, who had to worry about public opinion. More generously, one could argue that the four commissions testify to the seriousness with which the panel approached its task, in that they saw their role as recognizing different types of quality in the operas they selected.

Attempts to secure performance

The four composers awarded with commissions by the Arts Council represent a curious mix. Karl Rankl (1898–1968), the embattled Musical Director of the Covent Garden Opera Company, was a student of Schoenberg and Webern. As a conductor, he had worked his way up through the ranks in opera companies in eastern Europe before escaping to England after the German invasion of Czechoslovakia, but he was completely unperformed and unknown as a composer in Britain or, indeed, anywhere else. During his lifetime Rankl composed eight symphonies, few of which were ever performed, and numerous other orchestral and vocal works. Berthold Goldschmidt (1903–1996) was a German immigrant earning his keep as a conductor. In Germany he had a number of major compositions and performances, including one opera production (*Der gewaltige Hahnrei*), to his name, but little recognition in Britain. Arthur Benjamin (1893–1960), a student of Charles Stanford at the Royal College of Music from 1912 to 1914, and a resident of London since 1921, had seen his two comic one-act operas produced in London in 1931 (*The Devil Take Her*) and 1949 (*Prima donna*) with some success and was a regular presence on British concert programs.

Alan Bush (1900–1994) was a graduate of the Royal Academy of Music, where he served as Professor of Composition from 1925. Although *Wat Tyler* was his first opera, he was known in the world of English music both because of his Royal Academy connections (which doubtless resulted in a certain regularity of performances, if only by students) and through a number of high-profile commissions and premieres, such as the 1937 piano concerto (a massive and much-praised work with a choral finale, on the model of Busoni's piano concerto), and the 1949 *Nottingham* symphony. The chief feature that distinguished Bush from other English composers of his time, however, was his strongly held political beliefs. Bush was a committed communist and an outspoken supporter of the international workers' movement and Stalin's Soviet Union. His political opinions motivated a large part of his work outside of the Royal Academy and were often woven into his compositions, in the choice of both subjects and texts.

The operas by this disparate group of composers have varying performance histories, but none was particularly successful. In striking contrast to the ambitious hopes of the initiators of the scheme, in the 60 years since the announcement of the results, none of the four operas has ever been produced by a major British opera company. Not long after the announcement of the competition winners, the four composers, as well as critics and historians, began to voice the suspicion that a mixture of political unease and bad blood undercut the attempt to arrange performances:

> That none [of the operas] was performed in Britain at the time inevitably invites speculation: did the fact that of the four commissioned composers only one had been born in Britain, and he an avowed communist, play any role in events?
>
> (Banks 1988: 428)

Given the odd group of composers, none of whom was entirely presentable as an exemplary British composer, it was difficult to portray the scheme as a great success for national opera. During the Festival year especially it was perhaps easier to leave the whole episode unmentioned. In his memoir, Berthold Goldschmidt ascribed the failure of any of the commissioned works to attract a performance squarely to the troubling politics—personal as well as partisan—of the scheme's outcome:

> When [the jury] learned who they had awarded the prizes to, they were thunderstruck: Alan Bush, a communist; Karl Rankl, a fairly unpopular man, who was in a state of war with Lambert; Goldschmidt—I had had some serious arguments with Stewart [sic] Wilson regarding my conducting; and Arthur Benjamin—he came from Australia, so at least from the Commonwealth. The results were therefore not so pleasant from the patriotic point of view, and although the Arts Council had reserved for itself the performance rights to the opera for two years, nothing happened.
> (Goldschmidt 1994: 72)[4]

In this comment, Goldschmidt implied that the Arts Council had deliberately let the winners languish without performance rather than have to support the performance of works politically inappropriate to the national image that the Festival of Britain was trying to project. Of course, as a long-neglected composer, it was in Goldschmidt's interests in his 1994 autobiography to emphasize Britain's terrible parochialism, and thus his own victimization. But others have also repeated this suspicion. Whatever the specific circumstances were which prevented performances in each case, the disparity between the prize-winners and the Festival's image of Britishness was unmistakable.

This is not to say that there was no attempt made to obtain performances, or that the neglect which the commissioned operas suffered went unnoticed. By August 1950 the Arts Council, having run the entire scheme as the cornerstone of their Festival of Britain commissions, had determined that there was little chance any of the winning operas would receive a performance during the Festival. On August 16th, Gerald Barry, the Director General of the Festival of Britain, sent a memo to the Arts Council objecting to this state of affairs:

> We spoke recently about the apparent unlikelihood of any of the four operas which the Arts Council has commissioned in connection with the Festival being produced during the Festival season. I should like to record my dismay. It seems to me a glaring mistake that these operas, or at least some of them, specially appropriated for the purpose, should not be made available to the public until after the Festival is over. I am sure that it will bring the Arts Council and the Festival Office as well (for the uninformed public do not particularise in these matters) in for severe criticism and not a little ridicule. I would strongly urge that the inevitability of this decision should be

immediately questioned and every possible means investigated to enable it to be reversed.

(EL6/61, August 16, 1950)

On August 19, 1950, White responded to Barry's memo (EL6/61). He reminded Barry of the Arts Council's other operatic commissions, which at this point seemed evenly spread over the three existing opera companies: Covent Garden had finally accepted Vaughan Williams's *Pilgrim's Progress* for the Festival season, the Carl Rosa company had accepted George Lloyd's *John Socman*, and Britten's *Billy Budd* was still at this point proposed for Sadler's Wells. The thinking behind the separate commissioning scheme had been to bring to attention operas by composers less established than Vaughan Williams, Britten, and Lloyd, works which would probably not be taken up by the major companies.

White also pointed out that there simply was not time to arrange productions of the winning operas. Under the scheme's original schedule the final scores were not due until September 30, 1950, and that date was now postponed to December 31, 1950. This was far too late for any of the established companies to add a new full-scale work to their 1950–1951 seasons. Even if they attracted immediate interest, the operas could not receive productions until the 1951–1952 season at the earliest. Furthermore, the scheme was lagging behind schedule. True, Goldschmidt delivered the completed score of *Beatrice Cenci* in July 1950, but the other works would not be ready by the revised deadline: Benjamin projected that he would have *A Tale of Two Cities* complete in the spring of 1951, and Bush wasn't expecting to finish orchestrating *Wat Tyler* until Christmas 1951 (although in the event he delivered the full score on March 29) (EL6/70).

All these were good practical reasons, and White, at least, cannot be accused of deliberately dismissing the winning operas. To the extent he could, he worked to get them noticed by performing organizations, although even his advocacy lasted only so long before it was overwhelmed by the crush of his other ongoing commitments such as the elaborate concert plans for the Festival of Britain. In his note, White assured Barry that as the works became available they would be given run-throughs to stimulate the interest of the opera companies. A private reading of *Beatrice Cenci*, which Goldschmidt had completed in short score, had taken place as early as July 3, 1950, only one day after the public announcement of his commission (EL6/73). (Goldschmidt himself had learned of the commission in May.) *Beatrice Cenci* received another, more public, audition on December 3, 1950. On November 26, 1950 an audition of *Wat Tyler* was given with piano accompaniment. *A Tale of Two Cities* fared differently. On several occasions Benjamin or the Arts Council began to plan a reading—one with small chorus, soloists, and a small ensemble almost occurred in early 1952—but due to bad timing or concern over the great expense, none ever occurred (EL6/69). There is no evidence that any reading of *Deirdre of the Sorrows* ever took place, but Rankl would have had any number of opportunities to play it for David Webster at Covent Garden.

In the meantime, if stage productions were not likely any time soon, radio broadcasts might be. In November, White approached the BBC about arranging this. In July 1950, Leonard Isaacs, the Head of Music for the Third Programme at the BBC, expressed interest in broadcasting some of the operas as soon as summer 1951 (R27/11/4, EL6/70). In November, White responded that only Goldschmidt's score was already available, but White promised to pass along the others as they became available. Goldschmidt expressed delight at the opportunity and Bush also agreed, but the other composers were not happy with this compromise. Both Rankl and Benjamin expressed the desire for stage rather than broadcast premieres of their works. The Arts Council therefore passed on scores of *Wat Tyler* and *Beatrice Cenci* to the BBC music reading panel, where they languished for months. Although it seems that Rankl and Benjamin eventually relented, and that the Arts Council passed on their scores to the BBC as well some months later, there is no record that the BBC panel reviewed *Deirdre of the Sorrows* and *A Tale of Two Cities* at this time.

The first internal BBC reviewers' reports on *Wat Tyler* came from L. David Harris and Leonard Isaacs, who attended the read-through of the work with piano in November 1950. Although both made positive comments about the monologue for John Ball in Act 1, neither found the work particularly impressive overall. Harris condemned the "long stretches of developed declamation, punctuated with set songs of a traditional English flavour" and the dearth of "musical or dramatic development of any idea of the principle characters." Isaacs found the music "dull," "fragmentary," and "dreary," and felt "no musical sympathy with any of the characters." They agreed that the effect was of a "play set to music." When the score arrived at the BBC in April 1951, the readers' reports were more positive. Benjamin Frankel, William Alwyn, and Gordon Jacob all agreed that the work displayed more of the qualities of a cantata than an opera, and was not effective theater; Jacob and Alwyn were slightly put off (as Harris had been) by the work's overtly political expression. But all three advocated the broadcast of excerpts, Frankel praising the work's "lofty style," "great boldness," and "stark splendour," Alwyn the "great sincerity and ... simplicity of style which was often most moving," and Jacob the "passages of beauty and musical value" (R27/556).

Striking in its absence from these reports was any consideration that *Wat Tyler* was a national historical opera. Bush, while working on the project, had declared that it was the first such opera ever to be written (EL6/70, February 7, 1949), and hoped that this distinction would bring the work the attention both of producers and audiences. In typical fashion for the time, however, the BBC reading panel seems to have taken its charge to be evaluation of the score separate from any such contexts. Not one report suggests that an epic operatic treatment of a celebrated and controversial episode in national history might have an inherent interest that could counterbalance perceived flaws in style. This is not to say that the BBC *should* have accepted the work. But, as with the 1951 Proms, the bureaucratic processes at the BBC appear to have excluded creative possibilities, and cast the Arts Council's own ambivalent attempts in a more favorable light by comparison.

The February 1951 readers' reports on *Beatrice Cenci* by the same three composers were more equivocal than those of *Wat Tyler*, praising the score's lyrical moments, dramatic force, and sheer mass of invention, but expressing concerns about the score's "gloomy" tone, dense contrapuntal textures, and failure in vocal characterization (R27/578). After a unproductive prod from White around the same time, Herbert Murrill, the BBC Director of Music, returned Goldschmidt's score with a note which, while it assured the composer that no decision had yet been reached, pointed out the great expense of broadcasting opera, and suggested that only one of the operas would be chosen for broadcast (EL6/70, March 30, 1951). Goldschmidt reacted with alarm, showing the note to White, but John Denison cautioned patience (EL6/70, April 3, 1951). In April, Bush too wrote to White:

> I have still heard nothing definite from the BBC. Mr Leonard Isaacs has assured me that a decision will be made shortly. (In this connection a definition of the word "shortly" might be difficult, but I understand that the advisors of the BBC whose advice has been sought will have completed their examination of the score by the end of the week.)
>
> (EL6/70, April 20, 1951)

In May, admitting that the reading panel was having difficulty reaching a decision about the two operas, Murrill asked Steuart Wilson if the panel could read the competition judges' reports on *Beatrice Cenci* and *Wat Tyler* (the only scores they had in hand). Wilson agreed to pass on the reports, so long as they remained confidential and were not quoted. Finally, on May 17th, Murrill proposed a broadcast of excerpts from each opera:

> I have read very carefully the Panel reports on the two Arts Council commissioned operas submitted to us for possible first performance in our programmes. I have also had a preliminary conversation with you on the reports and (off the record) have discussed earlier reports made by the Arts Council Panel with Sir Steuart Wilson.
>
> The result of all this is that I feel it my duty to recommend that we do not, in the first instance, produce either the Goldschmidt or Alan Bush operas complete. Both are long and the Goldschmidt maintains an atmosphere of tense horror, whereas the Bush appears to have some moments of dramatic and musical dullness. We should probably serve both composers best, besides giving our listeners a more favourable view of the two commissioned works, if we decided to broadcast scenes from each.
>
> If the idea commends itself I will just confirm with the Arts Council that they would consider any obligation of ours to be satisfactorily discharged in the suggested broadcast, and there is, of course, no reason why one, or indeed both, of the operas should not later be mounted in its entirety if the selected scenes provoke enough interest and comment.
>
> (R27/556)

At Murrill's instigation, Leonard Isaacs estimated the cost of broadcasting excerpts from the two works at £850, but the matter then bogged down again (R27/11/5). In July, White queried the BBC again as to the status of their decision, and passed on Goldschmidt's and Bush's agreement to have only excerpts broadcast, but to no avail.

Bush, now attempting to get *Wat Tyler* broadcast in East Germany, wrote to White later in July suggesting glumly that little could be expected from the BBC, which seemed to be hesitating on financial grounds. White and Denison vented their frustration over the BBC's indecision on the confidential routing slip attached to Bush's letter:

> I wish the BBC would have the courage of its convictions, and if it doesn't want to broadcast Wat Tyler and Beatrice Cenci in whole or in part, it would say so! E[ric] W[alter] W[hite]
> As I mentioned to you verbally, there is an internal battle going on in the BBC over this. Murrill (who is ready to do extracts) cannot get agreement from [the] Third Programme controller. Meanwhile he is quite prepared for us to express consternation and frustration over BBC [slowness (?—word unclear)] . . . J[ohn]. D[enison].
> (EL6/70 July 28, 1951)

In September, Rudolf Bing, now the General Manager of the Metropolitan Opera, wrote to Denison commending the score of *Beatrice Cenci* and asking if anything could be done to secure a performance. Denison, seeing the opportunity to put some pressure on the BBC, forwarded the letter to Herbert Murrill in early October. Eric Warr, Murrill's assistant, replied that "the Goldschmidt and Bush operas worry me scarcely less than they worry you." As Denison reported to Bing in November, he then met with Murrill, who turned out to me more sympathetic to the operas than expected, but explained again that he could not sell the idea of the broadcasts to the Third Programme controllers, especially since the score readers had given such poor reports (ACGB 51/75). There the matter seems to have rested.

Eventually, the BBC broadcast all four of the operas in part or in whole, and three of them received stage productions, but this process took decades to unfold. Meanwhile, within the Arts Council, the "slight air of gloom" surrounding the scheme's ambiguous outcome settled into resignation. With the fall of the Labour government in 1951, the plug was pulled unceremoniously on the Festival of Britain. Furthermore, with the advent of another economic crisis government funding for the arts tightened in 1952 and Covent Garden's insolvency generated a new "opera crisis", while at the same time audience growth stagnated, further discouraging untested projects (EL4/76). More than fully occupied with its regular ongoing commitments, the Arts Council soon abandoned its advocacy of the four operas, as lost causes.

With the death of George VI in early 1952, the Arts Council began to gear up for another festival-like production, the gala performances surrounding the coronation of Elizabeth II in 1953. The agency helped to arrange the commission—

by the Covent Garden Opera Company, so that performance was assured—of Britten's *Gloriana*. Although this work, written specifically for the occasion to a libretto by William Plomer based on Lytton Strachey's *Elizabeth and Essex*, was Britten's deliberate attempt at "national opera," it turned out in its own way to be another fiasco for that cause. The Covent Garden premiere became the coronation gala, interrupted by long intermissions for various functions and attended by the young monarch and hundreds of visiting dignitaries and heads of state who were unfamiliar with and uninterested in contemporary opera. Given this inauspicious context, the expectations and demands brought to bear on the work were probably impossible to meet. As a national coronation opera, whose subject was the dynastic glory of Good Queen Bess, it was expected to celebrate the monarchy as a fixed and timeless institution above criticism and to represent what was best in England. Instead, the opera portrayed a less than heroic Elizabeth I with human weaknesses and a measure of spite and political deviousness. The critics, feeling that such a portrayal was inappropriate at the dawn of the "Second Elizabethan Age," were scandalized, and they panned the work. Although the Arts Council was less directly involved, the *Gloriana* disaster probably ended forever the hopes of individuals like Eric Walter White that state institutions like the Arts Council could foster national opera. The Festival competition and commissions became footnotes in British operatic history, and the Arts Council never attempted a competitive commissioning project again.

Arthur Benjamin, *A Tale of Two Cities*

Ironically, although Arthur Benjamin had initially rejected the idea of a radio broadcast and held out for a staged performance, in the end, his was the score that the BBC accepted first. *A Tale of Two Cities* was thus the first of the commissioned operas to receive a performance in Britain. The BBC's decision to give three radio performances of it in April 1953 may have been encouraged by the marketing and promotion of the composer by Boosey and Hawkes, who were similarly successful at arranging performances of Britten's works. It is also true that, of the four winners, Benjamin was the only composer near the mainstream of British concert life, and of the winning operas, his was the lightest in style, the most familiar in plot, and also arguably the most accomplished in its musical dramaturgy.

For an opera with a plot so familiar and so complimentary to Victorian British bourgeois values, *A Tale of Two Cities* at its radio premiere prompted an unusually vitriolic review in the journal *Opera* from Donald Mitchell, who decried "[t]he twin pillars which support the structure of Mr. Cliffe's widely acclaimed libretto . . . Sex and Sadism", and declared "revulsion" at the opera's "abundance of horror": "[W]e don't need to make the trip to the Camden Theatre to learn the truth about the French Revolution; we know that already from our history books, and from the knowledge we possess of the darker side to our own passions. In 1953—despite the gas-chamber and the atom-bomb—we don't enjoy the spectacle of the guillotine in action ('One two chop chop Off goes her head'), and this is about all *A Tale of Two Cities* has to offer us" (Mitchell 1953: 377). (The BBC forces performed the work before a select audience at the Camden Theatre.) Although Mitchell laid most of the blame at the door of the librettist, he faulted Benjamin's weak characterization and lack of "genuine inventiveness". This overblown condemnation was perhaps meant to serve Mitchell's favorite, Britten, whose own new opera, *Gloriana*, slated for premiere at Covent Garden shortly thereafter, might benefit by the comparison.

The radio performances attracted attention and led to a radio performance in Canada in 1954. The first stage production was given at the Sadler's Wells Theatre in July 1957, and again in 1958, by the New Opera Company, a mixed group of amateurs and professionals that started in Cambridge (Arundell 1965: 241). A BBC television production followed in 1958. Since then the work has been revived at various times by amateur groups and music schools.

Goldschmidt, *Beatrice Cenci*

Goldschmidt's *Beatrice Cenci* has little connection with any English tradition, other than the language of its libretto. It is based on Shelley's play *The Cenci*, set in Renaissance Rome, and is written in Goldschmidt's flexibly chromatic but tonally-rooted continental style.[5] Like Benjamin, who showed his score to Rankl and Webster at Covent Garden, Goldschmidt tried to interest several impresarios in his opera, even writing to Rudolf Bing at the Metropolitan Opera in New York in March 1951. Bing, smarting from the financial disaster of the 1948 production of *Peter Grimes*, responded that he could not afford premieres (ACGB 51/75).

A partial reading of the work with narration was originally scheduled for November 26, 1950 for the Opera Circle at the American Women's Club, but when Goldschmidt found out that Bush was planning the reading of *Wat Tyler* for the same evening, he generously postponed his reading a week to December 3rd (EL6/73, 27 October 1950). Although there was no chorus at this reading, it brought the work to the attention of several important figures (Jacobs 1951a: 37). Sadler's Wells considered it, but rejected it, probably on account of its gruesome plot:

> I contacted White many times, and finally he arranged a meeting where we presented the opera with a piano and a few singers. Several people were enthusiastic: Lord Harewood, Vaughan Williams, who, although he praised the music, still thought that the subject was frightful, as bad as *Tosca*.
>
> (Goldschmidt 1994: 72)[6]

As a contemporary report stated, "Shelley's play 'The Cenci' (1819) features murder, torture, incest, and execution in the Italy of 1599. Martin Esselin [sic], who has adapted it, has naturally produced a libretto to stand beside 'Tosca', 'Turandot', and 'Salome' in sadistic depravity" (Jacobs 1951a: 36).[7]

These responses, along with the interminable BBC indecision over whether to broadcast the score or not, were a serious blow to Goldschmidt, who although he had resided in Britain for 15 years was still having great difficulty breaking into the English musical scene. Goldschmidt had initially been permitted to enter the

148 *The opera commissioning scheme*

United Kingdom in 1935 on the unusual and draconian condition that he engage in no employment of any kind (Goldschmidt 1994: 57). This unreasonable condition was eventually lifted, and he began to work as a conductor, but it helps explain his failure in the first years to achieve any renown (Banks 1988: 426–428; Keeffe 1995: 14). He may have seen the opera commissioning scheme as his best opportunity, and, when its promise began to fade, he reacted with a measure of paranoia. As early as September 5, 1950, he wrote to White speculating that there was a secret policy to bar him from English stages as both a composer and conductor.

Even so, as Lewis Foreman recounts (2003: 77), in April 1952 Goldschmidt made another attempt to interest the BBC in *Beatrice Cenci*, writing to Eric Warr. In Foreman's analysis, Leonard Isaacs was Goldschmidt's champion within the BBC, and seems finally to have prevailed. In November 1952, Isaacs wrote to Goldschmidt suggesting a set of excerpts, and, with some additions, the BBC finally broadcast these April 13 and 14, 1953, with Goldschmidt himself conducting (Lawrence 1995: 11; Struck 2001). (Goldschmidt notably fails to mention this broadcast in his self-dramatizing autobiography.) Even at the last minute, there was some uncertainly within the BBC whether such a broadcast had ever been properly approved. In response to such a query on March 24th, Eric Warr responded somewhat testily, defending the broadcast:

> The reports on the *opera as a whole* being doubtful, C[ontroller of].T[hird].P[rogramme]. jibbed at the expense of mounting it. Nor was he keen on undertaking a cut version that would be less uneconomical. The April performance is not, of course, a cut version but a few bits extracted. They were chosen—I believe in consultation with L[eonard].I[saacs].—by the composer who must know the best bits to extract for an orchestral concert. We trust that they are the "lyric parts" & "impressive moments" noted by Alwyn and the "excellent", "lyrical" and "moving" parts to which Frankel refers.
>
> (R27/578)

After the broadcast, Leonard Isaacs made one last push for a full presentation of the opera:

> I heard a playback the other evening privately of a tape recording of the excerpts from the above opera given in the Third Programme last April or May under the composer's direction. . . . I was very considerably impressed with the sound of the music. It had dignity and here and there nobility and the composer's use of the orchestra was sometimes really imaginative and always completely professional. . . . With this in mind I must admit to having some doubts as to whether we were right in recommending to C.T.P. that he should not sponsor the whole work. . . . I remain under the impression that we ought perhaps to think again about the whole work.
>
> (R27/578)

But no further broadcast was forthcoming, and, although Goldschmidt's career as a conductor did improve, his failure to attract attention as a composer led him to abandon composition entirely from 1958 until 1982. In the 80s interest in his music began to increase, particularly as the press could portray him as unjustly neglected: a near-martyr to the dominance of atonal and avant-garde styles in the 60s and 70s. *Beatrice Cenci* was finally rescued from oblivion and premiered in a concert version in London as part of an "Emigré Composer" festival in 1988. The work's stage premiere in Magdeburg in 1994 was well received, and the Berlin German Symphony Orchestra recorded it in 1995 with an impressive line-up of English soloists.[8]

Bush, *Wat Tyler*

Like Berthold Goldschmidt's *Beatrice Cenci*, *Wat Tyler* was first heard in a private reading. Bush arranged for the Workers' Musical Association chorus and several soloists to perform the work with piano at the Salle Erard on November 26, 1950. The Workers Musical Assocation Singers and Opera Group and the Radlett Singers provided the chorus, and Bush himself accompanied. Invited were the competition judges, the members of the Arts Council, its music panel and staff, Bush's colleagues at the Royal Academy of Music, representatives of Covent Garden, Sadler's Wells, Glyndebourne, and the English Opera Group, as well as the other competition winners, Britten, Tippett, Rutland Boughton, John Ireland, and many others. Rankl and David Webster could not attend, but Bush played the score to them privately (EL6/70, EL6/75).

The Arts Council agreed to cover reasonable expenses for the event. The Arts Council paid for hiring the hall, but was unhappy with the high cost of copying the score and chorus parts—£149, 7s—which, it was felt, should be recoverable from Bush's publisher. Negotiations with the publisher, Joseph Williams Ltd., were unproductive, since until the work was performed they were unwilling to consider it published. The Arts Council therefore decided to give Bush a loan of £150, repayable upon publication. Joseph Williams published the vocal score after the 1953 Leipzig premiere and Bush reimbursed the Arts Council.

Some excerpts were also presented at the 50th-birthday concert for Bush given by the Workers' Musical Association on December 15, 1950 at Conway Hall in London. Bernard Stevenson (1981: 118) claims that Bush used the money from the commission to finance this performance. What little note in the press there was of these performances was positive. In the volume of essays published by the WMA in December 1950 to honor Bush's birthday, E. J. Dent published an appreciative article on the opera, declaring that it "ought to initiate a new and inspiring movement in national English opera" (Clark 1950: 52). Dent's piece reached a wider audience when *Musical Opinion* reprinted it, and the following notice appeared in *Musical Times*:

> Alan Bush's score quotes, in the chorus part, the old English revolutionary folk-song, "The Cutty Wren": and he has consciously borrowed from

mediæval musical idiom for his setting of the traditional couplet "When Adam delved and Eve span . . .". For the rest, he uses mainly a forthright not-too-modernist idiom which seems admirably suited to the theatre and to the expressive libretto by his wife, Nancy Bush. The chorus part is finely written and notably prominent: for "the people" plays a leading part in this story of the Peasants' Revolt and King Richard II. (No prizes are awarded for the first critic to call this opera "the English *Boris Godunov*".) . . . Both dramatically and musically, the production of this opera can be looked forward to with the liveliest hopes.

(Jacobs 1951a: 37)

Other journals praised the dramatic music, the choruses, and, especially, the more intimate, lyrical numbers such as the minstrel's songs and Margaret's lament in the epilogue. Despite this modest exposure, as we have seen, the opera was however not picked up for performance in Britain by either an opera company or the BBC. It seems likely that in the nervous political atmosphere of the gathering Cold War an outspoken communist with close connections in East Germany was deemed unsuitable for official patronage.

In April 1951, while attending a composers' conference in East Berlin, Bush played through the score for his colleagues there, and received assurances of a broadcast by Berlin Radio for the following season, with a decision on the basis of the broadcast whether to mount a production in an East German opera house (EL6/70, April 20, 1951). Upon his return to Britain, Bush wrote to the Arts Council to ascertain if they would object to a German performance, since the conditions of the commission reserved to the Arts Council the right "to nominate the first production" for a period of two years from the March 29, 1951 commission. Needless to say, the Arts Council, faced with the almost complete indifference of the British opera world to the winning operas, could raise no objection. Eric Walter White wrote back that the Arts Council would welcome such a production, opportunities in Britain being so few (EL6/70, April 25, 1951).

Bush therefore pursued the German radio offer, and in October 1951 he was invited to conduct *Wat Tyler* early in 1952. A somewhat abridged version of the work—two hours condensed from two hours 45 minutes—was recorded in German translation, with the full chorus and orchestra of Berlin Radio and several fine German singers. The broadcasts went out on April 3 and 11, 1952, and Bush made sure to inform musicians and opera house officials in Britain and abroad, including Norman Tucker at Sadler's Wells and Steuart Wilson at Covent Garden. Bush also wrote to the Earl of Harewood, a friend of Britten's, the editor of the journal *Opera*, and an important figure in the English opera world, to inform him of the broadcast. Bush hoped to engage Harewood's interest in the work and enlist his support in getting an English stage production: "This performance will be in German; but I am hoping—and not for purely selfish reasons—that the first public performance of this English historical opera will be in English!" (Bush Archive, October 26, 1951). Bush even went so far as to offer to play the work through privately for Harewood. Bush's letter also states: "I understand from Sir Steuart

Wilson that the work is again to be considered for the 1952/53 season," although there is no confirmation of this claim elsewhere. Harewood replied politely, but did not take up the opera's cause (Bush Archive, November 6, 1951).

The announcement of this broadcast generated another of the occasional bursts of political nervousness that attended the opera's early career. A staffer at the Arts Council Western Division sent a note to John Denison which read:

> As you may imagine, I was amused to receive the printed handout, which no doubt you have seen, announcing the world premiere of Alan Bush's Festival opera in the Berliner Rundfunk tomorrow. Knowing the importance ascribed by the populace to the "tendencies" expressed in any stage work and remembering past personal sessions with the political boys over British soloists broadcasting from the Russian controlled network, I can sympathise with whoever may be having a head-ache now! Let us hope that repercussions on the possible propaganda use of this "sponsored" work need get no further than the Foreign Office.
>
> (EL6/70, April 2, 1952)

Despite the worries expressed in the letter, the broadcast seems not to have led to any political difficulties. In fact, the broadcast was a success for Bush, with the notice in the *Musical Times* comparing Bush's work to that of Modest Musorgsky:

> [*Wat Tyler*] seems, astonishingly, to be the first opera on an English historical theme by a British composer.... The chorus, used somewhat in Moussorgskyan style, plays a leading part.... The subject—the peasants' uprising in 1381, and its failure—is one of intense and perennial interest.
>
> (Anderson 1952: 216)

The announcement in October 1951 of the upcoming Berlin Radio broadcast probably also gave the BBC reading panel a convenient excuse to drop the matter of British broadcast, assuming the matter was still under consideration. In November 1951, after a full year of waiting, Alan Bush could write: "[S]o far, there is no indication that [the BBC] are going ... to do anything at all about any of the operas which won the Arts Council's 'Festival of Britain' Awards" (Letter to Lord Harewood, Bush Archive, November 9, 1951).

As Bush had hoped, as a result of the German broadcast, *Wat Tyler* was taken up by the Leipzig Municipal Opera for German-language production the following season. He was clearly elated, although he wrote to Eric Walter White that he regretted that his opera should not have its premiere in his native language. Thus, Bush's *Wat Tyler* was the first of the four Festival of Britain operas to receive a fully staged performance anywhere. The opera had its stage premiere in Leipzig on September 6, 1953, with the Gewandhaus Orchestra in the pit.

Although the broadcast had not, the upcoming stage premiere produced some political embarrassment within the Arts Council. On April 7, 1953, Bush wrote to a number of representatives of the leading British cultural organizations, including W. E. Williams, the Secretary General of the Arts Council, to invite them to be guests of the Leipzig Opera House at the premiere (EL6/70, April 7, 1953). The offer was genuinely meant, but it also cannot have escaped the notice of either the East German government or the invitation recipients that there was a political advantage to be gained by treating British representatives to the spectacle of a fully professional premiere production of a major new British opera that no British opera house could or would touch. In the event, the British officials stayed away. John Denison, writing to decline the Arts Council invitation (which had been passed down to him and which he had even passed on to Eric Walter White), excused the entire staff on the grounds that the upcoming coronation of Elizabeth II demanded all their time (EL 6/70, April 16, 1953).

The Leipzig performances were successful, and the opera was repeated the following season, with another production later that season in Rostock and a third production in Magdeburg in 1959. In addition, the director of the Weimar opera commissioned a second opera from Bush; this work, *Men of Blackmoor*, received its premiere on November 1956. Bush's later two operas premiered in East Germany as well.

The stage premiere of *Wat Tyler* attracted more notice in the press than had the radio broadcast the previous year, with many reviewers besides the one for the *Musical Times* comparing the opera with Musorgsky's *Boris Godunov*. The British journal *Opera* reprinted the following review, translated from *Neues Deutschland*:

> This opera about the English Peasant Rising of 1381 is an important contribution to the problem of realism in opera. The great example of *Boris Godunov* has undoubtedly influenced and stimulated the character of this work ... In *Boris* the Russian people, not the Czar, are the hero of the drama. Likewise in *Wat Tyler* the peasants are the protagonists, led and represented by Tyler himself. Mussorgsky uses old Russian modal turns of phrase to characterize the historical period; in a similar manner Alan Bush employs the polyphonic technique of early English choral music and folk music, without pastiche or archaism. It is indeed the outstanding characteristic of Bush's music that in it the English national style is fused with an entirely personal mode of expression.
>
> (Petzold 1953: 743)

The reference to "the problem of realism" points to the post-1948 socialist-realist context of these comments, but the comparison to Musorgsky, as I discuss in Chapter 5, is not merely a *pro forma* obeisance to Russian cultural overlords.

In the wake of the successful production in Leipzig and the positive press reaction, Leonard Isaacs and Eric Warr wrote up newer, much more thorough reports on the opera for the BBC in late 1953. Neither recommended the work. Isaacs' report is largely negative, dwelling on the score's dullness and lack of melody, and the rigid moral polarity of the scenario, in which the heroes are all good and the villains all bad. Warr was more positive, finding much of the music "plain" but effective, but drew back from recommending broadcast (R27/556).

The successful premiere of Bush's next opera, *Men of Blackmoor*, in Weimar in 1956 finally provided the necessary impetus, and the BBC finally broadcast a condensed version of *Wat Tyler* on 9 and 10 December 1956, under the baton of Stanford Robinson. This was the opera's British premiere, and its first public performance in English.

Ernest Chapman, in his *Listener* preview of the broadcast, again made the familiar comparison, writing "'Wat Tyler' is concerned less with its hero's personal life than with the destiny of the people as a whole. It is thus a truly national opera, like Musorgsky's 'Boris Godunov', and, as in that work, the chorus representing the people, plays an outstanding part" (Chapman 1956: 965). Hugh Ottaway, previewing the broadcast in *Musical Times*, praised the libretto and the score, especially the final scene, of which he wrote: "I would attribute Bush's success here to his clinching the tragedy in both individual and collective aspects and to his complete avoidance of musical rhetoric. . . . With its restrained eloquence . . . and its wonderful synthesis of Tyler's music . . . this is among the most affecting moments in modern English opera" (Ottaway 1956: 635–636).

Despite such glowing recommendations, and the overt identification of the work's historical subject and national qualities, the BBC broadcast did little to encourage any English opera company to mount *Wat Tyler*. Indeed, the Leipzig premiere appears to have inaugurated the period of neglect of Bush's music by critics and performers in Britain from which his reputation never recovered; as performances multiplied in East Germany and other Soviet bloc countries, they dwindled in Britain. As a result, *Wat Tyler* had to wait almost 18 years for its British stage premiere. In 1974, a group of enthusiastic members and associates of the Workers' Musical Association, led by Bush himself as Artistic Director, founded a new, rather *ad hoc* semi-amateur opera company. This troupe, the Keynote Opera Society, "formed . . . to promote new or unfamiliar operas of this Century" (Stevens 1974: 5), began its first season by mounting three performances of *Wat Tyler* at the Sadler's Wells Theatre on June 19, 21, and 22, 1974, with financial assistance raised by the WMA and with grants from the Arts Council and the Greater London Arts Association. While the Society provided the opera chorus, it engaged a number of professional soloists, such as the baritone John Noble, who took the title part, as well as the Royal Philharmonic Orchestra. Bush entrusted the conducting to Stanford Robinson, who had conducted the BBC broadcast. By all accounts, the production was rather sketchy; with the limited resources available, full justice could not be done to the work in the realm of sets and costumes and some of the principals were weak. There have been no subsequent productions.[9]

It is tempting to read the sad fate of *Wat Tyler* as a kind of political object lesson, revealing the boundaries of acceptable state support for artistic expression. Despite being a professor at the Royal Academy of Music, a widely respected composition teacher and composer, Alan Bush, by virtue of his communism, seems to have been perceived as a shade too dangerous to receive the wholehearted support of the institutions—the Arts Council, the BBC, Covent Garden, publishers like Boosey and Hawkes, and the like—that could have brought his opera before the public. There is no evidence of outright rejection of the opera on political grounds, and Bush's inflexible and dogmatic personality probably did not aid his efforts. But unlucky timing and political unease based on the composer's broad political views and known sympathies—not anything dangerous or subversive within the opera itself—seem to have quashed the opera's chances for performance in Britain for decades. Bush's failure to find support for the work did not result from its content having genuinely offended, for there was nothing in the work that could truly offend. Instead, in a strange irony, the opera itself, like its hero, was first granted a state charter—the Arts Council commission—that proved worthless, and then the opera was, so to speak, murdered.

Rankl, *Deirdre of the Sorrows*

Rankl's opera was and remains the most obscure of the winners. Although known as a conductor, Rankl was never taken seriously as a composer. By 1950, Rankl had few friends left in London, and *Deirdre of the Sorrows* never seems to have attracted any interest. Indeed, by the time Rankl won his commission his position at Covent Garden was rapidly deteriorating; never popular or an acclaimed conductor, despite the tireless work he had put into the founding of the company, he was increasingly unhappy with his position, suffering the disapproval of David Webster, Covent Garden's General Administrator, and in the shadow of guest conductors. In 1951 Rankl wrote several annoyed letters to the Arts Council complaining about the BBC's failure to make any decision on radio broadcast of the score (EL6/74), but his resignation from Covent Garden that same year and withdrawal from London musical life eliminated any chance of its production, as he was not on hand to advocate for his score himself. Ironically, in the Arts Council correspondence file for the Royal Opera House (ACGB 50/208), the letter to Webster informing him that Rankl's score has won a commission, along with Webster's terse reply, lies right next to Webster's letter to the Arts Council concerning the search for Rankl's replacement.

From 1952 to 1959, Rankl was director of the Scottish National Orchestra, and with his move to Scotland he appears to have let the matter drop. Like Goldschmidt, he seems to have been quite bitter about the treatment (or lack thereof) of his competition opera. In 1963 he wrote a brief letter to an uninterested David Webster at the Royal Opera, "only to remind you that it is 12 years since the completion of my opera *Deirdre of the Sorrows*" (Haltrecht 1975: 152). From 1958 to 1960 he was music director of the Elizabethan Trust Opera Company in Sydney, which later became the Australian Opera. According to Haltrecht (1975: 152) and Wilson (1993: 70), Rankl set foot in the Royal Opera House only once again, in 1965, and then only as a member of the audience. In 1995, almost three decades after Rankl's death, the BBC broadcast a series of excerpts from the score, the first time that any of the music had ever been heard publicly, at which time it was revealed as "vividly imagined and approachable score on a grand scale" (Foreman, 2003: 76).

Assessment

Ironically, in September 1954, before any of the four operas that the panel had actually chosen for commission was produced in Britain, Lennox Berkeley's *Nelson* received a professional stage premiere, broadcast by the BBC, at the Sadler's Wells Opera Company, the second most prestigious company in the nation. In the judgment of Lewis Foreman (2003: 76) Berkeley's opera, over whose fate the judges had deliberated so excruciatingly for years, most nearly fit the Festival of Britain's requirements of popular opera and national celebration. As recounted in Chapter 3, three works rejected by the judges, Brian Easdale's *Sleeping Children*, Peter Tranchell's *Mayor of Casterbridge*, and Egon Wellesz's *Incognita*, had been produced during the Festival year, and, in addition to *Nelson*, two more rejected works, Inglis Gundry's *Tinners of Cornwall* and Arwel Hughes's *Menna*, received amateur productions in 1953 and 1954 respectively. Thus, by 1957, including *A Tale of Two Cities* and the East German production of *Wat Tyler*, eight of the operas submitted to the competition had been staged. (I discuss these works further in Chapter 5.)

Although in retrospect such a record can be deemed a modest success, at the time the Arts Council could take neither credit for it nor comfort from it; the staged operas were not the ones anointed with commissions. Indeed, the Festival opera commissioning scheme is one of the most ambitious, and, at the same time, least successful large projects ever undertaken by the agency. To be sure, for a short period of time, operatic composition in Britain could be said to have been artificially stimulated; if nothing else, the tremendous initial response to the announcement revealed how widespread dreams of operatic achievement were among British composers both amateur and professional. But the scheme failed to realize any of its explicit goals: None of the operas commissioned ever took a place in the national repertory, which, in its still nascent state, remained virtually unchanged, and the major opera companies, which dominated the Arts Council's time and funds, paid the works scant attention. The dismal performance record of the winners, if anything, dampened the optimism of boosters of national opera like Eric Walter White and those composers who, unlike Britten, did not command the automatic attention of opera producers. In the colorful assessment of Lewis Foreman (2003: 75), the scheme was "a classic British funding cock-up. It was a starry-eyed scheme which did not command the resources to implement its outcome."

How, then, did the Arts Council achieve its ends more or less successfully in the commissioning scheme for concert music but misjudge so terribly in the case of opera? First of all, the goals and mechanisms of the opera competition were different from those of the concert commission program. As the internal sources cited in Chapter 2 demonstrate, the concert commissions had (or could be portrayed to have) modest aims: The production of ephemeral occasional works was not beneath the dignity of the Arts Council in that case. For this reason, the concert commissions were placed with established composers whom the Arts Council could reasonably expect to complete their works. (Even so, several of the commissions were not finished in time.) The exception was the concerto competition for young composers, to whom it offered an entrée into the repertory. The essential attribute of the open opera scheme—the fact that it was judged anonymously—signals its higher ambitions. Far from a means to create occasional opera to celebrate the Festival, it was an attempt to advance the national repertory and to give great undiscovered opera composers their chance. It turned out to be far easier to open a path for a young composer's 25-minute violin or piano concerto than for a three-hour opera.

In further addressing the scheme's outcomes, it is useful to separate the process of selection from the attempts to secure performance. The selection was successful in the sense that it identified four varied operas, all worthy to an extent, and paid their composers handsome commissions for their work. The failure, as Berthold Goldschmidt sarcastically pointed out in his memoir, lay in the shape of the "national repertory" that these works implied. However liberal-minded and welcoming to immigrant talent the administrators of the scheme may have appeared in drawing up the rules, they really did intend and expect to stimulate native opera, composed by British citizens in the English tongue for British audiences, to the greater glory of the British nation. Although the operas of Benjamin, Bush, Goldschmidt, and Rankl were all accomplished works, it was hard to present any one of them clearly in such a light. Although they were not ready in time, none was ideal for the Festival of Britain anyway; then, with the Festival past, any reason to consider them also seemed to have passed.

Furthermore, the high moral principles implied by anonymous competition and independent judging drove the Arts Council directly into this web of political difficulties. As discussed above, the judges undoubtedly knew that *Deirdre of the Sorrows* and *Beatrice Cenci* were not really British in the common sense, or at least, if "British," certainly not English. It is clear that at least some of the judges also knew, from personal contacts or the press, the identities of the composers of *A Tale of Two Cities* and *Wat Tyler*. The panel's unwillingness to bend aesthetic judgment to political expediency is perhaps admirable in an abstract sense, and is a fine example of mandarin loftiness. As a committee given a single, circumscribed task—to select the winning scores—the panel probably considered questions of appropriateness to the occasion beneath their notice or beyond their purview. It is also possible that some of the judges were naïve or grandiose enough to believe that their choices would inevitably be embraced by performing institutions. Contrariwise, for some, the odd set of works may have advanced a concealed conviction that opera by English composers was not really as mature as the competition implied. Did any of them experience malicious gratification when they realized that a "suitable" work was missing from the list?

The failure to secure performances of the winning scores, on the other hand, resulted in part from the very practical circumstance that the competition ran behind schedule. In 1951, Britain had relatively few opera companies. It was unreasonable to expect any of them to mount financially risky productions under great time pressure in a climate where fear of alienating small and unsure audiences with unfamiliar repertory was great. But naivety and overreach on the part of the Arts Council also had a large role in the debacle. To conceive and mount such a competition in the first place implied tremendous faith in the maturation of British operatic institutions, not to mention the agency's own influence; it is obvious in retrospect that this confidence was unwarranted. Despite the growing clout granted by the Festival, the Arts Council discovered that its power did not extend to imposing a production of an entirely unknown work on an opera company. The agency could, with a little pressure, shoehorn the concert commissions into programs—although in a few cases that was difficult too—and it underwrote the productions of *John Socman* and *Billy Budd*. But with the open opera scheme, the Arts Council exerted only moral pressure on performing institutions, trusting that its own good name and the publicity surrounding the competition would prevail.

In the end, all the publicity merely spread the Arts Council's unrealistic expectations abroad and left the agency trapped. The progress of such a major national competition, with its attendant press coverage and extensive private communications with the composers, created an environment in which the Arts Council could not back away from the works once they were complete. Even when the operas were not ideal for the Festival season, when they were announced too late to be taken up in time, and in the face of continued apathy from producers, there was no way to publicly declare the competition a failure, or the works unsuitable, and be done with it. The Arts Council had to at least give the impression of supporting the works, even if figures in the organization had growing doubts as to their artistic merit or eventual success.

Finally, as discussed in Chapter 3, trends out of the Arts Council's control were working against it. In the increasingly internationalized and market-oriented postwar culture of Western Europe and America, opera companies found producing new works by untried composers financially unpromising. Company managers probably calculated that none of the four commissioned operas had the potential—a composer of great reputation, the ability to delight the audience, or even a score of great originality and genius—to generate enough interest in the opera-going community to make it a worthwhile investment. Engaged in a costly and highly public enterprise, they tended to follow international trends and rely on standard repertory and star singers to draw in an audience.

The Arts Council tried to interpose itself in this system, but did not have enough leverage to achieve its ends. The entire episode demonstrated the limits of the ability of modern institutions of state patronage to direct the course of the national culture, especially where insufficient power or will supports the mandarin approach to cultural provision, with its disregard for popular taste and the market. However close it may have seemed to come in the late forties, the Arts Council never took direct control over the opera houses themselves. Without this control, and the much larger, European-size budget which this would have entailed, the Arts Council could not initiate productions, so, in the end, at least in this sphere, it was left looking powerless and a bit foolish.

Notes

1 There is some uncertainty about the date of the judges' decision on this work. Wilson left it off the list of newly rejected projects that he forwarded to White after the October 23, 1949 meeting (EL6/71, 27 October 1949). Nevertheless, it is never listed as either still in the running or definitely rejected after that meeting, and in White's master table of all submissions it is marked as rejected on that date.
2 EL6/70 preserves the correspondence between Steuart Wilson and Eric Walter White, and between White and Bush concerning the passing of sections of the vocal and full score of *Wat Tyler* between the composer and the panel of judges.
3 There is no record of the work in Mellers's papers at the University of York.
4 "Als sie [die Jury] erfuhren, wem sie die Preise zugesprochen hatten, fielen sie aus allen Wolken: Alan Bush—ein Kommunist; Karl Rankl—ein reichlich unbeliebter Mann, der mit Lambert auf Kriegsfuß stand; Goldschmidt—ich hatte einige ernste Auseinandersetzungen mit Stewart Wilson bezüglich meiner Dirigierweise gehabt; und Arthur Benjamin—er kam aus Australien, also wenigstens aus dem Commonwealth. Die Ergebnisse waren aus patriotischer Sicht also nicht gerade erfreulich, und obwohl der Arts Council sich die Rechte für die Aufführung der Oper zwei Jahre lang vorbehalten hatte, passierte nichts."
5 Foreman (2003: 75–76) describes Goldschmidt's working methods while he composed the opera.
6 "Ich wandte mich mehrfach an White, und schließlich arrangierte er ein Treffen, bei dem wir die Oper am Klavier mit ein paar Sängern vorführten. Einige Leute waren begeistert—Lord Harewood, Vaughan Williams –, der meinte, obwohl er die Musik lobte, das Thema sei doch furchtbar, so schlimm wie *Tosca*."
7 See Banks 1988: 428–430, for a defense of the opera against such impressions, and a fine general discussion of the work.
8 Despite the by-then typical rhetoric about Goldschmidt's being a rediscovered master who spent decades wandering in the atonal wilderness, the review for *Opera* of the German performance makes comments about incessant and tedious orchestral counterpoint similar to those of the early BBC reviewers (Sutcliffe 1994).
9 I examine *Wat Tyler* in detail in Lew 2001, Chapter 6. Both in the fifties and in the seventies, the opera was unsuccessful with critics, largely for its haughty rejection of moral and political ambiguity. In my opinion, the invention of a wife and daughter for Tyler does much to humanize an otherwise starkly politicized drama.

5 This is our moment
National elements in Festival operas

As the last two chapters have shown, the programs that the Arts Council announced in 1949 for the Festival of Britain brought a large number of operatic projects to light. Between April and December 1951, four new scores received commissions from the Arts Council as a result of the Festival competition, with two unannounced runners-up. Although none of these six operas were performed during the Festival, three had premieres in the next few years, along with two works rejected earlier in the competition. During or soon after the Festival, four new works received professional productions, while three had semi-professional premieres at universities or schools. Table 5.1 lists these 15 works, along with two contemporaneous projects by major composers not directly associated with the Festival.[1]

While these pieces differ greatly, most invite readings as representations of national identity from a variety of perspectives. This may at first appear surprising. Although 1951 was a peak year for British opera, the compositional circumstances, thematic concerns, and artistic aims of the composers varied, and did not appear overnight upon an offer of money or performance. But even in those cases where composers in their studios seem remote from social questions, we can discern traces of the *Zeitgeist* in their works. In his study of British film from the same period, Allan Medhurst (1995: 289–290) defends such claims:

> [I]t seem incontrovertible to me that the films of an era must bear the traces of the times that produced them. As to whether those traces were consciously placed there by socially-conscious film-makers, have become apparent with the advantages of hindsight, or are the product of critical over-ingenuity—the jury is still out on that.

Of course, it is not only over-ingenious critics who interpret works decades later; meanings accrue in their own time. There are several reasons why the postwar environment was particularly conducive to such expression, which one would not find among any set of historically proximate works. The social engagement of the thirties, the sense of national unity forged during Second World War and the societal and cultural reforms advanced by the postwar Labour government formed the environment of the artists who contributed to the Festival of Britain. The late forties offered the excitement and challenge of a new era, a drive toward

Table 5.1 New operas associated with the 1951 Festival of Britain

Competitive Anonymous Commissions	Performances	Setting	Source
Arthur Benjamin, *A Tale of Two Cities*	Broadcast 1954, stage 1957	Paris & London, 1780s	Charles Dickens historical novel
Alan Bush, *Wat Tyler*	Broadcast 1952, stage 1953	Kent & London, 1381	History
Berthold Goldschmidt, *Beatrice Cenci*	Excerpts 1953, premiere 1988	Rome, 1599	History & Percy Bysshe Shelley play
Karl Rankl, *Deirdre of the Sorrows*	Excerpts 1995	Ireland, legendary times	Irish legend & John M. Synge play
Festival Year Premieres (*competition rejects)			
Benjamin Bitten, *Billy Budd*	Covent Garden Opera (Dec)	English naval ship, Napoleonic wars	Herman Melville historical novella
*Brian Easdale, *The Sleeping Children*	English Opera Group	English boarding school, 1945	(original story)
Antony Hopkins, *The Man from Tuscany*	Canterbury Choir School	Lepizig, early 18th century	(original story)
George Lloyd, *John Socman*	Carl Rosa Opera	Wiltshire village, 1415	(references historical events)
*Peter Tranchell, *The Mayor of Casterbridge*	Cambridge University	English town, early 19th century	Thomas Hardy historical novel

Ralph Vaughan Williams, *The Pilgrim's Progress*	Covent Garden Opera	17th-century allegorical landscape	John Bunyan allegory
*Egon Wellesz, *Incognita*	Oxford University Dec	Renaissance Florence	William Congreve novel

Other Significant Competition Rejects

Lennox Berkeley, *Nelson* (runner-up)	Premiere 1954	Europe & London, Napoleonic wars	History
Inglis Gundry, *The Tinners of Cornwall*	Premiere 1953	Cornish village, late 18th century	(references historical events)
Arwel Hughes, *Menna*	Premiere 1954	Traditional Welsh village	(original story)
Wilfrid Mellers, *Christopher Marlowe* (runner-up)	Never performed	Elizabethan England	History

Other Projects in Progress

Michael Tippett, *The Midsummer Marriage*	Premiere 1955	Timeless symbolic landscape	(original story)
William Walton, *Troilus and Cressida*	Premiere 1954	The Trojan War	Geoffrey Chaucer poem (loosely)

national redefinition which the coming Festival's rhetoric and focus on the arts accentuated. And by the forties, the English musical establishment regarded opera as the preeminent art-form for broad public statements that addressed such questions.

Regardless of composers' intent, and even when the conjunction with the Festival was largely coincidental, the context of all new operatic activity in Britain in 1951 was inescapably national. Funding by the government, association with the Festival in the press, presentation in major public venues as a Festival event, and public scrutiny as representative music in a time of national celebration—all these factors provided audiences with a lens that colored the works' reception. The Festival of Britain in effect catalyzed reflection on national themes in these opera. It highlighted explicit representations of national identity, and granted official status to implicit threads of meaning.

The analysis that follows looks mainly at the plots of the operas produced around the Festival, and examines their engagement with such themes. These reflections exist on a number of levels and have many sources; with different composers, audiences, and circumstances, the weights of these elements and their subtleties of meanings are different. Some operas overtly advance specific visions of the nation, while in others, characters, settings, and cultural referents are recognizably national. Source material drawn from history and canonic literature which audiences believe imbued with national character lends an aura of authenticity to some operas, as do subject matters and themes of particular national interest or resonance, and cherished ideals and symbols.

Musical style

Musical style on its own was a relatively weak marker of national identity in Britain in the late forties. The composers under review here represent a diverse range of idioms. Stylistic markers could certainly brand an opera *non-English*: The sophisticated Continental polyphony of Goldschmidt, Rankl, and Wellesz could not masquerade as English music, even though each of these composers chose a source by a prominent English-language author for his opera. But critics accepted the national *bona fides* of the operatic contributions of composers as disparate as Arthur Benjamin, Lennox Berkeley, and Peter Tranchell.

Nonetheless, at this period audiences continued to recognize certain pre-war musical tropes as an "English sound": most notably a rhapsodic flow of broad modal diatonic writing with idealized roots in folksong or Tudor polyphony. Of the Festival operas, only *The Pilgrim's Progress* and *Wat Tyler* fully inhabit this stylistic universe. When other composers reference this sound, they do so sparingly and at carefully planned moments merged into a broader stylistic matrix. To varying degrees, such procedures are found in *Billy Budd* and *John Socman*.

The transition between the scenes of Act 2 of Britten's *Billy Budd* provides an instructive example of deliberate reference to English stylistics. The chorus begins singing sea chanteys offstage at the end of the first scene, set in the Captain's cabin. The chanteys then continue in the orchestra through the following interlude, and grow into the rapturous choral crescendo on the chantey "Blow her away" that opens the next scene. Since the officers hear and comment on the crew's chanteys in the earlier scene, the sense of musical community momentarily encompasses the entire ship. It is significant that Britten casts this climactic moment of happy cohesion, the last moment before the action of the tragedy begins in earnest, in music of great national symbolic power: a great choral outburst, a sea chantey, and the profound "English pastoral" simplicity of a nearly pentatonic diatonic melody over very stable harmonic support. This is the most consonant and emotionally satisfying climax in the entire score, counterpart to the visionary apotheosis that ends *Wat Tyler* or any one of the many moments of musical transcendence in *The Pilgrim's Progress*.

As this example suggests, one musical element that many of the operas share that is truly nationally marked is a central role for the chorus. Operas concerned with the fate of peoples are often choral, not only because the chorus represents the masses, but also because the sound of choral singing can forge a sense of collectivity and even patriotism in the audience. Most of the operas famous for their national stature or reception—Giuseppe Verdi's *Nabucco*, Modest Musorgsky's *Boris Godunov*, Richard Wagner's *Parsifal*—have choral scenes of great importance. A harbinger of this development in England was Rutland Boughton's 1911 "Essay on Choral Drama," which called for the chorus to take the leading dramatic role in opera. Boughton's injunction was an article of artistic faith by the forties, especially but not exclusively among the politically engaged composers who gathered around him such as Gundry and Bush. Thus is not surprising to find dominant choral roles in their works, as well as in *A Tale of Two Cities*, *Billy Budd*, and *The Mayor of Casterbridge*. Even though less integrated into the plots, the choral parts of *The Sleeping Children*, *John Socman*, and *The Pilgrim's Progress* rise at moments to similar prominence. In postwar England the opera chorus arguably also had a deeper national resonance, representing the transfer of the characteristic oratorio chorus into a newly prestigious genre; it is hardly surprising that the first component of the Covent Garden Opera Company to achieve fully professional quality in the eyes of the critics was the chorus.

Address

In two cases, the composers of Festival operas deliberately undertook to address the nation on broad terms and to advance a specifically vision of national betterment. In *Wat Tyler*, Alan Bush created a visionary heroic opera that overtly concerns the historical fate of the English people, as well as a call to all the people of the country to join in support of a common social(ist) ideal. (Characteristically, he harbored grand if unrealistic ambitions to attract urban workers to performances of his work.)

Wat Tyler advances a specific partisan interpretation of English history. Bush was a committed communist, and his opera represents the national past, and, by extension, its present as well, as a period of inequality and oppression. The old order, while challenged in the opera, reestablishes itself: Although Tyler extracts a charter of emancipation from Richard II, William Walworth kills him at Smithfield, and Richard revokes the serfs' freedoms. But the opera does not end there; it also shows what the nation can and must become. The peasant army is as much a protagonist as Tyler himself, and its survival and future glory after the death of its champion provide the work's moral. In the closing pages the chorus foresees the inevitable overthrow of tyranny and a future Britain of free and equal citizens.

Although Bush's own political convictions are not in doubt, the precise nature of the victory foreseen in the opera's final chorus remains purposefully vague. The work offers no direct argument that the fulfillment of the peasants' hopes should be found in international revolutionary communism. Indeed, given its plot set in the remote past, the work's call to abolish unfair privilege and inequality, and its rousing affirmation that despite the forces of reaction such goals can be achieved, provide a relatively uncontroversial moral. Bush himself rejected postwar Labour socialism as tainted with bourgeois capitalism and insufficient to the nation's needs. But despite his ideological orientation, the opera's optimistic vision of a future order parallels the egalitarian and reformist zeal of the Labour period from 1945 to 1948, when a British style of socialism seemed achievable, as well as the obscuring of class differences in the Festival Exhibition. Nancy Bush's libretto, with its promise that "all that is great in Man still lives and once again shall rise," is as potentially inspiring to the mid-century liberal-minded reformer or the mildly socialist welfare capitalist as it is to the revolutionary communist. For this reason, although *Wat Tyler* might not have won a permanent place in the repertory, had it been performed in 1948, it might have captured the public's imagination. Bush, however, completed the work too late, just as the political period whose mood it captured was grinding to a dispirited close. (I give a fuller analysis and interpretation of *Wat Tyler* in Lew 2001: Chapter 6.)

Ralph Vaughan Williams's operatic testament, *The Pilgrim's Progress*, similarly addresses the entire nation, albeit from a very different perspective than that of *Wat Tyler*. Through use of John Bunyan's cherished text, *The Pilgrim's Progress* offers a compelling vision of England in symbolic, rather than historical or political terms. While *The Pilgrim's Progress* would have been a major premiere in any year, as Covent Garden's only English offering of the main Festival season, its national qualities attracted enormous—even overwhelming—attention in the press.[2] But ironically, although the work benefitted from the Festival context of its premiere, its vision strongly contrasts with that of the Festival. While the Festival emphasized modernity and efficiency, and in contrast to the national redemption that *Wat Tyler* locates in future political emancipation, Vaughan Williams's opera grounds the nation's moral security in an imaginary shared cultural past.

Vaughan Williams, who was 78 years old in 1951, served as the unofficial national composer to whom the country turned in times of trouble or celebration. He envisioned this timeless, hieratic opera as *heil'ge englische Kunst*: a representation of the best in the English literary, musical, and religious tradition, as well as a demonstration of how through the use of such materials opera could be remade into a ritual of universal salvation. In three scenes in Vaughan William's opera—The House Beautiful, The Arming of Pilgrim, and The Celestial City—the chorus, although it never takes part in the action, represents a collective will through which the Pilgrim's journey accrues its meaning. (Parallels with Wagner's *Parsifal* began even before the premiere.)[3]

With *The Pilgrim's Progress*, Vaughan Williams hoped to draw the entire nation together musically and culturally. He did not literally expect everyone in the nation to see the opera, but his desire, eventually frustrated, that students in Cambridge, rather than professionals at Covent Garden, perform the work reminds us that, as with so much of his oeuvre, he wanted it to make its impact more among the moderately musically cultivated and enthusiastic amateur populace, and particularly among impressionable young people, rather than solely among the musical and social elites of London.

Billy Budd, the best known of the Festival operas, serves as a counterexample to the two works just mentioned. Britten's work features a plot and music with strong national resonances—its maritime subject, sea chanteys, and depiction of shipboard life bring it into the realm of British national myth—but while fundamentally a political tale in the broadest sense, it is not an explicitly national work. Britten does not concern himself with speaking to the entire nation; his work is addressed to the elite audience of the operatically educated who will appreciate it. And, as discussed below, its critical engagement with English identity lies beneath the surface. In his later overt essay in "national opera", *Gloriana*, depicting the reign of Elizabeth I and composed in 1953 for the coronation of Elizabeth II, Britten engaged the question of "the fate of the nation," but to a more limited extent than *Wat Tyler* or *The Pilgrim's Progress*. The score draws substantially on nationally marked resources such as Elizabethan masques and lute songs, and choral episodes such as the Norwich scene and the London uprising give voice to the English people, but there is little trace of Bush's and Vaughan Williams's belief that an opera can address, much less heal, the nation as a whole. (For the origins of *Gloriana* as a "national opera" see Banks 1993: 11.)

Sources

As in the case of *Billy Budd*, even when composers writing for or around the Festival of Britain did not explicitly examine the nation's destiny, they still sought to realize the national potential of opera. The choice of subject is the most important means by which an opera can embody national expression. Both history and canonic literature contain figures, settings, and cultural referents that audiences perceive as authentic and native. The examples of local settings and subjects in the Festival operas fall into three overlapping categories: (1) fictional stories set in English historical contexts, (2) adaptations of canonical literary works that audiences believed to be imbued with national character, and (3) factual historical episodes. While none of these types of source is entirely new in English opera, their preponderance in the Festival period is striking.

The first category consists of works with original plots that lack the imprimatur of an esteemed literary source, such as George Lloyd's *John Socman* and Inglis

Gundry's *Tinners of Cornwall*. Both these works are number-operas in tonal styles modeled on the village romance of the nineteenth century. In these progeny of Donizetti's comic scores and Smetana's *Bartered Bride*, a pair of lovers surmounts the obstacles to their union in a folkloric setting. Although documentation suggests that both Lloyd and Gundry placed great importance on the national settings of their works, neither one deeply interrogates national identity. Indeed, in their hands, the genre appears hackneyed and undercuts what little national meaning the work might convey.

As discussed in Chapter 3, the chief defect leading to *John Socman*'s failure was its lack of dramatic sophistication: The work's structural and narrative similarity to pre-war operatic fare, more than its musical idiom, led critics to dismiss it as insubstantial and irrelevant. Neither George Lloyd nor his father seems to have considered the potential of opera to provide anything more than generic entertainment with incidental national color. The work's historical setting gave the work an aura of relevance in the Festival year, but fundamentally provided no more than an ornamental backdrop to the generic plot. The opera communicates little beyond the supposedly eternal values of Country Life and Young Love, and less about the English nation. Indeed, corrupt local officials being a universal scourge, the story, with its echoes of *Luisa Miller* and *Tosca*, could equally well take place in any country.

Unlike Lloyd, Inglis Gundry was ethnically nationalist. The plot and characters of *The Tinners of Cornwall*—the sixth of his 15 operas—are ostentatiously Cornish. Gundry's libretto is largely in dialect and his score is larded with genre numbers. Furthermore, Gundry was a politically engaged artist, who lectured for the Workers' Educational Association. The lovers in his village romance are caught up in a specific episode in British economic history: the decline of Cornish tin mining brought about by the discovery of copper in Anglesey. Gundry exploits this historical setting, depicting class conflict between farmers and miners and the social threat of mass unemployment.

Essentially a regional composer, Gundry viewed the Arts Council's opera competition as a potential path to a greater national reputation. He also submitted a fairy-tale opera based on *The Sleeping Beauty* but when instructed by the competition judges to advance only one project, he chose *The Tinners of Cornwall*, hoping that its relevance to contemporary social concerns would strike a chord with the Arts Council judges and with audiences. The judges of the Arts Council's opera competition clearly saw some value in the work, for they passed it through to the very last cut.

But while similar to Bush's *Wat Tyler*, or even more closely to Bush's second opera, *Men of Blackmoor*, *The Tinners of Cornwall* is not predominantly a work of social protest. Had it come before a broad national audience it is doubtful that they would have found much depth in its half-hearted political content. Gundry's musical style and dramaturgy felt outdated. He wrote all his operas in a "simple uncomplicated style" that has "made them suitable for amateur performers, with the result that they have rarely broken out beyond the fringe and semi-professional performing scene" (Rye 1995: 371). The simple, predictable romance plot and

Cornish folklore dominate the action, and the composer, as a later comment reveals, defanged his social critique by resolving the tragedy of the unemployed miners with an ahistorical plot twist that sends them off to be sailors or cultivate moorland. Gundry admitted that this "happy coda" was rather too neat even for his own comfort, and its avoidance of harsh reality earned him a rebuke from the composer Rutland Boughton, the unofficial political conscience to a number of composers at the time (Gundry n.d.: Chapter 15).

Michael Tippett's contemporary treatment of a village romance in symbolic terms in *The Midsummer Marriage* offers an instructive comparison to Lloyd's and Gundry's work. The idiosyncratic combination of Eastern, contemporary Western, and invented mythic elements in Tippett's opera largely precludes exploration of national traits. Although the typical village romance setting provides a nominally national element, Tippett rendered the genre contemporary by stripping it of common national topics. Thus, on the evidence of these three works it seems that by the forties the village romance's conventionality offered little scope for significant exploration of national identity.

Established works of English historical fiction were a different matter. They could confer *gravitas* upon native operas and spark considerations of national history and culture. In her study of the literary sources of twentieth century English operas, Irene Morra (2007: 5) discerns a new tendency among postwar composers to adapt the more esteemed literary works of the preceding 100 years. These novels, whose merit was widely acknowledged, provided sophisticated operatic characters and narratives, while at the same often time looking inward to English customs and locales.[4] Peter Tranchell and Arthur Benjamin, with their adaptations of novels by Hardy and Dickens, exemplify this class of postwar opera, as does Britten's *Billy Budd*, even though Herman Melville was American.

Curiously, while in nineteenth century Europe, Walter Scott had been one of the most productive sources for opera libretti, the best-selling Victorian and early twentieth century English novelists have attracted little operatic attention. Despite their enormous and continuing popularity, the works of neither Dickens nor Hardy have been much adapted for operatic purposes. There seem to have been only four English Dickens operas before Benjamin's, all based on less serious texts: Alexander Mackenzie's 1914 *Cricket on the Hearth*, Charles Wood's two modest essays composed for the Royal College of Music—*A Scene from Pickwick* (1921) and *The Family Party* (1923), based on a scene from *Martin Chuzzlewit*—and *Pickwick* by Albert H. Coates (1936). As for Hardy, Frederic Alfred D'Erlanger's 1906 Italian opera *Tess* seems to be the only predecessor to Tranchell's score (White 1983). While Melville's sprawling works were perhaps less amenable to operatic adaptation to begin with, his final unfinished novella was a different story: First published in 1924, it attracted the attention of both Italian composer Giorgio Federico Ghedini and Britten in the forties. (Ghedini's one-act version received its premiere in Venice in 1949.)

Unlike *John Socman*, and to a greater extent than Gundry's *Tinners of Cornwall*, the national-historical contexts of Tranchell's, Benjamin's, and Britten's operas are essential to their plots and drive the characters' conflicts, which are more

168 *National elements in Festival operas*

morally engaging than those in Lloyd's and Gundry's work. For native audiences, the familiar historical English events and customs and the characters' ostensibly national traits engendered a sense of recognition and pride. Even when such representations of authenticity were more nostalgic than critical, they had obvious appeal in the transitional postwar period, when changing fortunes rendered the definition of the nation problematic.

As we have seen, Festival-year commentary on Peter Tranchell's *Mayor of Casterbridge*, as well as on Hardy's original tale, emphasized its essential Englishness. Although the story arguably has little overt contemporary relevance, it unfolds in the markedly national setting of an eighteenth-century Wessex town, and encompasses an agricultural fair, a Mayor's reception, and a magistrate's court; the score features several real and imitation folktunes. Furthermore, while developing the work, Tranchell and his librettist Peter Bentley tightened both the work's focus on the flawed protagonist, whom they paint as an ambiguous but essentially sympathetic figure, and his conflict with and rejection by his community. In the opera's climactic chorus, the people of Casterbridge turn on their Mayor and denounce his misdeeds, deaf to his attempts at expiation. Clearly, Britten's *Peter Grimes*, with its critical portrayal of provincial English closedmindedness, exerted a powerful influence on the young Tranchell, who modeled this massive scene on Britten's similar scenes, but there is a crucial difference: Tranchell's townsfolk are enraged at a genuine violation of the social order, for Henchard did in fact sell his wife at auction years before.

Arthur Benjamin's *Tale of Two Cities* reveals a similar influence of *Peter Grimes* and its antagonistic chorus. Benjamin and his librettist Cedric Cliffe place the revolutionary Paris mob, baying ever more violently for blood, at the center of four of the work's six scenes. Perhaps because of Benjamin's Australian origin and use of continental and popular music elements, the London press often perceived him as a "cosmopolitan" composer rather than a naturalized Englishman. Indeed, his pre-war operas have continental settings. But his choice of one of the best-loved novels by the most successful of all English novelists for his postwar opera shows not merely an (unfortunately thwarted) instinct for popular success, but also a timely concern to make a specifically English statement. One central project of *A Tale of Two Cities* is to celebrate the admirable qualities of the English character. The familiar plot pits English domestic calm and honorable, heroic self-sacrifice against French revolutionary Terror. Its demonstration of English adherence to humane values and social order in the face of murderous continental madness cannot have failed to resonate with memories of the Second World War.

Britten, for his part, had by 1951 already revealed a penchant for English subjects, having composed *Peter Grimes*, *The Little Sweep*, and *Albert Herring* (its Maupassant source transferred to East Anglia). The setting of *Billy Budd*, a British Navy vessel during the Napoleonic wars, is no different, and indeed evokes a national significance even greater than those of *A Tale of Two Cities* and *The Mayor of Casterbridge*, "maritime et typiquement britannique" according the review of the Paris performances (Cooke and Reed 1993: 141). As I discuss below, a large and growing literature on the opera has examined its relationship to the postwar British experience in some detail.

As these examples suggest, operas based on Victorian historical literature had great potential to address contemporary Britain, through both the comfortable assurance of historical continuity and parallels with harsh recent experience. But this trend proved short-lived, quickly overtaken by more modernist aesthetic expectations. Irene Morra (2007: 6–7) observes that as the postwar period progressed,

> Composers turned increasingly to literary works characterized by their introspection and dense and ambiguous narrative. This is not to say that such staple operatic sources such as the plays of Shakespeare or popular nineteenth century novels did not achieve operatic status. Increasingly, however, the more popular plot-oriented and generally accessible the literary source, the more likely it was to be transcribed into the form of a musical . . . than an opera. This preference for the esoteric literary status of its original narrative sources has helped to differentiate British opera in particular from other forms of musical theater.

In other words, no sooner was Victorian literature taken up in English opera than it was shunted off to other genres as avant-garde figures came onto the scene, both in England and on the Continent, to whom the plots and themes of such literature were dated or tainted with populism. It seemed natural enough for Benjamin and Cliffe to turn *A Tale of Two Cities* into a grand romantic opera, while only nine years later, in the hands of Lionel Bart, *Oliver Twist* naturally became a musical. The West-End musical *Pickwick*, coming three years later, achieved a success denied to Wood and Coates's operatic efforts on the same theme.

If England's literature could infuse opera with national authenticity, then so could its actual history. There appear to be very few serious full-scale operas on true English historical subjects before the Festival of Britain. Eric Walter White, in his thorough if not exhaustive account starting in the sixteenth century (1983), lists only three: Henry Bishop's *Edward the Black Prince*, a setting of an imitation of Shakespeare by William Shirley, of 1828, George Macfarren's *King Charles II* of 1849; and Frederic H. Cowen's *Harold, or the Norman Conquest*, performed at Covent Garden in 1895. Ignorant of these precursors, Alan Bush, when he began work on *Wat Tyler* in 1948, believed that he was composing the first English historical opera (EL6/70, February 7, 1949). Unbeknownst to Bush, his was one of three projects, along with Lennox Berkeley's *Nelson* and Wilfrid Mellers's *Christopher Marlowe*, although because Mellers suppressed his work, it is impossible to know how he presented his historical figures and events.

Our post-modern sensibilities may recognize little difference between historical fiction and fictionalized history, but in the forties the stakes for historical opera were higher. Composers and critics repeatedly invoked the precedent of Musorgsky's *Boris Godunov* and *Khovanshchina* in discussions of national opera. These seminal works, which seemingly bared the true soul of the Russian people, demonstrated that opera best captured a nation's self-image when the audience knew that the plot derived from history. Before undertaking *Wat Tyler*, Alan Bush and his wife Nancy, who wrote the libretto, did significant research on the Peasants' Revolt of 1381, and claimed that they altered or simplified the historical record only when necessary for dramatic expediency. Indeed, their presentation of the Peasants' Revolt as a justifiable response to oppression undone by aristocratic treachery resonates with an emerging mid-century liberal historical consensus about it (Dobson 1983: 29–30, 392ff.). It is not surprising that the press repeatedly compared Bush's *Wat Tyler* with *Boris Godunov*.

Wat Tyler and *John Socman* are set a mere 34 years apart: The Battle of Agincourt occurred in 1415. Although *John Socman* is not strictly a historical opera, the same Musorgskian standard that motivated the Bushes sheds some light on the failure of *John Socman*. Arguably, in the wake of *Boris Godunov*, historical opera had to derive political, or at least contemporary meaning from its subject matter. But where the Bushes' opera found essential lessons for the future in the Peasants' Revolt, the Lloyds merely exploited Agincourt as a colorful backdrop.

Nelson offers yet a third approach to history. Eschewing the unwavering political sincerity of *Wat Tyler* and *John Socman*'s insignificant picturesque, Berkeley's opera examines history from an ironic distance. As we have seen, the work's dryness got the composer into trouble with the Arts Council competition judges. (In this regard, *Nelson* also prefigures Britten's *Gloriana*, with its unheroic portrayal of Elizabeth II.) The Second World War, with its echoes of the Napoleonic Wars, led to a resurgence (if such was possible) of Nelson-worship. But Berkeley and his librettist Alan Pryce-Jones evince little interest in the nation's military triumph or paeans to the great admiral. There is no significant role for the chorus, which never represents "the people," and, rather than ending with Nelson's death, Berkeley and Pryce-Jones give Emma Hamilton the last word (literally, "Nelson!"). Although the libretto encompasses the Battle of Trafalgar, it offers no overarching vision or interpretation. Of course, this is a matter of degree; as with *Khovanshchina*, which is often close to incomprehensible to non-Russian audiences, historical understanding can transmute domestic and political intrigue into the Fate of the Nation. The *English* audience, at least, knows full well that upon Nelson's duty hangs the very survival of Britain; with this knowledge come associations that can mute the opera's irony.

Furthermore, *Nelson*'s focus on personal relationship, downplaying the heroism of warfare in favor of the protagonist's untidy domestic attachments, gives the opera depth and an attention to character lacking in Bush's work. Because the central conflict concerns a man torn between love and duty, this focus also renders the work far less Musorgskian (the point of comparison for *Wat Tyler*), and more in line with a Verdian tragic love story.

A review of counterexamples brings the charged emphasis on English nationality on display in the works by native-trained composers into clearer relief. Honoring their adopted home, the three émigré composers, Berthold Goldschmidt, Karl Rankl, and Egon Wellesz, all chose operatic sources from prominent English-language writers (Shelley, Synge, and Congreve), but these sources offered them operatic potential in traditional, continental terms, with no immediate connection to British postwar experience or concerns. Shelley's gruesome family drama *The Cenci*, the source of Goldschmidt's opera, is set in the Italian Renaissance and concerns an aristocratic family caught up in church politics, while Wellesz's text, Congreve's comic novel *Incognita*, offers masked lovers and mistaken identities in an even more generic Italian Renaissance setting.

Synge's *Deirdre of the Sorrows*, set by Karl Rankl, derives from Irish mythology, and raises the question of the status of Celtic subjects. The emphasis on English subjects and settings in Festival operas contrasts with the frequency of exotic and Celtic subjects in earlier English opera.[5] Even after the severing of emotional ties with the Empire motivated a shift away from orientalist plots that had fed operatic fantasy in the nineteenth century, the "Celtic fringe" continued to provide English composers well into the twentieth century with a native orientalized realm. The Festival spirit, however, opposed both cultural regionalism and its exploitation by the center. As Becky Conekin notes (2003: 31–32), the chief sense of local belonging on display in the Festival was a *Britishness* that, while ostensibly supplementing ethnic identities, left little room for Imperial exoticism or peripheral Celticness. In an analogous manner, the Festival operas show the pre-war fascination with the Celtic world in retreat. The immigrant Rankl, out of touch, perhaps, with the prevailing mood, gravitated toward a legendary, magical plot, but not so the other composers. *The Tinners of Cornwall*, though thoroughly Cornish, betrays little glimmer of Celtic twilight. The exception here is Arwel Hughes's *Menna*, an invented tale of Welsh village magic and tragic love whose lushly romantic musical style would have been unexceptional in the nineteenth century. Hughes set the libretto in English, but when the opera was denied a Festival commission, he prepared a Welsh translation for the Welsh National Opera. Although one might accuse Hughes of *self-orientalizing* in the work, his pedigree grants the work a cultural authenticity, at least superficially, far above the assumed Celtic manner of earlier English composers.[6]

Shared themes

The parallels and points of contact among the Festival of Britain operas go beyond merely taking their subjects from English history and literature. Although not as overtly national as the source-texts just examined, beneath the widely varied settings, a set of shared themes and plot elements reveals deeply held collective concerns. The Second World War was a common experience for all the composers who wrote operas for and around the Festival. Among the legacies of the War, the problematic experience of the soldier's return to civilian society, and the consequent reintegration or disintegration of his family, weaves its way into many of their projects. Both *John Socman* and Brian Easdale's *Sleeping Children* concern a soldier who returns from war to find his fiancée or wife taken by another. Lloyd's own wartime experience was ghastly, and his recovery from terrible injury, nursed by his wife, slow and uncertain. It therefore makes sense that a tale of a heroic returning soldier facing challenges to marriage appealed to him. But as we

172 *National elements in Festival operas*

have seen, the stock characters and situations undermine any serious treatment of this theme in *John Socman*, and the critical response completely failed to notice its relevance.

The Sleeping Children is an altogether stranger case. Brian Easdale and Tyrone Guthrie envisioned the work as a serious examination of the plight of the returned soldier, and several critics agreed that it achieved this goal. Rather than sympathize with what was at its essence a timely predicament, however, audience members are more likely to have scratched their heads in bewilderment at the libretto's torrent of sententious symbolism and impersonal platitudes. At the climax of the opera the Schoolmaster, addressing no one in particular, sings "The Schoolmaster has learned how to love," after which the Janitor rings the school's Great Bell and it finally stops raining. This was not exactly the homecoming catharsis experienced by most demobbed servicemen.

Berkeley's *Nelson*, by contrast, inverts the pattern of these two works, in that the war hero, upon his return to London in Act 2, has himself fallen in love with a new woman and is estranged from his wife. His choice to return to war, duty, and death, abandoning both women, forms the central event of the plot. *Billy Budd*, in at least one reading, depicts an unsuccessful homecoming. In comparison with *John Socman*'s overcoming of adversity and happy reunion, *The Sleeping Children*'s fraught acceptance of loss in symbolic terms, and *Nelson*'s renunciation and death, Britten's opera illustrates what we might now recognize as Post-Traumatic Stress: Captain Vere struggles to come to terms with his wartime culpability for the death of Billy, but is incapable of fully achieving the closure that he so triumphantly pronounces for himself.[7] Analogues of all these experiences were widespread among the audiences for these works.

In *Billy Budd*, war is not confined to the past, but is a constant presence as a general condition coloring all action. Clifford Hindley (1989: 363) argues that Britten's opera condemns war itself:

> The theme, among other things, enabled the composer to deal with a victorious period in British naval history (not inappropriate to the commission), yet in a way which reflected his own concern with the evils of war. . . . This is no panegyric to the British Navy. On the contrary, protest against the evils of war is a significant part of the opera's message.[8]

In this reading, the war in the background of *Billy Budd*, a system of institutionalized violence, casts a pall over the entire opera, invading and distorting the actions and judgments of every character and engendering the brutality of naval discipline and the violence of the foreground plot. Even Billy's lethal outburst against Claggart derives from the environment of brutality which surrounds him.[9] By contrast, Robert Hewison (1993: 12) interprets *Billy Budd* as a cold-war allegory, a tragedy in which "the rules of war and the menace of revolution demand unbending conformity to public discipline, though at a great personal cost." Although this reading seems to contradict the attitude that Britten and his librettist E. M. Forster held towards oppression and violence, it is nonetheless fruitful, for there are political ambiguities at the core of the opera that seem to have escaped its creators' control. In readings such as Hewison's, the opera sits uneasily with the postwar political spirit of political idealism of the late forties out of which the Festival grew and that *Wat Tyler* so effectively plays into. It is thus ironically appropriate that *Billy Budd* was first performed after the fall of the Labour government that mounted the Festival. Indeed, the opera's debut followed only months after the defection to the Soviet Union of the spies Guy Burgess and Donald McLean, a crisis that brought to the surface of British political life many of the same themes—conspiracy, treason, betrayal (in Forster's famous terms) of one's country rather than one's friend—that haunt the opera. The subject was thus simultaneously in tune and discordant with the themes of the era.[10]

Furthermore, the specific war in which Britten's crew is engaged—an early stage of the Napoleonic war—was particularly topical in the postwar years, as Douglas Stevens (2011) points out, with England once again having faced down and defeated a megalomaniacal European tyrant. In Britten's work, the scarcely seen enemy is largely unreal: The French frigate externalizes the characters' internal conflicts, and the conflict with it brings out the worst in them. In *Nelson*, the very same historical war functions very differently. The French and the Battle of Trafalgar are real and decisive to the denouement of the opera, bringing out, if not what is best in the protagonist, at least what is necessary for the nation and the larger world.

The revolt against tyranny—its justification and its outcomes—is a second thematic thread connected to the Second World War that arises in a number of the Festival operas, and one whose presentation typically relies on the use of the chorus. Britten's *Billy Budd* again presents the most sophisticated case, demonstrating in the view of many critics the brutal operation of authority. For most of the opera, Britten uses the chorus to provide musical climaxes, the main ones being the Captain's Muster which ends Act 1 and the battle scene in Act 3.[11] These and similar passages provide an emotional and dramatic backdrop that gives poignancy to the divisive personal narrative played out by the three central characters. As Clifford Hindley points out, the chorus at these moments serves as a necessary foil to the darker elements of the story, particularly given the opera's Festival commission:

> [T]here is some irony in the fact that for a commemoration of national reconstruction the choice fell on a narrative which represents so graphically the wretchedness of life below decks in Nelson's navy and the inhumanity of naval discipline. The implicit criticisms of these evils as necessary concomitants of war would no doubt have commended the story to the pacifist in Britten. At the same time, the camaraderie among the men (in the shanty sequences) and the patriotic exhilaration at the prospect of action are positively portrayed.
>
> (Hindley 1999: 149)

In the final scene of the opera, the chorus briefly steps into a more active role, as the execution of Billy sparks a mutiny among his shipmates, but the revolt, set musically as grunts rather than words, appears to deprive the sailors of their humanity. Although quickly suppressed by the officers, the mutiny crystallizes the opera's central dilemma: It questions not only the morality of the military order that has hanged Billy but also the morality of struggle against such authority.

Wat Tyler similarly portrays a failed rebellion, and at greater length, but Bush's opera offers a clear moral division of characters, and the creators' hopes and sympathies are unambiguously with the struggle. The opera ends with a prophecy that the oppressive order will be successfully overthrown in the future. The meaning of the tragedy and the redemption of its victims come through the future struggle of the entire society, into which the individual is subsumed. (In *Billy Budd*, by contrast, the ultimate if problematic vision of redemption is found only in individual lives and relationships.) The background plot about the miners in *The Tinners of Cornwall*, and their short-lived rebellion in Act 3, touches on similar matters, although it advances no political orthodoxy other than sympathy for the downtrodden.

In *Wat Tyler* uprising becomes actual revolution, with the fortunes of an entire people hanging in the balance. Superficially, *Billy Budd* does not concern rebellion on this scale, but it does lie in the background. The new ideas of freedom which Vere's officers see as such a threat—the "infamous creed of 'the rights of man'"[12]—originated in the first, idealistic phase of the French Revolution, which, for all its sequelae, did overthrow an oppressive regime. The suspicion raised by the reiteration of this phrase and its accompanying musical motive is the chief instrument in the libretto and the score that brands the ship's officers and the system they serve as reactionary. The twentieth century British audience, in the context of the Festival of Britain and the incipient Cold War, recognizes that the "Rights of Man", while threatening to military order in 1797, will eventually prevail in British society.

The French Revolution also forms the context to *A Tale of Two Cities*, which thus provides an ironic counterpart to Britten's and especially Bush's opera, reminding its viewers how justified and necessary struggles for liberation can grow out of control. In contrast to the failed revolution in *Wat Tyler*, that in *A Tale of Two Cities* is of course successful, with dire consequences for the principals. As with the opening scene of *Wat Tyler*, where peasants are crushed by unfair taxes, the first scene of *A Tale of Two Cities* primes us to sympathize with another chorus seeking freedom from tyranny, when the carriage of an unconcerned nobleman runs over a child. But while Bush glosses over the ensuing bloody acts of his rioters, Benjamin's mob reveals itself as vengeful and bloodthirsty. Egged on by Madame Lafarge, it becomes the chief antagonist in the opera, in the manner of *Peter Grimes*. The massive choral ensemble in Act 2 of Peter Tranchell's opera analogously presents a chorus that becomes hostile to the protagonist. This scene, however, is only one episode in a longer plot that does not feature tyranny and rebellion, and addresses more complex moral questions than do Bush's and Benjamin's operas.

The moment we've been waiting for

In reviewing and analyzing these works as I do, I do not mean to suggest that in the years surrounding the Festival of Britain there was a secret compact by which composers agreed to address specifically national topics in opera. Nor did the Arts Council direct composers in any way toward such themes; in fact, the one time when such a course of action was proposed, when the Festival Office suggested that the Arts Council offer the subject of the Great Exhibition of 1851 to commissioned composers, the Council demurred. Nor were the means I have reviewed here by which composers imbued their works with national meaning particularly novel. A review of English opera through the preceding three centuries will turn up similar examples. But among the English settings and folkloric topics will be a heavy admixture of oriental and Celtic exotica, continental folk tales, aristocratic escapades, and *verismo* slices of life. It is unusual to find a concentration of English operas in such close temporal proximity that draw so consistently on such a range of nationally marked settings, subjects, characters, cultural referents, ideas, and symbols.

There is more to learn about how the elements I have outlined here interact with long-held nostalgic views and emerging critical ideas about the nation's identity, and how they function in other English narrative and dramatic genres of this time, which arguably address the state of the nation even more commonly than opera.[13] But it is clear that these themes had great appeal in the postwar period and the well-publicized run-up to the Festival of Britain, when changing fortunes opened up the definition of nation and its culture. Composers and their librettists responded, whether consciously or unconsciously, to newly urgent imperatives to make opera a specifically national genre and to express authentic English experiences.

Notes

1. Only limited information is available about several of these works. Mellers's opera is apparently lost. Scores of those by Gundry, Hopkins, Rankl, and Wellesz are not readily available, but I have consulted recorded excerpts of Rankl's opera and the secondary literature on Gundry, while neither the Hopkins nor Wellesz opera is central to my discussion. Of the remaining 12 works, I have examined the scores of all except the Goldschmidt, which is not germane to my discussion, and recordings of at least excerpts of all except the Benjamin and the Easdale. Tranchell's unpublished score is in the Cambridge University Library, and only brief excerpts have ever been recorded. Easdale's score is in the Britten Pears Foundation.
2. See Lew 2002 for a full consideration of national themes in this work.
3. The chorus in *The Sleeping Children* similarly represents a collective will, in that case the unconscious mind.
4. As I explain in Lew 2002, Bunyan's *Pilgrim's Progress*, as a revered seventeenth-century text, provides a similar national authenticity to Vaughan Williams's opera, although that work falls outside the categories I am analyzing here.
5. Examples include Rutland Boughton's Arthurian operas; Granville Bantock, *Caedmar* and *The Seal Woman*; Julius Benedict, *Lily of Killarney*, Charles Villiers Stanford, *Shamus O'Brien*; Ralph Vaughan Williams, *Riders to the Sea*; and Michael Balfe, *Bonny Kilmeny*.

6 Antecedents would be the Welsh and Scottish operas of Joseph Parry and Hamish MacCunn. See also Forbes 1987.
7 The insistent irruption of B-minor triads into the otherwise grandiloquent arrival in B-flat major in the opera's final pages undermines the finality of the cadence and supports this interpretation. Furthermore, the dovetailing of the opera's close with its opening suggests that Vere, like Coleridge's Ancient Mariner, has not truly found peace but is doomed to retell his tale forever.
8 See also Whittall 1990: 127.
9 Ironically for the work of an avowed pacifist, the war is the background that generates the moral ambiguity of Vere's position, and therefore offers him a chance of redemption. Only the shadowy presence of the hostile French frigate off the starboard bow justifies Vere's decision to hang Billy. If the events of the opera took place in peacetime, Billy's final cry of "Starry Vere, God bless you" could scarcely save the Captain.
10 The complexity with which *Billy Budd* deals with the effects of war stand in contrast to William Walton's contemporary *Troilus and Cressida*, which exploits the Trojan War as the setting for its tragic love story.
11 References are to the original four-act version of 1951. Britten, wanting a large-scale choral scene to end the first act, asked the librettists to insert the Captain's Muster during the revisions of the libretto in August 1949, but it attracted some of the sharpest criticism in the press—Ernest Newman likened it to *HMS Pinafore*—and Britten excised it in the 1960 revision (Crozier 1986: 21).
12 These are Claggart's words. Vere himself identifies the threat posed by Napoleonic France in more reasonable and justifiable terms: "France the tyrant who wears the cap of liberty, France who pretends to love mankind and is at war with the world. . . ."
13 For instance, a number of contemporary plays, such as George Grimaldi's *Close Combat* (1951) and Terrence Rattigan's *Deep Blue Sea* (1952) concern returning servicemen.

Afterword

The Festival of Britain generated widely conflicting impressions while it ran. In attempting to be comprehensive, historic, symbolic, entertaining, and culturally significant, it served too many constituencies and raised too many incompatible expectations not to scandalize some while it delighted others. It was simultaneously a great success and a great failure, its meaning and legacy debated ever since the day it opened, whether the topic is the architectural style and design of the exhibition, its contents, the larger programs of events and amusements, or the campaign of activities and renewal. Furthermore, as the culminating act in a contested period in British politics and culture, the Festival has attracted a wide variety of historical interpretations. The many analyses of state intervention in British culture in the forties almost all offer the Festival as a crucial piece of evidence, and in the light of each political and cultural opinion against which it is held to account it assumes a different significance.

For some, the Festival signaled the end of forties socialism: "that last flowering of wartime togetherness before the Tory government closed it down" (Fyrth 1995: 12). For others, it marked a genuine end to postwar gloom, signaling the beginning of fifties prosperity: "the conscious celebration of a settled, successful society vindicated in twentieth century war with its eye . . . on the technologies and markets of the century to come" (Hennessy 1992: 425). Arthur Marwick (1991: 8) similarly descries in the Festival real achievements and indications of future changes, such as the introduction of modern architecture and design and the advancement of media, especially the successful introduction of television. But for a third group, such as Adrian Forty, the Festival exaggerated the nation's recovery with superficial merrymaking: "The Festival provided the illusion that Britain was recovering, which was very much what people wanted to believe, but in reality the Festival concealed the fact that the patient was suffering a relapse" (Banham and Hiller 1976: 26).

Debate also continues on the kind of culture that the Festival promoted: a truly broad culture in the wartime "people's culture" mode, a diluted and popularized middlebrow culture, or unabashedly elitist highbrow culture. A similar diversity of opinion concerns its place in cultural history: as a high point, a low point, or just part of a gradual progress. Robert Hewison (1988: 48) views the Festival as a step forward, an opportunity to halt and correct the dismaying cultural disintegration and conservative drift of the foregoing six years; others see only a backward-looking, oddly Victorian affair, celebrating tradition rather than innovation despite the progressive rhetoric (Addison 1985; Hennessy 1992: 427–428).

There are similarly conflicting opinions of the Arts Council's contribution to the Festival. The Festival provided an essential stimulus in the development of the Council, allowing it to exert the full power of its advocacy and planning. The London Season of the Arts, the regional arts festivals, and the commissions and competitions for the Festival of Britain together constitute a project on a massive scale. Similar in its essentials but far greater than anything CEMA had accomplished during or after the war, the Festival helped solidify the agency's position within the government and in British culture. In the words of Robert Hewison (1988: 55–56), "For the Arts Council and the Council of Industrial Design, the Festival marks a coming of age, and the effect of the Festival was more important for these two institutions than for any individual. . . . [T]he Arts Council was confirmed in its role of leading public taste in the arts to the light, and acting as a judge of artistic quality." By accepting the additional money and responsibility to plan, organize, and realize the Festival's arts components, the Arts Council developed beyond its previous limited sphere into whole new areas of functioning, gaining "invaluable experience and information about the artistic resources of the country as a whole" (Arts Council Annual Report 1950–1951: 10). The Festival represents the high-point of the Arts Council's early existence, the first and only moment when substantial financial support backed up the philosophy under which it founded.

However, as socialist historians have pointed out, by excluding most amateur activity and demotic contributions from the Festival, the Arts Council missed a chance to open up the doors of culture to a wider public. One of the most polemical interpretations of the Festival of Britain is that of Alan Sinfield. In his 1995 essay "The Government, the People and the Festival," Sinfield views the Festival as an unequal conflict between a fading egalitarian, socialist vision of culture and the resurgent forces of traditional elitism. He reads the integration of temporary site-specific murals and sculptures into the South Bank buildings and the novel streamlined designs as indications of a new populism, breaking with old museum-based hierarchies. He further points out that elements of the Exhibition such as references to lower-class pastimes and language usage lent it a populist bent. Against these progressive features, present but underdeveloped, he holds up such traditional cultural projects as the "60 Paintings for '51" exhibit, organized by the Arts Council with the specific intent of generating lasting artworks for posterity. Similarly, Andy Croft (1995: 220), another champion of "people's culture", takes the judges of the Festival poetry contest to task, interpreting their assessment that most of the entries were of very poor quality as disdain for the genuine, if unsophisticated, poetic expression of the people. Croft offers the poetry competition—whose outcome Roy Fuller calls "a remarkable act of would-be popularization" (Banham and Hillier 1976: 187)—as an example of how "ivory tower elitists" took back control of British culture after a brief wartime and postwar golden age. In the final analysis, Sinfield and Croft regard the popular manifestations as too few and too feeble, overwhelmed by emphasis on the "posh" art of the elites and the paternalistic, top-down planning of cultural bureaucrats who presumed to know what the people wanted and how to make them happy.

It is difficult to imagine how the institutions of British governance in the late forties could have mounted a festival broad enough to satisfy critics such as Sinfield and Croft. They are largely correct in their diagnosis of the mandarinism of the Arts Council and its concentration on the professional "fine arts exclusively" (to quote its charter). But at this late date, assessments of the Council's achievement within its chosen sphere are more relevant than disparaging judgments. Considered from a high-culture perspective that values enduring contributions to the repertory, the artistic component of the Festival had its shortcomings. As time has passed, the architecture and design, if physically ephemeral, have attracted increasing respect. In music, the Festival bequeathed to the nation a major new publishing institution, *Musica Britannica*, and gave a boost to the Royal Festival Hall. But as the sensible if disillusioned member of the Music Panel predicted in his anonymous memorandum on commissions discussed in Chapter 2, for all the time and money spent, the lasting contribution to the stock of British music, literature, and fine art was not great. To be sure, a number of compositions are ripe for rediscovery; I can only hope that the present work will stimulate such interest. But at present, in concert music, only the *Three Shakespeare Songs*, Ralph Vaughan Williams's contribution to the National Competitive Music Festival, and Gordon Jacob's *Music for a Festival*, commissioned by the Arts Council, appear to have lasted. In opera, despite unprecedented breadth of offerings, only *Billy Budd* entered the permanent repertory, a fact for which neither the Festival nor the Arts Council can take much credit, since Britten probably would have written the opera anyway without a Festival commission, and Covent Garden would likely have produced it (although probably not as lavishly). At any rate, it did not become internationally successful until two decades after the Festival. Certainly, the Arts Council's opera competition was a textbook example of how not to create great art.

But even if the Festival of Britain did not bring into existence a significant new repertory of works, it incorporated the most concentrated effort in history to display British existing high-art creativity in all its forms. Nowhere was this effort more pronounced than in classical musical performance. Due to a combination of the maturing of institutions and Festival support, 1951 proved a banner year for both English concert music and opera, with a music festival of unmatched scope and size, a record number of new operas produced, and a record number of operatic revivals. Indeed, it is likely that more Britons saw a British opera in 1951 than in any previous year. Furthermore, this great survey was not merely retrospective and reactionary. The commissioning schemes, if mixed in their results, reflect a recognition that new works of art help define and celebrate past achievement. The compositions brought forth by the Festival served in this sense as a symbolic capstone, fixing the concept and parameters of the contemporary ideology of English Musical Renaissance. As I point out in Chapter 1, such a forceful demonstration of the cultural past in relation to the present might be expected to have generated a swifter reaction among contemporary artists. The fact that few composers and musical institutions responded with decisive moves in new avant-garde directions for several years suggests that in the realm of musical style and taste the Festival of Britain was not merely the culmination of previous trends and values but also an accurate representation of contemporary British classical music.

Appendix 1

British music performed in the London Season of the Arts

Composer	Work	Performers	Date	Venue
anon	Alleluia psallet	The Tudor Singers and Carl Dolmetsch Ensemble	May 16	Wigmore Hall
anon	Benedictus and Hosanna from Missa O quam suavis	The Renaissance Singers	May 30	Wigmore Hall
anon	Borey, Mr. Tollett	Carl Dolmetsch Ensemble	May 16	Wigmore Hall
anon	Coranto	Carl Dolmetsch Ensemble	May 16	Wigmore Hall
anon	Gloria on Custodi nos Domine	The Tudor Singers and Carl Dolmetsch Ensemble	May 16	Wigmore Hall
anon	Go Herte Hurte with Adversity	The Tudor Singers and Carl Dolmetsch Ensemble	May 16	Wigmore Hall
anon	Now Wel May We Mirthes Make	The Tudor Singers and Carl Dolmetsch Ensemble	May 16	Wigmore Hall
anon	Peggy Ramsay (traditional)	London Orpheus Choir	June 28	Wigmore Hall
anon	Sumer is Icumen In	The Tudor Singers and Carl Dolmetsch Ensemble	May 16	Wigmore Hall
anon	The Gipsies Round	Carl Dolmetsch Ensemble	May 16	Wigmore Hall
various	Elizabethan songs with virginals	Megan Foster and Margaret Hodson	May 21	Wigmore Hall
various	English church music	Southward Cathedral Choir	June 16	Southward Cathedral
various	Folksongs	London Philharmonic and National Youth Orchestras and mass children's choir	May 6	Royal Albert Hall
various	Folksongs	Patrick Shuldham-Shaw	June 11	Wigmore Hall
various	Folksongs and English songs	Workers Music Association Choir and Hanwell Silver Band	June 1	St Pancras Town Hall
various	Folksongs of the British Isles	Pipers Guild Quartet, etc	June 13	Cowdray Hall
Alwyn, William	Festival March	London Symphony Orchestra	May 20	Festival Hall
Alwyn, William	Festival March	London Junior and Senior Orchestras	June 1	Festival Hall

continued...

British music performed in the London Season of the Arts ... Continued

Composer	Work	Performers	Date	Venue
Alwyn, William	Festival March	massed brass bands	May 12	Royal Albert Hall
Armstrong Gibbs, Cecil	A Litany	London Orpheus Choir	June 28	Wigmore Hall
Armstrong Gibbs, Cecil	Cradle Song	London Orpheus Choir	June 28	Wigmore Hall
Armstrong Gibbs, Cecil	Five Eyes	various	June 11	Wigmore Hall
Armstrong Gibbs, Cecil	Hypochondriacus	(unrecorded)	June 20	Wigmore Hall
Armstrong Gibbs, Cecil	Silver	various	June 11	Wigmore Hall
Armstrong Gibbs, Cecil	The Flooded Stream	(unrecorded)	June 21	Central Hall, Westminster
Armstrong Gibbs, Cecil	The Listeners	British Federation of Music Festivals	June 23	Festival Hall
Armstrong Gibbs, Cecil	The Stranger	Fleet Street Choir	May 24	Wigmore Hall
Armstrong Gibbs, Cecil	Ye Spotted Snakes	London Philharmonic and National Youth Orchestras and mass children's choir	May 6	Royal Albert Hall
Arne, Thomas	Harpsichord Concerto in G minor	Goldsbrough Orchestra and Thurston Dart	May 23	Wigmore Hall
Arne, Thomas	Libera me	South London Bach Society	May 29	St Bartholomew the Great, Smithfield
Arne, Thomas	Now Phoebus Sinketh into the West	various	June 4	Wigmore Hall
Arne, Thomas	O Ravishing Delight	various	May 21	Wigmore Hall
Arne, Thomas	O salutaris hostia	Westminster Cathedral Choir	May 14	Westminster Cathedral
Arne, Thomas	Rule Britannia	joint orchestra and choir	May 3	Festival Hall
Arne, Thomas	Sonata 3 in G	George Malcolm	June 6	Wigmore Hall
Arne, Thomas	Sonata 5 in B flat	George Malcolm	June 6	Wigmore Hall
Arne, Thomas	Sweet Echo, from *Comus*	Goldsbrough Orchestra and Ena Mitchell	May 23	Wigmore Hall
Arne, Thomas	Thou Soft-flowing Avon	various	June 4	Wigmore Hall
Arne, Thomas	Under the Greenwood Tree	various	June 4	Wigmore Hall
Arne, Thomas	Where the Bee Sucks	various	June 4	Wigmore Hall
Arne, Thomas	Would You Taste the Noonday Air, from *Comus*	Goldsbrough Orchestra and Ena Mitchell	May 23	Wigmore Hall
Arnell, Richard	Ballet: *Punch and the Child*	Royal Philharmonic Orchestra	June 17	Royal Albert Hall

Composer	Work	Performer	Date	Venue
Arnold, Malcolm	Overture: The Smoke	London Philharmonic Orchestra	June 30	Festival Hall
Attwood, Thomas	Motet	Westminster Cathedral Choir	May 13	Westminster Cathedral
Austin, Frederick	Orpheus	(unrecorded)	June 18	Wigmore Hall
Babell, William	Concerto for Two Recorders and Strings	Dolmetsch Foundation	May 10	Wigmore Hall
Bairstow, Edward	Blessed City	Westminster Abbey Choir	July 1	Westminster Abbey
Bairstow, Edward	Let All Mortal Flesh	Westminster Abbey Choir and Purcell Club and Choral Scholars	July 6	Westminster Abbey
Balfour Gardiner, Henry	Cargoes	London Orpheus Choir	June 28	Wigmore Hall
Bantock, Granville	Coronach	London Orpheus Choir	June 28	Wigmore Hall
Bantock, Granville	Prometheus Unbound	massed brass bands	May 12	Royal Albert Hall
Bantock, Granville	The Lake Isle of Innisfree	London Orpheus Choir	June 28	Wigmore Hall
Bartlet, John	Wither Runneth My Sweetheart	various	May 21	Wigmore Hall
Bateson, Thomas	Have I Found Her?	The Tudor Singers	May 16	Wigmore Hall
Bateson, Thomas	Song: If Floods of Tears	Carl Dolmetsch Ensemble and Dorothy Langmaid	May 16	Wigmore Hall
Bax, Arnold	I Heard a Piper Piping	various	June 4	Wigmore Hall
Bax, Arnold	Nonet	Dennis Brain Wind Quintet and Wigmore Ensemble	June 5	RBA Galleries
Bax, Arnold	Oboe Quintet	Martin String Quartet and Evelyn Rothwell	May 23	Queen Mary Hall
Bax, Arnold	Overture: London Pageant	BBC Symphony	May 20	Royal Albert Hall
Bax, Arnold	Overture to a Picaresque Comedy	London Symphony Orchestra	May 27	Festival Hall
Bax, Arnold	Summer Music	Royal Philharmonic Orchestra	May 16	Royal Albert Hall
Bax, Arnold	Symphony 3	Bournemouth Municipal Orchestra	June 26	Festival Hall
Bax, Arnold	This Worldes Joie	St Michael's Singers	May 9	St Michael's Cornhill
Bax, Arnold	Tintagel	City of Birmingham Symphony Orchestra	June 20	Festival Hall
Benjamin, Arthur	A Tall Story	(unrecorded)	June 21	Central Hall, Westminster
Benjamin, Arthur	Ballade	Boyd Neel Orchestra	June 23	Wigmore Hall
Bennet, John	Weep O Mine Eyes	The Tudor Singers	May 16	Wigmore Hall
Berkeley, Lennox	Divertimento	Liverpool Symphony	June 6	Festival Hall

continued...

British music performed in the London Season of the Arts . . . Continued

Composer	Work	Performers	Date	Venue
Berkeley, Lennox	Five Songs of Walter de la Mare	Dennis Brain Wind Quintet and Wigmore Ensemble	June 5	RBA Galleries
Berkeley, Lennox	How Love Came In	various	June 11	Wigmore Hall
Berkeley, Lennox	Serenade for Strings	Riddick String Orchestra	June 26	Wigmore Hall
Berkeley, Lennox	Silver	various	June 11	Wigmore Hall
Berkeley, Lennox	Sonata for Recorder and Harpsichord	Dolmetsch Foundation	May 10	Wigmore Hall
Bishop, Henry Rowley	Bid Me Discourse	various	May 21	Wigmore Hall
Bliss, Arthur	A Colour Symphony	Modern Symphony Orchestra	May 26	Northern Polytechnic
Bliss, Arthur	Morning Heroes	BBC Symphony and Choral Society	May 13	Festival Hall
Bliss, Arthur	Pastorale	Tobin Chamber Orchestra and London Choral Society	June 1	Central Hall, Westminster
Bliss, Arthur	Piano Concerto	Yorkshire Symphony	May 23	Festival Hall
Bliss, Arthur	Seven American Poems	various	June 11	Wigmore Hall
Bliss, Arthur	String Quartet 1	Martin String Quartet	May 23	Queen Mary Hall
Blow, John	Ground in G	George Malcolm	June 6	Wigmore Hall
Blow, John	Lift Up Your Heads	Renaissance Singers and Basil Lam Sonata Ensemble	June 20	Church of All Souls, Langham Place
Blow, John	Ode for St Cecilia's Day	Goldsbrough Orchestra and Choir	May 23	Wigmore Hall
Blow, John	Salvator mundi	Renaissance Singers	June 20	Church of All Souls, Langham Place
Blow, John	Suite for Strings, from Venus and Adonis	Riddick String Orchestra	June 26	Wigmore Hall
Blow, John	The Fair Lover to His Black Mistress	various	June 4	Wigmore Hall
Blow, John	The Self-banished	Scott Joynt and Hubert Dawkes	May 23	Wigmore Hall
Blow, John	The Self-banished	various	May 21	Wigmore Hall
Blow, John	Toccata for Double Organ	Geraint Jones	June 20	Church of All Souls, Langham Place

Blow, John	Trio Sonata in A	Basil Lam Sonata Ensemble	June 20	Church of All Souls, Langham Place
Boughton, Rutland	Faery Chorus, from *The Immortal Hour*	London Orpheus Choir	June 28	Wigmore Hall
Boughton, Rutland	Final Scene, from *The Round Table*	London Philharmonic Orchestra and London Philharmonic Choir	May 17	Festival Hall
Boyce, William	Matins Service in C	Westminster Abbey Choir	July 7	Westminster Abbey
Boyce, William	Symphony 7 in B flat	Boyd Neel Orchestra	June 30	Wigmore Hall
Boyce, William	Symphony 8 in D minor	Goldsbrough Orchestra	May 23	Wigmore Hall
Boyce, William	The Lord is My Light and My Salvation	Renaissance Singers	June 20	Church of All Souls, Langham Place
Boyce, William	The Song of Momus to Mars	Scott Joynt and Hubert Dawkes	May 23	Wigmore Hall
Boyce, William	The Song of Momus to Mars	various	May 21	Wigmore Hall
Boyce, William	Trio Sonata in A	Basil Lam Sonata Ensemble	June 20	Church of All Souls, Langham Place
Bridge, Frank	Fantasy Trio	Rubbra-Gruenberg-Pleeth Trio	May 16	RBA Galleries
Bridge, Frank	Go Not, Happy Day	Peter Pears and Benjamin Britten	May 7	Wigmore Hall
Bridge, Frank	Love Went A-riding	Peter Pears and Benjamin Britten	May 7	Wigmore Hall
Bridge, Frank	Second Trio	(unrecorded)	May 15	RBA Galleries
Bridge, John Frederick	Bold Turpin	London Orpheus Choir	June 28	Wigmore Hall
Britten, Benjamin	A Spring Symphony	London Philharmonic Orchestra	May 24	Festival Hall
Britten, Benjamin	A Waly Waly (arr)	various	May 14	Wigmore Hall
Britten, Benjamin	Duets	Mewton-Woods	May 22	RBA Galleries
Britten, Benjamin	Fish in the Unruffled Lakes	Peter Pears and Benjamin Britten	May 7	Wigmore Hall
Britten, Benjamin	Les Illuminations	Philharmonia Orchestra and Suzanne Danco Moiseiwitsch	June 11	Festival Hall
Britten, Benjamin	My Beloved is Mine and I am His	Peter Pears and Benjamin Britten	May 7	Wigmore Hall
Britten, Benjamin	O Can Ye Sew Cushions (arr)	various	May 14	Wigmore Hall
Britten, Benjamin	O Come You Not from Newcastle (arr)	various	May 14	Wigmore Hall
Britten, Benjamin	Prelude and Fugue	Boyd Neel Orchestra	June 23	Wigmore Hall

continued...

British music performed in the London Season of the Arts . . . Continued

Composer	Work	Performers	Date	Venue
Britten, Benjamin	Simple Symphony	London Philharmonic Orchestra	May 28	Festival Hall
Britten, Benjamin	Sinfonia da Requiem	London Symphony Orchestra	May 15	Festival Hall
Britten, Benjamin	Spring Symphony	London Philharmonic Orchestra	May 10	Festival Hall
Britten, Benjamin	String Quartet 2	Martin String Quartet	May 23	Queen Mary Hall
Britten, Benjamin	Sweet Polly Oliver (arr)	various	May 14	Wigmore Hall
Britten, Benjamin	The Ashgrove (arr)	various	May 14	Wigmore Hall
Britten, Benjamin	The Miller of Dee (arr)	various	May 14	Wigmore Hall
Britten, Benjamin	The Ploughboy (arr)	various	May 14	Wigmore Hall
Britten, Benjamin	The Trees that Grow So High (arr)	various	May 14	Wigmore Hall
Britten, Benjamin	There's None to Soothe (arr)	various	May 14	Wigmore Hall
Britten, Benjamin	Variations on a Theme of Frank Bridge	Boyd Neel Orchestra	June 23	Wigmore Hall
Bull, John	Bull's Goodnight	Margaret Hodsdon	June 27	Wigmore Hall
Bull, John	Fantasia on a Flemish Chorale "Laet ons met herten reijne"	Geraint Jones	June 20	Church of All Souls, Langham Place
Bull, John	Regina Galliard	Margaret Hodsdon	June 27	Wigmore Hall
Bull, John	The Prince's Courante	Margaret Hodsdon	June 27	Wigmore Hall
Bull, John	Trumpet Pavan	Margaret Hodsdon	June 27	Wigmore Hall
Burt, Francis	Two motets	South London Bach Society	May 29	St Bartholomew the Great, Smithfield
Bush, Alan	Nottingham Symphony	London Philharmonic Orchestra	June 19	BBC Studio Maida Vale
Bush, Alan	Our Song	Workers Music Association Choir and Hanwell Silver Band	June 1	St Pancras Town Hall
Bush, Geoffrey	The Impatient Lover	various	June 4	Wigmore Hall
Bush, Geoffrey	Twelfth Night: An Entertainment	Tobin Chamber Orchestra and London Choral Society	June 1	Central Hall, Westminster
Butterworth, George	Love Blows as the Wind Blows	various	May 28	Wigmore Hall
Butterworth, George	Seventeen Come Sunday (arr)	various	June 11	Wigmore Hall
Butterworth, George	The Banks of Green Willow	Liverpool Philharmonic	June 7	Festival Hall

Butterworth, George	Three Songs from *A Shropshire Lad*	various	June 4	Wigmore Hall
Byrd, William	A Gigg	Carl Dolmetsch Ensemble	May 16	Wigmore Hall
Byrd, William	Alack When I Do Look Back	The Renaissance Singers	June 23	St Sepulchre's Holborn
Byrd, William	Assumpta est Maria	Golden Age Singers	June 13	Wigmore Hall
Byrd, William	Ave verum corpus	Schola Polyphonica	June 13	Wigmore Hall
Byrd, William	Ave verum corpus	Westminster Abbey Choir	July 5	Westminster Abbey
Byrd, William	Ave verum corpus	Westminster Abbey Choir and Purcell Club and Choral Scholars	July 6	Westminster Abbey
Byrd, William	Ave verum corpus	Westminster Cathedral Choir	May 17	Westminster Cathedral
Byrd, William	Awake Mine Eyes	Schola Polyphonica	June 13	Wigmore Hall
Byrd, William	Ballett: Tho Amaryllis Dance in Green	Schola Polyphonica	June 13	Wigmore Hall
Byrd, William	Beata viscera	Golden Age Singers	June 13	Wigmore Hall
Byrd, William	Canzonet: The Nightingale So Pleasant	Golden Age Singers	June 13	Wigmore Hall
Byrd, William	Christus resurgens	Schola Polyphonica	June 13	Wigmore Hall
Byrd, William	Christus resurgens	The Renaissance Singers	June 16	St Sepulchre's Holborn
Byrd, William	Civitas sancti tui	Schola Polyphonica	June 13	Wigmore Hall
Byrd, William	Come Jolly Swains	Golden Age Singers	June 13	Wigmore Hall
Byrd, William	Come to Me Grief for Ever	Golden Age Singers	June 13	Wigmore Hall
Byrd, William	Fantasia 1 for Viols in Six Parts	London Consort of Viols	June 13	Wigmore Hall
Byrd, William	Fantasia in 5 Parts	London Consort of Viols	June 13	Wigmore Hall
Byrd, William	Galliard: Wolsey's Wild	Margaret Hodsdon	June 13	Wigmore Hall
Byrd, William	Hear My Prayer	Westminster Abbey Choir and Purcell Club and Choral Scholars	July 6	Westminster Abbey
Byrd, William	I Thought that Love Had Been a Boy	Golden Age Singers	June 13	Wigmore Hall
Byrd, William	Justorum animae	Schola Polyphonica	June 13	Wigmore Hall

continued ...

British music performed in the London Season of the Arts . . . Continued

Composer	Work	Performers	Date	Venue
Byrd, William	Justorum animae	Westminster Abbey Choir	June 30	Westminster Abbey
Byrd, William	Laudibus in sanctis	Fleet Street Choir	June 27	Wigmore Hall
Byrd, William	Lullaby for Solo Voice and Viols	London Consort of Viols and Margaret Field-Hyde	June 13	Wigmore Hall
Byrd, William	Mass for Five Voices	Westminster Abbey Choir	July 8	Westminster Abbey
Byrd, William	Mass for Five Voices	Westminster Cathedral Choir	May 20	Westminster Cathedral
Byrd, William	Mass for Four Voices	Westminster Cathedral Choir	May 14	Westminster Cathedral
Byrd, William	Mass for Three Voices	Westminster Abbey Choir	June 27	Westminster Abbey
Byrd, William	Motet	Westminster Cathedral Choir	May 13	Westminster Cathedral
Byrd, William	O Rex gloriae	Golden Age Singers	June 13	Wigmore Hall
Byrd, William	Pavan: The Earl of Salisbury	Margaret Hodsdon	June 13	Wigmore Hall
Byrd, William	Pavane and Galliard: Bray	London Consort of Viols	June 27	Wigmore Hall
Byrd, William	Praise Our Lord All Ye Gentiles	Golden Age Singers	June 13	Wigmore Hall
Byrd, William	Praise Our Lord All Ye Gentiles	Westminster Abbey Choir	July 6	Westminster Abbey
Byrd, William	Psalm 114	The Renaissance Singers	June 23	St Sepulchre's Holborn
Byrd, William	Senex puerum portabat	Golden Age Singers	June 13	Wigmore Hall
Byrd, William	Sing Joyfully	Westminster Abbey Choir	July 8	Westminster Abbey
Byrd, William	The Great Service	Westminster Abbey Choir	June 28	Westminster Abbey
Byrd, William	The Great Evensong Service	Westminster Abbey Choir	July 6	Westminster Abbey
Byrd, William	The Leaves Be Green	London Consort of Viols	June 13	Wigmore Hall
Byrd, William	Tu es pastor ovium	Westminster Abbey Choir	June 29	Westminster Abbey
Byrd, William	Tu es Petrus	Westminster Abbey Choir	June 28	Westminster Abbey
Byrd, William	Turn Our Captivity	Schola Polyphonica	June 13	Wigmore Hall
Byrd, William	Variations on Mistress Mine	Margaret Hodsdon	June 13	Wigmore Hall
Byrd, William	Veni sancte spiritus	Westminster Cathedral Choir	May 14	Westminster Cathedral
Campion, Thomas	Awake Sweet Love	Peter Pears and Benjamin Britten	May 7	Wigmore Hall
Campion, Thomas	Shall I Come, Sweet love	Peter Pears and Benjamin Britten	May 7	Wigmore Hall
Campion, Thomas	The Cypress Curtain of the Night	Peter Pears and Benjamin Britten	May 7	Wigmore Hall
Campion, Thomas	There is a Garden in Her Face	various	May 21	Wigmore Hall

Causton, Thomas	Eucharist Service (excerpts)	St Bartholomew's Choir	June 12	St Bartholomew the Great, Smithfield
Cavendish, Michael	Down in the Valley	various	May 21	Wigmore Hall
Cavendish, Michael	Wandering in This Place	Golden Age Singers	June 27	Wigmore Hall
Clarke, Rebecca	Viola Sonata	Pipers Guild Quartet, etc	June 13	Cowdray Hall
Coleridge-Taylor, Samuel	Rhapsodic Dance: The Bamboula	Band and Trumpeters of Kneller Hall	May 14	Festival Hall
Cosyn, Benjamin	The Goldfinch	Margaret Hodsdon	May 9	Wigmore Hall
Darke, Harold	Advenante Deo	St Michael's Singers	May 9	St Michael's Cornhill
Darke, Harold	Choral Prelude on a Theme	St Michael's Singers	May 9	St Michael's Cornhill
Darke, Harold	O Brother Man	St Michael's Singers	May 9	St Michael's Cornhill
Davies, William Hubert	Festival Overture	London Philharmonic Orchestra and Welsh Festival Choir	May 19	Festival Hall
Davy, Richard	Excerpts from the Passion	The Renaissance Singers	May 30	Wigmore Hall
Delius, Frederick	*A Mass of Life*	Royal Philharmonic Orchestra and London Philharmonic Choir	June 7	Royal Albert Hall
Delius, Frederick	Brigg Fair	London Symphony Orchestra	May 27	Festival Hall
Delius, Frederick	Intermezzo from *Fennimore and Gerda*	Halle Orchestra	May 25	Festival Hall
Delius, Frederick	Love's Philosophy	various	June 4	Wigmore Hall
Delius, Frederick	Paris, Song of a Great City	Yorkshire Symphony	May 23	Festival Hall
Delius, Frederick	The Splendour Falls on Castle Walls	Fleet Street Choir	May 24	Wigmore Hall
Delius, Frederick	The Walk to the Paradise Garden	City of Birmingham Symphony Orchestra	June 21	Festival Hall
Delius, Frederick	To Be Sung of a Summer's Night on the Water	London Orpheus Choir	June 28	Wigmore Hall
Delius, Frederick	Violin Concerto	Modern Symphony Orchestra and Frederick Grinke	May 26	Northern Polytechnic
Dowland, John	Can She Excuse My Wrongs	various	May 28	Wigmore Hall
Dowland, John	Come Again Sweet Love	Dorian Singers and London Consort of Viols	May 30	Wigmore Hall
Dowland, John	Daphne Was Not So Chaste	London Consort of Viols	May 30	Wigmore Hall

continued...

British music performed in the London Season of the Arts . . . Continued

Composer	Work	Performers	Date	Venue
Dowland, John	Fantasia: Farewell	Basil Lam	May 30	Wigmore Hall
Dowland, John	Fantasia: Forlorn Hope	Basil Lam	May 30	Wigmore Hall
Dowland, John	Fine Knacks for Ladies	various	May 28	Wigmore Hall
Dowland, John	Flow My Tears	London Consort of Viols	May 30	Wigmore Hall
Dowland, John	From Silent Night	London Consort of Viols	May 30	Wigmore Hall
Dowland, John	In Darkness Let Me Dwell	various	May 28	Wigmore Hall
Dowland, John	Lachrymae antiquae	London Consort of Viols	May 30	Wigmore Hall
Dowland, John	Mr John Langton's Pavan	London Consort of Viols	May 30	Wigmore Hall
Dowland, John	Partsong: Come Heavy Sleep	Dorian Singers	May 30	Wigmore Hall
Dowland, John	Partsong: Fine Knacks for Ladies	Dorian Singers	May 30	Wigmore Hall
Dowland, John	Partsong: Sleep Wayward Thoughts	Dorian Singers	May 30	Wigmore Hall
Dowland, John	Say Love If Ever Thou Didst Find	Dorian Singers and London Consort of Viols	May 30	Wigmore Hall
Dowland, John	Semper Dowland semper dolens	London Consort of Viols	May 30	Wigmore Hall
Dowland, John	Sleep Wayward Thoughts	London Consort of Viols	May 30	Wigmore Hall
Dowland, John	The Earl of Essex Galliard	London Consort of Viols	May 30	Wigmore Hall
Dowland, John	The King of Denmark's Galliard	Basil Lam	May 30	Wigmore Hall
Dowland, John	Thou Mighty God	Peter Pears and Benjamin Britten	May 7	Wigmore Hall
Dowland, John	To Ask for All Thy Love	London Consort of Viols	May 30	Wigmore Hall
Dowland, John	Weep You No More Sad Fountains	Dorian Singers and London Consort of Viols	May 30	Wigmore Hall
Dowland, John	What If I Never Speed	London Consort of Viols	May 30	Wigmore Hall
Dunstable, John	Crux fidelis	The Tudor Singers and Carl Dolmetsch Ensemble	May 16	Wigmore Hall
Dunstable, John	O rosa bella	The Tudor Singers and Carl Dolmetsch Ensemble	May 16	Wigmore Hall
Dunstable, John	Sancta Maria	The Tudor Singers and Carl Dolmetsch Ensemble	May 16	Wigmore Hall

Dunstable, John	Veni sancte spiritus	The Tudor Singers and Carl Dolmetsch Ensemble	May 16	Wigmore Hall
Dyson, George	Song for a Festival	London Philharmonic Orchestra	May 19	Central Hall, Westminster
Dyson, George	Song for a Festival	London Symphony Orchestra	May 26	Central Hall, Westminster
Dyson, George	Song for a Festival	London Philharmonic and National Youth Orchestras and mass children's choir	May 6	Royal Albert Hall
Dyson, George	Song for a Festival	Workers Music Association Choir and Hanwell Silver Band	June 1	St Pancras Town Hall
Dyson, George	*The Canterbury Pilgrims*	London Symphony Orchestra and Alexandra Choir	June 12	Festival Hall
Dyson, George	Who Would True Valour See	London Philharmonic Orchestra and Free ChurchUnion Choir	June 23	Royal Albert Hall
East, Michael	Pavane and Galliard	London Consort of Viols	May 9	Wigmore Hall
East, Michael	Triumphavi 7 in five parts	London Consort of Viols	May 9	Wigmore Hall
East, Michael	Two Four-part Fantasias	London Consort of Viols	June 27	Wigmore Hall
Eccles, John	The Jolly Jolly Breeze	various	June 4	Wigmore Hall
Edwardes, Richard	Partsong: On Going to My Naked Bed	The Tudor Singers	May 16	Wigmore Hall
Elgar, Edward	Benedictus	London Philharmonic Orchestra and Free Church Union Choir	June 23	Royal Albert Hall
Elgar, Edward	Cello Concerto	London Symphony Orchestra and Pierre Fournier	May 28	Royal Albert Hall
Elgar, Edward	Cockaigne	London Symphony Orchestra	May 9	Festival Hall
Elgar, Edward	Cockaigne	London Symphony Orchestra	May 20	Festival Hall
Elgar, Edward	Cockaigne	London Philharmonic Orchestra	June 30	Festival Hall
Elgar, Edward	Cockaigne	London Philharmonic and National Youth Orchestras	May 6	Royal Albert Hall
Elgar, Edward	Death on the Hills	London Orpheus Choir	June 28	Wigmore Hall

continued ..

British music performed in the London Season of the Arts . . . Continued

Composer	Work	Performers	Date	Venue
Elgar, Edward	Enigma Variations	London Philharmonic Orchestra	June 30	Central Hall, Westminster
Elgar, Edward	Enigma Variations	Halle Orchestra	May 25	Festival Hall
Elgar, Edward	Enigma Variations	Philharmonia Orchestra	June 28	Festival Hall
Elgar, Edward	Enigma Variations	Modern Symphony Orchestra	May 26	Northern Polytechnic
Elgar, Edward	Falstaff	City of Birmingham Symphony Orchestra	June 20	Festival Hall
Elgar, Edward	Introduction and Allegro	London Symphony Orchestra	May 28	Royal Albert Hall
Elgar, Edward	Introduction and Allegro	Riddick String Orchestra	June 5	St Bartholomew the Great, Smithfield
Elgar, Edward	Introduction and Allegro	Jacques String Orchestra	May 31	Victoria and Albert Museum
Elgar, Edward	It's to Be a Wild Wind	London Orpheus Choir	June 28	Wigmore Hall
Elgar, Edward	Motet	Westminster Cathedral Choir	May 13	Westminster Cathedral
Elgar, Edward	My Love Dwelt in a Northern Land	Fleet Street Choir	May 24	Wigmore Hall
Elgar, Edward	O salutaris hostia	Westminster Cathedral Choir	May 20	Westminster Cathedral
Elgar, Edward	Overture: In the South	London Philharmonic Orchestra	May 17	Festival Hall
Elgar, Edward	Piano Quintet	Aeolian String Quartet and Rene Soames	May 30	Queen Mary Hall
Elgar, Edward	Pomp and Circumstance March 1	joint orchestra and choir	May 3	Festival Hall
Elgar, Edward	Pomp and Circumstance March 4	Band and Trumpeters of Kneller Hall	May 14	Festival Hall
Elgar, Edward	Prologue from *The Apostles*	London Philharmonic Orchestra and mass choir	June 2	Royal Albert Hall
Elgar, Edward	Sea Pictures	London Symphony Orchestra and Kathleen Ferrier	May 28	Royal Albert Hall
Elgar, Edward	Serenade for Strings	Riddick String Orchestra	June 27	Queen Mary Hall
Elgar, Edward	Severn Suite	massed brass bands	May 12	Royal Albert Hall
Elgar, Edward	Symphony 1	London Philharmonic Orchestra	May 7	Festival Hall
Elgar, Edward	Symphony 1	London Symphony Orchestra	June 17	Festival Hall
Elgar, Edward	Symphony 2	London Symphony Orchestra	May 28	Royal Albert Hall

Elgar, Edward	*The Apostles*	London Symphony Orchestra and Royal Choral Society	May 10	Royal Albert Hall
Elgar, Edward	*The Dream of Gerontius*	London Symphony Orchestra and Royal Choral Society	May 24	Royal Albert Hall
Elgar, Edward	*The Dream of Gerontius*	Southward Cathedral Choir	May 19	Southward Cathedral
Elgar, Edward	*The Kingdom*	London Symphony Orchestra and Royal Choral Society	May 17	Royal Albert Hall
Elgar, Edward	The Music Makers	London Symphony Orchestra and Alexandra Choir	June 12	Festival Hall
Elgar, Edward	Wand of Youth Suite 1	London Symphony Orchestra	May 26	Central Hall, Westminster
Farmer, John	Fair Phyllis I Saw	The Tudor Singers	May 16	Wigmore Hall
Farnaby, Giles	Construe My Meaning	The Tudor Singers	May 16	Wigmore Hall
Farnaby, Giles	Farnaby's Dream	Margaret Hodsdon	June 27	Wigmore Hall
Farnaby, Giles	His Humour	Margaret Hodsdon	June 27	Wigmore Hall
Farnaby, Giles	His Rest	Margaret Hodsdon	June 27	Wigmore Hall
Farnaby, Giles	Pawles Wharf	Margaret Hodsdon	June 27	Wigmore Hall
Farnaby, Giles	Tower Hill	Margaret Hodsdon	June 27	Wigmore Hall
Farrant, Richard	Magnificat	St Bartholomew's Choir	June 12	St Bartholomew the Great, Smithfield
Fayrfax, Robert	Aeternae laudis lilium	The Renaissance Singers	May 30	Wigmore Hall
Fayrfax, Robert	Aeternae laudis lilium	The Renaissance Singers	June 16	St Sepulchre's Holborn
Fayrfax, Robert	O Johannes beatissimus	The Renaissance Singers	May 30	Wigmore Hall
Ferrabosco, Alfonso	Four-part Fantasia	London Consort of Viols	June 27	Wigmore Hall
Finzi, Gerald	Three Songs from *Earth and Air and Rain*	various	June 11	Wigmore Hall
Forde, Thomas	Almighty God Who Has Me Bought	London Philharmonic Orchestra and Free Church Union Choir	June 23	Royal Albert Hall
Foster, Arnold	Piano Concerto on English Country Dance Tunes	Arnold Foster Choir and Orchestra	June 7	Central Hall, Westminster

continued . .

British music performed in the London Season of the Arts . . . Continued

Composer	Work	Performers	Date	Venue
Frankel, Benjamin	Violin Concerto	London Philharmonic Orchestra	June 19	BBC Studio Maida Vale
Fricker, Peter Racine	String Quartet	Amadeus String Quartet	May 9	Queen Mary Hall
Fricker, Peter Racine	Violin Concerto	Jacques String Orchestra	May 3	Victoria and Albert Museum
Fricker, Peter Racine	Wind Quintet	Dennis Brain Wind Quintet	June 5	RBA Galleries
Gibbons, Orlando	Ah Dear Heart	Golden Age Singers	May 9	Wigmore Hall
Gibbons, Orlando	Almighty and Everlasting God	Westminster Abbey Choir	July 2	Westminster Abbey
Gibbons, Orlando	Behold Thou Hast Made My Days	Renaissance Singers	June 20	Church of All Souls, Langham Place
Gibbons, Orlando	Fantasia in Four Parts	Geraint Jones	June 20	Church of All Souls, Langham Place
Gibbons, Orlando	Fantasia no 5 in Three Parts	London Consort of Viols	May 9	Wigmore Hall
Gibbons, Orlando	Faux-bourdons Evensong Service	Westminster Abbey Choir	June 25	Westminster Abbey
Gibbons, Orlando	Great King of Gods	The Renaissance Singers	June 23	St Sepulchre's Holborn
Gibbons, Orlando	Hosanna to the Son of David	Westminster Abbey Choir and Purcell Club and Choral Scholars	July 6	Westminster Abbey
Gibbons, Orlando	If Ye Be Risen Again with Christ	The Renaissance Singers	June 23	St Sepulchre's Holborn
Gibbons, Orlando	In Humble Faith I Dedicate to Thee	London Philharmonic Orchestra and Free Church Union Choir	June 23	Royal Albert Hall
Gibbons, Orlando	O Clap Your Hands	Westminster Abbey Choir	June 30	Westminster Abbey
Gibbons, Orlando	O Lord Increase My Faith	Westminster Abbey Choir	July 3	Westminster Abbey
Gibbons, Orlando	Short Evensong Service	Westminster Abbey Choir	June 26	Westminster Abbey
Gibbons, Orlando	Short Matins Service	Westminster Abbey Choir	July 5	Westminster Abbey
Gibbons, Orlando	The Fairest Nymphs	Margaret Hodsdon	May 9	Wigmore Hall
Gibbons, Orlando	What Is Our Life?	Cambridge University Madrigal Society	May 9	Wigmore Hall
Gibbons, Orlando	Why Art Thou So Heavy O My Soul	The Renaissance Singers	June 23	St Sepulchre's Holborn

Composer	Work	Performer	Date	Venue
Gibbs, Joseph	Violin Sonata in D minor	Neville Marriner and Thurston Dart	May 23	Wigmore Hall
Goss, John	Motet	Westminster Cathedral Choir	May 13	Westminster Cathedral
Grainger, Percy	Six Dukes Went A-fishin (arr)	various	June 11	Wigmore Hall
Greaves, Thomas	Ballett: Come Away, Sweet Love	Golden Age Singers	June 27	Wigmore Hall
Greene, Maurice	O Praise the Lord	Westminster Abbey Choir	June 28	Westminster Abbey
Gurney, Ivor	Epitaph	various	June 4	Wigmore Hall
Gurney, Ivor	Hawk and Buckle	various	June 4	Wigmore Hall
Gurney, Ivor	Sleep	(unrecorded)	June 21	Wigmore Hall
Gurney, Ivor	Sleep	various	June 4	Wigmore Hall
Gurney, Ivor	Spring	various	June 4	Wigmore Hall
Hamerton, Ann	Song: A Memory	Pipers Guild Quartet, etc	June 13	Cowdray Hall
Hamerton, Ann	Song: The Persian Flute	Riddick String Orchestra	June 27	Queen Mary Hall
Hamerton, Ann	Song: The Wind and the Sea	Pipers Guild Quartet, etc	June 13	Cowdray Hall
Handel, George Frideric	Arm Arm Ye Brave, from *Judas Maccabeus*	Band and Trumpeters of Kneller Hall	May 14	Festival Hall
Handel, George Frideric	Concerto Grosso op 6 no 12	Riddick String Orchestra	May 22	St Bartholomew the Great, Smithfield
Handel, George Frideric	Concerto Grosso op 6 no 4	Riddick String Orchestra	June 5	St Bartholomew the Great, Smithfield
Handel, George Frideric	Excerpts from *Israel in Egypt*	Westminster Choral Society	May 19	Central Hall, Westminster
Handel, George Frideric	Excerpts from *Israel in Egypt*	Philharmonia Orchestra and mass Yorkshire choir	June 24	Royal Albert Hall
Handel, George Frideric	Excerpts from *Judas Maccabeus*	Westminster Choral Society	May 19	Central Hall, Westminster
Handel, George Frideric	Excerpts from *Messiah*	Westminster Choral Society	May 19	Central Hall, Westminster
Handel, George Frideric	Excerpts from *Messiah*	Philharmonia Orchestra and mass Yorkshire choir	June 24	Royal Albert Hall

continued ..

British music performed in the London Season of the Arts . . . Continued

Composer	Work	Performers	Date	Venue
Handel, George Frideric	Hallelujah and Amen, from *Messiah*	joint orchestra and choir	May 3	Festival Hall
Handel, George Frideric	Haste Thee Nymph from *L'Allegro*	London Orpheus Choir	June 28	Wigmore Hall
Handel, George Frideric	*Messiah*	Tobin Chamber Orchestra and London Choral Society	June 30	St Marylebone Parish Church
Handel, George Frideric	*Messiah*	Westminster Abbey Choir and Jacques String Orchestra	July 3	Westminster Abbey
Handel, George Frideric	Music for the Royal Fireworks	London Symphony Orchestra	May 9	Festival Hall
Handel, George Frideric	Oboe Concerto in G minor	Riddick String Orchestra	June 26	Wigmore Hall
Handel, George Frideric	Ode for St Cecilia's Day	Tobin Chamber Orchestra and London Choral Society	June 1	Central Hall, Westminster
Handel, George Frideric	Overture in D minor	London Junior and Senior Orchestras	June 1	Festival Hall
Handel, George Frideric	Overture in D minor	City of Birmingham Symphony Orchestra	June 20	Festival Hall
Handel, George Frideric	Overture to *Alcina*	Jacques String Orchestra	May 31	Victoria and Albert Museum
Handel, George Frideric	*Solomon*	Royal Philharmonic Orchestra and London Philharmonic Choir	May 29	Royal Albert Hall
Handel, George Frideric	Songs	Jenny Tourel	June 4	Festival Hall
Handel, George Frideric	Trio for Recorder, Violin, and Harpsichord	Dolmetsch Foundation	May 10	Wigmore Hall
Handel, George Frideric	Water Music	London Philharmonic Orchestra	May 19	Central Hall, Westminster
Handel, George Frideric	Water Music	London Symphony Orchestra	May 20	Festival Hall
Handel, George Frideric	Ye Boundless Realms of Joy	London Philharmonic Orchestra and Free Church Union Choir	June 23	Royal Albert Hall
Handel, George Frideric	Zadok the Priest	joint orchestra and choir	May 3	Festival Hall
Harris, William Henry	Praise the Lord	St Michael's Singers	May 9	St Michael's Cornhill
Harty, Hamilton	Herrin's in the Bay	various	June 4	Wigmore Hall
Harty, Hamilton	The Mystic Trumpeter	Philharmonia Orchestra and Goldsmith's Choral Union	June 29	Festival Hall

Hatton, John Liptrot	To Anthea	various	May 21	Wigmore Hall
Henderson, Thomas	The Villagers' Round	London Orpheus Choir	June 28	Wigmore Hall
Henry VIII	Fantasie	Carl Dolmetsch Ensemble	May 16	Wigmore Hall
Holbrooke, Joseph	Labour Songs	Workers Music Association Choir and Hanwell Silver Band	June 1	St Pancras Town Hall
Holbrooke, Joseph	Ulalume	Royal Philharmonic Orchestra	June 17	Royal Albert Hall
Holst, Gustav	A Little Music	various	June 4	Wigmore Hall
Holst, Gustav	Ballet Music, from *The Perfect Fool*	Arnold Foster Choir and Orchestra	June 7	Central Hall, Westminster
Holst, Gustav	Ballet Music, from *The Perfect Fool*	London Philharmonic Orchestra	May 10	Festival Hall
Holst, Gustav	Ballet Music, from *The Perfect Fool*	London Philharmonic Orchestra and mass choir	June 2	Royal Albert Hall
Holst, Gustav	Betelgeuse	various	June 4	Wigmore Hall
Holst, Gustav	Hammersmith	London Philharmonic Orchestra	June 30	Festival Hall
Holst, Gustav	Hymn: Lord Who Has Made Us for Thine Own	London Philharmonic and National Youth Orchestras and mass children's choir	May 6	Royal Albert Hall
Holst, Gustav	Jupiter from The Planets	London Philharmonic Orchestra	June 30	Central Hall, Westminster
Holst, Gustav	My Sweetheart's Like Venus	London Orpheus Choir	June 28	Wigmore Hall
Holst, Gustav	Ode on a Grecian Urn	Arnold Foster Choir and Orchestra	June 7	Central Hall, Westminster
Holst, Gustav	Persephone	Peter Pears and Benjamin Britten	May 7	Wigmore Hall
Holst, Gustav	Rhyme	various	June 4	Wigmore Hall
Holst, Gustav	Second Suite for Military Band	Band and Trumpeters of Kneller Hall	May 14	Festival Hall
Holst, Gustav	Suite in E flat	massed brass bands	May 12	Royal Albert Hall
Holst, Gustav	The Planets	BBC Symphony	May 20	Royal Albert Hall
Holst, Gustav	The Song of the Blacksmith (arr)	Fleet Street Choir	May 24	Wigmore Hall
Hook, James	Hush Every Breeze	various	May 21	Wigmore Hall
Hopkins, Antony	A Melancholy Song	various	June 4	Wigmore Hall
Howells, Herbert	A Maid Peerless	British Federation of Music Festivals	June 22	Festival Hall

continued ..

British music performed in the London Season of the Arts … Continued

Composer	Work	Performers	Date	Venue
Howells, Herbert	Collegium Regale Evensong Service	Westminster Abbey Choir	July 7	Westminster Abbey
Howells, Herbert	Gavotte	various	June 4	Wigmore Hall
Howells, Herbert	Rhapsody in D flat	St Michael's Singers	May 9	St Michael's Cornhill
Howells, Herbert	Salve Regina	Westminster Cathedral Choir	May 20	Westminster Cathedral
Howells, Herbert	Song: King David	Pipers Guild Quartet, etc	June 13	Cowdray Hall
Hughes, Arwell	Song of Deliverance	London Philharmonic Orchestra and Welsh Festival Choir	May 19	Festival Hall
Hume, Tobias	Fain Would I Change That Note	various	May 21	Wigmore Hall
Humfrey, Pelham	By the Waters of Babylon	Renaissance Singers and Basil Lam Sonata Ensemble	June 20	Church of All Souls, Langham Place
Humfrey, Pelham	I Pass All My Days in a Shady Old Grove	Scott Joynt and Hubert Dawkes	May 23	Wigmore Hall
Hyde	Nunc dimittis	Westminster Cathedral Choir	May 20	Westminster Cathedral
Ireland, John	A London Overture	London Philharmonic Orchestra	May 10	Festival Hall
Ireland, John	A London Overture	London Symphony Orchestra	June 17	Festival Hall
Ireland, John	A London Overture	London Philharmonic Orchestra	June 30	Festival Hall
Ireland, John	Concertino Pastorale	Boyd Neel Orchestra	June 23	Wigmore Hall
Ireland, John	Fantasy Sonata for Clarinet and Piano	(unrecorded)	May 15	RBA Galleries
Ireland, John	Fantasy Trio	Rubbra-Gruenberg-Pleeth Trio	May 16	RBA Galleries
Ireland, John	Hymn for a Child	various	May 14	Wigmore Hall
Ireland, John	Man in His Labour Rejoiceth	Workers Music Association Choir and Hanwell Silver Band	June 1	St Pancras Town Hall
Ireland, John	My Fair	various	May 14	Wigmore Hall
Ireland, John	Piano Concerto 1	London Symphony Orchestra	May 27	Festival Hall
Ireland, John	Piano Concerto 1	Philharmonia Orchestra and Eileen Joyce	May 6	Royal Albert Hall
Ireland, John	The Advent	various	May 14	Wigmore Hall
Ireland, John	The Land of Lost Content	various	May 14	Wigmore Hall
Ireland, John	The Salley Gardens	various	May 14	Wigmore Hall

Ireland, John	The Scapegoat	various	May 14	Wigmore Hall
Ireland, John	The Soldier's Return	various	May 14	Wigmore Hall
Ireland, John	These Things Shall Be	London Philharmonic Orchestra and mass choir	June 2	Royal Albert Hall
Ireland, John	These Things Shall Be	Workers Music Association Choir and Hanwell Silver Band	June 1	St Pancras Town Hall
Ivimey, Ella	Songs from the 18th Century (arr)	Riddick String Orchestra	June 27	Queen Mary Hall
Jacob, Gordon	A William Byrd Suite	Arnold Foster Choir and Orchestra	June 7	Central Hall, Westminster
Jacob, Gordon	Concerto for Horn and Strings	Riddick String Orchestra and Dennis Brain	May 8	Wigmore Hall
Jacob, Gordon	Music for a Festival	Band and Trumpeters of Kneller Hall	May 14	Festival Hall
Jacob, Gordon	Prelude to Revelry	massed brass bands	May 12	Royal Albert Hall
Jacob, Gordon	Suite 3	Bournemouth Municipal Orchestra	June 27	Festival Hall
Jacobson, Maurice	Ariel	British Federation of Music Festivals	June 22	Festival Hall
Jenkins, John	Fantasia in Five Parts	Boyd Neel Orchestra	June 6	Wigmore Hall
Jones, Robert	Love's God is a Boy	Peter Pears and Benjamin Britten	May 7	Wigmore Hall
Jones, Robert	Sweet Kate	various	May 21	Wigmore Hall
Lambert, Constant	Dirge, from *Cymbeline*	London Philharmonic Orchestra	June 19	BBC Studio Maida Vale
Lambert, Constant	Summer's Last Will and Testament	London Symphony Orchestra and Goldsmith's Choral Union	May 29	Festival Hall
Lawes, Henry	Fantasia in Six Parts	Boyd Neel Orchestra	June 6	Wigmore Hall
Lawes, Henry	Night and Day	various	June 4	Wigmore Hall
Leveridge, Richard	Advice	various	June 4	Wigmore Hall
Lidel, Andreas	Divertimento in A	Riddick String Orchestra	June 27	Queen Mary Hall
Lidel, Andreas	Divertimento in A	Riddick String Orchestra	May 8	Wigmore Hall
Linley, Thomas (Jr)	O Bid Your Faithful Ariel Fly	various	June 4	Wigmore Hall
Locke, Matthew	Excerpts from *Cupid and Death*	Boyd Neel Orchestra	June 6	Wigmore Hall
Locke, Matthew	Toccata	Geraint Jones	June 20	Church of All Souls, Langham Place

continued...

British music performed in the London Season of the Arts . . . Continued

Composer	Work	Performers	Date	Venue
Lutyens, Elisabeth	Nativity	Riddick String Orchestra and Edith Lake	June 5	St Bartholomew the Great, Smithfield
Maconchy, Elizabeth	String Quartet 6	Martin String Quartet	May 22	RBA Galleries
Maconchy, Elizabeth	Theme and Variations for Strings	Riddick String Orchestra	June 27	Queen Mary Hall
Malcolm, George	Te lucis ante terminum	Westminster Cathedral Choir	May 20	Westminster Cathedral
Malcolm, George	Veni creator	Westminster Cathedral Choir	May 13	Westminster Cathedral
Malcolm, George	Veni creator	Westminster Cathedral Choir	14 May 14	Westminster Cathedral
Malcolm, George	Veni creator	Westminster Cathedral Choir	15 May 15	Westminster Cathedral
Moeran, Ernest John	In Youth is Pleasure	Peter Pears and Benjamin Britten	7 May 7	Wigmore Hall
Moeran, Ernest John	Lonely Waters (arr)	various	11 June 11	Wigmore Hall
Moeran, Ernest John	Nutting Time (arr)	various	June 11	Wigmore Hall
Moeran, Ernest John	Overture to a Masque	City of Birmingham Symphony Orchestra	June 21	Festival Hall
Moeran, Ernest John	Said I that Amaryllis	Fleet Street Choir	May 24	Wigmore Hall
Moeran, Ernest John	Seven Poems of James Joyce	various	May 28	Wigmore Hall
Moeran, Ernest John	Sinfonietta	Arnold Foster Choir and Orchestra	June 7	Central Hall, Westminster
Moeran, Ernest John	Spring, the Sweet Spring	Fleet Street Choir	May 24	Wigmore Hall
Moeran, Ernest John	Symphony in G Minor	Scottish National Orchestra	June 14	Festival Hall
Moeran, Ernest John	The Jolly Carter	London Philharmonic and National Youth Orchestras and mass children's choir	May 6	Royal Albert Hall
Moeran, Ernest John	The Treasure of My Heart	London Orpheus Choir	June 28	Wigmore Hall
Morley, Thomas	Agnus Dei	Westminster Abbey Choir and Purcell Club and Choral Scholars	July 6	Westminster Abbey
Morley, Thomas	Ballett: About the Maypole New	Golden Age Singers	May 9	Wigmore Hall
Morley, Thomas	Canzonet: I Go Before, My Darling	Golden Age Singers	June 27	Wigmore Hall
Morley, Thomas	Canzonet: Joy, Joy Doth So Arise	Golden Age Singers	June 27	Wigmore Hall
Morley, Thomas	Canzonet: Miraculous Love's Wounding	Golden Age Singers	June 27	Wigmore Hall
Morley, Thomas	Faux-bourdons Evensong Service	Westminster Abbey Choir	June 27	Westminster Abbey

Morley, Thomas	Hard by a Crystal Fountain	Cambridge University Madrigal Society	May 9	Wigmore Hall
Morley, Thomas	Ho! Who comes here?	Golden Age Singers	May 9	Wigmore Hall
Morley, Thomas	Ho! Who comes here?	Golden Age Singers	June 27	Wigmore Hall
Morley, Thomas	Il Lamento	Carl Dolmetsch Ensemble	May 16	Wigmore Hall
Morley, Thomas	In Dew of Roses	Golden Age Singers	May 9	Wigmore Hall
Morley, Thomas	It Was a Lover and His Lass	various	May 21	Wigmore Hall
Morley, Thomas	Out of the Deep	The Renaissance Singers	June 23	St Sepulchre's Holborn
Morley, Thomas	The Frog Galliard	Carl Dolmetsch Ensemble	May 16	Wigmore Hall
Morley, Thomas	Will Ye Buy a Fine Dog	various	May 28	Wigmore Hall
Morris, Reginald Owen	Brisk Young Sailor (arr)	Fleet Street Choir	May 24	Wigmore Hall
Mundy, William	O Lord the Maker of All Things	The Tudor Singers	May 16	Wigmore Hall
Mundy, William	O Lord the Maker of All Things	The Renaissance Singers	June 23	St Sepulchre's Holborn
Mundy, William	O Lord the Maker of All Things	Westminster Abbey Choir	July 3	Westminster Abbey
Murray	Motet	Westminster Cathedral Choir	May 14	Westminster Cathedral
Newman, Master	A Pavyon	Carl Dolmetsch Ensemble	May 16	Wigmore Hall
Nicholas, John Morgan	Ysbryd yw Duw	London Philharmonic Orchestra and Welsh Festival Choir	May 19	Festival Hall
Orr, Charles Wilfred	Song: Plucking the Rushes	Pipers Guild Quartet, etc	June 13	Cowdray Hall
Parcham, Andrew	Violin Sonata in G major	Neville Marriner and Thurston Dart	May 23	Wigmore Hall
Parry, C. H. Hubert	Blessed Pair of Sirens	London Philharmonic Orchestra and mass choir	June 2	Royal Albert Hall
Parry, C. H. Hubert	Come Pretty Wag	Fleet Street Choir	May 24	Wigmore Hall
Parry, C. H. Hubert	Crabbed Age and Youth	various	June 4	Wigmore Hall
Parry, C. H. Hubert	Fantasia and Fugue in G	St Michael's Singers	May 9	St Michael's Cornhill
Parry, C. H. Hubert	Hear My Words	Westminster Abbey Choir	July 8	Westminster Abbey
Parry, C. H. Hubert	I Was Glad	Westminster Abbey Choir	June 30	Westminster Abbey
Parry, C. H. Hubert	If Thou Would'st Ease Thine Heart	various	June 4	Wigmore Hall
Parry, C. H. Hubert	Lord Let Me Know Mine End	St Michael's Singers	May 9	St Michael's Cornhill
Parry, C. H. Hubert	Love is a Babe	various	June 4	Wigmore Hall

continued...

British music performed in the London Season of the Arts ... Continued

Composer	Work	Performers	Date	Venue
Parry, C. H. Hubert	Never Weatherbeaten Sail	Fleet Street Choir	May 24	Wigmore Hall
Parry, C. H. Hubert	Ode at a Solemn Music	joint orchestra and choir	May 3	Festival Hall
Parry, C. H. Hubert	There is an Old Belief	Westminster Abbey Choir and Purcell Club and Choral Scholars	July 6	Westminster Abbey
Parry, C. H. Hubert	Through the Ivory Gate	various	May 31	Wigmore Hall
Parry, C. H. Hubert	To Althea from Prison	various	June 4	Wigmore Hall
Parry, C. H. Hubert	Why So Pale, Young Lover	various	May 31	Wigmore Hall
Parsley, Osbert	Magnificat and Nunc dimittis	The Renaissance Singers	June 23	St Sepulchre's Holborn
Pearsall, Robert Lucas De	Salve Regina	Westminster Cathedral Choir	May 19	Westminster Cathedral
Peerson, Martin	The Fall of the Leafe	Margaret Hodsdon	May 9	Wigmore Hall
Peerson, Martin	The Primrose	Margaret Hodsdon	May 9	Wigmore Hall
Pepusch-Dent	Excerpts from *The Beggar's Opera*	Boyd Neel Orchestra	June 6	Wigmore Hall
Philips, Peter	Tibi laus tibi gloria	Westminster Cathedral Choir	May 20	Westminster Cathedral
Pilkington, Francis	Care For Thy Soul	The Tudor Singers	May 16	Wigmore Hall
Playford, John	Suite of Dances from *The Dancing Master*	Boyd Neel Orchestra	June 6	Wigmore Hall
Poston, Elizabeth	Sonata for Pipes and Piano	Pipers Guild Quartet, etc	June 13	Cowdray Hall
Poston, Elizabeth	Song Cycle: A Garland of Laurel 'In Praise of Woman'	Riddick String Orchestra	June 27	Queen Mary Hall
Poston, Elizabeth	Sweet Suffolk Owl	various	June 4	Wigmore Hall
Priaulx Rainier, Ivy	String Quartet	Amadeus String Quartet	May 9	Queen Mary Hall
Price, Richard Maldwyn	English Folk Fantasia	Workers Music Association Choir and Hanwell Silver Band	June 1	St Pancras Town Hall
Purcell, Henry	A Dialogue between Strephon and Dorinda	various	May 29	Victoria and Albert Museum
Purcell, Henry	Air	Philharmonia Orchestra and Birmingham University Special Choir	May 22	Victoria and Albert Museum

Purcell, Henry	Anthem: Praise the Lord O My Soul	Boyd Neel Orchestra and Kings College Cambridge Choir and Westminster Abbey Choir	June 26	Westminster Abbey
Purcell, Henry	Bess of Bedlam	various	May 14	Wigmore Hall
Purcell, Henry	Bess of Bedlam	various	May 29	Victoria and Albert Museum
Purcell, Henry	Bonduca	Philharmonia Orchestra and Morley College Choir	June 19	Victoria and Albert Museum
Purcell, Henry	Catch: An Ape, a Lion, a Fox, and an Ass	Boyd Neel Orchestra and Oxford University Opera Club Chorus	June 12	Victoria and Albert Museum
Purcell, Henry	Catch: Bartholomew Fair	Boyd Neel Orchestra and Oxford University Opera Club Chorus	June 12	Victoria and Albert Museum
Purcell, Henry	Catch: Bring the Bowl and Cool Nants	Boyd Neel Orchestra and Oxford University Opera Club Chorus	June 12	Victoria and Albert Museum
Purcell, Henry	Catch: Once, Trice, Thrice I Julia Tried	Boyd Neel Orchestra and Oxford University Opera Club Chorus	June 12	Victoria and Albert Museum
Purcell, Henry	Catch: Since Time So Kind to Us Does Prove	Boyd Neel Orchestra and Oxford University Opera Club Chorus	June 12	Victoria and Albert Museum
Purcell, Henry	Catch: To Lovers of Music	Boyd Neel Orchestra and Oxford University Opera Club Chorus	June 12	Victoria and Albert Museum
Purcell, Henry	Catch: Who Comes There?	Boyd Neel Orchestra and Oxford University Opera Club Chorus	June 12	Victoria and Albert Museum
Purcell, Henry	Cebell	Philharmonia Orchestra and Birmingham University Special Choir	May 22	Victoria and Albert Museum
Purcell, Henry	Celemene	various	May 14	Wigmore Hall
Purcell, Henry	Chacony in G minor	Philharmonia Orchestra and Covent Garden Opera Chorus	May 8	Victoria and Albert Museum
Purcell, Henry	Come Unto These Yellow Sands	London Philharmonic and National Youth Orchestras and mass children's choir	May 6	Royal Albert Hall

continued ...

British music performed in the London Season of the Arts ... Continued

Composer	Work	Performers	Date	Venue
Purcell, Henry	Coronation Anthem: My Heart is Inditing	Boyd Neel Orchestra and Kings College Cambridge Choir and Westminster Abbey Choir	June 26	Westminster Abbey
Purcell, Henry	Crown the Altar, Deck the Shrine	Philharmonia Orchestra and Covent Garden Opera Chorus	May 8	Victoria and Albert Museum
Purcell, Henry	Ducibella	various	May 29	Victoria and Albert Museum
Purcell, Henry	Evening Hymn	various	May 29	Victoria and Albert Museum
Purcell, Henry	Evensong Service in G minor	Westminster Abbey Choir	July 3	Westminster Abbey
Purcell, Henry	Fantasia of Four Parts 2 in B flat	Boyd Neel Orchestra and Oxford University Opera Club Chorus	June 12	Victoria and Albert Museum
Purcell, Henry	Fantasia of Four Parts 4 in F minor	Boyd Neel Orchestra and Oxford University Opera Club Chorus	June 12	Victoria and Albert Museum
Purcell, Henry	Fantasia of Four Parts 8 in G	Boyd Neel Orchestra and Oxford University Opera Club Chorus	June 12	Victoria and Albert Museum
Purcell, Henry	Fantasia Upon One Note in Five Parts	Goldsbrough Choir and Orchestra	June 5	Chapel of the Royal Hospital, Chelsea
Purcell, Henry	Frost scene, from *King Arthur*	Philharmonia Orchestra and Birmingham University Special Choir	May 22	Victoria and Albert Museum
Purcell, Henry	Harpsichord Suite no 5 in G	various	May 29	Victoria and Albert Museum
Purcell, Henry	Harpsichord Suite no 7 in D minor	Philharmonia Orchestra and Birmingham University Special Choir	May 22	Victoria and Albert Museum
Purcell, Henry	Hear My Prayer	Westminster Abbey Choir	June 26	Westminster Abbey
Purcell, Henry	I Will Give Thanks unto Thee O Lord	Goldsbrough Choir and Orchestra	June 5	Chapel of the Royal Hospital, Chelsea
Purcell, Henry	I will Sing unto the Lord	Westminster Abbey Choir and Purcell Club and Choral Scholars	July 6	Westminster Abbey

Purcell, Henry	If Music be the Food of Love (1st and 3rd versions)	Philharmonia Orchestra and Morley College Choir	June 19	Victoria and Albert Museum
Purcell, Henry	In nomine of Seven Parts	Boyd Neel Orchestra and Oxford University Opera Club Chorus	June 12	Victoria and Albert Museum
Purcell, Henry	In nomine of Six Parts	Goldsbrough Choir and Orchestra	June 5	Chapel of the Royal Hospital, Chelsea
Purcell, Henry	Lesson from Musick's Handmaid	Philharmonia Orchestra and Birmingham University Special Choir	May 22	Victoria and Albert Museum
Purcell, Henry	Lord, How Long wilt Thou Be Angry	Westminster Abbey Choir and Purcell Club and Choral Scholars	July 6	Westminster Abbey
Purcell, Henry	Lost is My Quiet	various	May 14	Wigmore Hall
Purcell, Henry	Man is for the Woman Made	various	May 14	Wigmore Hall
Purcell, Henry	Masque from *Diocletian*	Philharmonia Orchestra and Covent Garden Opera Chorus	May 8	Victoria and Albert Museum
Purcell, Henry	Masque from *Timon of Athens*	Philharmonia Orchestra and Birmingham University Special Choir	May 22	Victoria and Albert Museum
Purcell, Henry	Music for a While	Philharmonia Orchestra and Covent Garden Opera Chorus	May 8	Victoria and Albert Museum
Purcell, Henry	Music from *Don Quixote*	various	May 29	Victoria and Albert Museum
Purcell, Henry	My Beloved Spake	Philharmonia Orchestra and Morley College Choir	June 19	Victoria and Albert Museum
Purcell, Henry	No, No, Resistance is But Vain	London Chamber Orchestra and Chamber Singers	May 15	Victoria and Albert Museum
Purcell, Henry	Not All My Torments	various	May 29	Victoria and Albert Museum
Purcell, Henry	O dive custos auricae domus	London Chamber Orchestra and Chamber Singers	May 15	Victoria and Albert Museum
Purcell, Henry	O Sing unto the Lord	Westminster Abbey Choir	July 5	Westminster Abbey
Purcell, Henry	Ode for Queen Mary's Birthday 1693: Come Ye Sons of Art	Philharmonia Orchestra and Morley College Choir	June 19	Victoria and Albert Museum

continued...

British music performed in the London Season of the Arts ... *Continued*

Composer	Work	Performers	Date	Venue
Purcell, Henry	Ode for St Cecilia's Day 1682: Welcome to All the Pleasures	Boyd Neel Orchestra and Oxford University Opera Club Chorus	June 12	Victoria and Albert Museum
Purcell, Henry	Ode for St Cecilia's Day 1692: Hail Bright Cecilia	Goldsbrough Choir and Orchestra	June 5	Chapel of the Royal Hospital, Chelsea
Purcell, Henry	Ode for the Duke of Gloucester's Birthday 1695	London Chamber Orchestra and Chamber Singers	May 15	Victoria and Albert Museum
Purcell, Henry	Overture Airs and Dances from *The Married Beau*	London Chamber Orchestra and Chamber Singers	May 15	Victoria and Albert Museum
Purcell, Henry	Overture in D from *The Fairy Queen*	Boyd Neel Orchestra and Kings College Cambridge Choir and Westminster Abbey Choir	June 26	Westminster Abbey
Purcell, Henry	Rejoice in the Lord Always	Goldsbrough Choir and Orchestra	June 5	Chapel of the Royal Hospital, Chelsea
Purcell, Henry	Remember Not, Lord	Westminster Abbey Choir	June 26	Westminster Abbey
Purcell, Henry	Remember Not, Lord	Westminster Abbey Choir and Purcell Club and Choral Scholars	July 6	Westminster Abbey
Purcell, Henry	Rigadoon from Musick's Handmaid part II	Philharmonia Orchestra and Birmingham University Special Choir	May 22	Victoria and Albert Museum
Purcell, Henry	Saul and the Witch of Endor	Goldsbrough Choir and Orchestra	June 5	Chapel of the Royal Hospital, Chelsea
Purcell, Henry	Saul and the Witch of Endor	various	May 14	Wigmore Hall
Purcell, Henry	Sonata 7 in C for Two Violins, Cello, and Harpsichord	London Chamber Orchestra and Chamber Singers	May 15	Victoria and Albert Museum
Purcell, Henry	Song Tune from Musick's Handmaid part II	Philharmonia Orchestra and Birmingham University Special Choir	May 22	Victoria and Albert Museum
Purcell, Henry	Songs	Jenny Tourel	June 4	Festival Hall
Purcell, Henry	Soul of the World, from Ode for St Cecilia's Day	joint orchestra and choir	May 3	Festival Hall
Purcell, Henry	Sound the Trumpet	various	May 14	Wigmore Hall

Purcell, Henry	Suite for Strings	London Philharmonic Orchestra and mass choir	June 2	Royal Albert Hall
Purcell, Henry	Suite from *Abdelazer*	Boyd Neel Orchestra and Oxford University Opera Club Chorus	June 12	Victoria and Albert Museum
Purcell, Henry	Suite from *King Arthur*	Philharmonia Orchestra and Covent Garden Opera Chorus	May 8	Victoria and Albert Museum
Purcell, Henry	Suite from *The Virtuous Wife*	Philharmonia Orchestra and Birmingham University Special Choir	May 22	Victoria and Albert Museum
Purcell, Henry	Sylvan scene from *King Arthur*	Philharmonia Orchestra and Birmingham University Special Choir	May 22	Victoria and Albert Museum
Purcell, Henry	Te Deum and Jubilate in D	Boyd Neel Orchestra and Kings College Cambridge Choir and Westminster Abbey Choir	June 26	Westminster Abbey
Purcell, Henry	The Blessed Virgin's Exposition	Philharmonia Orchestra and Covent Garden Opera Chorus	May 8	Victoria and Albert Museum
Purcell, Henry	*The Indian Queen*	London Chamber Orchestra and Chamber Singers	May 15	Victoria and Albert Museum
Purcell, Henry	The Meditation	various	May 29	Victoria and Albert Museum
Purcell, Henry	The Queen's Epicedium	Philharmonia Orchestra and Morley College Choir	June 19	Victoria and Albert Museum
Purcell, Henry	The Vision of Britain, from *King Arthur*	Philharmonia Orchestra and Birmingham University Special Choir	May 22	Victoria and Albert Museum
Purcell, Henry	There's Not a Swain	various	May 14	Wigmore Hall
Purcell, Henry	Thou Knowest Lord	Westminster Abbey Choir	July 6	Westminster Abbey
Purcell, Henry	Toccata for Double Organ	Boyd Neel Orchestra and Kings College Cambridge Choir and Westminster Abbey Choir	June 26	Westminster Abbey
Purcell, Henry	Trio Sonata 12 in D major	Boyd Neel Orchestra and Oxford University Opera Club Chorus	June 12	Victoria and Albert Museum

continued...

British music performed in the London Season of the Arts ... *Continued*

Composer	Work	Performers	Date	Venue
Purcell, Henry	Trio Sonata 2 in B flat	Boyd Neel Orchestra and Oxford University Opera Club Chorus	June 12	Victoria and Albert Museum
Purcell, Henry	Trio Sonata 3 in A minor	Philharmonia Orchestra and Covent Garden Opera Chorus	May 8	Victoria and Albert Museum
Purcell, Henry	Trio Sonata 5 in A minor	various	May 29	Victoria and Albert Museum
Purcell, Henry	Trio Sonata 6 in G minor	Boyd Neel Orchestra and Oxford University Opera Club Chorus	June 12	Victoria and Albert Museum
Purcell, Henry	Trio Sonata 7 in E minor	various	May 29	Victoria and Albert Museum
Purcell, Henry	Trio Sonata 9 in C minor	various	May 29	Victoria and Albert Museum
Purcell, Henry	Trio Sonata 9 in F	Philharmonia Orchestra and Covent Garden Opera Chorus	May 8	Victoria and Albert Museum
Purcell, Henry	Trumpet Voluntary	London Philharmonic Orchestra	June 30	Central Hall, Westminster
Purcell, Henry	What Can We Poor Females Do?	various	May 29	Victoria and Albert Museum
Purcell, Henry	What Can We Poor Females Do?	various	May 14	Wigmore Hall
Quilter, Roger	Blow Blow Thou Winter Wind	various	June 4	Wigmore Hall
Quilter, Roger	Go Lovely Rose	various	June 4	Wigmore Hall
Quilter, Roger	Love's Philosophy	various	June 4	Wigmore Hall
Quilter, Roger	Non nobis Domine	London Philharmonic Orchestra and mass choir	June 2	Royal Albert Hall
Quilter, Roger	Over the Mountains (arr)	various	June 11	Wigmore Hall
Rawsthorne, Alan	Away Delights	various	June 4	Wigmore Hall
Rawsthorne, Alan	Cortege	Scottish National Orchestra	June 15	Festival Hall
Rawsthorne, Alan	God Lyceus	various	June 4	Wigmore Hall
Rawsthorne, Alan	Piano Concerto 2	London Symphony Orchestra and Clifford Curzon	June 17	Festival Hall

Rawsthorne, Alan	Quartet for Clarinet and Strings	(unrecorded)	May 15	RBA Galleries
Redford, John	Rejoice in the Lord	St Bartholomew's Choir	June 12	St Bartholomew the Great, Smithfield
Redford, John	Rejoice in the Lord	Westminster Abbey Choir and Purcell Club and Choral Scholars	July 6	Westminster Abbey
Roberton, Hugh S	Dream Angus	London Orpheus Choir	June 28	Wigmore Hall
Roseingrave, Thomas	Three movements from The Harpsichord Lessons	George Malcolm	June 6	Wigmore Hall
Rosseter, Philip	What Then is Love But Mourning	various	May 28	Wigmore Hall
Rosseter, Philip	When Laura Smiles	Peter Pears and Benjamin Britten	May 7	Wigmore Hall
Roy Henry	Sanctus	The Tudor Singers and Carl Dolmetsch Ensemble	May 16	Wigmore Hall
Rubbra, Edmund	Amoretti	various	May 28	Wigmore Hall
Rubbra, Edmund	Missa in honorem Sancti Dominici	Fleet Street Choir	May 24	Wigmore Hall
Rubbra, Edmund	Te Deum	London Philharmonic Orchestra and London Philharmonic Choir	June 30	Festival Hall
Rubbra, Edmund	Trio	Rubbra-Gruenberg-Pleeth Trio	May 16	RBA Galleries
Sampson, Godfrey	Awake My Soul, and With the Sun	London Philharmonic Orchestra and Free Church Union Choir	June 23	Royal Albert Hall
Scott, Cyril	Irish Serenade	Riddick String Orchestra	June 26	Wigmore Hall
Sharp, Cecil	O No John (arr)	various	June 11	Wigmore Hall
Shaw, Geoffrey	Ring Out, Ye Crystal Spheres	London Philharmonic and National Youth Orchestras and mass children's choir	May 6	Royal Albert Hall
Sheppard, John	I Give You a New Commandment	Westminster Abbey Choir	June 27	Westminster Abbey
Sheppard, John	Playnsong Mass for a Mene	Westminster Cathedral Choir	May 16	Westminster Cathedral
Smyth, Ethel	Overture to *The Wreckers*	Royal Philharmonic Orchestra	June 17	Royal Albert Hall
Somervell, Arthur	Poems from *A Shropshire Lad*	various	June 4	Wigmore Hall
Stanford, Charles Villiers	Beati quorum via	St Michael's Singers	May 9	St Michael's Cornhill

continued ..

British music performed in the London Season of the Arts ... Continued

Composer	Work	Performers	Date	Venue
Stanford, Charles Villiers	Beati quorum via	Westminster Abbey Choir and Purcell Club and Choral Scholars	July 6	Westminster Abbey
Stanford, Charles Villiers	Caelos ascendit hodie	Westminster Abbey Choir and Purcell Club and Choral Scholars	July 6	Westminster Abbey
Stanford, Charles Villiers	Coelos ascendit hodie	Fleet Street Choir	May 24	Wigmore Hall
Stanford, Charles Villiers	Cuttin' Rushes	various	June 11	Wigmore Hall
Stanford, Charles Villiers	Evensong Service in A	Westminster Abbey Choir	July 8	Westminster Abbey
Stanford, Charles Villiers	Evensong Service in B flat	Westminster Abbey Choir	June 28	Westminster Abbey
Stanford, Charles Villiers	Evensong Service in C	Westminster Abbey Choir	July 1	Westminster Abbey
Stanford, Charles Villiers	Heraclitus	Fleet Street Choir	May 24	Wigmore Hall
Stanford, Charles Villiers	Heraclitus	various	June 11	Wigmore Hall
Stanford, Charles Villiers	Justorum animae	Westminster Abbey Choir and Purcell Club and Choral Scholars	July 6	Westminster Abbey
Stanford, Charles Villiers	La Belle Dame sans merci	various	June 11	Wigmore Hall
Stanford, Charles Villiers	Magnificat	St Michael's Singers	May 9	St Michael's Cornhill
Stanford, Charles Villiers	Matins Service in B flat	Westminster Abbey Choir	July 8	Westminster Abbey
Stanford, Charles Villiers	Matins Service in C	Westminster Abbey Choir	June 30	Westminster Abbey
Stanford, Charles Villiers	My Gentle Harp	London Orpheus Choir	June 28	Wigmore Hall
Stanford, Charles Villiers	Songs of the Fleet	London Philharmonic Orchestra and mass choir	June 2	Royal Albert Hall
Stanford, Charles Villiers	Songs of the Sea	London Philharmonic Orchestra and Welsh Festival Choir	May 19	Festival Hall
Stanford, Charles Villiers	The Blue Bird	London Orpheus Choir	June 28	Wigmore Hall
Stanford, Charles Villiers	The Fairy Lough, from An Irish Idyll	various	June 11	Wigmore Hall
Stanford, Charles Villiers	The Fairy Lough, from An Irish Idyll	various	May 31	Wigmore Hall
Stanford, Charles Villiers	The Monkey's Carol	various	June 11	Wigmore Hall
Stanford, Charles Villiers	The Witch	Fleet Street Choir	May 24	Wigmore Hall

Composer	Work	Performers	Date	Venue
Stanford, Charles Villiers	When Mary Through the Garden Went	Fleet Street Choir	May 24	Wigmore Hall
Stevens, Bernard George	Go and Catch a Falling Star	various	June 11	Wigmore Hall
Stevens, Bernard George	Trio	Rubbra-Gruenberg-Pleeth Trio	May 16	RBA Galleries
Sullivan, Arthur	O Gladsome Light, from *The Golden Legend*	London Philharmonic Orchestra and mass choir	June 2	Royal Albert Hall
Sullivan, Arthur	Overture di ballo	London Philharmonic Orchestra	May 17	Festival Hall
Tallis, Thomas	Bone pastor, panis vere	Westminster Cathedral Choir	May 19	Westminster Cathedral
Tallis, Thomas	Faux-bourdons Evensong Service	Westminster Abbey Choir	July 2	Westminster Abbey
Tallis, Thomas	Hear the Voice and Prayer of Thy Servants	Renaissance Singers	June 20	Church of All Souls, Langham Place
Tallis, Thomas	If Ye Love Me	Westminster Abbey Choir	July 4	Westminster Abbey
Tallis, Thomas	Mass for Four Parts	Westminster Cathedral Choir	May 19	Westminster Cathedral
Tallis, Thomas	Matins Service in the Dorian mode	Westminster Abbey Choir	July 3	Westminster Abbey
Tallis, Thomas	Motets	The Renaissance Singers	June 16	St Sepulchre's Holborn
Tallis, Thomas	Salvator mundi	St Bartholomew's Choir	June 12	St Bartholomew the Great, Smithfield
Tallis, Thomas	Spem in alium	Philharmonia Orchestra and Morley College Choir	May 30	Festival Hall
Tallis, Thomas	Te Deum and Benedictus	St Bartholomew's Choir	June 12	St Bartholomew the Great, Smithfield
Tallis, Thomas	Te lucis ante terminum	Westminster Cathedral Choir	May 13	Westminster Cathedral
Tate, Phyllis	Songs of Sundry Natures	Dennis Brain Wind Quintet and Wigmore Ensemble	June 5	RBA Galleries
Tate, Phyllis	The Cock	various	June 11	Wigmore Hall
Tate, Phyllis	The Falcon	(unrecorded)	June 19	Wigmore Hall
Tate, Phyllis	The Falcon	various	June 11	Wigmore Hall
Taverner, John	Gloria from Missa O Michael	The Renaissance Singers	May 30	Wigmore Hall
Taverner, John	In pace in idipsum	The Renaissance Singers	May 30	Wigmore Hall

continued...

British music performed in the London Season of the Arts . . . Continued

Composer	Work	Performers	Date	Venue
Taverner, John	Mass Sine nomine	Westminster Cathedral Choir	May 17	Westminster Cathedral
Taverner, John	Mass: Small Devotion	The Renaissance Singers	June 16	St Sepulchre's Holborn
Terry, Richard	Tantum ergo sacramentum	Westminster Cathedral Choir	May 20	Westminster Cathedral
Thiman, Eric	O Gladsome Light, O Grace	London Philharmonic Orchestra and Free Church Union Choir	June 23	Royal Albert Hall
Tippett, Michael	A Child of Our Time	Philharmonia Orchestra and Morley College Choir	May 30	Festival Hall
Tippett, Michael	Concerto for Double String Orchestra	Boyd Neel Orchestra	June 30	Wigmore Hall
Tippett, Michael	String Quartet 2	Amadeus String Quartet	May 9	Queen Mary Hall
Tippett, Michael	The Heart's Assurance	Peter Pears and Benjamin Britten	May 7	Wigmore Hall
Tomkins, Thomas	O Give Thanks	Westminster Abbey Choir	July 4	Westminster Abbey
Tomkins, Thomas	Praise the Lord O My Soul	Renaissance Singers	June 20	Church of All Souls, Langham Place
Tomkins, Thomas	Preces	The Renaissance Singers	June 23	St Sepulchre's Holborn
Tomkins, Thomas	See, See the Shepherd's Queen	The Tudor Singers and Carl Dolmetsch Ensemble	May 16	Wigmore Hall
Tomkins, Thomas	See, See the Shepherd's Queen	Fleet Street Choir	June 27	Wigmore Hall
Tomkins, Thomas	Weep No More Thou Sorry Boy	Golden Age Singers	May 9	Wigmore Hall
Trimble, Joan	Song: Girls' Song	Pipers Guild Quartet, etc	June 13	Cowdray Hall
Tye, Christopher	I Will Exalt Thee	St Bartholomew's Choir	June 12	St Bartholomew the Great, Smithfield
Tye, Christopher	In nomine in 5 Parts	London Consort of Viols	May 9	Wigmore Hall
Tye, Christopher	Mass Euge bone	Westminster Cathedral Choir	May 13	Westminster Cathedral
Tye, Christopher	Nunc dimittis	St Bartholomew's Choir	June 12	St Bartholomew the Great, Smithfield
Tye, Christopher	O Come Ye Servants of the Lord	The Tudor Singers	May 16	Wigmore Hall

Tye, Christopher	Omnes gentes	St Bartholomew's Choir	June 12	St Bartholomew the Great, Smithfield
Tye, Christopher	Praise the Lord, Ye Children	St Bartholomew's Choir	June 12	St Bartholomew the Great, Smithfield
Vaughan Williams, Ralph	A London Symphony	London Symphony Orchestra	May 20	Festival Hall
Vaughan Williams, Ralph	A Pastoral Symphony	BBC Symphony	May 13	Festival Hall
Vaughan Williams, Ralph	A Sea Symphony	London Symphony Orchestra and Royal Choral	May 9	Royal Albert Hall
Vaughan Williams, Ralph	A Sea Symphony	Royal Choral Society	June 9	Royal Albert Hall
Vaughan Williams, Ralph	Benedicite	London Philharmonic Orchestra and Welsh Festival Choir	May 19	Festival Hall
Vaughan Williams, Ralph	Benedicite	Bach Choir	May 22	Royal Albert Hall
Vaughan Williams, Ralph	Benedicite	London Philharmonic Orchestra and mass choir	June 2	Royal Albert Hall
Vaughan Williams, Ralph	Concerto Grosso for Strings	London Junior and Senior Orchestras	June 1	Festival Hall
Vaughan Williams, Ralph	Fantasia on the Old 104th	Arnold Foster Choir and Orchestra	June 7	Central Hall, Westminster
Vaughan Williams, Ralph	Five Tudor Portraits	Philharmonia Orchestra and Goldsmith's Choral Union	June 29	Festival Hall
Vaughan Williams, Ralph	Flourish for Brass Band	Workers Music Association Choir and Hanwell Silver Band	June 1	St Pancras Town Hall
Vaughan Williams, Ralph	I Will Give My Love an Apple (arr)	various	June 11	Wigmore Hall
Vaughan Williams, Ralph	Job	BBC Symphony and Women's Chorus	May 20	Royal Albert Hall
Vaughan Williams, Ralph	Let Beauty Awake	various	May 21	Wigmore Hall
Vaughan Williams, Ralph	Magnificat	Tobin Chamber Orchestra and London Choral Society	June 1	Central Hall, Westminster
Vaughan Williams, Ralph	Mass in G	Westminster Abbey Choir	June 29	Westminster Abbey
Vaughan Williams, Ralph	Mass in G	Westminster Abbey Choir	July 1	Westminster Abbey
Vaughan Williams, Ralph	O vos omnes	Fleet Street Choir	May 24	Wigmore Hall
Vaughan Williams, Ralph	Oboe Concerto	Riddick String Orchestra	June 26	Wigmore Hall

continued...

British music performed in the London Season of the Arts . . . Continued

Composer	Work	Performers	Date	Venue
Vaughan Williams, Ralph	On Wenlock Edge	Aeolian String Quartet and Lance Dossor	May 30	Queen Mary Hall
Vaughan Williams, Ralph	On Wenlock Edge	various	May 28	Wigmore Hall
Vaughan Williams, Ralph	See the Chariot at Hand	(unrecorded)	June 19	Wigmore Hall
Vaughan Williams, Ralph	Serenade to Music	joint orchestra and choir	May 3	Festival Hall
Vaughan Williams, Ralph	Song: The Watermill	Pipers Guild Quartet, etc	June 13	Cowdray Hall
Vaughan Williams, Ralph	Suite for Pipes	Pipers Guild Quartet, etc	June 13	Cowdray Hall
Vaughan Williams, Ralph	Symphony 4	Halle Orchestra	May 25	Festival Hall
Vaughan Williams, Ralph	Symphony 5	Yorkshire Symphony	May 22	Festival Hall
Vaughan Williams, Ralph	Symphony 6	BBC Symphony and Choral Society	May 6	Festival Hall
Vaughan Williams, Ralph	Tallis Fantasia	London Philharmonic Orchestra	May 10	Festival Hall
Vaughan Williams, Ralph	Tallis Fantasia	London Philharmonic Orchestra	May 31	Festival Hall
Vaughan Williams, Ralph	Tallis Fantasia	Jacques String Orchestra	May 3	Victoria and Albert Museum
Vaughan Williams, Ralph	The Lark Ascending	London Philharmonic Orchestra	June 30	Central Hall, Westminster
Vaughan Williams, Ralph	The Lark Ascending	various	May 31	Wigmore Hall
Vaughan Williams, Ralph	The Lover's Ghost (arr)	Fleet Street Choir	May 24	Wigmore Hall
Vaughan Williams, Ralph	The New Commonwealth	Workers Music Association Choir and Hanwell Silver Band	June 1	St Pancras Town Hall
Vaughan Williams, Ralph	The New Ghost	various	May 21	Wigmore Hall
Vaughan Williams, Ralph	The Sons of Light	London Philharmonic and National Youth Orchestras and mass children's choir	May 6	Royal Albert Hall
Vaughan Williams, Ralph	The Turtle Dove	London Philharmonic and National Youth Orchestras and mass children's choir	May 6	Royal Albert Hall
Vaughan Williams, Ralph	The Wasps	Modern Symphony Orchestra	May 26	Northern Polytechnic
Vaughan Williams, Ralph	The Water Mill	various	May 21	Wigmore Hall
Vaughan Williams, Ralph	Three Shakespeare Songs	British Federation of Music Festivals	June 23	Festival Hall
Vaughan Williams, Ralph	Toward the Unknown Region	London Philharmonic Orchestra and University of London Choir	June 23	Central Hall, Westminster

Composer	Work	Performers	Date	Venue
Vautor, Thomas	Ballett: Come Forth Sweet Nymphs	The Tudor Singers and Carl Dolmetsch Ensemble	May 16	Wigmore Hall
Walford Davies, Henry	Hymn Tune Preludes	London Philharmonic Orchestra and Welsh Festival Choir	May 19	Festival Hall
Walford Davies, Henry	The Blessed Birth	London Philharmonic Orchestra and Free Church Union Choir	June 23	Royal Albert Hall
Walker, Ernest	One Generation Passeth Away (arr)	Fleet Street Choir	May 24	Wigmore Hall
Wallbank, Newell S	Mass of St Andrew	South London Bach Society	May 29	St Bartholomew the Great, Smithfield
Walmisley, Thomas Attwood	Evensong Service in D minor	Westminster Abbey Choir	June 29	Westminster Abbey
Walsworth, Ivor Williams	Here Where the World is Quiet	various	June 4	Wigmore Hall
Walton, William	*Belshazzar's Feast*	London Symphony Orchestra, Royal Choral Society and Huddersfield Choral Society	May 9	Royal Albert Hall
Walton, William	*Belshazzar's Feast*	Royal Choral Society	June 9	Royal Albert Hall
Walton, William	Crown Imperial	London Symphony Orchestra	May 26	Central Hall, Westminster
Walton, William	Crown Imperial	Band and Trumpeters of Kneller Hall	May 14	Festival Hall
Walton, William	In Honour of the City of London	London Philharmonic Orchestra	June 30	Festival Hall
Walton, William	Scapino	London Philharmonic Orchestra	June 19	BBC Studio Maida Vale
Walton, William	Scapino	Philharmonia Orchestra	June 25	Festival Hall
Walton, William	Scapino	Philharmonia Orchestra	June 28	Festival Hall
Walton, William	String Quartet	Aeolian String Quartet	May 30	Queen Mary Hall
Walton, William	Symphony in B flat minor	London Symphony Orchestra	May 27	Festival Hall
Walton, William	Viola Concerto	London Symphony Orchestra and Walter Primrose	May 9	Festival Hall
Walton, William	Violin Concerto	Liverpool Symphony and Alfredo Campoli	June 6	Festival Hall
Ward, John	Out from the Vale	The Tudor Singers	May 16	Wigmore Hall
Ward, John	Upon a Bank with Roses	Fleet Street Choir	June 27	Wigmore Hall

continued ..

British music performed in the London Season of the Arts . . . Continued

Composer	Work	Performers	Date	Venue
Warlock, Peter	And Wilt Thou Leave Me Thus	various	May 21	Wigmore Hall
Warlock, Peter	Captain Stratton's Fancy	various	May 21	Wigmore Hall
Warlock, Peter	Mr Belloc's Fancy	various	May 21	Wigmore Hall
Warlock, Peter	Passing By	various	May 21	Wigmore Hall
Warlock, Peter	Piggesnie	various	May 21	Wigmore Hall
Warlock, Peter	Pretty Ring Time	various	May 21	Wigmore Hall
Warlock, Peter	Sleep	various	May 21	Wigmore Hall
Warlock, Peter	Sweet-and-twenty	(unrecorded)	June 22	Kingsway
Warlock, Peter	The Bally Beareth the Bell Away	various	May 21	Wigmore Hall
Warlock, Peter	The Countryman	various	May 21	Wigmore Hall
Warlock, Peter	The Fox	various	May 21	Wigmore Hall
Warlock, Peter	The Passionate Shepherd	various	May 21	Wigmore Hall
Warlock, Peter	The Sweet o' the Year	(unrecorded)	June 22	Kingsway
Warlock, Peter	When May is in his Prime	various	May 21	Wigmore Hall
Warlock, Peter	Willow, Willow (arr)	various	May 21	Wigmore Hall
Webbe, Samuel	Regina caeli	Westminster Cathedral Choir	May 14	Westminster Cathedral
Weelkes, Thomas	As Vesta was Descending	Cambridge University Madrial Society	May 9	Wigmore Hall
Weelkes, Thomas	As Vesta was Descending	Fleet Street Choir	June 27	Wigmore Hall
Weelkes, Thomas	Ballett: Hark All Ye Lovely Saints Above	Golden Age Singers	May 9	Wigmore Hall
Weelkes, Thomas	Ballett: To Shorten Winter's Sadness	Golden Age Singers	June 27	Wigmore Hall
Weelkes, Thomas	David's Lamentation	Fleet Street Choir	June 27	Wigmore Hall
Weelkes, Thomas	Gloria in excelsis	The Renaissance Singers	June 23	St Sepulchre's Holborn
Weelkes, Thomas	Gloria in excelsis	Westminster Abbey Choir	July 1	Westminster Abbey
Weelkes, Thomas	Gloria in excelsis	Westminster Abbey Choir and Purcell Club and Choral Scholars	July 6	Westminster Abbey
Weelkes, Thomas	Hence Care, Thou Art Too Cruel	Fleet Street Choir	June 27	Wigmore Hall
Weelkes, Thomas	Let Thy Merciful Ears	Westminster Abbey Choir	June 25	Westminster Abbey

Weelkes, Thomas	Like Two Proud Armies	Cambridge University Madrial Society	May 9	Wigmore Hall
Weelkes, Thomas	O Care, Thou Wilt Despatch Me	Fleet Street Choir	June 27	Wigmore Hall
Weelkes, Thomas	The Andalusian Merchant	Golden Age Singers	June 27	Wigmore Hall
Weelkes, Thomas	The Nightingale, the Organ of Delight	Golden Age Singers	May 9	Wigmore Hall
Wesley, Samuel	Anima nostra erepta est	St Michael's Singers	May 9	St Michael's Cornhill
Wesley, Samuel	In exitu Israel	St Michael's Singers	May 9	St Michael's Cornhill
Wesley, Samuel	In exitu Israel	Westminster Abbey Choir	June 30	Westminster Abbey
Wesley, Samuel Sebastian	Almight God Give Us Grace	London Philharmonic Orchestra and Free Church Union Choir	June 23	Royal Albert Hall
Wesley, Samuel Sebastian	Cast Me Not Away	Westminster Abbey Choir and Purcell Club and Choral Scholars	July 6	Westminster Abbey
Wesley, Samuel Sebastian	Evensong Service in E	Westminster Abbey Choir	July 5	Westminster Abbey
Wesley, Samuel Sebastian	The Wilderness	Westminster Abbey Choir	July 7	Westminster Abbey
Whittaker, William Gillies	Bobbie Shaftoe (arr)	London Orpheus Choir	June 28	Wigmore Hall
Whittaker, William Gillies	Bobby Shaftoe (arr)	various	June 11	Wigmore Hall
Whittaker, William Gillies	The Keel Row (arr)	various	June 11	Wigmore Hall
Whittaker, William Gillies	The Waters of Tyne (arr)	various	June 11	Wigmore Hall
Wilbye, John	Adieu Sweet Amaryllis	Golden Age Singers	May 9	Wigmore Hall
Wilbye, John	Draw on Sweet Night	Cambridge University Madrial Society	May 9	Wigmore Hall
Wilbye, John	Oft Have I Vowed	Fleet Street Choir	June 27	Wigmore Hall
Wilbye, John	Sweet Honey-sucking Bees	Golden Age Singers	June 27	Wigmore Hall
Wilbye, John	Weep O Mine Eyes	Golden Age Singers	May 9	Wigmore Hall
Wood, Charles	Eucharist Service in the Phrygian Mode	Westminster Abbey Choir	July 1	Westminster Abbey
Wood, Charles	Evensong Service in E	Westminster Abbey Choir	July 4	Westminster Abbey
Wood, Charles	Evensong Service in F	Westminster Abbey Choir	June 30	Westminster Abbey
Wood, Charles	Hail Gladdening Light	Fleet Street Choir	May 24	Wigmore Hall
Wood, Charles	Hail Gladdening Light	Westminster Abbey Choir	June 30	Westminster Abbey

continued...

British music performed in the London Season of the Arts ... Continued

Composer	Work	Performers	Date	Venue
Wood, Charles	Music When Soft Voices Die	Fleet Street Choir	May 24	Wigmore Hall
Wood, Charles	O Thou Sweetest Source	London Philharmonic Orchestra and Free Church Union Choir	June 23	Royal Albert Hall
Wood, Charles	Oculi omnium	Westminster Abbey Choir	July 7	Westminster Abbey
Wood, Charles	The Ride of the Witch	London Philharmonic and National Youth Orchestras and mass children's choir	May 6	Royal Albert Hall
Wood, Charles	Tis the Day of Resurrection	St Michael's Singers	May 9	St Michael's Cornhill
Wood, Thomas	*The Rainbow: A Tale of Dunkirk*	massed brass bands and choirs	May 12	Royal Albert Hall

Appendix 2
British works commissioned or premiered during the Festival of Britain

A. Official Arts Council concert music commissions

1. William Alwyn, *Festival March*
2. George Dyson, "Song for a Festival", to a text by Cecil Day Lewis
3. Peter Racine Fricker, Concerto for Violin and Small Orchestra (winner of the young composers competition)
4. Gordon Jacob, *Music for a Festival* for military band and additional ensemble of trumpets
5. Alan Rawsthorne, Piano Concerto no. 2
6. Edward Rubbra, *Festival Te Deum* for soprano solo, chorus, and orchestra, op. 71
7. Thomas Wood, *The Rainbow, a Tale of Dunkirk*, to a text by Christopher Hassall, for male voices and one or more brass bands (orchestrated by Frank Wright)

B. Welsh and Scottish commissions

In July 1949, the Arts Council's Welsh committee on music suggested five commissions, which the Festival Council, after the usual delays and financial consideration, accepted on March 1, 1950 (EL4/95). All of these works received premieres in the Festival except the psalm by Nicholas, which payment records suggest was never completed.

1. William Hubert Davies, *Festival Overture*
2. Arwel Hughes, *Dewi Sant* (Saint David) an oratorio on the life of St. David
3. Daniel Jones, Symphony no. 2
4. John Morgan Nicholas, *Psalm 130* (in Welsh) for baritone, chorus, and orchestra
5. David Wynne (pen name of D. W. Thomas), *Chwe Chan i Denor a Thelyn* (Six Songs for Tenor and Harp)

In 1950, the Scottish committee decided to hold competitions (EL6/172). A panel of judges consisting of Herbert Wiseman, Arthur Bliss, and Herbert Howells was to judge scores submitted by composers who were Scottish by parentage or birth, or who had resided in Scotland for at least four years. The Committee would grant prizes for works in the five genres listed below. This competition was initiated very late in the Festival planning process (the first mention of it in the files is in 1951). No winners were recorded, and there are no records of disbursements or performances, which suggests that the competition was either abandoned or not completed on time.

1. A Festival overture or short orchestral work at least 10 minutes in length (£200)
2. A short choral work accompanied by string or small orchestra lasting around 10 minutes (£150)
3. An unaccompanied part song (£75)
4. A unison song with piano or string orchestra accompaniment (£50)
5. A march or other work for military or brass band lasting around 10 minutes (£150)

C. Arts Council expenses for concert music commissions

1. Rawsthorne, Piano Concerto no. 2	£262, 10s
2. Fricker, Concerto for Violin	£200
3. Vaughan Williams, *The Sons of Light*	£200[1]
4. Dyson, Song for a Festival	£157, 10s
Day Lewis, poem	£52, 10s
5. Jacob, Music for a Festival	£157, 10s
6. Rubbra, Festival Te Deum	£157, 10s
7. Wood, The Rainbow	£105
Hassall, poem	£31, 10s
8. Alwyn, Festival March	£105
9. Jones, Symphony no. 2	£100
10. Hughes, *Dewi Sant*	£100
11. Arnold, *A Sussex Overture*	£50
12. Davies, *Festival Overture*	£50
13. Nicholas, *Psalm 130*	£50[2]
14. Thomas (Wynne), *6 Chan i denor a thelyn*	£50
15. Copying costs for Welsh commissions	£300
16. CPNM expenses for young composer competition	£112
TOTAL	£2,298

D. Concert music commissions and competitions by other organizations

In addition to the works listed here, the Hallé Concerts Society announced a competition with a prize of 100 guineas for an overture to commemorate the 1951 opening of the renovated Free Trade Hall in Manchester. The judges were the conductors John Barbirolli and Malcolm Sargent and H. Proctor Gregg, the Head of the Music Department at Manchester University. I have found no record of a winner: There was no announcement of a premiere in Manchester, which was not a Festival center, nor did the Hallé perform a premiere at their only London appearance during the London Season of the Arts.

1. Matthew Arnold, *A Sussex Overture* (Brighton Festival, with funding from the Arts Council)
2. Francis Burt, two motets (South London Bach Choir)
3. Geoffrey Bush, *Twelfth Night: An Entertainment* (London Choral Society)
4. Norman Fuller, *Sinfonia Pastorale* (Bournemouth and Wessex Festival, Bournemouth Municipal Orchestra)[3]
5. Antony Hopkins, *Cutty Sark* (Rural Schools Music Association)
6. Herbert Howells, *A Maid Peerless* (National Competitive Music Festival)
7. Gordon Jacob, Concerto for French Horn and Strings (Riddick String Orchestra)
8. Elisabeth Lutyens, *Nativity*, cantata for soprano and strings to a text by W. R. Rogers (Riddick String Orchestra)
9. R. Maldwyn Price, *English Folk Fantasia for Brass Band* (Worker's Musical Association)
10. Cyril Scott, *Irish Serenade* (Riddick String Orchestra)
11. Ralph Vaughan Williams, *Flourish for Brass Band* (Workers' Musical Association)[4]
12. Ralph Vaughan Williams, *The Sons of Light* (Schools Music Association of Great Britain, with funding from the Arts Council)
13. Ralph Vaughan Williams, *Three Shakespeare Songs* (National Competitive Music Festival)
14. Newell Wallbank, Mass of Saint Andrew (South London Bach Choir)

E. Uncommissioned concert music premieres

Given the enormous quantity of music-making in the Festival, the following list may not be complete.

1. Matthew Arnold, Symphony no. 1 (Cheltenham)
2. Arthur Bliss, String Quartet no. 2 (Cheltenham)
3. Benjamin Britten, *Six Metamorphoses after Ovid* (Aldeburgh)
4. Alan Bush, *Piers Plowmans' Day* (Symphonic Suite) (BBC Proms)
5. Arnold Cooke, Concerto for Strings (composed 1948, Malvern)
6. Benjamin Frankel, String Trio (Cheltenham)
7. Benjamin Frankel, Three Poems for Cello (Wigmore Hall)
8. Peter Racine Fricker, Symphony no. 2 (Liverpool and BBC Proms)
9. John Gardner, Symphony (composed 1947, Cheltenham)
10. Roberto Gerhard, Concerto for Piano and String Orchestra (Aldeburgh)
11. Cecil Armstrong Gibbs, Pastoral Suite (Colchester)

12. Patrick Hadley, Rhapsody for Soprano and Orchestra on lines from Shelley's *Cenci* (Norwich)
13. Hubert Hales, *Pastoral Music* (Norwich)
14. Gordon Jacob, *Galop Joyeux* (BBC Proms)
15. Maurice Jacobson, Symphonic Suite (Cheltenham and BBC Proms)
16. Maurice Johnstone, *A Cumbrian Rhapsody, Tarn Hows* (BBC Proms)
17. Arthur Oldham, *The Commandment of Love* (song cycle on lyrics of Richard Rolle) (Aldeburgh)
18. Robin Orr, *Te Deum* (Cambridge)
19. Franz Reizenstein, Serenade for Winds (Cheltenham)
20. Edmund Rubbra, String Quartet (Cheltenham)
21. Edmund Rubbra, *The Dark Night of the Soul* (Norwich)
22. Philip Sainton, Serenade Fantastique for Oboe and Strings (BBC Proms)
23. Humphrey Searle, Poem for Twenty-Two Strings (Cheltenham—UK premiere)
24. Martin Shaw, *The Changing of the Year* (Colchester)
25. Michael Tippett, *The Heart's Assurance* (song cycle on poems of Alun Lewis and Sidney Keyes) (Aldeburgh)
26. Arnold van Wyk, Symphony no. 1 in A minor (Cheltenham)
27. Thomas Wood, *Daniel and the Lions* (Colchester—local premiere)
28. William Wordsworth, Piano Quartet (Cheltenham)
29. William Wordsworth, Symphony no. 2 (Edinburgh)[5]

F. Opera commissions and premieres

1. Arthur Benjamin, *A Tale of Two Cities* (Arts Council competition winner, unperformed)
2. Benjamin Bitten, *Billy Budd* (Covent Garden Opera, Arts Council commission)
3. Alan Bush, *Wat Tyler* (Arts Council competition winner, unperformed)
4. Brian Easdale, *The Sleeping Children* (English Opera Group)
5. Berthold Goldschmidt, *Beatrice Cenci* (Arts Council competition winner, unperformed)
6. Antony Hopkins, *The Man from Tuscany* (Canterbury Cathedral choristers)
7. George Lloyd, *John Socman* (Carl Rosa Opera, Arts Council commission)
8. Karl Rankl, *Deirdre of the Sorrows* (Arts Council competition winner, unperformed)
9. Peter Tranchell, *The Mayor of Casterbridge* (Cambridge University)
10. Ralph Vaughan Williams, *The Pilgrim's Progress* (Covent Garden Opera)
11. Egon Wellesz, *Incognita* (Oxford University)

G. Opera and theater music revivals

1. Thomas Arne, *Artaxerxes* (excerpts in concert)
2. Thomas Arne, *The Cooper* (Riddick String Orchestra)

Appendix 2   223

3. Thomas Arne, *Thomas and Sally* (Intimate Opera)
4. Michael Balfe, *The Bohemian Girl* (Liverpool and Covent Garden)
5. Julius Benedict, *The Lily of Killarny* (BBC broadcast)
6. Benjamin Britten, *Albert Herring* (English Opera Group)
7. Benjamin Britten, *Let's Make an Opera!* (English Opera Group)
8. Benjamin Britten, *The Rape of Lucretia* (English Opera Group)
9. Geoffrey Bush, *The Spanish Rivals* (Intimate Opera)[6]
10. Henry Carey, *True Blue* (Intimate Opera)
11. Frederick Delius, music to James Elroy Flecker's *Hassan* (Open-Air Theatre in Regents Park)
12. Charles Dibdin (arr Geoffrey Bush), *The Grenadier* (Intimate Opera)
13. John Eccles, *The Judgment of Paris* (London Chamber Orchestra and Singers)
14. Gustav Holst, *The Wandering Scholar* (English Opera Group)
15. Hamish MacCunn, *Jennie Dean* (Glasgow Grand Opera Society)
16. Bruce Montgomery, *Amberley Hall* (Intimate Opera)
17. Johann Christoph Pepusch, *The Beggar's Opera* (British Poetry-Drama Guild)
18. Elizabeth Poston, arr., *Michael and Frances* (Elizabethan Stage Jig) (London Opera Club)
19. Henry Purcell, *Dido and Aeneas* (English Opera Group, Sadler's Wells Opera, and a commercial production starring Kirstin Flagstad)
20 Henry Purcell, *The Fairy Queen* (Haslemere semi-amateur and Covent Garden)
21. Henry Purcell, *The Tempest* (Cambridge, amateur)
22. Henry Purcell, masque from *Timon of Athens* (Intimate Opera)
23. Charles Villiers Stanford, *The Traveling Companion* (Swindon, amateur)
24. Stephen Storace (arr Sumner Austin), *Le Bal Masqué* (adapted from *My Grandmother*) (Intimate Opera)
25. Stephen Storace (arr Sumner Austin), *The Glorious First of June* (Riddick String Orchestra)
26. Arthur Sullivan, *Cox and Box / The Pirates of Penzance* (D'Oyly Carte)
27. Arthur Sullivan, *Iolanthe* (D'Oyly Carte)
28. Arthur Sullivan, *Patience* (D'Oyly Carte)
29. Arthur Sullivan, *Ruddigore* (D'Oyly Carte)
30. Arthur Sullivan, *The Gondoliers* (D'Oyly Carte)
31. Arthur Sullivan, *The Mikado* (D'Oyly Carte)
32. Arthur Sullivan, *The Yeomen of the Guard* (D'Oyly Carte)
33. Arthur Sullivan, *Trial By Jury / HMS Pinafore* (D'Oyly Carte)
34. Ralph Vaughan Williams, *Hugh the Drover* (Sadler's Wells Opera)
35. Ralph Vaughan Williams, *Sir John in Love* (Stratford-upon-Avon, amateur)

H. Ballet commissions, premieres, and revivals

In September 1948, along with the proposal for the three opera commissions, the short-lived Arts Council Opera and Ballet Panel recommended commissions for each of the nation's five established ballet companies (Sadler's Wells Ballet,

224 Appendix 2

Sadler's Wells Theatre Ballet, International Ballet, Metropolitan Ballet, and Ballet Rambert). The companies themselves were to choose the composers, choreographers, and designers. In December 1949, the Metropolitan Ballet folded, and at the same time the International Ballet made clear that their focus on the classics largely precluded the use of new music. Thus, three new ballets were eventually commissioned.

1. Richard Arnell/John Cranko, *Harlequin in April* (Sadler's Wells Theatre Ballet, Arts Council commission)
2. Lord Berners, *A Wedding Bouquet* (Sadler's Wells Ballet)
3. Arthur Bliss, *Checkmate* (Sadler's Wells Ballet)
4. William Boyce (arr Constant Lambert), *The Prospect Before Us* (Sadler's Wells Theatre Ballet)
5. Gavin Gordon, *The Rake's Progress* (Sadler's Wells Ballet)
6. Constant Lambert/Frederick Ashton, *Tiresias* (Sadler's Wells Ballet at Covent Garden, Arts Council commission)[7]
7. Peter Racine Fricker/David Paltenghi, *The Canterbury Prologue* (Rambert Ballet, Arts Council commission)
8. Arthur Sullivan arr. Charles Mackerras, *Pineapple Poll* (Sadler's Wells Ballet, premiere in March 1951)
9. Geoffrey Toye, *The Haunted Ballroom* (Sadler's Wells Theatre Ballet)
10. Peter Tranchell, *Fate's Revenge* (Rambert Ballet, premiere)

Notes

1. Vaughan Williams accepted only £50 for himself and £25 for Ursula Wood, the librettist of *The Sons of Light*. The remaining £125 was given to the Schools Music Association for the placing of later commissions (ACGB paper 159).
2. The Arts Council expense summary at the end of the Festival (WORK 25/6/A1/A6/1) shows the commission for Nicholas as unpaid and not expected to be paid, and there is no announcement of a performance of Psalm 130, which implies that Nicholas did not complete this work.
3. Fuller's work won a £150 prize for "a suite, divertimento, sinfonietta, or symphony playing from 20 to 35 minutes" put forward by the London music-seller Harold Reeves. The selection committee consisted of the composer Gordon Jacob and the conductors Boyd Neel and Rudolf Schwarz.
4. The Arts Council press release (WORKS 25/67/A6/B4, AC/PRESS/9/51) for the big Festival concert in London by the Workers' Music Association announces that they have commissioned a new work for brass band from Vaughan Williams. The London Season of the Arts program lists a work entitled *Flourish for Brass Band*. This may be an arrangement of the 1939 *Flourish for Wind Band*, or a later uncatalogued work.
5. Wordsworth's symphony, although not a Festival commission, had won a competition in 1949. This was the only performance of note of British music at the expressly "international" Edinburgh Festival.
6. Some publicity materials announced the performances of Bush's *Spanish Rivals* as a premiere. Bush wrote the work in 1941 as a puppet opera, and it had received several performances in that form. The Intimate Opera production may have been the first one using singing actors rather than puppets.

7 Lambert barely completed *Tiresias*, his last work, before succumbing to alcoholism. He himself prepared the scenario, a troubling exploration of human gender that found little favor with the conservative ballet public. For more on the work's genesis, see Macfarlane 2010.

Appendix 3
Timeline of the open opera commissioning scheme (compiled from EL6/71)

I. Composers who applied but did not submit proposals for consideration

* = Applicants who wrote to ask for the reasons that their application had been rejected.

A. Rejected immediately by Eric Walter White and John Denison on the basis of the February 1949 application (44)

1. Gordon George Baker
2. Eric Bander
3. Elizabeth Bantock
4. John P. Barrett
5. Wilfred Burns
6. William Bromhead Coates
7. Guirve Creith
8. Frederick Thomas Durrant*
9. Kenneth James Eade
10. Martin Fogell
11. Julian Gardiner
12. John L. Gardner*
13. Alfred J. H. Garland
14. Terence White Gervais*
15. John Gilligan
16. David G. Gow
17. Thomas Henderson*
18. Norman Kay
19. Josef Klein
20. John A. Neill Lambert
21. Ralph Letts
22. John McNeil
23. Robert Frederick Eric Miller
24. Margaret More*
25. G. F. Oldham

228   *Appendix 3*

26. John C. K. Peterson
27. Roy A. Phillips*
28. Harry William Pile
29. P. Platt
30. Godfrey Sampson
31. Leonard Scott
32. George Muir Simpson
33. James A. Smith
34. Samuel Soden
35. Frank Spitori [Malta]
36. John Cole Stokes
37. David Tidboald*
38. Brian J. M. Tovey
39. Mervyn Vicars
40. Evelyn Herbert Webb
41. Margaret Rosalind Wegener
42. Geoffrey Winters
43. Ernest John Wright
44. Agnes Yendall

B. Considered further but rejected by Eric Walter White and John Denison on the basis of the February 1949 application (12)

1. Alastair Kennedy Casselsbrown
2. Kenneth Essex
3. Herbert Ferrers
4. Robert Gill
5. Hubert J. Hales*
6. Florence Mary Hill Holmes
7. Daniel Jones
8. Vivien Lambelet
9. Peter John Pirie
10. Leonard Rafter*
11. Bernard Wilson
12. Christopher Neame Wood*

C. Accepted into round one but voluntarily withdrawn (4)

1. Richard Arnell
2. Lionel Heudebert
3. Antony Hopkins
4. Bernard D. K. Lewis

II. Proposals considered by judges

Composers are listed in the left column with their pseudonyms, where known, and countries of residence if this was not the United Kingdom. (British subjects resident abroad were eligible to apply, as were foreigners who had taken up permanent residence in the United Kingdom.) Titles of opera projects are given in the right column. The "outline" consisted of a full synopsis of the plot, a synopsis of the dramatic and musical treatment, and one scene of the libretto.

D. Outlines found ineligible (2)

1. Brian Easdale ([pseudonym unknown])   *The Sleeping Children*
    Supposedly ineligible because one act only, but possibly because of existing commission from English Opera Group.
2. Cecil Armstrong Gibbs ("Feste")   *Twelfth Night*
    Reasons for ineligibility not recorded.

E. Outlines rejected at 9 September 1949, judges' meeting (22)

1. David Branson ("Strephon")   *Jonah*
2. Alexander Brent-Smith ("Edmund Seaton")   *Catherine Morland*
3. Hugo Cole ("Seithenyn")   *The Cure for Melancholy*
4. Arnold Cooke ("Manounian")   *Mary Barton*
5. Christian Darnton ("Petronius")   *Fantasy Fair*
6. Shula Doniach ("Syrinx")   *The Shulamite*
7. Isobel V. S. Dunlop ("Dunedin")   *Valiant Fury*
8. Christopher Edmunds ("Harlequin")   *Herod*
9. Hubert Foss ("Josiah Peacock")   *Prince Otto*
10. Arnold Foster ("Pipe and Tabor")   *Lord Bateman*
11. John Harvey Frost ("A. Shepherd")   *The Lost Sheep*
12. Dudley Glass ("Lyrico")   *Gerda*
13. Robert Watson Hughes ("Anthony Almond") [Australia]   "Lyric Drama" [no title]
14. Maurice Johnstone ("David Bowman")   *Jane Eyre*
15. Michael S. C. Maxwell ("Genseric")   "Opera" [no title]
16. Kenneth John Pakeman ("Dangu")   *The Silent Knight*
17. H. Ian Parrott ("Figaro")   *Will o' the Weekend*
18. Thomas B. Pitfield ("Tadpole")   *College Courtship*
19. Leonard Salzedo ("Lionhard Wolf Willowgrove")   *Deirdre of the Sorrows*
20. Cyril Scott ("Charles Lundy")   *Maureen O'Mara*
21. Peter Tranchell ("James")   *The Mayor of Casterbridge*
22. Grace Williams ("February")   *Dic Penderyn*

F. Outlines rejected at 25 October 1949, judges' meeting (13)

1. Warwick Braithwaite ("Atearoa")   *Pendragon*
2. Alexander Brent-Smith ("Edmund Seaton")   *The Lost Elixir*
3. Albert H. Coates ("Die Pieteri") [South Africa]   *The Boy David*

230 *Appendix 3*

    4. Norman Demuth ("Mars")   *Volpone*
    5. Norman Fulton ("Ian Balva")   *Honeypot*
    6. Peter Hodgson ("Richard Moat")   *The Lady of the Lake*
    7. Robin Humphrey Milford ("Gabriel")   *The Summer Stars*
        Judges' *"special mention for high poetic quality of libretto."*
    8. Clifton Parker ("Arquebus")   *Aucassin and Nicolette*
    9. Bernard Stevens ("Terpander")   *Mimosa*
   10. Freda Swain ("Scorpio")   *The Quest*
   11. Gilbert Vinter ("Pablo Parino")   *Ines de Castro*
   12. R. W. Wood ("Seps")   *The Hand of Isa*
   13. [unknown] ("Richard Jones")   *Orestes*
        Accepted into scheme late.

G. Outlines rejected at 9 December 1949, judges' meeting (11)

    1. Malcolm Arnold ("Orsino")   *Henry Christophe*
    2. Manuel Frankell ("Nomos")   *David the King*
    3. Ruth Gipps ("Neptune")   *Chanticleer*
    4. Arwel Hughes ("Madog")   *Menna*
    5. Benton Jackson ("I. P. Kshessinsky")   *Postwar People*
        [Canada]
    6. Christabel Marillier ("Thalia")   *A Rogue Unmasked*
    7. Kenneth Donald Morrison   *The Seal Woman*
        ("Richard Perry")
    8. Francis Stephen Rhys ("Tavis Mate")   *Out of Egypt*
    9. Egon J. Wellesz ("Incognitus")   *Incognita*
   10. Stanley Wilson ("Lamed")   *King Midas*
   11. William B. Wordsworth ("Michael")   *The Two Drovers*

H. Project withdrawn December 1949 at request of judges (1)

    1. Inglis Gundry ("Melopoios")   *The Sleeping Beauty*
        Withdrawn because Gundry had two submissions under consideration.

I. Outlines rejected at January 20, 1950, judges' meeting (5)

    1. Dennis ApIvor ("Spalanzani")   *She Stoops to Conquer*
    2. Allan Hawthorne Baker ("A. Pibroch")   *Arthur*
    3. Inglis Gundry ("Melopoios")   *The Tinners of Cornwall*
    4. Humphrey Searle ("Quo Vadis")   *The Life of the Insects*
    5. Diccon Shaw ("C.K.A.")   *Agamemnon*

J. Projects accepted for commissions at April 20, 1950 judges' meeting (3)

    1. Arthur Benjamin ("Stagestruck")   *A Tale of Two Cities*
    2. Berthold Goldschmidt ("Squirrel")   *Beatrice Cenci*
    3. Karl Rankl ("Charles Francis")   *Deirdre of the Sorrows*
        Passed to round two at 9 September 1949 meeting.

K. Project accepted for commission later (1)
   1. Alan Bush ("Dudley Underwood")   *Wat Tyler*
      Accepted for commission June 1950.
L. Projects considered for commission but eventually rejected (2)
   1. Wilfrid H. Mellers ("Nicholas Howe")   *Christopher Marlowe*
      Rejected March 1951.
   2. Lennox Berkeley ("Timotheus")   *Nelson*
      Almost rejected on April 20, 1950, finally rejected February 1952.

Bibliography

Archives Consulted

Alan Bush Papers, Histon, Cambridgeshire. Now housed in the British Library, Euston, London.
Archive of the Arts Council of Great Britain (The Victoria and Albert Museum), Blythe House, West Kensington, London. Citations begin "EL" or "ACGB."
Archive of the Royal Opera House, Covent Garden, London. Citations begin "AROHCG."
BBC Written Archive, Caversham, Berkshire. Citations begin "R."
Britten-Pears Foundation, Aldeburgh, Suffolk. Citations begin "BPF."
National Archive, Kew, Richmond, Surrey. Citations begin "WORKS."
Peter Tranchell Papers, Cambridge University Library. Citations begin "CUL."

Published Sources

Addison, Paul. 1985. *Now the War is Over: A Social History of Britain 1945–51*. London: BBC/Jonathan Cape.
Anderson, W.R. 1952. "Round About Radio." *Musical Times* 93/1311 (May): 216.
Arundell, Dennis. 1965. *The Story of Sadler's Wells*. London: Hamish Hamilton.
Banfield, Stephen. 1997. "Lloyd, George." *New Grove Dictionary of Opera*. London: Oxford University Press.
Banham, Mary and Bevis Hillier. 1976. *A Tonic to the Nation: The Festival of Britain*. London: Thames & Hudson.
Banks, Paul. 1988. "The Case of *Beatrice Cenci*." *Opera* 39/4 (April): 426–432.
Banks, Paul. 1993. *Britten's* Gloriana: *Essays and Sources*. Woodbridge: Boydell.
Boughton, Rutland. 1911. *Music Drama of the Future*. London: W. Reeves.
Briggs, Asa. 1965. *The Golden Age of Wireless*. The History of Broadcasting in the United Kingdom, vol. 2. Oxford: Oxford University Press.
Britten, Benjamin. 1969. "Some Notes on Forster and Music." In *Aspects of E. M. Forster*, edited by Oliver Stalleybrass. London: Edward Arnold.
Carpenter, Humphrey. 1992. *Benjamin Britten: A Biography*. London: Faber & Faber.
Carpenter, Humphrey. 1996. *The Envy of the World: Fifty Years of the BBC Third Programme and Radio 3, 1946-1996*. London: Weidenfield & Nicholson.
Chapman, Ernest. 1956. "Wat Tyler." *Listener* 56 (6 November): 965.
Chowrimootoo, Chrisopher. 2014. "Reviving the Middlebrow, or: Deconstructing Modernism from the Inside." *Journal of the Royal Musical Association* 139/1: 177–204.
Clark, Edward. 1950. *A Tribute to Alan Bush on his Fiftieth Birthday*. London: Workers' Music Association.

Conekin, Becky. 2003. *The Autobiography of a Nation: The 1951 Festival of Britain.* Manchester and New York: Manchester University Press.
Connolly, Cyril. 2008. *Enemies of Progress.* Chicago: University of Chicago. First published 1938.
Cooke, Mervyn and Philip Reed. 1993. *Benjamin Britten: Billy Budd.* Cambridge Opera Handbooks. Cambridge: Cambridge University Press.
Croft, Andy. 1995. "Betrayed Spring: The Labour Government and British Literary Culture." In *Labour's Promised Land: Culture and Society in Labour Britain, 1945–1951*, edited by Jim Fyrth, 197–223. London: Lawrence & Wishart.
Crozier, Eric. 1965. "Peter Grimes." *Opera* 16/6 (June): 415.
Crozier, Eric. 1986. "The Writing of Billy Budd." *Opera Quarterly* 4 (Autumn): 11–27.
Dobson, R.B. 1983. *The Peasants' Revolt of 1381.* 2nd edition. London & Basingstoke: Macmillan.
Doctor, Jennifer. 1999. *The BBC and Ultra-modern Music, 1922–1936: Shaping a Nation's Tastes.* Music in the 20th Century, vol. 10. Cambridge, Cambridge University Press.
Donaldson, Frances. 1988. *The Royal Opera House in the 20th Century.* London: Weidenfeld & Nicholson.
Dyment, Christopher. 2012. *Toscanini in Britain.* Woodbridge: Boydell.
Evans, Peter. 1995. "Instrumental Music I." In *The 20th Century*, edited by Stephen Banfield. The Blackwell History of Music in Britain, vol. 6: 179–277. Oxford: Blackwell.
Festival Council. 1952. *The Story of the Festival of Britain.* London: Festival Council.
Forbes, Anne-Marie H. 1987. "Celticism in Opera." *The Music Review* 47/3: 176–183.
Foreman, Lewis. 2003. "Alan Bush, Arthur Benjamin, Berthold Goldschmidt, Karl Rankl, Lennox Berkeley and the Arts Council's 1951 Opera Competition. *British Music Society News* 100 (December): 75–78.
Frayn, Michael. 1980. "Festival." In *Age of Austerity*, edited by Michael Sissons and Philip French, 305–328. Oxford: Oxford University Press. First published 1963.
Furbank, P.N. 1978. *E. M. Forster: A Life.* Vol. 2. London: Seckler & Warburg.
Fyrth, Jim. 1995. "Days of Hope: The Meaning of 1945." In *Labour's Promised Land: Culture and Society in Labour Britain, 1945–1951*, edited by Jim Fyrth. 3–15. London. Lawrence & Wishart.
Gilbert, Susie. 2011. *Opera for Everybody: The Story of English National Opera.* London: Faber & Faber.
Glendinning, Nigel. 1995. "Art and Architecture for the People?." In *Labour's Promised Land: Culture and Society in Labour Britain, 1945–1951*, edited by Jim Fyrth, 276–288. London: Lawrence & Wishart.
Goldschmidt, Berhold. 1994. *Komponist und Dirigent: Ein Musiker-Leben zwischen Hamburg, Berlin und London.* Hamburg: Bockel Verlag.
Gundry, Inglis. n.d. "The Last Boy in the Family." www.musicweb-international.com/gundry/front.htm.
Haltrecht, Montague. 1975. *The Quiet Showman: Sir David Webster and the Royal Opera House.* London: Collins.
Hamburger, Paul. 1951. "Cheltenham. English Opera Group. The Sleeping Children (Easdale). July 9." *Opera* 2/9 (September): 504–508.
Harrington, Paul. 1989. "Holst and Vaughan Williams: Radical Pastoral." In *Music and the Politics of Culture*, edited by Christopher Norris, 106–127. New York: St Martin's.
Harris, Alexandra. 2010. *Romantic Moderns.* London: Thames & Hudson.
Harwood, Elain and Alan Powers. 2001. *Festival of Britain.* Modern Architecture, no. 5. London: 20th Century Society.

Hennessy, Peter. 1992. *Never Again: Britain 1945–1951.* London: Jonathan Cape.
Hewison, Robert. 1988. *In Anger: British Culture in the Cold War 1945–1960.* Revised edition. New York: Oxford University Press.
Hewison, Robert. 1993. "'Happy Were He': Benjamin Britten and the *Gloriana* Story." In *Britten's Gloriana: Essays and Sources*, edited by Paul Banks. Woodbridge: Boydell.
Hindley, Clifford. 1989. "Love and Salvation in Britten's Billy Budd." *Music and Letters* 70/3 (August): 363–381.
Hindley, Clifford. 1999. "Eros in Life and Death: Billy Budd and Death in Venice." In *The Cambridge Companion to Benjamin Britten*, edited by Mervyn Cooke, 147–164. Cambridge: Cambridge University Press.
Howes, Frank. 1951. *Musical Britain 1951. Compiled by the Musical Critic of the Times.* London: Oxford University Press.
Howkins, Alun. 1986. "The Discovery of Rural Britain." In *Englishness: Politics and Culture 1880–1920*, edited by Robert Colls and Philip Dodd, 62–88. London: Croom Helm.
Howkins, Alun. 1989. "Greensleeves and the Idea of National Music." In *Patriotism: The Making and Unmaking of British National Identity*, edited by Raphael Samuel. Vol. 3: 89–98. London and New York: Routledge.
Hutchison, Robert. 1982. *The Politics of the Arts Council.* London: Sinclair Brown.
Ifor Evans, Benjamin and Mary Glasgow. 1949. *The Arts in England.* London: Falcon.
Jacobs, Arthur. 1951a. "Festival of Britain Operas." *Musical Times* 92/1295 (January): 36–37.
Jacobs, Arthur. 1951b. "The Mayor of Casterbridge." *Musical Times* 92/1303 (September): 421.
Keeffe, Bernard. 1995. "The Composer." In *Berthold Goldschmidt, Beatrice Cenci* (program booklet). Sony Classical CD S2K 66 836, 14.
Kennedy, Michael. 1980. *The Works of Ralph Vaughan Williams.* 2nd edition. Oxford: Oxford University Press.
Kennedy, Michael. 1993. *Britten.* The Dent Master Musicians. London: J. M. Dent.
Kildea, Paul. 2002. *Selling Britten.* London and New York: Oxford University Press.
Lawrence, Helen. 1995. "Berthold Goldschmidt's Beatrice Cenci: The Discovery of an Opera." In *Berthold Goldschmidt, Beatrice Cenci* (program booklet). Sony Classical CD S2K 66 836, 11.
Lebrecht, Norman. 2000. *Covent Garden, the Untold Story: Dispatches from the English Culture Wars, 1945–2000.* Boston: Northeastern University Press.
Leventhal, F.M. 1990. "'The Best for the Most': CEMA and the State Sponsorship of the Arts in Wartime, 1939–1945." *20th Century British History* 1/3: 289–317.
Lew, Nathaniel G. 2001. *A New and Glorious Age: Constructions of National Opera in Britain, 1945–1951.* Ph.D. dissertation, University of California, Berkeley.
Lew, Nathaniel G. 2002. "'Words and music that are forever England': The Pilgrim's Progress and the Pitfalls of Nostalgia." In *Vaughan Williams Essays*, edited by Byron Adams and Robin Wells, 175–205. Aldershot: Ashgate.
Lindsay, Jack. 1945. *British Achievement in Arts and Music.* London: Pilot.
Macfarlane, Helen. 2010. "The Sources of Constant Lambert's *Tiresias.*" Paper delivered at the conference of the North American British Music Studies Association, Des Moines IA.
Martin, Steven Edward. 2010. *The British 'Operatic Machine': Investigations into the Institutional History of English Opera, c. 1875–1939.* Ph.D. dissertation, University of Bristol.
Marwick, Arthur. 1991. "Britain 1951." *History Today* 41 (April). 5–11.

236 Bibliography

Medhurst, Andy. 1995. "Myths of Consensus and Fables of Escape: British Cinema 1945–51." In *Labour's Promised Land: Culture and Society in Labour Britain, 1945–1951*, edited by Jim Fyrth, 289–301. London: Lawrence & Wishart.

Mellers, Wilfred. 1952. "Recent Trends in British Music." *Musical Quarterly* 38/2 (April): 185–201.

Minihan, Janet. 1977. *The Nationalisation of Culture*. London: Hamish Hamilton.

Mitchell, Donald. 1953. "BBC Third Programme. A Tale of Two Cities (Benjamin). April 20th." *Opera* 4/6 (June): 376–377.

Morra, Irene. 2007. *20th-century British Authors and the Rise of Opera in Britain*. Farnham: Ashgate.

Murrill, Herbert. 1951. [Autumn programming preview]. *Radio Times* 112/1455 (28 September).

Oldham, Arthur. 1951. "Music For Opera." *Times* [London] 23 July, 7.

Ottaway, D. Hugh. 1956. "Alan Bush's Wat Tyler." *Musical Times* 97/1366 (December): 633–636.

Payne, Anthony. 1951. "John Socman." *Musical Times* 92/1301 (July): 318.

Petzold, Richard. 1953. [Dispatch about *Wat Tyler* in Leipzig]. *Opera* 4/12 (December): 743–744.

Richards, Jeffrey. 2001. *Imperialism and Music: Britain 1876–1953*. Manchester and New York: Manchester University Press.

Riley, Matthew. 2010. *British Music and Modernism, 1895–1960*. Farnham: Ashgate.

Rosenthal, Harold D. 1951. "The Arts Theatre, Cambridge. The Mayor of Casterbridge (Peter Tranchell). July 28 to August 4." *Opera* 2/11 (October): 595–597.

Routh, Francis. 1972. *Contemporary British Music: The Twenty-five Years from 1945 to 1970*. London: Macdonald.

Rye, Matthew. 1995. "Music and Drama." In *The 20th Century*, edited by Stephen Banfield. The Blackwell History of Music in Britain, vol. 6: 343–401. Oxford. Blackwell.

Saunders, Graham. 2012. "Prizes for Modernity in the Provinces: The Arts Council's 1950–1951 Regional Playwriting Competition." *History Research* 2/6: 391–397.

Shawe-Taylor, Desmond. 1951. [Review of Festival events]. *New Statesman and Nation* (May), 617.

Sheridan, David. 2007. *"Give Us More Music": Women, Musical Culture, and Work in Wartime Britain, 1939–1946*. Ph. D. dissertation, University of Southern California.

Sinclair, Andrew. 1995. *Arts and Cultures: The History of the 50 Years of the Arts Council of Great Britain*. London. Sinclair-Stevenson.

Sinfield, Alan. 1989. *Literature, Politics, and Culture in Postwar Britain*. Berkeley and Los Angeles: University of California Press.

Sinfield, Alan. 1995. "The Government, the People, and the Festival." In *Labour's Promised Land: Culture and Society in Labour Britain, 1945–1951*, edited by Jim Fyrth, 181–196. London. Lawrence & Wishart.

Sterndale Bennett, R. 1951. "Britain's Music in 1851." *Radio Times* 111/1432 (April 20th).

Stevens, Bernard. 1974. "Alan Bush's Wat Tyler." *Composer* 51 (Spring): 5.

Stevens, Douglas. 2011. *Lennox Berkeley: A Critical Study of His Music*. Ph.D. dissertation, University of Bristol.

Street, Sarah. 2012. "Cinema, Colour and the Festival of Britain, 1951." *Visual Culture in Britain* 13/1: 83–99.

Struck, Michael. 2001. "Goldschmidt, Berthold." *New Grove Dictionary of Music and Musicians*. 2nd edition. New York: Grove's Dictionaries.

Sutcliffe, James Helme. 1994. "Germany: Goldschmidt's 'Cenci'." *Opera* 45/12 (December): 1412–1414.
Taylor, Basil. 1951. *The Official Book of the Festival of Britain 1951.* London: H.M. Stationery Office.
Turner, Barry. 2011. *Beacon of Change: How the 1951 Festival of Britain Helped to Shape a New Age.* London: Aurum.
Walton, Susana. 1988. *William Walton: Behind the Façade.* London: Oxford University Press.
Weber, William. 1999. "The History of Musical Canons." In *Rethinking Music*, edited by Mark Everist and Nicholas Cook, 340–359. London and New York: Oxford University Press.
White, Eric Walter. 1972. *The Rise of English Opera.* New York: Da Capo. First published 1951.
White, Eric Walter. 1975. *The Arts Council of Great Britain.* London: Davis-Poynter.
White, Eric Walter. 1983. *A Register of First Performances of English Operas.* London: Society for Theatre Research.
Whittall, Arnold. 1990. *The Music of Britten and Tippett: Studies in Themes and Techniques.* Second edition. Cambridge: Cambridge University Press.
Whittall, Arnold. 1995. "British Music in the Modern World." In *The 20th Century*, edited by Stephen Banfield. The Blackwell History of Music in Britain, vol. 6: 9–26. Oxford: Blackwell.
Wiebe, Heather. 2012. *Britten's Unquiet Pasts: Sound and Memory in Postwar Reconstruction.* Cambridge: Cambridge University Press.
Williams, Raymond. 1989. *Resources of Hope: Culture, Democracy, Socialism.* London: Verso.
Williams, Stephen. 1951. [Review of *Billy Budd* at Covent Garden]. *Evening News* (London), 3 December.
Wilson, Conrad. 1993. *Playing for Scotland: The History of the Royal Scottish National Orchestra.* Glasgow: Harper Collins.
Witts, Richard. 1998. *Artist Unknown: An Alternative History of the Arts Council.* London: Little, Brown. The 1998 Warner Books paperback is an abridgement with different pagination.
Wolf, Benjamin. 2010. *Promoting New Music in London, 1930–1980.* Ph.D. dissertation, Royal Holloway, University of London.

Index

60 Paintings for '51 178

Addinsell, Richard 73n1
Agincourt, Battle of 83, 85–86, 170
Albert (Prince) 45–46
Aldeburgh Festival 16, 18, 73n7, 91, 98, 101, 221
Alwyn, William 48, 71, 143, 148; *Festival March* 42, 64, 66, 69, 219–220
architecture and industrial design 2–4, 6, 14–15, 21n1, 24, 177–179
Armstrong Gibbs, Cecil 37, 41, 73n7, 124, 221, 229
Arne, Thomas 1, 28, 39–41, 98, 222
Arnell, Richard 224, 228
Arnold, Malcolm 27, 54n9, 123, 220–221, 230
Arts Council of Great Britain: funding 33–34, 65, 75–76, 81, 109–110, 220, 224n1–3; Music Panel 9, 31–32, 55, 58, 60–63, 66–67, 70–72, 76–77, 88, 122–123, 149, 179; Opera and Ballet Panel 9, 76–78, 80, 90, 115, 117, 119–120, 223; organization and functioning 9–12, 42; regional directors and committees 10, 18, 20, 65, 87, 102–103, 219–220; royal charter 5, 8–10, 13–14, 42, 58, 61, 80, 179
Arundell, Dennis 82, 127
Ashton, Frederick 224
atonality 24, 149, 158n8
audiences for concerts 8, 12–13, 23–27, 34–35, 47, 49–50, 52
Austin, Frederick 119–120, 131, 134–136
avant-garde *see* modernism

Bach, Johann Sebastian 45, 109
Balfe, Michael 46, 56, 83, 175n5; *The Bohemian Girl* 109–110, 223
ballet 10–11, 14, 19, 26–27, 33, 42, 75–77, 109–110, 223–224; *see also* individual companies
Ballet Rambert 223–224
Bantock, Granville 37, 39, 54n9, 175n5
Barbirolli, John 221
Barry, Gerald 3–4, 17–18, 31, 79, 120, 141–142
Bart, Lionel *see Oliver* (musical)
Bartók, Béla 51
Battersea Pleasure Gardens 3, 8, 34, 47
Bax, Arnold 20, 41, 48, 51, 62–64, 70, 73n1, 73n6
Baylis, Lillian 78
BBC (British Broadcasting Corporation) 1, 16, 27, 31, 33, 75, 86, 119, 127, 137, 223; 1851 Week 45–46, 53, 54n8; 1951 Promenade Concerts (Proms) 19, 23, 35, 42–44, 47–53, 54n9, 143, 221–222; broadcast of Festival operas 87, 89, 97–98, 108, 112, 136, 143–155, 158n8; Home and Light Services 42–45, 50, 61, 69; organization and functioning 12, 24, 42–45; other Festival plans 8, 19, 43, 54n3, 65; Third Programme 36–37, 42–43, 45–46, 50, 97, 143–145, 148; *see also* television
BBC Symphony 32
Beecham, Thomas 31–33, 54n3, 110
Beethoven, Ludwig van 45–46, 49, 51, 110
Beggar's Opera, The 109, 223
Benedict, Julius 109, 175n5, 223

240 Index

Benjamin, Arthur 20, 124, 129, 140, 146; *A Tale of Two Cities* 113, 126–130, 137–139, 142–143, 146–147, 155–156, 160, 162–163, 167–169, 174, 175n1, 222, 230
Bennet, John 46
Bentley, Peter 104–108, 114n8, 168
Berkeley, Lennox 9, 123, 128, 131; *Nelson* 82, 126–131, 134–136–138, 155, 161–162, 169–170, 172–173, 231
Berlioz, Hector 59–60
Berners, Lord (Gerald Hugh Tyrwhitt-Wilson) 26, 54n9, 224
Beuler, John 46
Bing, Rudolf 132, 145, 147
Birmingham 112
Bishop, Henry 39, 46, 169
Bizet, Georges 76
Blake, William 1, 66
Blewitt, Jonathan 46
Bliss, Arthur 26, 34, 37, 51, 61–62, 64, 73n6, 82, 119, 219, 221, 224
Blow, John 39, 41
Boosey and Hawkes 27, 78–79, 93, 111, 124, 127, 146, 153
Boughton, Rutland 52–53, 54n9, 119, 149, 163, 167, 175n5
Boulanger, Nadia 130
Boult, Adrian 1, 32–33
Bournemouth Municipal Orchestra 129, 221
Boyce, William 39, 224
Boyd Neel Orchestra 54n3
Braham, John 46
brass bands 8, 28, 33, 44, 56, 58, 61–65, 67–69, 71, 73n2
Brian, Havergal 52–53
Bridge, Frank 54n9
Bristol 69, 83
British Council 34, 54n3, 121
British Empire 15–16, 57–58, 71, 171
British Empire Exhibition 15–16, 56–57
British Federation of Music Festivals 33, 54n3
British Museum 30
British National Opera Company 119
Britten, Benjamin 9, 27, 41, 63, 72, 79–80, 90–91, 102, 106, 114n5, 114n6, 123, 131–132, 136, 149–150, 155, 168, 176n9; *Albert Herring* 90, 98, 110, 168, 223; *Billy Budd* 82, 87–98, 100, 109, 111–113, 114n4, 118, 142, 157, 160, 162–163, 165, 167–168, 172–174, 176n7, 176n10, 176n11, 179, 222; *Gloriana* 145–147, 165, 170; *Let's Make an Opera (The Little Sweep)* 91, 98, 110, 168, 223; *Peter Grimes* 75, 78–79, 90–93, 96, 106, 112, 147, 168, 174; *Six Metamorphoses after Ovid* 73n7, 221; performances with Peter Pears 36–37; *The Rape of Lucretia* 98, 110, 223
Bruce, Michael 46
Buesst, Aylmer 120
Bull, John 41
Bunyan, John 1, 86–87, 161, 164, 175n4
bureaucratic culture 6–7, 9, 19, 23–24, 47, 52, 57, 61, 70, 122–123, 138, 143, 179; *see also* mandarinism
Burt, Francis 221
Bush, Alan 26, 48, 127, 140, 221; *Men of Blackmoor* 152–153, 166; *Wat Tyler* 82, 113, 126–130, 137–140, 142–145, 147, 149–156, 158n2, 158n9, 160, 162–166, 169–170, 173–174, 222, 231
Bush, Geoffrey 34, 37, 221, 223, 224n6
Bush, Nancy 164, 170
Busoni, Feruccio 140
Butterworth, George 54n9
Byrd, William 36, 39–41, 46

Cambridge Arts Theatre 87–89, 92, 104, 107
Cambridge Philharmonic 104
Cambridge University 18, 102–104, 116, 119, 147, 223; *The Mayor of Casterbridge* 98, 102–105, 107–108, 110–111, 132, 160, 175n1, 222; *The Pilgrim's Progress* 87–89, 165
Campion, Thomas 40
canons 5, 19, 23–24, 37, 53
Canterbury 17, 86, 109, 160, 222
Cardiff 112
Carey, Henry 223
Carl Rosa Opera 77–85, 93, 100, 109, 113, 142, 160, 222
Carner, Mosco 120
Carver, Robert 45

CEMA (Council for the Encouragement of Music and the Arts) 9–10, 22n2, 55, 58, 72, 178
Cheltenham Festival of Contemporary British Music 16, 18, 69, 72, 98–101, 221–222
Chichester 86
choral ode 56–57
Christie, John 95
Clarke, Rebecca 40
Cliffe, Cedric 147, 168–169
Coates, Albert H. 20, 124, 167, 169; *The Boy David* 124, 133–135, 229
Coates, Eric 48, 54n9, 124
Cold War 3, 150, 172, 174
Coleman, Basil 97
Coleridge, Samuel Taylor 62, 73n4, 176n7
Collingwood, Lawrance 119–120, 131, 134–136
Colonial and Indian Exhibition 56
Committee for the Promotion of New Music 54n3, 64, 121
communism 140–141, 150, 153–154, 163–164
Composers' Guild of Great Britain 54n3, 121
Congreve, William 109, 132, 161, 170–171
conservatories 25, 27, 65, 114, 137; *see also* individual conservatories
Cooke, Arnold 221, 229
Cornwall 20, 81, 161, 166–167, 171
Cosyns, Benjamin 36
Covent Garden Opera Company 1, 19, 44, 75, 77–79, 110, 119–120, 125–127, 129, 140, 145–146, 163, 179, 223; and competition operas 147, 149–151, 153–154; *Billy Budd* 90–92, 94–98, 111–113, 160, 179, 222; funding 11, 75–76, 109–110; *The Pilgrim's Progress* 82, 86–89, 142, 161, 164–165, 222
Cowen, Frederic H. 169
Cranko, John 224
Croft, Andy 4, 22n2, 178–179
Cross, Joan 9, 97, 119–120
Crozier, Eric 90–93, 114n4
Crystal Palace 2, 15, 57

Cundell, Edric 64
Curzon, Clifford 69
Curzon, Frederick 44

dance *see* ballet
dance bands 8, 28, 61
Darnton, Christian 123, 229
Davenant, William 104
Davies, William Hubert 70, 219–220
Davy, Richard 35–36
Day Lewis, Cecil 1, 64, 66, 219–220
de los Angeles, Victoria 44
de Sabata, Victor 44
Delius, Frederick 37, 41, 48, 51, 109, 223
Demuth, Norman 123, 230
Denison, John 28–29, 58, 62–64, 67, 71, 73n5, 86–87, 89, 103–104, 119–124, 129, 132, 139, 144–145, 150–151, 227–228
Dent, Edward J. 89, 119–120, 126, 131, 134–136, 149
D'Erlanger, Frederic Albert 167
Dibdin, Charles 223
Dickens, Charles 126, 138–139, 146, 160, 167–169
drama (spoken) *see* theater
Donizetti, Gaetano 166
Dowland, John 37, 40–41, 136
D'Oyly Carte Company 28, 110, 223
Dryden, John 104
Dunkirk Evacuation 67–68
Dunstable, John 35–36
Dvorak, Antonin 50
Dykes-Bower, John 69
Dyson, George 63–64, 71–72; *Song for a Festival* 1, 42, 64, 66, 68, 219–220

Easdale, Brian 98–99, 101, 106, 108, 112, 114n5; *The Sleeping Children* 29, 98–102, 109–111, 114n6, 124, 132, 138, 155, 160, 163, 171–172, 175n1, 175n3, 222, 229
Ebert, Carl 94
Eccles, John 223
Edinburgh International Festival 16, 18, 50, 83, 92, 94–96, 224n5
eisteddfodau 20, 69

Index

Elgar, Edward 1, 15–16, 39–42, 48, 51, 57–58, 66; *The Dream of Gerontius* 30, 42, 104
Eliot, T. S. 31
Elizabeth I (Queen) 146, 165
Elizabeth II (Queen) 145–146, 152, 165, 170
émigré musicians in Britain 5, 15, 21, 62, 118, 139, 147–9, 156, 162, 170–171
English Musical Renaissance 5, 25–26, 39, 48, 53, 179
English National Opera *see* Sadler's Wells Opera
English Opera Group 29, 75, 77, 90–92, 98, 101–102, 109–110, 114n5, 116, 124, 131–132, 149, 160, 222–223, 229
ethnic identities in Britain 20–21, 65, 171

Farmer, Henry 46
Farnaby, Giles 41
Fayrfax, Robert 35, 104
Fell, William 87, 103
Ferrier, Kathleen 37
Festival of Britain: ballet commissions 61–62, 77, 109, 178, 223–224; competition for young composers 1, 61, 64, 67, 71–72, 156, 178–179, 219, 220; concert music commissions 12, 17, 19, 29, 55–73, 77, 85, 115, 117, 138, 155, 178–179, 219, 220; Council 16, 65, 80, 86, 219; Executive Committee 18, 34, 61–62, 80, 102; local festivals 3, 17–19, 28–29, 31, 44, 87, 102, 109, 178, 221; Office 31, 34, 79, 141, 175; Opening Ceremony 1, 44, 68; opera commissions 19, 61, 75–98, 109, 111, 113, 114n4, 118, 142, 159, 173–179, 222; opera competition 12, 19, 92–93, 98, 103–104, 108–109, 113, 115–159, 166, 170–171, 178–179, 222, 227–231; playwriting competition 21n1, 73n3, 178; poetry competition 73n3, 178; South Bank Exhibition 1–4, 6, 27, 31–34, 47, 49, 53, 80, 178; Welsh and Scottish musical commissions 20, 65, 70, 178, 219–220
Festival of Empire 15–16, 56–57
film 14–15, 21n1, 27, 58, 73n1, 80, 98, 159

Finzi, Gerald 25, 42, 61–62, 71
First World War 1, 25, 66, 78
Fisher, Geoffrey (Archbishop of Canterbury) 2, 89
Flagstad, Kirstin 223
Fletcher, Percy 57
folksong 25, 27, 37, 105, 107, 149, 152, 162, 168
Fonteyn, Margot 97
Ford, Thomas 46
Forster, E. M. 79, 91–93, 95, 172–173, 176n10
Foulds, John 52–53
Frankel, Benjamin 143, 148, 221
French Revolution 2, 138, 146, 168, 174
Fricker, Peter Racine 1, 27, 48, 51, 72, 221, 224; Concerto for Violin and Small Orchestra 1, 64, 67–68, 219–220
Fuller Maitland, John 37, 224n3
Fuller, Norman 73n7, 221

Gardner, John 221, 227
Gaylor, Frank 82
Gellhorn, Peter 97
George I (King) 57
George VI (King) 33, 97, 145
Georgian (era) music 31, 39, 57, 66, 71
Gerhard, Roberto 221
German, Edward 48, 54n9
Ghedini, Giorgio Federico 93, 167
Gibbons, Christopher 28
Gibbons, Orlando 36, 41, 46
Gibbs, Joseph 36
Gilbert, W. S. 28, 110, 223
Glasgow 112, 223
Glasgow, Mary 10, 13, 16, 22n2, 33, 65, 81, 96
Glastonbury Festival 119
Glock, William 53
Glover, Stephen 46
Glyndebourne Opera 44, 75, 77, 95, 109–110, 116, 149
Goldschmidt, Berthold 128, 140–141, 147–148; *Beatrice Cenci* 126–130, 135, 137–139, 142–145, 147–149, 154, 156, 158n5, 158n7, 158n8, 160, 162, 170–171, 175n1, 222, 230
Gonville and Caius College 110
Goossens, Eugene 54n9

Index

Gordon, Gavin 224
Gounod, Charles 110
GPO Film Unit 98
Grainger, Percy 54n9
Great Victorian Exhibition of 1851 2–3, 13, 56, 57, 71, 80, 175
Gregg, H. Proctor 221
Grimaldi, George 176n13
Guernsey, Wellington 46
Gundry, Inglis 166–167; *The Sleeping Beauty* 126, 166, 230; *The Tinners of Cornwall* 126, 155, 161, 163, 165–168, 171, 174, 175n1, 230
Guthrie, Duncan 16–18, 30, 55, 72, 79–80
Guthrie, Tyrone 98, 100–102, 114n6, 120, 172

Haas, Karl 56
Hadley, Patrick 87, 103, 221–222
Hales, Hubert 73n7, 222, 228
Hallé Orchestra 69, 220–221
Hamerton, Ann 54n6
Hamilton, Emma 126, 135, 170
Handel, George Frideric 1, 30, 34, 39–42, 46, 48, 56–57, 64
Hardy, Thomas 86, 103, 108, 114n8, 160, 167–168
Harewood, Lord (George Lascelles) 102, 111, 147, 150–151, 158n6
Harris, L. David 143
Harrison, Julius 120
Harriss, Charles 57
Harty, Hamilton 54n9
Hassall, Christopher 65, 68, 219–220
Hatton, John 39, 46
Henderson, Thomas 54n6, 227
Herbage, Julian 35, 47–52
Herold, Ferdinand 46
Herrmann, Bernard 73n1
Hindemith, Paul 138
Hippodrome, Bristol 83
historical fiction 97, 165, 167–169
Holst, Gustav 26, 36, 41–42, 58, 98, 110, 223
Home Service *see* BBC
Hook, James 39
Hopkins, Antony 37, 221, 228; *The Man from Tuscany* 109, 160, 175n1, 222

Howells, Herbert 9, 25, 42, 54n9, 104, 219, 221
Howes, Frank 9, 30, 39, 54n5, 84–85, 101, 114n6
Hughes, Arwel: *Dewi Sant* (Saint David) 65, 219–220; *Menna* 123, 155, 161, 171, 230

International Ballet 223–224
Intimate Opera 109–110, 116, 222–223, 224n6
Ireland, John 40–42, 48, 50, 63–64, 70, 149
Isaacs, Leonard 37, 143–145, 148, 152
ISCM (International Society for Contemporary Music) 16, 44, 54n3
Ivirney, Ella 54n6

Jacob, Gordon 27, 57, 61–62, 64, 67, 143, 221, 224n3; *Galop Joyeux* 48, 50, 222; *Music for a Festival* 64, 67, 69, 71, 73n7, 179, 219–220
Jacobson, Maurice 48, 222
Jacques String Orchestra 1, 54n3, 68
Janá?ek, Leo? 110
jazz 8, 26 *see also* dance bands
Johnson, Robert 45
Johnstone, Maurice 48, 123, 222, 229
Jones, Daniel 48–49, 219–220, 228
Joseph Williams Ltd. 149

Keynes, John Maynard 10, 58, 72, 78
Keynote Opera Society 153
Kildea, Paul 29, 70–72, 73n7, 114n4
Kipling, Rudyard 58
Krips, Josef 97
Kubelík, Rafael 44

Lady Margaret Singers 104
Laloux, Fernand 114n9
Lam, Basil 36, 39
Lambert, Constant 26, 62, 64, 70, 110, 119–120, 128, 130–131, 134–135, 141, 224, 225n7
Last Night of the Proms 1, 50
Leipzig 149, 151–153
light music 28, 48, 60, 123–124, 137
light opera *see* operetta
Light Service *see* BBC

244 Index

Linley, Thomas (Jr.) 39
Listener (journal) 44, 101, 153
Liverpool 86, 101, 110, 221, 223
Llanrwst 69
Lloyd, George 20, 27, 78–81, 85, 106, 112, 114n2, 123, 171; *John Socman* 80–86, 93, 97, 100, 105, 108–109, 111, 113, 118, 138, 142, 157, 160, 162–163, 165–168, 170–172, 222
Lloyd, William 81, 166, 170
Locke, Matthew 28
London Choral Society 30, 34, 54n3, 221
London Contemporary Music Centre 54n3, 121
London County Council 29, 32–33, 69
London Philharmonic Orchestra 1, 34, 54n3, 69–70
London Season of the Arts 10, 12–13, 17–19, 23–24, 27–42, 44, 47–53, 54n4, 54n5, 69–70, 72, 110, 138, 178, 221, 224n4; three special concert series 30, 35–42, 53, 115
London Symphony Orchestra 54n3, 69
Lutyens, Elisabeth 27, 40, 54n9, 72, 221
Lyric Theatre, Hammersmith 98, 110

MacCunn, Hamish 176n6, 223
Macfarren, George 169
Mackenzie, Alexander 15, 84, 167
Mackerras, Charles 224
Maconchy, Elizabeth 40
Maldwyn Price, Richard 221
Maluczinski, Witold 44
Manchester 78, 112, 220
mandarinism 7–9, 13, 52–53, 59, 156–157, 179
march 1, 42, 57–58, 61, 64, 66–69, 71
Marchant, Stanley 55, 119
Mascagni, Pietro 117
masque 110, 165
mass song (unison song) 58, 61–63, 66, 220
Master Newman 36
medieval music 35, 39, 45
Mellers, Wilfred: *The Tragicall History of Chrisopher Marlowe* 126–131, 136–138, 158n3, 161, 169, 175n1, 231
Melville, Herman 91–93, 160, 167
Mendelssohn, Felix 42, 45–46

Menuhin, Yehudi 44
Metropolitan Ballet 223–224
Metropolitan Opera 93, 132, 145, 147
Meyerbeer, Giacomo 45–46
military band 16, 31, 44, 52, 56–58, 64, 67, 70–71, 104
Milton, John 1, 28
Mitchell, Donald 146–147
modernism 23–26, 71–73, 113, 137–139, 149–150, 169, 180
Moeran, Ernest J. 37, 41, 49–50
Monteverdi, Claudio 98, 110
Montgomery, Bruce 223
Morley College 54n3, 64
Morley, Thomas 36–37, 41
Mozart, Wolfgang Amadeus 45–46, 110
Murrill, Herbert 31, 39–40, 49, 51, 53, 112–113, 144–145
Musica Britannica 28, 179
musical comedy 8, 28, 169
Musical Times (journal) 68, 149, 151–153
music hall 28, 61
Musicians' Union 81–82
Musorgsky, Modest 150–153, 163, 169–170

Napoleonic Wars 92, 160–161, 168–170, 172–173, 176n9, 176n12
National Brass Band Club 33, 54n3, 69
National Competitive Music Festival 33, 179, 221
National Youth Orchestra 1, 54n3, 69
Neel, Boyd 54n3, 224n3
Nelson, Horatio 46, 126, 130, 134–135, 170, 172–173
neoclassicism 130, 135
New London Opera Company 116
New Opera Company 147
Newman, Ernest 119–120, 176n10
Nicholas, John Morgan 219–220, 224n2
Noble, John 153
Norfolk and Norwich Festival 16, 222
number opera 81, 83–84, 101, 106, 118, 137–138, 166

Old Vic 78, 119
Oldham, Arthur 98, 114n5, 222
Oliver (musical) 169

Index

opera chorus 77, 79, 82–84, 90–91, 94–94, 105–107, 126, 149–151, 153, 162–165, 168, 170, 173–174, 175n3
Opera (journal) 102, 106, 111, 116, 146, 150, 152, 158n8
opera revivals 19, 78, 108–110, 112, 179, 222–223, 224n6
operetta 39, 80, 118
Oppenheimer, Hans 120
oratorio 17, 30, 40, 42, 46, 58–59, 64–65, 67, 73n5, 104, 123, 136, 163
Orr, Robin 104, 222
Oxford University 18, 102–103, 108, 110, 132, 161, 222

Pageant of Empire *see* British Empire Exhibition
Pageant of London *see* Festival of Empire
Parcham, Andrew 36
Paris 112, 168
Parker, Clifton 123; *Aucassin and Nicolette* 125–126, 132, 158n1, 230
Parrott, Ian 123, 229
Parry, C. Hubert H. 1, 15, 39–41, 57–58, 63, 66
Parry, Joseph 176n6
pastoralism 7, 25–26, 54n2, 71, 73n7, 163
Pears, Peter 36–37, 92
Peasants' Revolt of 1381 126, 150–152, 170, 174
Peerson, Martin 36
Phillips, Annette 78, 81–82
piano concerto 40, 51, 58, 60, 62–64, 69, 71, 140, 156, 219–220
Pickwick (musical) 169
Piper, John 94, 97
Plomer, William 146
Pooley, Ernest 29, 93, 102, 122, 127, 129
popular music 8, 61, 114, 168
Poston, Elizabeth 223
Poulenc, Francis 130
Priaulx Rainier, Ivy 40
progressivism *see* modernism
Proms *see* BBC
Pryce-Jones, Alan 170
psychoanalytic theory 100–101
Puccini, Giacomo 76, 84, 110, 117, 147, 166

Purcell, Henry 1, 25, 30, 35–43, 46, 57, 103–104, 136, 223; *Dido and Aeneas* 98, 109–110, 119, 223; *The Fairy Queen* 103–104, 110, 223

Queen's Hall 29–30
Quilter, Roger 37

Rachmaninov, Sergei 73n1
Radio Times (journal) 44–45, 51, 54n8, 112
Raimondi, Pietro 73n5
Rankl, Karl 86, 126–129, 140, 147, 149, 154; *Deirdre of the Sorrows* 125–130, 136, 138–139, 142–143, 154, 156, 160, 162, 170–171, 175n1, 222, 230
Rattigan, Terrence 176n13
Ravel, Maurice 130
Rawsthorne, Alan 51, 64–65, 69, 219–220
Reeves, Harold 224n3
Reizenstein, Franz 222
Renaissance Singers 40
Richard II (King) 150, 164
Riddick String Orchestra 54n3, 109, 221–223
Robinson, Joseph 46
Robinson, Stanford 153
Rossini, Gioacchino 45–46
Roy Henry 35
Royal Academy of Music 55, 127, 140, 149, 153
Royal Albert Hall 1, 17, 23, 29–30, 33, 47, 54n3, 69
Royal Artillery Band 44
Royal Ballet *see* Sadler's Wells Ballet
Royal Choral Society 30, 54n3
Royal College of Music 63, 107, 140, 167
Royal Festival Hall 1, 6, 13, 17, 30–35, 44, 69–70, 179
Royal Military School of Music, Kneller Hall 67, 69
Royal Opera *see* Covent Garden Opera Company
Royal Opera House, Covent Garden 32, 78, 87–89, 96–97, 154, 169, 223–224
Royal Philharmonic Society 34, 54n3, 94, 153

Index

Rubbra, Edmund 9, 61–62, 82, 222; *Festival Te Deum* 33, 64, 66, 69, 219–220
Rural Music Schools Association 54n3, 221

sacred music 20, 30–31, 33, 35, 38–41, 45
Sadler's Wells Ballet 11, 62, 119, 223–4
Sadler's Wells Opera Company 19, 44, 77–78, 82, 86–88, 90, 92–96, 109–110, 125, 142, 147, 149–150, 155, 223; funding 11, 75–76, 119–120
Sadler's Wells Theatre Ballet 11, 223–224
Sainton, Philip 46, 48–49, 222
Salzedo, Leonard 125, 229
Sargent, Malcolm 1, 9, 32–33, 97, 221
Schoenberg, Arnold 54n1, 136, 138, 140
Schools Music Association 33, 221, 224n1
Schreker, Franz 137
Schubert, Franz 51
Schwarz, Rudolf 129, 224n3
Scotland 15, 20–21, 45, 65, 107–108, 154, 176n6, 219–220
Scott, Cyril 123, 221, 229
Scott, Walter 167
Scottish National Orchestra 154
Searle, Humphrey 27, 54n9, 72, 123, 138, 222, 230
Second World War 2–5, 15, 21, 24–26, 42, 46, 50, 81, 128, 159, 168, 170–173, 176n10, 176n13
Shakespeare, William 1, 17, 27, 46, 169
Sharp, Cecil 37
Shaw, Martin 222
Shawe-Taylor, Desmond 33, 84, 101–102
Shelley, Percy Bysshe 126–127, 147, 160, 170–171
Shield, William 46
Sinfield, Alan 7, 9, 21n1, 22n2, 178–179
Smetana, Bed?ich 166
Smyth, Ethel 40, 54n9, 109–110
Somervell, Arthur 37
Sorabji, Kaikhosru 52–53
South Bank Exhibition *see* Festival of Britain, South Bank Exhibition
Soviet Union 3, 140, 152–153, 173
Spohr, Louis 45
St. Bartholomew Choir 40
St. David's 70
St. John's Waterloo (Festival Church) 35, 39
St. Michael's Singers 40
St. Paul's Cathedral 2, 33, 56, 66, 69
Stalin, Josef 140
Stanford, Charles Villiers 15, 20, 40–41, 54n9, 109, 140, 175n5, 223
Sterndale Bennett, Robert 45
Sterndale Bennett, William 45
Stevens, Bernard 54n9, 123, 230
Storace, Stephen 223
Strachey, Lytton 146
Stradella, Alessandro 46
Strauss, Richard 85, 109–110, 147
Stravinsky, Igor 24, 26, 94, 130, 135
Striggio, Alessandro 46
Sullivan, Arthur 46, 48, 57, 110, 176n11, 223–224
Sumer is icumen in 35
Swansea 69
Synge, John Millington 125, 160, 170–171

Tallis, Thomas 39, 41
Tchaikovsky, Pyotr Ilyich 50–51
Telegraph (journal) 32, 84
television 10, 80, 86–87, 112, 114, 147, 177
Tempo (journal) 111, 127
theater (spoken drama) 4–6, 9–11, 13–14, 17, 19, 27, 32, 45, 78, 100, 102, 175, 176n13
Third Programme *see* BBC
Thomas, D. W. *see* Wynne, David
Thomas, Goring 84
Thompson, W. W. 49
Three Choirs Festival 16–18, 42, 50
Tippett, Michael 9, 26, 37, 51, 79, 123–124, 149; *The Midsummer Marriage* 79, 82, 123, 161, 167
Tobin Chamber Orchestra 34
Toscanini, Arturo 32–33
Toye, Geoffrey 224
Trafalgar, Battle of 170, 173
Tranchell, Peter 103–104, 110–112, 114n7, 224; *The Mayor of Casterbridge* 98, 102–111, 113, 114n8, 132, 155, 160, 162–163, 167–168, 174, 175n1, 222, 229
Trinity College of Music 81

Index 247

Tucker, Norman 78, 86, 95–96, 120, 150
Tudor music 25, 28, 36, 39–41, 46, 53, 136–137, 162, 165
Tye, Christopher 41, 46

universities 20–21, 27, 43, 75, 102; *see also* individual universities

van Wyk, Arnold 222
Varlamov, Alexander 46
Vaughan Williams, Ralph 8, 25–27, 31, 34, 36, 40–42, 48, 57–58, 62–63, 70, 73n2, 78–80, 104, 123, 147, 175n5, 224n4; *Flourish for Brass Band* 221, 224n4; *Hugh the Drover* 108–110, 223; *On Wenlock Edge* 37, 41; *Sir John in Love* 109, 223; *Tallis Fantasia* 1, 42; *The Pilgrim's Progress* 1, 82, 86–90, 92, 94, 97, 100, 103, 109–110, 113, 118, 142, 161–165, 175n2, 175n4, 222; *The Sons of Light* 220–221, 224n1; *Three Shakespeare Songs* 179, 221
Vaughan Williams, Ursula *see* Wood, Ursula
Venice 91, 167
Verdi, Giuseppe 76, 83–85, 94, 106, 110, 163, 166, 170
Victoria and Albert Museum 1, 21, 21n1, 68
Victoria (Queen) 45
Victorian music 16, 39, 45–46, 53, 71, 73
visual art 5, 9–10, 13–14, 17, 26–27, 27, 73n9, 178

Wagner, Richard 49, 76, 85, 101, 106, 110, 163, 165
Wales 16, 20–21, 65, 70, 77, 81, 109, 161, 171, 176n6, 219–220
Wallace, William Vincent 109
Wallbank, Newell 221
Walton, Susana 75
Walton, William 26, 41–42, 48, 51, 61–62, 64, 66, 71, 75; *Troilus and Cressida* 62, 79, 82, 161, 176n10

Warlock, Peter (Philip Heseltine) 41, 54n9
Warr, Eric 145, 148, 152
Webern, Anton 54n1, 136, 140
Webster, David 76, 79, 86, 88–89, 95–97, 119, 120, 127, 129, 142, 147, 149, 154
Weelkes, Thomas 36, 41, 46
Wellesz, Egon 108, 123–124, 170; *Incognita* 108–109, 132, 155, 161–162, 170–171, 175n1, 222, 230
Welsh National Opera 77, 109, 171
Wesley, Samuel Sebastian 39
Westminster Abbey 35, 37, 40
Westminster Cathedral 35, 40
White, Eric Walter 10, 22n2, 55, 60, 63, 73n2, 82, 84, 103–104, 155, 169; support for opera commissions and revivals 76, 81, 85–87, 90–96, 98, 109, 112–113, 116–134, 139, 142–148, 150–152, 158n1, 158n2, 227–228
Wigmore Hall 11, 30, 33, 54n3, 221
Wilbye, John 41, 46
Williams, Charles 73n1
Williams, Grace 229
Williams, William Emrys 97, 152
Wilson, Steuart 14, 76, 82, 86, 96, 119–120, 122, 124, 126–128, 131–133, 139, 141, 144, 150–151, 158n1, 158n2
Wiseman, Herbert 219
Witts, Richard 9, 12, 22n2
Wolf-Ferrari, Ermanno 110
Wood, Anne 131–132
Wood, Charles 40–41, 167, 169
Wood, Henry 15
Wood, Thomas 8, 58, 62–64, 72, 122–123, 222; *The Rainbow, A Tale of Dunkirk* 65, 67–69, 71, 219–220
Wood, Ursula 224n1
Woolf, Virginia 116
Wordsworth, William 222, 224n5, 230
Workers' Music Association 54n3, 149, 153, 221, 224n4
working class 20, 52, 58, 67–68, 73n2
Wright, Denis 64
Wright, Frank 65, 67, 219
Wynne, David 65, 67, 219–220

Taylor & Francis eBooks

Helping you to choose the right eBooks for your Library

Add Routledge titles to your library's digital collection today. Taylor and Francis ebooks contains over 50,000 titles in the Humanities, Social Sciences, Behavioural Sciences, Built Environment and Law.

Choose from a range of subject packages or create your own!

Benefits for you
- Free MARC records
- COUNTER-compliant usage statistics
- Flexible purchase and pricing options
- All titles DRM-free.

Benefits for your user
- Off-site, anytime access via Athens or referring URL
- Print or copy pages or chapters
- Full content search
- Bookmark, highlight and annotate text
- Access to thousands of pages of quality research at the click of a button.

REQUEST YOUR **FREE** INSTITUTIONAL TRIAL TODAY

Free Trials Available
We offer free trials to qualifying academic, corporate and government customers.

eCollections – Choose from over 30 subject eCollections, including:

Archaeology	Language Learning
Architecture	Law
Asian Studies	Literature
Business & Management	Media & Communication
Classical Studies	Middle East Studies
Construction	Music
Creative & Media Arts	Philosophy
Criminology & Criminal Justice	Planning
Economics	Politics
Education	Psychology & Mental Health
Energy	Religion
Engineering	Security
English Language & Linguistics	Social Work
Environment & Sustainability	Sociology
Geography	Sport
Health Studies	Theatre & Performance
History	Tourism, Hospitality & Events

For more information, pricing enquiries or to order a free trial, please contact your local sales team:
www.tandfebooks.com/page/sales

www.tandfebooks.com